Collaborative Resilience

Collaborative Resilience

Moving Through Crisis to Opportunity

edited by Bruce Evan Goldstein

The MIT Press
Cambridge, Massachusetts
London, England

For information about special quantity discounts, please email special_sales@mitpress.mit .edu

This book was set in Sabon by Graphic Composition, Inc., Bogart, Georgia. Printed and bound in the United States of America.

Library of Congress Cataloging-in-Publication Data

Collaborative resilience : moving through crisis to opportunity / edited by Bruce Evan Goldstein.
    p. cm.
Includes bibliographical references and index.
ISBN 978-0-262-01653-7 (hbk. : alk. paper)—ISBN 978-0-262-51645-7 (pbk. : alk. paper).
1. Community development. 2. Community organization. 3. Crises—Social aspects.
4. Sociology, Urban. 5. City planning. I. Goldstein, Bruce Evan, 1963–
HN49.C6C576 2012
307.1'16—dc22

                                                                    2011011592

10 9 8 7 6 5 4 3 2 1

Contents

Acknowledgments

I would like to thank my friends, colleagues, and family who contributed to creating this book, as well as those who helped to organize the "Symposium on Enhancing Resilience to Catastrophic Events through Communicative Planning" held at Virginia Tech on November 16–18, 2008.

In particular I'd like to thank:

- My "brain trust" at Virginia Tech: William Butler, Max Stephenson, John Randolph, Paul Knox, and Bruce Hull.
- The three symposium cosponsors:
  The Institute for Policy and Governance at Virginia Tech (VTIPG);
  The School of Public and International Affairs (SPIA), Virginia Tech;
  The Virginia Tech Center for Peace Studies and Violence Prevention (CPSVP).
- Symposium manager extraordinaire Thomas Sheffer.
- The doctoral students who took part in the 2008 Virginia Tech seminar on resilience and who served as symposium discussants:
  Nicole Rishel, Jane Ann Williams, Travis Bland, Courtney Kimmel, Allison Stephenson, William Butler, and Tracy Cooper.
- Skilled editors Jana Carp, Moira Zellner, and Margaret Knox.
- My editor at MIT Press, Clay Morgan.

I dedicate this volume to my wife, Vicki; children Ari and Melina; and to my parents, Bernard and Patricia Goldstein, brother Mark, and sister Nancy, who supported the symposium and preparation of this volume through the Patricia and Bernard Goldstein Family Foundation.

About the Contributors

Derek Armitage is an associate professor of geography and environmental studies at Wilfrid Laurier University in Waterloo, Ontario, Canada. He coedited *Adaptive Co-Management: Collaboration, Learning, and Multi-Level Governance* (2007), published by the University of British Columbia Press.

Robert Arthur is a consultant with MRAG Ltd, based in London, U.K. His research on small-scale fisheries explores the role of natural resources in livelihoods, how policymakers and practitioners innovate in response to complex social and ecological challenges, and in particular how research supports these transformative processes.

Luis A. Bojórquez-Tapia is the director of the Sustainability Science Laboratory, Institute of Ecology, National Autonomous University of Mexico, in Mexico City. He focuses on decision theory and spatial modeling within the fields of sustainability science, environmental conflict resolution, and biological conservation.

Ryan Bullock is a postdoctoral fellow with the School of Environment and Sustainability at the University of Saskatchewan, Canada. His forthcoming coauthored book *Community Forestry: Conflict, Integration and Forest Land Management* provides an appraisal of local involvement in northern forest ecosystem governance in developed countries.

William Hale Butler is an assistant professor at Florida State University in the Department of Urban and Regional Planning. He completed his dissertation "Learning to Burn, Burning to Learn: Transforming Fire Management through the US Fire Learning Network" in 2009, and he continues to examine approaches to building resilience through collaborative planning.

Jana Carp is an assistant professor in the Department of Geography and Planning at Appalachian State University in Boone, North Carolina. She coedited *Under One Roof: Issues and Innovations In Shared Housing* (1996). Her work examines creative initiatives in the social production of space, particularly concerning the nature–culture relationship.

E. Franklin Dukes directs the Institute for Environmental Negotiation at the University of Virginia. He authored *Resolving Public Conflict: Transforming Community and Governance* (2006) and coauthored *Reaching for Higher Ground* (2009).

Hallie Eakin is an assistant professor at the School of Sustainability, Arizona State University, in Tempe, Arizona. She is the author of *Weathering Risk in Rural Mexico: Economic, Climatic and Institutional Change* (1996). She collaborates with colleagues across Latin America in research on smallholder decision making in contexts of globalization and vulnerability to global environmental change.

Bruce Evan Goldstein is an associate professor in the Department of Planning and Design at the University of Colorado in Denver. He examines how activists, managers, and other stakeholders develop innovative responses to social-ecological challenges, including wildfire, biodiversity loss, and climate change.

Charles J. Hoch is a professor in the Urban Planning and Policy Department at the University of Chicago. He is the editor of *The Practice of Local Government Planning* (2000).

Sanda Kaufman is a professor at the University of Cleveland in Ohio. She also directs the Master of Environmental Studies Program.

Steven Kelban is founding executive director of the Andrus Family Fund, a foundation concentrating its efforts in the areas of community reconciliation and the transition from foster care to independence. He was previously the executive director of the Public Interest Law Center at New York University School of Law.

Melissa Marschke is an assistant professor at the School of International Development and Global Studies, University of Ottawa, Canada. She authored *Resource Governance at the Margins: Experiences from Coastal Cambodia* (2011).

Patrick McConney is a senior lecturer at the Centre for Resource Management and Environmental Studies at the University of the West Indies, Cave Hill Campus, in Barbados. His research is on networks, resilience, socio-economics, and governance related to small-scale fisheries and marine protected areas around the Caribbean.

Bruce Mitchell is an associate provost (resources) and professor of geography and environmental management at the University of Waterloo in Ontario. A Fellow of the Royal Society of Canada, he is coauthor of *Environmental Change and Challenge: A Canadian Perspective* (2009).

Connie P. Ozawa is the director of urban studies and planning at Portland State University in Oregon, where she is a professor. She authored *Recasting Science: Consensus-Based Procedures in Public Policy Making* (1991) and edited *The Portland Edge* (2004).

Terrence Phillips is the program manager for fisheries management and development at the Caribbean Regional Fisheries Mechanism, St. Vincent and the Grenadines. He plans and implements the fisheries management and development program, which includes such areas as the strengthening of fisherfolk organizations and improved community participation, and the development and promotion of risk-reduction programs for fishers.

John Randolph is a professor of urban affairs and planning at Virginia Tech in Blacksburg. He authored *Environmental Land Use Planning and Management* (2011) and coauthored *Energy for Sustainability: Technology, Planning, Policy* (2008).

Karen E. Till is a lecturer in the Department of Geography at the National University of Ireland in Maynooth. She authored *The New Berlin: Memory, Politics, Place* (2005).

Edward P. Weber directs the School of Environmental and Public Affairs at the University of Nevada (Las Vegas), where he is a professor. He wrote *Bringing Society Back In: Grassroots Ecosystem Management, Accountability, and Sustainable Communities* (2003).

Eric W. Welch is an associate professor in the Department of Public Administration at the University of Illinois in Chicago, where he directs the Science, Technology, and Environment Policy Lab. His research concerns issues such as voluntary environment policy, the integration of science in environment policy, and the role of network structure in the implementation of policy.

Jill Williams is a program officer of the Andrus Family Fund in the city of New York. She was formerly the executive director of the Greensboro Truth and Reconciliation Commission. Jill supports community truth-seeking and reconciliation programs around the United States.

Moira L. Zellner is an assistant professor in the Department of Urban Planning and Policy at the University of Illinois in Chicago. Her research focuses on how policy and behavioral changes can address complex environmental problems, and she applies complexity theory and complexity-based models to policy exploration and social learning.

1

Introduction: Crisis and Collaborative Resilience

Bruce Evan Goldstein

This book originated in response to the Virginia Tech murders of Monday, April 16th, 2007. As a member of the university community, I observed how our response to this horror promoted global solidarity that supported our grieving while resisting other, more divisive framings of the tragedy. Such a constructive response to the shootings was the catalyst for a symposium that I organized a year later. Twenty-five researchers from planning and natural resource management were invited to Virginia Tech to discuss how collaboration in its many forms could promote resilience to crisis.

The resulting essays, collected in this book, consider the topic of collaborative resilience. We seek to answer if resilience can be cultivated among communities that face a wide array of challenges, including legacies of violence, collapse of timber and fisheries industries, and the impact of climate change. These essays explore how various collaborative processes can foster intentional communities as participants exchange ideas, stretch assumptions, and develop greater self-awareness. Chapters tackle the challenges of creating safe spaces in which people can learn together and reinvent their communities, even in complex circumstances that can be threatening and disruptive to social practices and relationships. In addition, you will read about how to aid communities in framing a common understanding of crisis, cultivating new forms of knowledge, identity, and governance that can enable far-reaching changes.

The Virginia Tech massacre inspired and defined the main themes of this volume. But even before the tragedy, planning and natural resource scholars had begun developing a shared interest in the notion of resilience as a basis for crisis response. Both fields have much to offer in helping communities develop what I call "communicative resilience." The essays in *Collaboration for Resilience* show the ways in which people in crisis collaborate. Herein are the stories of communities that have survived and thrived through adaptive consensus-building and transformative social change, altering assumptions, behaviors, processes, and structures for the greater good.

Unity in the Face of Crisis

On the day of the massacre, I was off campus preparing for a class; I was a professor in the Virginia Tech Urban Affairs and Planning program. Between 9:00 and 10:00 AM, student Seung-Hui Cho shot more than 50 people in the classrooms of Norris Hall, killing 27 students, 5 faculty, and then himself. I did not know those killed or wounded, but I grieved for them.

In the aftermath of that horrific event, I struggled to understand why the shootings occurred and how the community should respond. Other people likely were asking themselves the same questions, because crises do not come with a ready-made frame of reference. Even the Holocaust initially lacked a common narrative framework or distinct place in collective memory in the decade after the Second World War, when many survivors were stigmatized and silent (Mintz, 2001).

Has Virginia Tech recovered? I think that the school has recovered, but not just from the passage of time. The people had to intentionally *unify* in order to recover, heal, and to function again. They had to face an act that attacked the essence of what the university is and does. The killing of faculty and students in classrooms violated the trust and openness that allows a university to operate. It threatened the school's ability to maintain a safe space so that students can encounter ideas of all sorts, learn, and grow.

Ten thousand people attended a convocation at Cassell Coliseum the day after the shootings. Students organized a memorial vigil that night on the Drillfield in the center of campus. Classes were canceled for the remainder of the week, and most students went home to be with their families. While they were away, I asked my students to respond on a class Webblog to this question: "Did campus memorial events help you connect with others and help heal the rift that this disaster has created in our community?" Here are some of their responses:

Just the day before, I stood at the same spot on the Drillfield, as people yelled at me to turn around and run. The candlelight vigil restored my perception of the campus as a 'safe place.' Knowing that we were not alone was powerful.

The amazing thing about the love and friendship and support we shared is that it trumps the anger and hate which started this tragedy. I wish Cho could see that as a community we have not dissolved into bitterness, that hate does not beget hate.

It suggested that people are bound up with one another, sharing, despite differences, a common identity. That is why we wore orange and maroon. That is why we yelled 'Let's go. . . Hokies' together. With all our sadness, anger and fear, we needed this time to be together and to be around our fellow students, because we are the only ones who understand how we feel.

When students returned the following week, I invited Andy Morikawa, who directs the New River Valley Community Foundation, to join my Community Involvement class for a roundtable discussion. Andy described how his Japanese-American family was forced into internment camps during WW II. He told them how he had fought with bitterness, joined the Peace Corps, and devoted his life to building community. Thousands of other conversations took place that week in and out of classrooms, as we all tried to understand our relationship to the tragedy and develop a collective sense of what mattered and what needed to be done. Virginia Tech sociologists John Ryan and James Hawdon (2008) describe the shared frame of reference that emerged during this time. People began to understand that the shootings were an isolated incident, carried out by a mentally ill individual who held himself apart from the contact and interaction that defined the community. As Ryan and Hawdon (2008) explain, people came to these conclusions:

- This act could not have been foreseen or reasonably prevented.
- The surviving members of the university community were not responsible for this event.
- This was an attack not just on the victims, but also on the whole community.
- Everyone was victimized by what happened.
- The effects on the community will be devastating and long lasting, but the community will prevail.
- The whole country—and indeed the whole world—is watching and supporting the community in its grief.

Thus people judged the attack as being carried out against their entire community. They responded in a way that was dignified, unified, brave, and composed (Ryan and Hawdon 2008). In turn, their solidarity promoted support throughout the world.

Although unity often follows tragedy or disaster, solidarity is not always the case, and not always to the same degree (Carroll et al. 2006). For example, national solidarity with the people of New Orleans in the aftermath of hurricane Katrina (in August, 2005) was tempered by sensationalized initial coverage of violence in the Super Dome shelter and looting in the streets. Although accounts of the dignity and bravery of rescuers and residents were plentiful, the community as a whole was not associated with these characteristics, and this situation made national solidarity more equivocal.

Just as in New Orleans, the national media was eager to share stories that might have fostered less solidarity with Virginia Tech. Some journalists sought to identify who was to blame for the shootings. They asked why the campus had not been locked down earlier, and how Cho was allowed to reach his senior year without medical or disciplinary intervention. Some people adopted this blame-framing of the story, including, most visibly, parents of some of the students who were killed, overwhelmed as they were by grief and a sense of violated trust. To this day, a few people continue to pursue legal action aimed at securing a clear target of blame or pathway to accountability.

However, many of those closest to the victims did adopt the shared frame of reference, for example, horticulture professor Jerzy Nowak. Cho killed Jerzy's wife, Jocelyne M. Couture-Nowak, while she was trying to defend her French class. Jerzy wrote a heartbreaking account of learning of her death, of how he told his young daughter, and of how he handled the aftermath (Nowak and Veilleux 2008). Jerzy did discuss his delay in learning of Jocelyne's death and his difficulty in navigating some aspects of campus bureaucracy. Nevertheless, Jerzy reserved his contempt for "snooping journalists" and their immediate and relentless efforts to get material for their "ready-made scripts accusing the VT administration of neglect." He concludes, "The compassion and support that we have received from our community, including co-workers and university colleagues, are so unique that I never considered leaving Blacksburg." Building on this support network, Jerzy created the Virginia Tech Center for Peace Studies and Violence Prevention (http://www.cpsvp.vt.edu/). This center became a cosponsor of the symposium that led to this book.

Beyond the Intrinsically Resilient University

Virginia Tech's swift response was spontaneous. The shootings were an unexpected assault, one that focused and motivated the school to engage in collective deliberation and coordinated action. Anthropologist S. M. Hoffman (1999, 140) has widely studied disasters (as well as dealing with the loss of her house in the 1991 fire in Oakland, California). Hoffman says that after the initial shock of the disaster and social atomization, "an aura of purpose, almost a higher purpose, arises and immerses victims."

These words certainly do describe Virginia Tech; drawn together, the university community engaged in open and honest dialogue. They began to forge a common narrative that became a source of strength and solidarity. This common narrative enabled them to reject divisive stories that others wanted to tell about the tragedy. Our ability to tell our own story promoted resilience, and we quickly restored our ability to be an effective learning community.

I suspect that universities have an intrinsic capacity to respond to crises. They are ever-renewing community; people remain in close proximity and they have common experiences and loyalties that develop trust. They share a "language" and ways of interacting. The very intention of a school is to promote cooperative interaction that fosters student learning. As such, students can reinvent themselves within the society of the wider world.

Conditions are rarely so conducive, as at a school, to collaborative engagement in response to a crisis. Nor are all crises as clearly identifiable or immediate as the Virginia Tech shootings. In some crises, threats may have multiple causes or operate at multiple scales. There are those threats that combine social and ecological features. A crisis can be slow to build, episodic, loom in the distant future, or have occurred in the distant past. The circumstances leading to crisis may be complex and indeterminate, and thus the ways to recovery may be difficult to comprehend or beyond human ability to pursue.

When a crisis occurs in a neighborhood, region, or state, these societies (unlike a school) may not share a common language, habits, or interests. Communities riven by hostility or distrust may interpret crises in disparate ways, so that even discussing an issue can be emotionally and cognitively taxing, as well as personally and professionally threatening. These are the tough cases. A group may need to build a capacity for communication before it can even begin to engage effectively. Responding to crises may require challenging closely held institutional and normative commitments.

I organized the 2008 symposium at Virginia Tech for us to consider how collaboration can promote crisis resilience in the tough cases: when crises are complex, when communities lack cohesion and capacity, and when resilience may require system transformation instead of merely recovery. I was inspired by the unity that I saw after the shootings. I wanted to explore how different collaborative designs and approaches to facilitation might catalyze the collective energy and purpose that is released during a crisis (before it is possibly eclipsed by helplessness and hopelessness). I discovered that this area of inquiry has been relatively unexplored; most efforts to anticipate and respond to crises have focused on enhancing top-down managerial capacity (e.g., Fukuyama 2007), and such efforts do little to promote broader participation and collaborative engagement. But in the past decade, collaborative resilience has attracted the interest of scholars within both Natural Resource Management and Planning. These were fields of most of the symposium participants. They brought distinct assumptions that complement and challenge each other as they debated strategies for promoting resilience to crisis.

Crisis and Convergence

In both the fields of Natural Resource Management and Planning, interest in increasing resilience to crisis through collaboration began a half-century ago. What initiated this interest were threats to the legitimacy of both fields, an unexpected consequence of their longstanding faith in managerial acumen and scientific expertise.

For their part, natural resource managers were confronted by the depletion of seemingly inexhaustible fisheries stocks, including cod in Atlantic and pollock in the Pacific. Systematic efforts to suppress fire had led to more than a hundred million acres of biologically impoverished, fire-starved forests in the United States. These failures to optimize resource flows grew from their mechanistic perspective. They had thought that nature was composed of parts that could be redesigned, discarded, or exchanged to fine-tune outputs for optimal satisfaction of human wants and needs (Botkin 1990; Worster 1994).

Likewise, planners' faith in reason and expert guidance underlay the regrettable urban renewal programs of the 1960s and 1970s, which displaced vibrant communities and produced great suffering. Urban renewal produced the permanent "root shock" of displacement, an impact that continues to affect communities decades after their removal (Fullilove 2004).

These crises initiated a period of self-critique, and both fields embarked on a path to self-renewal. Within planning, the story of our redemption begins with Jane Jacobs's (1961) communitarian vision of the "Death and Life of American Cities." Planners urged each other to start listening to the people for whom they were planning. Initially they used client-centered "advocacy planning." Later they used a facilitated, collaborative process that enabled stakeholders to understand each other's interests and resolve conflict through consensus (Susskind 1987). As collaborative planning developed, scholars began investigating how trust and interdependence acquired by stakeholders could not only resolve disputes but also transform adversarial relationships and catalyze new institutions. Such connections could heal root causes of conflict (Booher and Innes 2002; Healey 1997). They could address social and ecological crises that played out over both long time scales and across multiple spatial scales (Innes and Booher 2010; Margerum and Whitall 2004).

Some natural resource management scholars questioned the assumed natural equilibrium that underlay strategies to optimize resource outputs. These scholars adopted insights about nonlinear system dynamics and feedback processes (Botkin 1990; Levin 1999). They embraced adaptive management, an iterative and precautionary practice (Gunderson, Holling, and Light 1995; Holling 1978). Scholars explored, too, the possibilities of broader participation, drawing inspiration from Ostrom's (1990) work on common property resource regimes as an alternative to a "tragedy of the commons" (Hardin and Baden 1977).

Social-ecological resilience lies at the juncture of this new scholarship in resource dynamics and institutions. The concept emphasizes the capacity to absorb stress and reorganize (as opposed to seeking the highest degree of efficiency at a single equilibrium point). As you will read in many of the chapters in this book, social-ecological resilience highlights the advantages of institutional flexibility. Resilience scholars suggest that even if centralized and hierarchical institutions could promote restoration of system function and structure in the face of perturbation, their rigidity might inhibit transition to a more desirable state when existing conditions are untenable (Berkes and Folke 1998; Gunderson and Holling 2002).

Chapter Overviews

Understanding Collaboration
This book explores the meeting point of planning and natural resource management in their attempt to understand how to intervene to enhance community resilience. They must intervene while at the same time preserving the autonomy and agency that both energize collaboration. The integrative and theoretical chapters of the first section of the book, "Understanding Collaboration," discuss various ways that collaborative processes contribute to resilience in the face of technological breakdown, disease, homelessness, and climate change. Describing in joint fact-finding as well as holistic sensemaking and storytelling, authors suggest that these techniques develop trust and empathy, foster understanding of interdependent relationships, and enhance cognitive capacity.

In chapter 2, Connie Ozawa considers how trust shapes a community's capacity to respond to catastrophe. While some people are more trusting than others, Ozawa notes that trust is also a group cognitive process, created or lost through social interaction. Cognitively based trust is grounded in the expectation that individuals (or organizations) will act in ways that are competent, committed, caring, and predictable. Ozawa suggests that trust is fragile and can rapidly disappear when norms of civic engagement are violated. She examines the Three Mile Island nuclear accident and a proposal to cover an open reservoir in Portland, Oregon, to prevent terrorism. Through these examples, Ozawa shows how quickly trust can be undermined by decision makers who feel that a situation is too urgent to submit to collective deliberation.

Chapter 3, by Moira L. Zellner, Charles J. Hoch, and Eric W. Welch, describes how the complexity of social-ecological system dynamics can inhibit or degrade trust. These dynamics can make it hard for individuals to understand how their actions matter or why they should change. The system can make it easy for defectors to operate undetected. The authors suggest that building trust can convert mutual vulnerability into recognition of interdependence. Collaboration helps by facilitating this recognition, building faith that others will act in concert, and thus enhancing capacity to respond to a crisis. The authors examine two case studies: a homelessness initiative in Chicago, and an attempt to change farming practices in a vulnerable water-supply watershed in upstate New York. They show how collaboration, in both cases, linked stakeholder diversity and vulnerability in ways that promoted equity and increased capacity to generate innovative responses. The solutions worked well for stakeholders at various organizational scales in the system. In both cases, collaborative dialogue built enduring relationships. The dialogue allowed and fostered recognition of interdependence that fostered social solidarity.

In chapter 4, Sanda Kaufman proposes that there are limits to an individual's capacity to process the information required to understand social-ecological systems and to respond appropriately to crisis. She suggests that collaborative planning can compensate for these cognitive deficiencies. Her proposal draws on an array of ideas, from psychology, linguistics, social psychology, social-ecological systems theory, complexity theories, and planning. She offers the possibility that collaboration can address inherent limits on individual cognition. Limits can be expanded by introducing a diversity of views, interests, preferences, values and solutions. Further, such efforts can support and encourage social interaction that enables mutual framing, trust building, social learning, and co-construction of shared stories.

Chapter 5 pinpoints a fundamental factor behind successful collaborative resilience: time. Jana Carp reflects on the Slow Food and Slow Cities movements in the context of collaborative planning. She suggests that increasing resilience requires resisting the pace of our hurried world by intentionally slowing down the pace of interaction and information. This provides the longer time period required for storytelling, deliberating, and empathizing. Like Kaufman, Carp recognizes the time required to move beyond simple mental models. People must engage with the social and ecological complexity of variables and processes that are slow-acting, incremental, or tightly coupled. In addition, Carp suggests that these "slow practices" are necessary to "reclaim our capacities at human scale" through trust-building, group learning, and building a sense of history and place.

In chapter 6, John Randolph provides a broad appraisal of collaborative approaches to climate change. His ideas touch on research, international goal-setting, and planning for mitigation and adaptation. He emphasizes that building climate-resilient communities is part social mobilization and part expert practice. Both approaches are necessary; they develop social capital and self-organizing abilities, they expand social acceptance and political support, and they build capacity to prepare for and cope with climate change. Randolph urges careful diagnosis of social-ecological context and opportunities to enhance the circumstantial advantages of particular collaborative designs.

Collaborative Resilience Case Studies

The eight case studies in the second part consider how collaboration can increase resilience to oppression, natural disasters, natural resource scarcity, and climate change. The first four cases describe collaboratives that tend to be highly inclusive and that are intended to maintain system continuity and integrity by reorganizing in response to changing conditions. All of the collaboratives show adaptive resilience (Walker et al. 2004). In contrast, the collaboratives described in the next four cases tend to exclude certain stakeholders in their pursuit of transformative resilience. When ecological, economic, or social conditions make an existing system untenable, they seek to "create untried beginnings from which to evolve a new way of living" (Walker et al. 2004, 7).

Reaching Consensus

In chapter 7, Luis A. Bojórquez-Tapia and Hallie Eakin describe a highly inclusive collaborative process organized in response to a federal requirement to create environmental assessments. On the hurricane-prone island of Cozumel, Mexico, unrestrained tourist development and urbanization were increasing human vulnerability and degrading terrestrial and marine ecosystems. In this instance, participants tried a new approach. They used a systematic technique—a combination of GIS and multicriteria decision analysis. The strategy enabled a synthesis of diverse forms of knowledge and reduction in power inequities. As they constructed a land suitability map, stakeholders voiced conflicting visions, probed for underlying interests, and develop shared criteria. After the collaborative process ended, continued availability of the map placed a check on efforts to circumvent the stakeholder's collective vision. Circulation of the map extended the influence of this relatively brief collaborative process and fostered greater accountability in decision making.

In contrast, Edward Weber describes, in chapter 8, a long-lived collaborative. The Blackfoot Challenge, organized by entrepreneurial stakeholders in the Blackfoot Valley of western Montana pursued a much broader mandate over fifteen years. In a community that was at first deeply divided, the Challenge created trust, cohesion, and capacity for innovation. Weber ties its effectiveness to several factors: a supportive regulatory structure, ample resources for program design and implementation, and the presence of organizers with a common-sense, strategic approach to problem-solving. The chapter covers the relationship between private and public responsibilities. It answers questions about the expectations of mutual aid, and the ways in which stakeholders can reach agreement about desirable change.

In chapter 9, Patrick McConney and Terrence Phillips describe an effort to enable community-based fisherfolk organizations to participate more effectively in collaborative regional governance of Caribbean fisheries. The authors began their participatory-action research by facilitating a discussion among fisherfolk, fisheries officers, and other stakeholders about the meaning and practical significance of the concepts of adaptive capacity, resilience, and networks. Through a series of site visits, workshops, and collaborative dialog, the authors helped stake-holders apply these ideas to design a voluntary network. This network would help to preserve fisherfolk's individual autonomy as well as enable them to express a collective voice in emerging consensus-based governance arrangements.

Chapter 10 is by Franklin Dukes, Jill Williams, and Steven Kelban. They begin by asserting that a group of people who have suffered "unrightable wrongs" (such as slavery or segregation) might be less resilient to new crises. Society may have shown an unwillingness to acknowledge and address past wrongs against these people. This unwillingness can reduce the group's trust, social cohesion, and collective will. The authors examine several cases, such as the Greensboro Truth and Reconciliation Commission, the Bainbridge Island Superfund cleanup, and efforts to address slavery's legacy at the University of Virginia. The authors emphasize that outsiders can provide neutral facilitation during times of crisis. Outsiders can help communities to reach consensus about past injuries and to address issues that perpetuate social division and inequality.

Advocating Change

The four chapters in the section "Advocating Change" describe transformative resilience. Such resilience requires collaborative efforts by disempowered actors to engage in critical discussion. In this way, people can mobilize to reinvent institutions, overcoming an entrenched status quo.

In chapter 11, Robert Arthur, Richard Friend, and Melissa Marschke draw on decades of experience in Southeast Asia's Mekong region. Arguing that resource management is unavoidably politicized and unfair, they suggest that reducing conflict to promote greater collaboration may only perpetuate inequities. Alternatively, they urge consultants and expert advisors to support local communities' efforts to organize collaboratives that strive for social change. They suggest that prioritizing local needs and aspirations can lead to institutional and discursive shifts that can bring about transformative change.

In chapter 12, Karen Till describes how in Cape Town, South Africa, the "District Six Museum" enabled descendents of non-white people who were forcibly relocated during Apartheid to imagine what it might mean to inhabit their city again. The museum's collaborative spaces and processes facilitated acknowledgment of long-silenced wrongs and communicated an experience of the city as a reservoir of living memory and emotional attachment. This museum enabled community dialog about possible shared futures, many of which were not yet visible in dominant representations of the urban landscape. Till critiques systems science for supporting a singular and hegemonic temporal and spatial conception of resilience. She suggests that urban resilience relies on the capacity to create stories that challenge dominant understandings about the past and future. Such stories strengthen diverse claims to inheritance and citizenship.

In chapter 13, Ryan Bullock, Derek Armitage, and Bruce Mitchell consider collaborative efforts to address the long-term decline in economic conditions and forest health in Northern Ontario, Canada. Disempowered actors met informally in what the authors call "shadow networks" that allowed them to speak openly without alarming the provincial government, forest companies, and labor groups who dominated the region. Through collaborative dialog, participants were able to reflect on community needs and ecological limits. They organized to advocate controversial proposals for land tenure reform and changes in forest management.

Chapter 14 examines how a group of collaboratives called the U.S. Fire Learning Network (FLN) addressed institutional obstacles to restoring natural fire regimes in the nation's forests. William Hale Butler and I describe how the FLN developed a common "social imaginary" across a dispersed network of collaboratives. Disrupting old assumptions and habits in favor of a shared practice of ecological restoration, network participants were able to work autonomously while engaging in a coordinated challenge to long-standing professional and organizational commitments to fire suppression.

In chapter 15, I identify ways that the fields of natural resource management and planning can benefit from understanding how both professions have approached collaborative resilience. Social-ecological scholarship can benefit from an understanding of how collaboration can reshape collective knowledge, identity, and governance possibilities. Planning scholarship likewise can benefit from an appreciation of how resilience informs an expanded range of collaborative processes that can enable communities to do more than just rapidly recover from an immediate crisis. I also suggest that the productive tension between the two fields informs us on several questions: How can communities reach agreement on what social and ecological relationships they should attempt to make more resilient? What approach should they use? Who will benefit? This approach (which I call "communicative resilience") can enable communities to better understand their place within complex adaptive systems. As communities engage with power and politics, they can make a just resilience possible.

Conclusion

At the convocation in Cassell Coliseum on April 17, 2007, the day following the shootings, professor and poet Nikki Giovanni delivered a poem called "We Are Virginia Tech."[1] Giovanni urged the university to take time to reflect and learn, rather than strive to "move on" quickly from the tragedy: "We are better than we think we are and not quite what we want to be. We are alive to the imaginations and the possibilities. We will continue to invent the future through our blood and tears and through all our sadness." Giovanni asked us to broaden our compassion to include those suffering from other crises, such as AIDS, warfare, and water scarcity, as well as the suffering that humans inflict on other species.

In this spirit, *Collaboration for Resilience* examines the potential to apply the collaborative energy that Virginia Tech demonstrated after the shootings to a broad range of challenges, including systematic oppression, natural disaster, resource scarcity, and climate change. This book shows how collaboration can create and build community by fostering trust and the capacity for mutual reinvention. Collaboration can create new kinds of knowledge, identity, and institutions. You can read in these chapters about communities that have resolved disputes and recovered from crises. This book considers how crises may offer a challenge to injustice and how crisis may promote greater resilience. The concept of resilience is a complex and irreducibly uncertain and contingent goal, consigning hope for speedy return to an optimized equilibrium to an earlier, more innocent time.

You will not learn from this book any specific guidelines for practice. We do not mean to offer modeled futures and or firm policy recommendations. Instead, this book offers to you some stories of what may happen. You will come away with situated knowledge, contingencies, details, analogies, and interpretations. We encourage you to adopt a precautionary humility in seeking to promote resilience. We hope no one will approach this challenge with an illusory sense of mastery and control. Rather, we encourage you to enable participants in collaborative processes to come to their own understanding of resilience by drawing on their own knowledge and telling their own stories. This method can aid consensus. This strategy can also enable a committed group to challenge dysfunctional but durable institutions. Such a capacity is especially useful during times of rapid transformation, when existing governance models often fail.

Note

1. Transcript and video online at http://www.americanrhetoric.com/speeches/nikkigiovannivatechmemorial.htm.

References

Berkes, F., and C. Folke. 1998. *Linking social and ecological systems.* Cambridge, U.K.: Cambridge University Press.

Booher, D. E., and J. E. Innes. 2002. Network power in collaborative planning. *Journal of Planning Education and Research* 21:221–236.

Botkin, D. B. 1990. *Discordant harmonies: A new ecology for the twenty-first century*. New York: Oxford University Press.

Caro, R. A. 1974. *The power broker: Robert Moses and the fall of New York*. 1st ed. New York: Knopf.

Carroll, M. S. H., L. Lorie, P. J. Cohn, and J. Burchfield. 2006. Community wildfire events as a source of social conflict. *Rural Sociology* 71:261–280.

Fukuyama, F. 2007. *Blindside: How to anticipate forcing events and wild cards in global politics*. Washington, D.C.: Brookings Institution Press.

Fullilove, M. 2004. *Root shock: Upheaval, resettlement and recovery in urban America*. New York: Random House.

Gunderson, L., and C. S. Holling. 2002. *Panarchy: Understanding transformations in human and natural systems*. Washington, D.C.: Island Press.

Gunderson, L., C. S. Holling, and S. Light, eds. 1995. *Barriers and bridges to the renewal of ecosystems and institutions*. New York: Columbia University Press.

Hardin, G. J., and J. Baden. 1977. *Managing the commons*. San Francisco: W. H. Freeman.

Healey, P. 1997. *Collaborative planning: Shaping places in fragmented societies*. London: Macmillan Press.

Hoffman, S. M. 1999. The worst of times, the best of times: Toward a model of cultural response to disaster. In *Catastrophe and culture: The anthropology of disaster*, ed. S. M. Hoffman and A. Oliver-Smith, 134–155. Santa Fe, NM: School of American Research Press.

Holling, C. S. 1978. *Adaptive environmental assessment and management*. New York: John Wiley and Sons.

Innes, J. E., and D. E. Booher. 2010. *Planning with complexity: An introduction to collaborative rationality for public policy*. New York: Routledge.

Jacobs, J. 1961. *The death and life of great American cities*. New York: Random House.

Levin, S. 1999. *Fragile dominion: Complexity and the commons*. Reading, MA: Perseus Books.

Margerum, R. D., and D. Whitall. 2004. The challenges and implications of collaborative management on a river basin scale. *Journal of Environmental Planning and Management* 47 (3): 407–427.

Mintz, A. 2001. *Popular culture and the shaping of Holocaust memory in America*. Seattle; London: University of Washington Press.

Nowak, J., and R. E. Veilleux. 2008. Personal reflections on the Virginia Tech tragedy from a victim's spouse with commentary by a close colleague. *Traumatology* 14:89–99.

Ostrom, E. 1990. *Governing the commons: The evolution of institutions for collective action*. Cambridge, U.K.: Cambridge University Press.

Ryan, J., and J. Hawdon. 2008. From individual to community: The "framing" of 4–16 and the display of social solidarity. *Traumatology* 14:43–51.

Susskind, L. C. J. 1987. *Breaking the impasse: Consensual approaches to resolving public disputes*. New York: Basic Books.

Walker, B., C. S. Holling, S. R. Carpenter, and A. Kinzig. 2004. Resilience, adaptability and transformability in social ecological systems. *Ecology and Society* 9(2): 5.

Worster, D. 1994. *Nature's economy: A history of ecological ideas*. Cambridge, U.K.: Cambridge University Press.

I
Understanding Collaboration

2

Planning Resilient Communities: Insights from Experiences with Risky Technologies

Connie P. Ozawa

This chapter explores the factors of social trust and communicative planning in the development of communities resilient to crisis. A "resilient system" is "one that can withstand shocks and surprises, absorb extreme stresses, and maintain its core functions, though perhaps in an altered form (Innes and Booher 2010, 205). A "resilient community" may be defined as a community that is able to respond to unexpected and unwelcomed events in ways that enable groups and individuals to work together to minimize the adverse consequences of such crises. A resilient community is adaptable, not rigid. Understanding how to build such communities is a pressing issue, given the frequency of crises such as the 9/11 tragedy, the recent flooding in the Midwest, electrical blackouts to several states from a bird on a power line, the hurricane in New Orleans, coastal areas battered by oil spills, and wildfires encroaching on residential subdivisions in Southern California.

Technology-based risks are more predictable than natural disasters or terror acts. Risky technologies, such as nuclear power plants, inherently pose dangers to people. Moreover, planning for the use of such technologies entails deliberate decisions by one group of people to place others in harm's way, albeit to an unknowable degree of certainty. These technologies run a danger spectrum that varies in terms of severity, nature, and scale of harm and intentionality; but they all share a positive probability of disaster occurring.

Since the 1986 Superfund Amendment Reauthorization Act (SARA), communities have invested in planning to anticipate crises resulting from the accommodation of risky technologies. Emergency mitigation plans are one example of this effort to mitigate harm or to remove populations from imminent danger. Such plans can create and clarify the social organization and technological infrastructure that will be needed in a crisis. If a crisis were to arise, the community would be better able to respond, minimize damage, reassess its assets, and resume normal livelihoods and lives.

Planning for risky technologies is a social effort that involves people: the decision makers, the implementers, public managers, planners, and the population at risk. They work together to plan, weigh risks, and make decisions. Relationships among these people are established long before the event, as well as during crises, and remain long after.

What we want to know is this: How can communities enhance their coherence in ways that go beyond simply the preparation of disaster recovery plans? What can we learn from these experiences that can help to build resilient communities?

In this chapter, I posit that social trust is an important ingredient in achieving the type of working relationships that fuel resilient communities. I propose that we can learn from both the experiences of a community dealing with a crisis and from one struggling to invest resources appropriately in technologies intended to reduce risks.

Communicative planning (CP) theory has emerged to challenge the "rational" planning model. CP theory focuses on the communications among actors and provides a framework for examining social trust in the community. In this chapter, two examples of crises will be viewed in light of this theory. Pivotal points in the dynamics of ongoing relationships emerge. After an analysis of how trust was lost and regained in these cases, this chapter will summarize how CP theory, with its linkages to negotiation theory, can help inform planners and other public managers who plan for risky technologies to plan for resilient communities.

Communicative Planning (CP) Theory and Social Trust

Communicative planning (CP) theory is about the *objects* of planning: gathering data, conducting analyses, generating alternatives, and recommending an optimum course. It is also about the *subjects* of planning and their relationships: the decision makers, the implementers, the people affected by the decision or plan, the planners, and the public managers. The theory intertwines substance (or the topics addressed in the product), process, and relationships. As Healey (1997, 29–30) notes, the theory is grounded in such factors as the acceptance that knowledge is socially constructed, that individuals learn about their "preferences" through interaction with others, and that public policies intended to manage "coexistence in shared spaces" must involve all with a "stake" in a given place. The communications that occur during the planning process explicitly (and implicitly) create and define the relationships among the individuals involved.

CP researchers have highlighted different aspects of the planning process and the relationships among the actors. Some authors focus on the blow-by-blow details of specific encounters and draw insights for theory from them (Forester 1999; Sandercock 2000). The new institutionalists consider how structures and relationships affect agency (Healey 1997), while still others note the apparent spontaneity of self-organizing forces among individuals (Innes and Booher 1999). There are two things in common among these writers: recognition of the interpersonal and inter-institutional dynamics of planning practice, and the importance of these dynamics in planning outcomes.

CP theory borrows heavily from the fields of negotiation, public dispute resolution, and consensus building (Forester 1999; Healey 1997; Hillier 2002; Innes 1996). Such cross-fertilization makes sense because planning is joint decision making; planning is, at its core, a negotiation among many parties (Shmueli et al. 2008). It is not surprising to find that the negotiation literature similarly identifies the importance of the same three elements: substance, process, and relationships. In fact, authors from the consensus-building field have long noted the primacy of these key components of negotiations (Carpenter and Kennedy 1988). Considerable attention has been directed toward the people and relationship aspects of negotiations (Bush and Folger 2005; Carlson 2007; Fisher and Brown 1987; Fisher and Shapiro 2005; Kolb and Williams 2000, 2003). Relationships are obviously crucial in negotiations; they set the context for individuals to interpret the meaning of everyone else's words and actions.

We can inquire further into relationships in communicative planning by exploring how they are considered in the rich negotiation literature. Books with titles such as *Getting Together, Beyond Reason,* and *The Shadow Negotiation* underscore the importance of relationships (Fisher and Brown 1987; Fisher and Shapiro 2005; Kolb and Williams 2000).

One critical factor in relationships and how they are structured is trust. On the interpersonal level, negotiation theorists emphasize the need for negotiators to pay attention to how their words and actions affect trust and their ability to achieve their goals. CP writers Kumar and Paddison have suggested that the "glue" that holds communities together is social trust (Kumar and Paddison 2000). It is social trust that allows individuals and organizations to work together with the expectation that their collective efforts will result in the collective good. "Trust is generally understood as 'a leap of faith' . . . [whereby stakeholders] believe that each is interested in the others' welfare and that neither will act without first considering the action's impact on the other" (Kumar 1996, p. 95). Where does the leap of faith come from? It may derive from peoples' belief in the altruism or paternalism of others. Alternatively, trust may develop when people come to understand that their own interests will not be met without an agreement that is acceptable and that fills the needs of the other parties. It is this alternative view that negotiation theorists would suggest (Fisher, Ury, and Patty 1991; Susskind and Cruikshank 1987). Let us suppose that recognition of mutual interdependency is indeed a factor in demonstrating that one is trustworthy. If so, then a closer examination of trust in risky situations may offer insights to planners and public managers. Kumar and Paddison (2000) explain the link between trust and planning theory:

Actively seeking trust would, therefore, engage professionals with the stakeholders in a process of continuous interaction under the conditions of communicative rationality leading to shared understanding and mutually agreed upon decisions. (p. 209)

In summary, communicative planning theory stresses the importance of relationships as part of the planning process. Kumar and Paddison have suggested that generating trust is a necessary ingredient of the work. An intentional effort to build trust requires a more detailed examination of the constitutive elements of trust. The next section will point out specific factors in the content of communications and actions that enhance trust among individuals.

Operationalizing Social Trust

Social psychologists refer to the terms "affect-based trust" and "cognition-based trust." *Affect-based trust* is generally perceived as innate in individuals to varying degrees. It is the sort of trust that elicits comments such as "She is a trusting person and does not expect ill of anyone." This ability to trust is associated with a social-emotional bond. It is elusive in the sense that researchers are not quite sure how an individual comes to have this emotional ability (Johnson and Grayson 2005; Kim 2005; McAllister 1995). Interestingly, scientists have identified that a hormone, oxytocin, is associated with social attachment and affiliation (Kosfeld et al. 2005). In experiments, when human subjects were administered a dose of oxytocin, they exhibited higher levels of affect-based trust.

In contrast, *cognition-based trust* comes from the mind, not the heart. It is the type of trust that must be built. A person may gain it, only to later lose it. It includes the type of trust that is based in observable behaviors, actions, and experience. Because cognition-based trust can be intentionally shaped, it is particularly relevant to planners and public managers anticipating risky situations.

In their work about choosing sites for hazardous facilities, Kasperson, Golding, and Tuler (1992) define social trust as "a person's expectation that other persons and institutions in a social relationship can be relied upon to act in ways that are competent, predictable, and caring" (Kasperson et al. 1992, p. 169). They then go on to add one more dimension: commitment. They describe the four factors in this way:

1. *Competence*   Trust is gained only when the individual or institution) in a social relationship is judged to be reasonably competent in its actions over time. While expectations may not be violated if these individuals or institutions are occasionally wrong, consistent failures and discoveries of unexpected incompetence and inadequacies can lead to a loss of trust.

2. *Commitment*   Trust relies on perceptions of uncompromised commitment to a common mission or goal (such as protection of the public health), and fulfillment of fiduciary obligations or other social norms.

3. *Caring*   Trust relies on a perception that an individual (or institution) will act in a way that shows concern for and beneficence to trusting individuals.

4. *Predictability*   Trust rests on the fulfillment of expectations and faith . . . predictability does not necessarily require consistency of behavior. Complete consistency of behavior would require unchanging actions or beliefs, even in the face of contradictory information, and also more consistency in values and related behavior than most individuals, groups, or institutions possess. (Kasperson, et al. 1992, p. 170)

This framework is useful for examining how trust is eroded, lost, and has the potential to be rebuilt. Viewing protracted public planning and decision-making sequences as a negotiation sequence may yield lessons relevant to planning for risky technologies. By extension, such a view can also help in developing resilient communities. There is, however, an important caveat. In the public sector, issues rarely arise and get settled quickly. More often, issues are negotiated over a period of time during which words are confirmed by actions, which then inform the interpretation of subsequent words and actions. Individuals may come and go; policies and laws may change. There is an increase in the influence of the media (and other "keepers and promulgators" of the public memory) in shaping longer-term memories. Trust in the public sphere in some cases is especially complicated. It resides in relationships not just among people, but also among institutions.

The following sections offer two cases in which public officials and managers lost the public trust. In the unfolding of the events, the reactions of planners and public managers either reinforced trust or a lack of trust in the public. After the narratives, examples from the two cases will be used to show how trust, negotiation theory, and communicative planning are connected.

Nuclear Power and Three Mile Island

The first case is the crisis that occurred at the Three Mile Island (TMI) nuclear power plant near Harrisburg, Pennsylvania in 1979. Federal emergency response requirements enacted through SARA were largely a response to Three Mile Island and other subsequent industrial accidents, including Union Carbide's tragic chemical releases at their plants in Bhopal, India and Institute, West Virginia. In their book, *Dealing with an Angry Public*, Susskind and Field (1996) describe the period immediately following the TMI crisis to instruct how principles of mutual gains bargaining could have been employed to mitigate the fears and distrust that arose in the days following the event. In this chapter, the case will include relations both before the event and a full thirty years after.

Nuclear power epitomizes risky technology. There is a low but persistent probability that this technology could cause a devastating event. Facility design, construction, and operation are conducted with multiple redundancies in safety systems. But as the events at Chernobyl in 1986 show, devastations can (and do) occur. According to research into TMI conducted by Goldsteen and Schorr (1991), the physical and mental well-being of nearby residents was seriously affected. The legitimacy of the facility operator, government spokespersons, and agencies involved was severely diminished. At the national level, the TMI event is a significant factor behind the long dormancy of the U.S. nuclear industry. No new licenses were sought for nuclear facilities in the United States for twenty-five years following the event.

The nuclear power industry generated considerable angst among residents in many regions of the country in the 1970s. Rather sophisticated organizations such as the Clamshell Alliance (in Seabrook, New Hampshire), the Oyster Shell Alliance (near New Orleans, Louisiana), and the Abalone Alliance (in California), emerged and raised serious doubts about the safety of nuclear power. Organized opposition did not arise, however, at Three Mile Island (TMI). This facility is located on an island in the Susquehanna River about ten miles from Harrisburg, the state capital of Pennsylvania. As Goldsteen and Schorr (1991) note, the Nuclear Regulatory Commission's (NRC) Special Inquiry Group reported no dissension. Preliminary hearings were virtually devoid of rancor. There were no charges of land grabbing. There were no residential dislocations. To be sure, some farmers were apprehensive about the effects of releases from the plant; but the apprehension of a few farmers seemed hardly more ominous to decision makers "than the potential smog and soot from a fossil fuel plant" (p. 11).

Most residents in the TMI environs were relatively indifferent about the risks of nuclear power until the fateful near-meltdown and release of radioactivity that occurred on March 28, 1979. That morning, residents were handed a series of conflicting and contradictory press releases from Metropolitan Edison, the owner/operator of the TMI plant, and state and federal government officials. These press reports mentioned a malfunction at the plant, the release of radioactive gases, and the progress in stabilizing the crisis. (It is noteworthy that *local* government seemed to be relatively out-of-the-loop in the making of official reports.) At the time, plant operators had only a limited sense of the scope of the problem. It was learned later that it took several days for the operators to know fully what was wrong. Government officials, particularly then-Governor Thornburgh, attempted to convey reassuring yet appropriately precautionary statements, such as encouraging the evacuation of only pregnant women and young children. On the second day, the NRC spokesperson issued a statement to the public declaring (prematurely) that the "danger was over," despite continuing confusion among facility managers. By the evening of the third day, news anchor Walter Cronkite broadcast this startling admission to the nation: "The world has never known a day quite like today. It faced the considerable uncertainties and dangers of the worst nuclear power plant accident of the atomic age. And the horror tonight is that it could get much worse" (Seaman 2006). Cronkite's dire report arose from an expert's assessment of the situation. The NRC promptly attempted to discredit the news report with press releases on the fourth day. On the fifth day, in an effort to calm fears and nerves, President Jimmy Carter and Governor Thornburgh visited the control room at TMI to demonstrate to the public the lack of danger of a core meltdown or any other catastrophic event.

Metropolitan Edison withheld and misinformed government officials (Susskind and Field 1996). Authorities and the media disseminated conflicting information apparently without attempting to reconcile competing statements. Some residents believed the miscommunications were not inadvertent, but a result of flat-out lies (Goldsteen and Schorr, 1991 p. 82). Clearly postevent communications were not handled well. According to the President's commission in 1979:

The response to the emergency was dominated by an atmosphere of almost total confusion. There was lack of communication at all levels. Many key recommendations were made by individuals who were not in possession of accurate information, and those who managed the accident were slow to realize the significance and implications of the events that had taken place. (President's Commission on the Accident at Three Mile Island 1979)

Contradictory communications contributed to a growing distrust of authorities. Over the subsequent months and years, community members continued to express unease with Metropolitan Edison and government regulators. One resident, in response to a question about how she felt six months after the crisis event, talked about Metropolitan Edison's plans to decontaminate the plant:

"I heard yesterday . . . [that they] are going to let this gas [Krypton-85] out, and it's the best and it's the safest [approach]. How can they say it's the safest? . . . We're just experiments. . . . We are their experiments because it's cheaper that way, and it's easier all around." (Goldsteen and Schorr, 1991 pp. 38–39)

Inevitably, unscheduled releases also occurred, which then had to be admitted and explained after-the-fact. These releases further eroded the community's sense of confidence in the competency of plant operators. One resident stated bluntly, "I don't think that they know what they're doing" (Goldsteen and Schorr, 1991 p. 57).

Residents expressed skepticism about how highly their health and safety were valued by Metropolitan Edison or the government regulators. One citizen said, "I kind of feel that money talks louder than voices, and they [Metropolitan Edison] have the influence and money behind them" (Goldsteen and Schorr, 1991 p. 53). An editorial in the *Philadelphia Inquirer* amplified that sentiment: "There are alternatives to venting into the atmosphere the radioactive krypton gas. . . . Venting is by far the cheapest and easiest method" (*Philadelphia Inquirer* 1980). Residents believed that neither the plant operators nor the government regulators considered their health or welfare a priority.

When their utility rates were increased (presumably to cover clean-up costs), residents suddenly learned another highly unsettling fact: that the power generated at the Three Mile Island facility was not for their use, but was delivered to residents hundreds of miles away in New Jersey! This incongruency again served to reinforce the sense that Metropolitan Edison, and the regulators by their complicity, were concerned more about their own fiscal viability than the well-being of the nearby residents.

The decontamination process entailed additional planned and controlled releases of radioactive materials into the air and water of the Susquehanna River. Accusations of mismanagement and incompetence continued to flood out of the media (Lyons 1983). Experts dueled in the press over the health risks of low-level exposures to radiation. The local authorities did little to allay resident concerns. When a public health study was commissioned to investigate health impacts of the radioactive releases, local authorities selected a health official who had stated publicly, *prior to the study*, that in his opinion the risks were not significant (Goldsteen and Schorr 1991).

Residents in the area continued to suffer anxiety from the 1979 event for years after. When the facility applied for permits to restart power generation, residents strenuously voiced concerns about the competency and candor of nuclear plant operators. In 1982, voters in three countries opposed restarting any of the TMI reactors (Dickinson College 2007). Twenty years after the event, residents continued to suspect radioactivity for things such as incidences of cancer, the remains of a two-headed calf born two years after the event, and other oddities. They continued to keep radiation monitors turned on in their homes. And, they continued not to trust Metropolitan Edison and government regulators (World Media Foundation 1999).

The next case is about planning to prevent a potentially disastrous contamination of drinking water in a city's open-air reservoir. Through this example we see that relational information is not only part of responding to crises but also part of planning for preventive technologies around risky events. The community is struggling to define the nature and acceptability of risk. Like the Three Mile Island experience, we see how trust among the community can be eroded and lost.

Mt. Tabor Reservoir

In 2002, the Portland, Oregon Water Bureau announced that they were planning to replace two of the city's main reservoirs with buried tanks. Their decision stemmed from the terrorist attacks of Sept. 11, 2001. The open reservoirs that supplied the city's residents with their drinking water seemed like a sitting target. But the bureau did not expect the public opposition that erupted. The affected public arrived uninvited to contest the tank plan. Several hundred citizens joined hands and stood in a circle around the Mt. Tabor reservoir in a symbolic gesture to protect it from the city's bulldozers. Their stand forced not only a reconsideration of the plan, but ultimately a reversal of the decision by city leaders. In this case, how the city dealt with the public clearly shaped the relationship among city residents, the Water Bureau, and elected officials.

As far back as the 1970s, the city had considered covering its largest open air reservoirs, built in 1894 and 1911. These reservoirs were located inside two city parks: Washington Park on the west side of town just above downtown, and Mt. Tabor Park on the east side of the Willamette River, atop an ancient volcanic cinder cone. The then-newly organized federal Environmental Protection Agency (EPA) issued a statement discouraging new construction of uncovered reservoirs to ensure drinking water quality. The city contracted with engineering firm CH2MHill to conduct a study of the facilities, but they then abandoned plans to retrofit due to the magnitude of the estimated costs. In 1981, Oregon passed rules requiring all new open reservoirs to be equipped with watertight roofs, reflecting concerns about the safety of open reservoirs. In 1999, the EPA passed rules requiring the covering of open reservoirs (or treatment of water from open reservoirs) serving populations of 10,000 persons or more (United States Office of Water 1999). By definition, those rules covered Portland effective October, 2008. The covering of open reservoirs was hardly a new idea.

Portland obtains water from the Bull Run reservoir, deep in the Cascade Mountains. Bull Run is one of the purest municipal water sources in the continental United States and until 1999 had met all EPA drinking-water standards without treatment or filtering. Late in 1999, the Water Bureau commissioned another study of its aging reservoirs, contracting with Montgomery Watson Harza (MWH). This company was a 6,000-person global engineering firm with an office staff of 40 located in Portland. Its vice president was a former chief engineer at the bureau. The firm's March 2001 assessment concluded that the reservoirs indeed were in need of significant repairs, but that no major overhaul of the system would be required for another twenty to twenty-five years.

After the September 11, 2001 attack on the World Trade Center in New York City, MWH returned to Portland city leaders to recommend covering the reservoirs in order to avoid deliberate contamination by terrorists. The city council members believed it was right to take such defensive action and in spring 2002, committed an estimated $76 million to the Water Bureau. The contract to facilitate public involvement was awarded to MWH, which also had the expertise to bid on the infrastructure project itself. The council gave permission to Commissioner Dan Saltzman, who was overseeing the reservoir project, to move ahead. (Saltzman was one of four commissioners who along with the mayor comprised the council.) The city decided to hold public meetings to discuss how the land placed atop the proposed capped facilities might be used, but not to discuss whether or not to cover the reservoirs. This relatively swift action alarmed neighbors of the Mt. Tabor reservoir. Portlanders are proud of their water's natural purity, fiscally prudent, and wary of add-on treatments that bear their own risks of chemical contamination. They also expected consultation on large public works projects. Residents formed a group called "Friends of Mt. Tabor Reservoir" and began demanding that the issue be reviewed through a more open process. In the group's document (2004), the Friends stated that neighbors were shocked by the city's "careless, even arrogant approach to citizen involvement." The Friends researched how other communities were dealing with uncovered reservoirs and found an example of an alternative to burial: in Pittsburgh, a micro-filtration plant was added to the water system at half the cost of covering the reservoir. They were skeptical of MWH's reports and legal documents, which they contended included "a significant amount of boilerplate material." Further, they said that the reports were "heavily self-referential." The group suspected that the consultants were not neutral parties, but instead had their own business interests to promote. That is, by arguing for increased security or highlighting the necessity of new water quality requirements, the consultants were making the case for additional studies and creating new opportunities for design and construction contracts for which their firm could compete (Friends of Mt. Tabor Reservoir 2004, p. 1).

Portland's neighborhoods are organized into city-supported neighborhood associations. Volunteer members in designated districts assume responsibility for organizing residents' concerns and coordinating responses to planning-related initiatives. This system is emblematic of Portland's commitment to public involvement in city decisions. As such, the process implements the first goal of the state's land-use law: citizen involvement. Neighborhood associations near the city parks where the reservoirs were located submitted to Commissioner Saltzman written requests to slow down the process in order to allow for the airing of additional concerns. A letter from the Pearl District Neighborhood Association states, "It is incomprehensible that proposed significant changes to the visual character of the reservoirs should not be subject to extensive discussion, planning, and public debate" (Case 2002). The Arlington Heights Neighborhood Association sent a letter acknowledging the city's security concerns but questioning whether planned actions would be effective or fiscally wise (Boly 2003).

Residents flooded into public meetings. However, throughout 2002 and 2003, their requests to the city to reconsider the plan were ignored and rebuffed by Commissioner Saltzman and the Water Bureau. In January, 2003, Commissioner Saltzman insisted, "The public health and safety threats are real. We are acting on behalf of all citizens of Portland. If we're going to do this in the three-year timetable that we had planned to, it doesn't allow for a timeout" (Jacklet 2003). He continued to deny any further review as specifically requested by the Friends, and he refused to engage the citizens entirely.

By the summer of 2003, fifteen local businesses publicly questioned the city's decision, noting a lack of consultation in the process and suggesting that the final costs of the project could run higher than twice the city's estimate of $107 million. Commissioner Saltzman noted the businesses' input by saying "They're coming in quite late" (Neves and Giedwoyn 2003). To their concern about cost overruns, he simply insisted that the project would stay below the official cost estimate.

In August 2003, a majority of the members of the city-sponsored Mt. Tabor Reservoir Replacement Project public advisory committee assembled to provide input on landscaping the covered reservoirs. Instead, they sent a memo to the mayor and the city council underscoring the historic value of the reservoirs and concluded that "the decision to bury the reservoirs was made under a false sense of urgency, without proper public process, and that creative alternatives were not considered." They requested the council to "defer further effort on this expensive and controversial project until there has been an independent analysis of alternatives, and full and open public discussion of those findings" (Members of Mt. Tabor Reservoir Replacement Project 2003).

In the fall of 2003, the Friends filed a lawsuit. The group alleged that the bond measure that provided the source of funds for the reservoir project could not be used legally for these purposes. Although the Friends would ultimately lose this lawsuit, public criticism of the Water Bureau was growing and a small group of influential local leaders met with Commissioner Saltzman in December, 2003, to persuade him to delay the project long enough to form a new citizen advisory panel and hear the panel's recommendations. Although Saltzman agreed, he allowed only ninety days for the new panel to come up with its findings. Further, no Friends were allowed on the panel; he said that the Friends were not impartial.

The Mt. Tabor and Washington Park reservoirs were listed on the National Register of Historic Places in January 2004. In June 2004, the second citizen advisory panel recommended that the city revisit the decision to bury the water and in the meanwhile, to implement interim water-security measures. The council accepted this recommendation. By the fall of 2004, a new mayor was elected and he reshuffled the commissioner assignments, asking Commissioner Randy Leonard to oversee the Water Bureau. Leonard promptly sent e-mails to many citizen leaders apologizing for the past dismissive responses to their concerns. The reservoir project was put on indefinite hold and the city set out to request waivers from federal EPA drinking water standards. Although these exemptions appear unlikely (as late as March 2011), the city says it is also prepared to seek congressional action to allow Portland to continue to take advantage of their exceptionally pure drinking water.

Findings and Discussion
There is no evidence in either of these cases that the residents began with a strong distrust of public officials and managers. However, residents quickly came to believe that these figures were not to be trusted. What did public officials and public managers do to evoke this reaction? Sheer lack of responsiveness to residents was a huge factor shaping public perceptions. A closer look at the various elements of trust, as presented by Kasperson, Golding, and Tuler (1992) can provide more insight into exactly how trust was lost.

In both cases, official decision makers and "those in charge" quickly came to be regarded as incompetent. In the TMI event, the plant operators and managers added to the public's perception of their incompetence by their repeated releases of contradictory information without coherent explanations of the discrepancies. In the Portland reservoir case, decision makers were viewed as being (mis)led by a consulting firm that could potentially benefit financially by presenting a limited range of options for ensuring safe drinking water. The public demonstrated their ability to become strong advocates and technical experts surprisingly quickly. The city's technical competency was drawn into question because the city, with its sole focus on terrorist attacks, did not demand a thorough examination of water-treatment alternatives (whereas the citizens' group did examine such alternatives).

In both cases, residents had reason to doubt that the decision makers shared a commitment to common goals. In the TMI case, local utility users were horrified about rate increases imposed after the accident. They were even more incensed when they learned that the Three Mile Island facility supplied power not to their homes and businesses, but to markets hundreds of miles away in New Jersey. In the Portland case, a city commissioner repeatedly signaled to community groups that their concerns were discounted. He sidestepped their worries about escalating project costs, and complained openly about how the turmoil was resulting in project delays. The public wondered if safe water was ever really the issue. The city had acknowledged that the water supply would remain vulnerable to other sources of contamination and that the city would not take steps to prevent this. This acknowledgment underscored residents' suspicions about the commitment of the City and their consultants to the putative goal of ensuring safe drinking water. In the minds of both TMI neighbors and Portland residents, dollars seemed to trump their welfare and safety.

The third factor contributing to trust (Kasperson et al. 1992) is "caring." In the years following the near-meltdown at Three Mile Island, residents have continued to express anxieties about the safety of the facility and the impact of prior radioactive releases on their long-term health. They were not comforted by the state's decision to contract a health study with a researcher who had publicly expressed doubt of significant adverse health effects from TMI. In the minds of some residents, the mere act of ignoring residents' feelings indicated a lack of sincere concern for their well-being.

In the reservoir case, the city failed to understand the core concerns of the residents. While covering a beloved, historic water feature was the focal point of the dialog, the commissioner's lack of engaging the Friends group (and later the business group) did not convey the level of respect that Portlanders expected. His refusal to talk with citizens appeared to indicate that he saw himself independent of the electorate. In contrast, the second official on the project issued an apology, signaling that the city did value the residents' perspectives. The apology paved the way for working together productively. In both cases, the refusal to engage residents closed off opportunities to exchange information that could have been useful in building trust. Negotiation theory provides useful concepts here. Fisher, Ury, and Patton (1991) offer a prescription of "focusing on interests, not positions." They advise negotiators to look beyond the demands that others make. Negotiators must find out why people are making those demands. What are the concerns and needs motivating their behavior? Whereas positions are often diametrically opposed, the multiple interests obscured by these positions may be shared (different but not conflicting), as well as conflicting. Negotiators who separate out these interests are more likely to develop options that offer something of value to all parties above what they may attain away from the negotiations. Robust agreements are pacts that recognize the interdependence of parties. More dialogue and exchange of information increases the likelihood trust will develop.

Finally, lack of predictability and consistency can fuel suspicions among the public. Communications after the toxic releases at Three Mile Island were plagued with inadvertent and even deliberate falsehoods, delays, and contradictions. In the reservoir case, the inconsistency of the city's response to residents' outcries was not only baffling and highly frustrating, but also raised questions about the city's underlying motives behind the reservoir projects. Portland is known for open decision-making. Whether this reputation is fully deserved or not, the apparently abrupt decision after the events of 9/11 by the city council to hurriedly move forward on the project without additional public input (despite the public outcry) struck many as out-of-character with the city's culture. This "lack of predictability" further fueled citizens' doubts and distrust.

While these cases provide examples of the ways in which the actions and communications of key actors worked to erode trust, how can this knowledge be translated into efforts to build trust and strong relationships in the community?

Implications for Planning for Risky Technologies

Planning for risky technologies is dicey not only for the vulnerable populations but also for public institutions. Conventional approaches by authorities rely on the wall of protection offered by the shield of expertise (Ozawa 1996). Clearly, disaster planning is tricky. Which official wants to be the one to say that the proposed (or in place) technology will impose a chance of horrendous harm or exorbitant costs? Instead, authorities often take the course of building up a case for the need of the technology, downplaying the chance of operations malfunctioning, and minimizing the risks by developing and implementing mitigation plans. But even the best-laid plans can go awry. Despite all the failsafes at Three Mile Island plant, we know now that power plants can erupt. When a plan to ward off danger does not work, the failure is usually at great expense to the groups ostensibly in charge: public regulators and industry.

What does communicative planning (CP) suggest to us about planning for risky technologies? As a descriptive theory, CP helps to understand how thirty years after TMI, public managers and planners can continue to enact the same cycle leading to public distrust. The political/economic structure of government and private actors (with their own agenda) creates incentives for self-interested, defensive, and obfsucatory action. Taken as normative theory, CP suggests an approach quite different from expert-driven or narrowly conceived, political processes. Communicative planning suggests that an initial step is to ensure that relationships among the managers, decision makers, and the populations at risk are explicitly acknowledged. In this strategy, operators and regulators would of course try to anticipate undesirable events by developing disaster relief plans and providing additional emergency response resources. But also they would try to build a strong social foundation in the community—not just with local elected leaders.

There are four guidelines for planning for risky technologies:

1. Identify and notify those likely to be affected.
2. Together, establish a knowledge base.
3. Discuss alternatives and choose an option acceptable to all.
4. Be transparent and share long-term commitment.

Identify and Notify Those Likely to be Affected

The first guideline is early identification and notification of the likely affected populations. Who are they? These people need to be notified so that they can be involved. This task of careful outreach might entail publicizing proposals widely at the initial planning stages, as well as actively seeking out special communication methods to reach affected populations. While this guideline is not a novel one by any stretch, it is one that is often ignored in planning for technologically sophisticated facilities.

Together, Establish a Knowledge Base

The second guideline is to foster an exchange of ideas. Two-way communication channels must be opened and structured to facilitate this information exchange. Public managers, elected officials, technology operators, and residents need a chance to hear and listen to one another's worries and concerns. Potential risks surrounding the technology should be shared openly. Identifying the bounds of certainty and uncertainty will add a level of candidness to discussions and, counter-intuitively, may bolster the perception of competency of the operators and regulators, especially if a low-probability crisis later occurs (Ozawa 2005). In the consensus-building literature this guideline is known as joint fact-finding (Susskind et al. 1999). But this second guideline might be labeled more accurately "socially constructing a shared knowledge base," because uncertainty will frustrate a search for "facts" on both technical issues as well as political issues. A knowledge base must be created in order to conduct planning. Including the community in the creation of the knowledge base demonstrates a caring for community concerns and the residents' well-being.

The community may then better respect the facility developer or operator, regulators, elected officials, and planners.

Mutual respect is not the only reason for the second guideline. In negotiations, understanding what others care about and why a particular alternative solution satisfies their needs are crucial to crafting an agreement that is stable, durable, and implementable. Moreover, when agreements are mutually acceptable because basic priorities of each party are satisfied, each party has something to gain by seeing the agreement implemented (which de facto acknowledges interdependency).

Discuss Alternatives and Choose an Option Acceptable to All
The third guideline is to facilitate discussions to reveal how the needs of groups will be met through various alternative courses of action. Then, select one that is acceptable to all and make this reasoning transparent.

It is a fact that communities live with risk. What is unacceptable is the involuntary imposition of risk, and the distribution of benefits that emanate from risky technologies (Fischhoff, et al. 1981). Indeed, every reduction in risk comes with a cost and, at some point a community may elect to incur a certain level of risk to reap the expected gains (or so that the additional public dollars may be better spent elsewhere). In anticipation of the inevitable acceptance of some level of risk, the common benefits of the use of the technology should be made clear. Risk bearers will likely expect that benefits are dispersed and commensurate with the attending chance, magnitude, and nature of harm or loss. For example, a community may be more willing to accept a nuclear facility whose size and operations correspond to the power consumption of that community. By contrast, in the TMI case, residents were forced to take on risks from a plant sized to meet the demands of remote populations.

Be Transparent and Share Long-term Commitment
The fourth guideline is identifying (and keeping clear and salient) a collective commitment to the varied interests of the sponsors of risky technologies and the most at-risk population.

Everyone must respond to one another's legitimate concerns, whenever they arise: elected officials, regulators, planners, technology operators, and members of the public. All of these people and the organizations they represent are interdependent; mutual recognition of that fact is crucial. When everyone has a shared commitment to the long-term health of the community, good working relationships can develop. When there is transparency in decision making, everyone benefits. A forum and process for fostering strong community relationships does not require some minimum frequency of use. But it does require consistency among the parties to use it.

Conclusion

A community's ability to recover from a disaster is contingent on the level of social trust among individuals and institutions. Communicative planning theory helps us to examine not just planning analysis, decisions, and outcomes, but also the process and its social relationships. When we view the interactions as an implicit negotiation, the focus is sharpened on how specific behaviors affect social trust. However, as in negotiations, communicative planning is not simply about on-the-spot reactions. Rather, such planning entails a comprehensive view of an entire process and set of relationships from the early stages of planning.

Accidents cannot always be avoided. The Mt. Tabor Reservoir case illustrates well the mishandling of planning for risky technologies. But that case also suggests the possibility of redemption through the power of a simple apology (although apologies are not always easy to execute).

Communities are made up of people. People are highly resilient. But a resilient community requires trusting relationships among its members, including the elected officials, planners, public managers, industry, and the general population. Communicative planning theory, with its links to the negotiation field, can offer guidance. The theory proposes that when groups attend to the elements of trust that can be acted upon deliberately, they can strengthen a community's ability to deal with an uncertain future.

References

Boly, J. 2003. Personal communication to Commissioner Dan Saltzman.

Bush, R., A. Baruch and J. P. Folger. 2005. *The promise of mediation: The Transformative approach to conflict.* San Francisco: Jossey-Bass.

Carlson, C. 2007. *A practical guide to collaborative governance.* Portland, OR: Policy Consensus Initiative.

Carpenter, S., and W. J. D. Kennedy. 1988. *Managing public disputes.* San Francisco: Jossey-Bass.

Case, C. 2002. Personal communication to Commissioner Dan Saltzman.

Dickinson College. 2007. Three Mile Island emergency timeline. Accessed 1-23-2011. Available at http://www.threemileisland.org/virtual_museum/index.html.

Fischhoff, B., S. Lichtenstein, P. Slovic, S. L. Derby, and R. Keeney. 1981. *Acceptable risk*. New York: Cambridge University Press.

Fisher, R., and S. Brown. 1987. *Getting together: Building a relationship that gets to yes*. Boston: Houghton Mifflin Company.

Fisher, R., and D. Shapiro. 2005. *Beyond reason: Using emotions as you negotiate*. New York: Viking.

Fisher, R., W. Ury, and B. Patton. 1991. *Getting to yes: Negotiating agreement without giving in*. New York: Penguin Books.

Forester, J. 1999. *The deliberative practitioner*. London; New York: Oxford University Press.

Friends of Mt. Tabor Reservoir. 2004. Introduction to the organization and its goals. Unpublished document.

Goldsteen, R. L., and J. K. Schorr. 1991. *Demanding democracy after Three Mile Island*. Gainesville, FL: University of Florida Press.

Healey, P. 1997. *Collaborative planning: Shaping places in fragmented societies*. Vancouver, BC: UBC Press.

Hillier, J. 2002. *Shadows of power: An allegory of prudence in land-use planning*. New York: Routledge.

Innes, J. 1996. Planning through consensus building: A new view of the comprehensive planning ideal. *Journal of the American Planning Association* 62(4): 460–472.

Innes, J., and D. Booher. 1999. Consensus building and complex adaptive systems: A framework for evaluating collaborative planning. *Journal of the American Planning Association* 65(4):412–423.

Innes, J., and D. Booher, 2010. *Planning With Complexity: An introduction to collaborative rationality for public policy*. New York: Routledge.

Jacklet, B. 2003. City won't budge on reservoirs. *The Portland Tribune,* January 3.

Johnson, D., and K. Grayson. 2005. Cognitive and affective trust in service relationships. *Journal of Business Research* 58:500–507.

Kasperson, R., D. Golding, and S. Tuler. 1992. Social distrust as a factor in siting hazardous facilities and communicating risks. *Journal of Social Issues* 48(4):161–187.

Kim, D. J. 2005. Cognition-based versus affect-based trust determinants: A cross-culture comparison study. In Proceedings of ICIS 2005. Las Vegas, NV, December 11–14.

Kolb, D., and J. Williams. 2000. *The Shadow negotiation: How women can master the hidden agendas that determine bargaining success*. New York: Simon & Schuster.

Kolb, D., and J. Williams. 2003. *Everyday negotiation: Navigating the hidden agendas in bargaining*. San Francisco: Jossey-Bass.

Kosfeld, M., M. Heinrichs, P. J. Zak, U. Fischbacher, and E. Fehr. 2005. Oxytocin increases trust in humans. *Nature* 435(2):673–676.

Kumar, N. 1996. The power of trust in manufacturer-retailer relationships. *Harvard Business Review* 74:92–106.

Kumar, A. and R. Paddison. 2000. Trust and collaborative planning theory: The case of the Scottish planning system. *International Planning Studies.* 5(2): 205–223.

Lyons, R. D. March 28, 1983. Crews at reactor criticize cleanup. *The New York Times* A1.

McAllister, D. J. 1995. Affect- and cognition-based trust as foundations for interpersonal cooperation in organizations. *Academy of Management Journal* 38(1): 24–59.

Members of Mt. Tabor Reservoir Replacement Project. August 27, 2003. Memo to Mayor Katz, Commissioner Francseconi, Commissioner Leonard, Commissioner Saltzman, and Commissioner Sten.

Neves, R., and A. Giedwoyn. 2003. Reservoir capping project receives further criticism. Accessed 7-25-2003. Available at http://www.kgw.com/cgi.bin-/bi/gold_print.cgi .

Ozawa, C. P. 1996. Science in environmental conflicts. *Sociological Perspectives* 39(2): 219–230.

Ozawa, C. P. 2005. Putting science in its place. In *Adaptive governance and water conflict: New institutions for collaborative governance*, ed. J. T. Scholz and B. Stiftel, 186–195. Washington, D.C.: RFF Press.

Philadelphia Inquirer. March 23, 1980. What's venting at TMI is frustration and fear . . . as alternatives are ignored. 6L.

President's Commission on the Accident at Three Mile Island. October 30, 1979. *Report of the President's Commission on the Accident at Three Mile Island.* Accessed 1-23-2011. Available at http://www.pddoc.com/tmi2/kemeny/.

Sandercock, L. 2000. When strangers become neighbours: Managing cities of difference, *Planning Theory & Practice* 1 (1): 13-3.

Seaman, P. 2010. Three Mile Island: BBC gets it wrong. http://paulseaman.eu/2010/04/three-mile-island-bbc-gets-it-wrong/ Accessed 3/5/11.

Shmueli, D., S. Kaufman, and C. Ozawa. 2008. Mining negotiation theory for planning insights. *Journal of Planning Education and Research* 27(3): 359–364.

Susskind, L., and J. Cruikshank. 1987. *Breaking the Impasse: Consensual approaches to resolving public disputes.* New York: Basic Books.

Susskind, L., and P. Field. 1996. *Dealing with an angry public: The mutual gains approach to resolving disputes.* New York: The Free Press.

Susskind, L., S. McKearnan, and J. Thomas-Larmer. 1999. *The Consensus Building Handbook.* Thousand Oaks, CA: Sage Publications.

United States Office of Water. April, 1999. *Uncovered finished water reservoirs guidance manual.* Environmental Protection Agency. EPA 815-R-99–011.

World Media Foundation. March, 1999. Three Mile Island: 20 years later. *Living on Earth.* Somerville, MA. Accessed 10-25-2008. Available at http://www.loe.org/series/three/part1.htm

3

Leaping Forward: Building Resilience by Communicating Vulnerability

Moira L. Zellner, Charles J. Hoch, and Eric W. Welch

Overview

Modern life requires a complex flow of goods and services. The institutional relationships that organize this complexity are based in trust in the competence, sincerity, honesty, and legitimacy of others. The more complex the flows and the more heterogeneous the actors involved, the greater the vulnerability to violations of these social habits. Violations become more attractive and they can more easily be hidden in the web of interactions. When violations occur, they generate ripples of uncertainty that undermine everyone's confidence in the institutions and infrastructure that make the conduct of modern living reliable, predictable, and secure. Lacking social resilience, human systems may fail to adapt to either internal or external disruptions. This chapter proposes that purposeful democratic deliberation provides an important resource against disruptions. Such deliberation can improve the prevention of (and the response to) serious crises. It can help identify the shared vulnerability that these disruptions produce. It can help motivate collaborative responses. Through democratic deliberation, human diversity and ingenuity can be harnessed to collaboratively create innovative responses that enhance adaptability. This chapter offers a comparison of two empirical planning cases, covering both a housing plan for homeless populations and a farmland management plan to prevent disease outbreaks. We compare the effectiveness of civic deliberation against adversarial and bureaucratic response strategies to disruptions, identifying the conditions and incentives that are required to support each approach. We argue that civic deliberation among diverse constituents can improve the grasp of system complexity—the interactions between individuals' decisions and their social and environmental consequences—allowing stakeholders to identify their shared vulnerability and find opportunities for adaptability and long-term resilience to complex problems. Thus, we see a joint vulnerability and interdependence linked to a resilient social solidarity as a sign of strength tied to a durable social hierarchy, against the view of social autonomy and independent resources. In this chapter we propose a framework for comparison and an agenda for testing the social resilience of plans for different resource and infrastructure threats.

Introduction to Planning

Rational planning identifies the elements of order in a system. It uses this pattern to predict future behaviors of that system. Complicated systems submit to rational planning because despite the greater number of linked components of such systems, the behavior still remains predictable. True, if one component fails, the entire system fails; but rational plans duplicate components to ensure redundancy and avoid system failure. Engineering has predominated as the preferred discipline to address problems in complicated systems. Planning becomes challenging, and the scope of engineering limited, when the systems for which we plan are complex. Complex systems are characterized by a large number of components that selectively interact with other components and with their environment in nonlinear ways. These selective interactions enable self-organization and make the system adaptable to external changes, but the interactions also often make its behavior unpredictable (Amaral and Ottino 2004). Comprehending complex urban and regional systems requires planning and management that prepare the system to adapt to a range of plausible futures (rather than engineering a future). People use cultural beliefs, conventions, and rules to make sense of the continuous generation of novelty and to keep order among all the shifting relationships. But interdependence among all their behaviors generates precisely the complexity that they try to make sense of, and that defies any single set of rules and any hopes for social engineering. The litany of social and environmental problems describes the cumulative externalities (e.g., congestion, pollution, crime) that accompany interactions across the specialized layers of order. How can we plan for (and cope with) these messy complex interaction effects?

Markets have offered perhaps the most powerful institution for managing the complex interaction among people. Markets are quite effective in producing and allocating goods and services without costly centralized coordination, using conventions and rules of behavior that work well for private contracts and possessions. Markets, however, also rely upon, and often fail to provide, efficient levels of public and common goods.[1] The provision of infrastructure and the establishment of sanctions to discourage private gain at public and community expense are predictable scaffolding for exchange. Additionally, social solidarity directs investment for purposes other than efficiency. This chapter proposes that private, public, and community goods each rely upon knowledge and respect for social norms of reciprocity and collaboration. If most people comply, markets are stable and reduce uncertainty. But individuals often take this social trust for granted and tend to free ride. In this situation, uncertainty reigns. Communities can use plans to help mobilize these norms to help cope with uncertainty.

Take, for example, the problem of cheating. Many people enjoin unfair contracts (e.g., predatory lending), avoid paying for public goods consumed (e.g., tax evasion), and deplete common goods for private gain (e.g., aquifer exhaustion). Once a critical mass of defection occurs, individual participants abandon the norm and lose trust in one another. Systems crises in a housing market, municipality, or aquifer stem from cascades of defection tied to breakdowns in trust. The breakdown may start from various causes: random actions, ignorance of interaction and long-term effects, purposeful exploitation of system vulnerability, or from breakdowns in the use and enforcement of rules designed to find and punish defectors. Distrust erodes the adaptability of the rational system, as each individual seeks gains that translate into losses for one another, reducing the ability to organize an effective response to the problem. When additional external disturbances hit the system (e.g., a hurricane or a drought), distrust makes it hard to establish cooperative strategies to collectively come up with fair and acceptable solutions, particularly when these solutions require significant and quick coordination among multiple actors.

Once broken, trust is hard to rebuild. Trust and relationship building are intimately linked, because you trust the people you know. You know them through repeated interactions, communication, and the sharing of concerns. Trust improves our learning about unfamiliar purposes and methods because we rely on the social scaffolding we share to consider the future implications of adopting these purposes and tools. New beliefs are adopted within the context of relationships that reduce risk of betrayal or defection. Trust contributes not only to social resilience, but also to an improved capacity to develop and consider innovative ideas addressing diverse purposes. It is no accident that the vast literature on conflict resolution offers many strategies for trust building among suspicious antagonists in environmental or labor disputes. The innovation required for complex problem solving and resilience will more likely emerge as stakeholders drop their mistrust and learn to listen to each other. Stakeholder differences based on antagonistic presuppositions may be recast as plausible strategies offering practical insights about the problem. Paradoxically, diversity can also play against trust building by fueling conflict. The differences in belief, strategy, and method may persist and even sharpen as they come to light. Therein is the challenge for planners: fostering a balance between the cosmopolitan demands of diversity and the provincial solidarity of trust. Keeping balance requires attending to forms of shared vulnerability generated by the uncertainties that bring stakeholders together, such as unemployment, displacement, flooding, and congestion.

This chapter describes some efforts at collaborative planning that improve social trust—and consequently, system resilience—through communicating vulnerability among diverse participants. This strategy can offset the temptation to defect and it can enhance the promise of joint gains. These cases are framed within a conceptual framework to help in their examination in terms of trust, diversity, and communication (as they relate to each other and to resilience). Adaptive planning and management relies on time-consuming participation as people learn together how to replace suspicious self-protection with mutual understanding and agreement. We believe that a collaborative planning and management activity that recognizes and acknowledges joint vulnerability to uncertainty[2] (both human uncertainty, such as the susceptibility to free-riding, and natural uncertainty, such as hurricane and flooding) can tap and mobilize the level of trust in society and thereby improve social resilience. We describe how preparation for future uncertainty can be improved by combining the social diversity of participants in the conduct of strategies for joint planning.

The Framework: Trust, Diversity, Communication, and Resilience

Trust

Social trust has many antecedents. Political scientists measure trust as the level of confidence that citizens place in government as a provider of social, economic, and political goods and services (Nye 1997). Political corruption undermines public trust in government, as this behavior misdirects public resources into private hands. Scholars in business and economics explain the role of trust in ensuring efficient markets, as the markets rely upon respect for contracts to enable cooperation among investors, lenders, consumers, and regulators (Blomqvist et al. 2008). Research on risk finds that trust depends on the fit between competence and authority. People will entrust themselves to group problem solving if they believe that they possess the ability to devise a solution and the power to implement it (Paton et al. 2008). Sociologists distinguish different kinds of trust, such as interpersonal, institutional, and generalized. They find that we may trust a colleague whose actions we know but at the same time not trust our joint employer and its distant leadership (Ahnquist, Lindström, and Wamala 2008; Putnam 2000).

There is a difference between passive and active trust. In passive trust, one submits one's future to the decisions and actions of an authority who is a stranger. His or her competence remains a promise based on reputation or testimony. In active trust, one chooses to join with a familiar partner with a known track record to prepare for the future. This chapter examines active trust: how people relate to each other, and how they take purposeful steps to create and sustain trust in social settings. Trust is best conceived as "generalized trust . . . in other people, [which] is related to informal participation" in social networks, rather than to more formal network structure, which is a hallmark of institutional trust (Ahnquist, Lindström, and Wamala 2008).

Trust helps to allow for the changes in belief and values that need to happen in effective solution building. People can have confirmation bias (Lord, Ross, and Lepper 1979), such that they will only believe what they already know, unless they trust the new source of information. This situation is particularly true when dealing with complex problems (see Kaufman in chapter four of this book). As explained previously, the multi-scale characteristic of complex systems (how local-level interactions build up into large-scale effects) poses some obstacles to collective solution building due to two factors: (1) inaccurate perception (how individual decisions lead to system-wide problems), and (2) the incentive to free ride on common and public goods, including natural resources like water and social resources like community services. In the first case, people cannot understand the effects of their decisions and do not see a reason why they should change them (Zellner 2008). In the second case, knowing the effects is not enough to change their attitudes because the impediment to control the multiple actions affecting the shared goods creates a disincentive that is difficult to overcome. Collective settings allow for relationship building that fosters the trust necessary to overcome these obstacles.

Diversity
Planning involves problem setting and solving as stakeholders conceive and compare future outcomes. Collective judgments about how to prepare

for the future improve with greater diversity in four elements: *perspectives* (the representations of a problem), *interpretations* (the classification systems used to understand problems), *heuristics* (tools or rules of thumb used to solve problems, which are intimately linked to a perspective) and *predictive models* (the connection between cause and effect) (Page 2007). Coordinating these differences among collaborators helps them to compose a wider range of explanations and responses. The judgments made are especially sensitive to collaborators' knowledge and experience relevant to the problems at hand. While preference diversity may enhance collective problem solving, it may also encourage conflicting interpretations that impede collaboration and frustrate agreement. Interpretations may lead in different directions. Building trust in this context is a challenge. Nevertheless, empirical evidence supports the claim that, overall, diversity does help solve complex problems better (Page 2007), as compared with conventional expert planning.

Communication and Collaboration
Collaborative planning combines the building blocks of trust and diversity to foster improved social resilience within organizations and communities (Healey 1998a, 1998b; Innes and Booher 2003). Collaborative planning taps the experience of diverse members familiar with the causes, conditions, and consequences of a serious unexpected problem. Planning puts that experience to practical use by helping others learn from it. For people to participate and listen to others different from themselves, they must recognize their shared vulnerability and interdependence in the face of the problem shock. They must trust strangers and one another in ways strong enough to allow for changes in belief about the future. Strong trust can motivate a shift in willingness to change their response to the future. Interpersonal communication proves more effective in changing individuals' attitudes regarding an issue than impersonal expertise and argument (Katz, Elihu, and Lazarsfeld 1955; Rogers 1982; both cited in Shibanai, Yasuno, and Ishiguro 2001). A community can improve social resilience to serious, unexpected problems by anticipating and preparing for them. Purposeful, collaborative planning can help prepare for crisis because diverse stakeholders learn to recognize shared vulnerability and entrust each other to compose innovative responses together, using their differences in knowledge and experience as a resource. A homogeneous group of people may share the same vulnerability, but they will not have as many resources to innovate. A heterogeneous group of people will likely not be able to focus their collective skills into devising

practical and appropriate solutions in a timely manner, unless they find some common ground around which to foster empathy and trusting relationships. Planning that links stakeholder diversity and vulnerability enhances prospects for collective innovation and cooperation in the face of complex common goods problems. This capacity for collective innovation and response accounts for the resilience collaborative planning can offer.

Resilience

We distinguish two aspects of resilience: physical and social. *Physical resilience* is the flexible and adaptive response of physical infrastructure to external shocks, such as an earthquake, flood, heat wave, or terrorist attack. Two measures of physical resilience include the severity of physical damage to a structure and the length of time required to return the structure to normal use after the shock. Compared to a rigid infrastructure, resilient infrastructure sustains less damage and thus can be repaired more quickly after a disaster. Physical resilience depends upon the design and materials used for constructing a structure in relation to the physical characteristics of the surrounding environment. *Social resilience* describes how quickly individuals, groups, organizations, and institutions respond practically to external or internal shocks. If they are resilient, they understand their vulnerability and use this knowledge to prepare for disaster. As a result, they suffer less severe adverse outcomes (e.g., displacement, injury, death, and crime), they are more likely to maintain routine behaviors during, and return to routine behaviors after, an extreme event. The extent to which society is resilient to shocks will not only depend on the characteristics of its actors—income, education, skills—but also on the interactions of those individuals through social, professional, and institution-based relationships. These relationships in turn may be affected by (and affect) the physical environment and infrastructure.

What is the difference between resilience and persistence? We consider resilience to be a purely positive attribute of a system, its ability to adapt and retain its integrity—perhaps with some variation—over time. Persistence, on the other hand, may sometimes be a negative trait. A persistent feature may be negative if it does not allow for adaptation to changing conditions, making the system rigid and prone to eventual collapse. Corruption, for example, is a very persistent trait in social systems. In the long term, this type of persistence decreases the ability of the system to adapt to changes, as can be observed in recent financial and political crises across the world.

Next are two cases illustrating how communicating vulnerability, trust, and diversity come together to support building resilience in social-environmental systems.

Case One: Blended Management in a Supportive Housing Nonprofit
Consider the problem of the homeless: The central issue is not simply the lack of shelter, but the uncertainty about the possession and use of a dwelling place. Impoverished rural and urban families can end up homeless due to illness, abuse, eviction, or job loss. A staggering number of people became homeless after Hurricane Katrina. So we know that homelessness can be preceded by both natural calamity and poverty. These people bear a huge burden of uncertainty. In wealthy urban societies in North America and Europe, homeless people can find an empty building, a transit stop, or rail car to spend the night. But their hold is precarious and their security is severely limited. The homeless are vulnerable to the elements, social predators, and the police. Some find their way into the shelter system, obtaining a place to sleep in a dormitory.

Practical efforts to remedy homelessness include the provision of shelter and social services. The formal two-solution approach flows from the long-standing economic and social division of labor between real estate and social work. The caretakers for the homeless organize their response in relation to the occupational specializations and hierarchy from each domain of employment.

Social workers at an emergency shelter for the homeless may admit a person for a one-night stay (or longer). They may offer referrals to an addiction counseling agency, food pantry, and financial assistance resource—including public funds and other social supports. The social workers judge need and seek direct remedy from different government and philanthropic resources. The homeless person or family do not make a home of the shelter, but use it as a service. The shelter offers little privacy and a short stay.

Housing providers focus less on persons or households and more on the provision and care of dwellings. On the front end are the housing developers/builders and at the tail end are the property managers. In the affordable housing arena, these building developers and managers expect the dwellings to be inhabited by low-income, needy households; but that goal is not the focus of their work. They use their skill to provide physical dwellings and associated utilities and amenities that meet high quality standards and pass the test of economic viability. The developers produce subsidized rental dwellings for the possession and use of needy inhabitants. Property managers ensure the long-term economic stability of the rental dwellings (usually a building with many dwellings). They expect the clientele to pay rent on time and properly maintain the unit.

The growth of social service and housing agencies has accompanied the persistence of homelessness over the past twenty-five years. For decades, reformers, advocates, and policy makers recognized the importance of developing a coordinated response between services and housing provision. The federal government sponsored a national plan to end homelessness that focused on integrating these two dimensions in preventive efforts that would reduce the risk of homelessness among the poor (United States Department of Housing and Urban Development 1994). The most promising program response was the development of supportive housing: affordable rental housing that includes an on-site mix of social services geared to the needs of the resident clientele (Ridgway et al. 1994). But the ideal of coordinated and integrated provision proved difficult. The social plans for individual and family security did not correspond with the housing plans for the provision and management of viable dwelling units. Simultaneously addressing economically focused housing provision with socially focused service provision poses significant challenges.

Mercy Lakefront Housing started out as a neighborhood-based housing developer. It was designed to acquire and rehabilitate the few remaining single-room hotels in Chicago's Uptown neighborhood to provide affordable permanent rental housing for homeless people. Started by advocates and organizers, the organization emphasized the creation of affordable units. The organizers had snapped up the dilapidated Moreland Hotel because it offered a lot of small units in a single development. More important was the learning that ensued as the project took shape and a social worker/tenant organizer/executive director took charge. She and her board members had experience with the aging hotel stock and the important role these buildings played for sheltering destitute individuals. The hotel structure was kept for the post-rehab organization, using a 24-hour desk clerk to monitor the public entrance and provide security. Additionally, the property managers and social workers were expected to work together; to discover ways to both screen applicants and to help tenants stay in the building regardless of social problems (e.g., a return to drinking) or economic problems (e.g., spent rent money). The leadership and staff together adapted a community-focused approach that blended social and economic management (Butzen 1996; Hoch and Slayton 1989).

The blending combined egalitarian beliefs with community sensitivity. But these beliefs were disciplined by the economic realities of managing the economic value of the housing asset. The leadership and staff recognized that the successful provision of each individual room required careful attention to the management of the common resources. The principles of need and efficiency that guide conventional service and housing provision were recast. The new outlook was reciprocity tied to the shared vulnerability of the tenants and the mutual teamwork of the social workers and property managers.

The previous separation of property management from social provision had generated problems. Efficient management for low-income tenants in an affordable building means more evictions, greater turnover, and higher eviction rates. Managers cannot test the validity of tenants' social claims about temporary need, nor do managers possess knowledge to help remedy those needs. Social workers do not understand the economics of rental housing and the effects that rent arrears generates for the long-term physical and economic viability of the building. In contrast, in working together, the property managers and social workers shifted the focus of vulnerability away from individual tenants to the building-wide community and the diversity of needs—individual, social, and economic—that required attention. Diverse collaboration improved their ability to respond effectively to the frequent ups-and-downs that low-income tenants face on a regular basis. The blended management strategy they developed was the product of a form of collaborative planning that integrated professional and social differences at the community scale. The security of the building was not the result of professional systems of provision acting in parallel. Rather, the building's security derived from jointly merged practical judgments tied to the collaboration of social workers and property managers. The "common good" features of the hotel-type building fostered the innovative merging of functions (Hoch and Slayton 1989). For example, as mentioned previously, the 24-hour desk clerk monitors the entrance to reduce the risk of predatory strangers. Residents rely on informal social networks among the diverse clientele on different floors to leverage their position in the hotel community. Residents employ the geographic location of the building to access resources. (For instance, a handicapped old-timer lets a newcomer "in" on who the hallway neighbors are, and then asks the newcomer to run an errand for him in return.) The professional blending improves the social capacity of residents to cope with unexpected disruptions (whether it is a fire drill or a drug dealer). The chaotic vulnerability of the streets is replaced with the complex vulnerability of managed supportive care in a vertical neighborhood.

As the Lakefront group expanded, it exhausted the supply of hotels available for rehab and started to develop new buildings. The growth in scale required more sophisticated development practices and more sys-tematic ways to foster the blended management collaboration as new employees were hired.

An important policy shift in compensation proved important. Property managers usually earn more than social workers in conventional occupa-tions. The egalitarian conception of collaboration at the center of blended management encouraged a change in compensation. Property manager and social worker positions receive equivalent compensation at Lakefront, thus reducing resentment and fostering trust. The employees take pride in their collaboration because they are rewarded for doing it. And collaboration works better in coping with the vulnerable clientele, because their shared effort uses vulnerability as a resource, reducing the stigma of client de-pendence (a move that improves resilience). For example, sociopaths find they cannot play a case worker against a property manager, and addicts and the mentally challenged obtain practical assistance before a relapse becomes cause for eviction. Individual resident case work plans for per-sonal improvement draw upon the purposeful collaboration of staff and residents. In this case study, we see a residential community that is able to help very poor tenants overcome their many handicaps, not as passive recipients, but as active community partners. This goal is accomplished by joint learning across function, focus on tenant outcomes, and respect for economic and social vulnerability.

In the most successful instances, previously destitute tenants recover from addictions and illness, get a job and participate in civic activities that include voter registration, art work, and theater groups. With the applica-tion of blended management, the tenants' individual vulnerability becomes a resource for collaborative community-building. Ironically, the residents' autonomy and security increase with collaborative work, as housing and service providers find ways to overcome the division of knowledge and skill, using reciprocity with each other and tenants. The collaborative plan for blending shifts attention away from disciplinary norms and clientele need. Instead, attention is paid to strategies for joint practical action.

Implications for Collaborative Planning to Combat Homelessness
Any plan to end homelessness must remember the profound vulnerabil-ity of the homeless. Mainstream traditional approaches imagine social workers and housing providers doing their respective work as specialized professionals using organizational schemes to help individuals move from the insecurity of the streets to the security of an apartment. The continuum of care remains a central guiding strategy for this coordination. Ironically,

the traditional response does little to remedy the uncertainty of the streets for most homeless people.

The Lakefront case illustrates a very different approach, one that focuses on creating collaborative communities as a basis for developing permanent improvements in individual autonomy and security. The Lakefront projects use collaborative planning to foster blended management. In this way, the Lakefront group creates what Leavitt and Saegert (1990) term *community households*—buildings whose residents share social and economic resources to reduce their vulnerability and improve prospects for individual development.

Case Two: Adoption of Whole Farm Plans to Prevent Disease Outbreaks
Adoption of whole farm plans in the early 1990s in upstate New York demonstrates the integration of diversity, trust, and resilience at the community level. About forty-five small farms surround the Skaneateles Lake (which is the water supply for Syracuse, New York, located some distance away). Many of these farms raise cattle and other farm animals. In the early 1990s there was increasing recognition among state and local environment and health officials that the farm animals represent a potential public health threat, as they are known carriers of protozoan parasites (such as giardia and cryptosporidium), and wastes from farm animals in a watershed can pollute the water supply (Anderson 1991; AWWA 1998; National Animal Health Monitoring System 1993).

The concern was especially high for cryptosporidium. Since the early 1990s, the incidence of cryptosporidium outbreaks had risen substantially. Cryptosporidiosis, the gastrointestinal disease resulting from cryptosporidium infection, had become more prevalent (Yoder and Beach 2007). At the time, there were uncertainties regarding the monitoring, behavior, and control of these waterborne parasites:

• Sampling and detection methods were unreliable.

• Water-treatment plants did not remove all cryptosporidium oocysts.

• Normal chlorine levels did not kill the parasite.

• It was not clear how many oocysts were sufficient to cause cryptosporidiosis.

• Water-quality indicators did not reliably predict the occurrence of cryptosporidium (Avery, Lemley, and Hornsby 1998).

No drug can cure cryptosporidiosis. While it is not often fatal, symptoms are the most severe for children, the elderly, and immune-compromised individuals.

To mitigate uncertainty and minimize the risk of outbreaks, state and federal agencies began to develop several approaches designed to reduce or inhibit the ability of the pathogens to reach the water supply. These options included water-filtration plants, public-education programs, and control measures on farms. In the case of Skaneateles Lake, state government developed a cooperative approach to environmental planning and management. In this approach, the government and the farmers would work together to improve farm facilities and alter farm practices to reduce the potential contamination of the watershed. The New York Department of Health and the U.S. Environmental Protection Agency (EPA) granted the city of Syracuse "filtration avoidance," which meant that Syracuse would not need to install a filtration plant to filter Skaneateles Lake water if a condition was met. The condition was that the farmers by the lake would cooperatively develop and implement whole farm plans that would alter their farming behavior in ways that reduced the risk for cryptosporidium from animal wastes to enter the water supply.

In 1994, the Skaneateles Lake Watershed Agricultural Program (SL-WAP) was established to gain cooperation from a diverse group of already heavily regulated farmers. SLWAP is a small interagency pollution prevention program, set up to work with watershed farmers on a cooperative basis. The goal of SLWAP was to help the farmers create operational plans that promised to mitigate risks of pollution and ensure water quality. Farmers would develop whole farm plans that integrated best management practices, ones that reduced the potential for parasite outbreaks. SLWAP was made up of eight-to-ten individuals from a variety of different government agencies and professional backgrounds: farm planning and finance, non-point pollution, engineering, construction management, and communications, among others. While the individuals represented different organizations, they were committed to the SLWAP and its mission of enabling farmer-led revisions to farming techniques that would reduce the potential for parasite outbreaks.

SLWAP was physically located near to the farmers to enable visibility and ease of interaction, as the officials and farmers would need to negotiate how farm plans would be developed and implemented on a one-to-one basis. Farmers were responsible for implementation of whole farm plan activities on their farms, while SLWAP was to provide a regulatory buffer between the farmer and other traditional regulatory agencies. The general approach was to engage farmers in an open and transparent process that would build trust in a traditionally regulated community. The aim was to change farming behaviors in ways that would increase social and physical resilience, to reduce the potential for future outbreaks. Such an approach would require success on several fronts (Welch and Marc-Aurele 1999):

• *Community Commitment*   Most (if not all) of the farmers would need to join the whole farm plan effort. Adoption of best practices by a subset of farmers would not be sufficient to demonstrate the viability of a new system of pollution prevention. However, obtaining full participation was not easy. Some of the farmers were part-time or weekend farmers who had day jobs because their family farms did not produce sufficient income to be full-time. Others were full-time farmers. Additionally, some dairy farmers had numerous livestock, a key source of parasites, while others were merely vegetable or grain farmers. Because the goals and interests of farmers varied substantially, switching to the whole farm planning system by the entire community would require a high level of consensus not so easily attained.

• *Flexible Authority*   SLWAP would need to be able to demonstrate concrete improvements and behavioral changes on farms to justify continuation of the program. It would need to simultaneously maintain authority and insist on key changes in farm plans and operations, while at the same time flexibly integrate the farmers' perspectives and constraints. The dialog would need to be constructive; SLWAP and the farmers would need to negotiate in full faith. The potential for regulatory capture was clear: the proximity and interaction of SLWAP and the farmers meant that SLWAP could easily have begun to side with farmers over time, especially given the need for full participation.

• *Community-Individual Perspectives*   SLWAP would need to integrate the farmers' specific needs and solutions with the community's demands for safe water. Negotiation outcomes would need to be fair for both the individual and for the community. Similarly, farmers and regulators would need to see the benefits and costs of the whole farm plans at both the farm and the watershed-community level. Initially the program received little attention from the farmers or the watershed community. A few farmers, those whose livelihoods depended most upon the farm, negotiated whole farm plans soon after the arrival of SLWAP. It is not clear what drove their thinking. Perhaps they were most exposed to traditional regulatory agencies and perceived the greatest risk to ignoring SLWAP. Perhaps they recognized greatest benefit in the SLWAP promise of a regulatory buffer. Whatever the reason, the initial actions by these few farmers did not result in a flood of other farmers wanting to adopt whole farm plans. SLWAP saw the possibility that the cooperative whole farm plan approach would not succeed as hoped. Several reasons for the early lack of attention exist: (a) limited understanding or acceptance of the relationships between farm practices and human health risks, (b) complexity of whole farm plans, (c) diversity of area farmers' interest and enthusiasm, and (d) general mistrust of what appeared to be another new local government agency.

Three communication strategies were important for the ultimate success of the programs: consistent and continuous depiction of the costs and benefits of whole farm plans, focus on the opinions of community leaders, and community-wide interaction and forums.

While the farmers' adoption of the program was voluntary, SLWAP did promise them two long-term benefits. First, SLWAP would foot the bill. Farmers were to be held economically harmless; any improvements agreed to in the plan would be paid for by SLWAP. This benefit meant that farmers would be compensated for changes in operations, equipment, or reduction of acreage due to new property buffers. Such changes would not just fit the farmers to the plan, but they might also improve the farmers' economic viability in the long-term.

In addition, farmers were assured that adoption and implementation of the plan would result in less regulatory oversight by external government agencies. Because costs to the farmer from regulatory oversight can be substantial, this assurance may have created strong incentives for farmers over time.

The whole farm plan was meant to be a negotiated deal between the farmer and the government. As long as the farmer demonstrated compliance through consistent implementation of the plan, and as long as SLWAP demonstrated continued acceptance of the plan, there was a basis for ongoing trust and a precedent for resilient planning in the community. Because these elements of the whole farm plan system were communicated and demonstrated to the farming community, barriers to widespread adoption began to fall.

SLWAP consciously engaged several of the leaders of the Skaneateles farming community in a dialog about the benefits and costs of the whole farm plans. These leaders were less dependent upon farming for their incomes, but they were also more suspicious of regulators. They believed that in the past, they had not been fairly treated by regulators. Additionally, they believed that community, which included several low-income farms, was already overburdened with regulatory demands. SLWAP sought common ground with these leaders on several fronts: community health benefits and risks, economic principles, regulatory buffers, and transparency of the planning process. Over time, the leaders agreed to engage in a cooperative process and to help develop the whole farm plans. Adoption by the leaders signaled the viability of the plans for most of the other members of the farming community.

Finally, SLWAP worked with farmers, extension agencies, and members of the university and professional communities to create opportunities for broader dialog among farmers and between farmers and other experts. For example, Syracuse University's Environmental Finance Center held workshops and charrettes (work intensives) to discuss concerns about (and barriers to) adoption of whole farm plans. Adopters and nonadopters from the Skaneateles farm community were invited and given the opportunity to present their opinions and experiences. Similarly, SLWAP members were given an opportunity to transparently commit to their roles as coordinators, planners, and experts. Over time, leading farmers took a strong role in these forums, and an open effort was made by all parties to address the diverse concerns of nonadopters. In the end, forty-three of forty-five farmers adopted the whole plan farm process.

The community now has a system based on trust, communication, and negotiation, by which it can respond to future potential crises more quickly. This case does not demonstrate the speed of recovery from a crisis. But the facts of this case do show that the cooperative response did improve the quality of outcomes for individuals and farming communities, and that the plan did reduce the likelihood of outbreaks in the drinking water supply. The SLWAP model was considered to be a successful cooperative effort to reduce the environmental risk related to non-point source pollution. The model was replicated across the state. While this experiment in whole farm planning represents one possible mechanism for building trust among a diverse spectrum of interests for the purpose of long-term resilience, research has also recently produced evidence of its success with regards to water quality (Miller et al. 2008).

Implications for Collaborative Planning for the Prevention of Outbreaks

The Skaneateles Lake watershed case demonstrates the viability of planning and management processes that seek to simultaneously engage diverse stakeholders, build trust, and enhance resilience. Success hinged on three elements: community commitment, flexible authority, and community–individual perspectives. To accomplish each of these three requirements, SLWAP and the farmers focused on a communicative process aimed at increasing exposure and acceptance of individual and community perspectives. Everyone sought to accommodate both individual and community needs and vulnerability within the context of long-term reduction of human health risks from parasite outbreaks.

Synthesis and Future Directions

The problems of these case studies, homelessness and water pollution, are products of individual and system-wide vulnerabilities. These problems prove difficult to communicate to those people who perpetuate them. Each case study describes how current popular responses to each complex problem fall short, and how purposeful collaborative planning and management work better. The participants in each effort adopted perspectives that changed the interpretation of the problem (from one that shed responsibility, to one that shared responsibility). The recognition and communication of vulnerability not only inspired joint deliberation, but also helped to develop trust among diverse people. This strategy enabled the creation of innovative and effective remedies. The method built up the people's capacity to respond to novelty, through the establishment of enduring relationships. The participants moved from fixed positions (as antagonists, victims, or experts) to a position where they could empathize and comprehend the consequences of alternative actions for others who shared the same common good.

Both case studies stress the importance of communicating the various forms of vulnerability to generate two outcomes: (1) the trust needed to encourage changes in beliefs and behaviors, and (2) innovative solutions. By communicating joint vulnerability, people in the case studies addressed the cognitive and behavioral challenges associated with complexity, and thus improved the community's capacity to collectively respond to unexpected crises. They both found and fostered trust as they invented and adapted institutional conventions and roles to serve new purposes. In each case study, collaborative planning helped tame complexity to different degrees. Certainly there is room for further study and improvement, as the narratives raise important questions for future research.

For innovation to arise from cooperation, the collection of participants must be diverse. Participatory planning processes tend to emphasize consensus-building. But focusing on consensus-building can be problematic, because the "desire to conform" to the main ideas in a group may lead to everyone adopting the wrong perspective and consequently making bad decisions (Page 2007; Zellner 2008). The "desire to reach consensus" may also be an incentive to leave those players with different mindsets out of the discussion! If the emphasis is instead more broadly on solution building, diversity should be actively sought out. Diversity ensures equity through the representation of affected constituents. Perhaps more importantly, diversity increases the ability of the collective to generate understanding and innovative solutions that work at various scales (for example, at the individual level and at the system-wide level). The greater the number of relevant skills and perspectives represented in a group, the greater the chances of finding globally optimal solutions to real-world problems. The challenge for planners, then, is to determine the appropriate set of "cognitive toolboxes" (Page 2007) for each situation.

There are, however, two problems with collective processes involving diverse stakeholders: power imbalances and potentially conflicting values.

Power imbalances   On one hand, power imbalances can hamper the collective process by undermining trust and the collective ability to find globally optimal solutions. Crowds can be manipulated, distorting the problem-solving abilities of the group, making the crowd more prone to error (Page 2007). Planners must therefore be trained to detect and counteract such power imbalances. This goal introduces an interesting dilemma: leadership can encourage trust, but leadership can also eliminate the benefits of diversity in promoting collective problem solving. In the case about housing, leadership worked to eliminate the power imbalances from the traditional approach to homelessness (where the economic sector tends to predominate over the social). Eliminating the power asymmetries was essential to make the collective process improve the conditions at all scales: the individual, the administrative, and the community level. In the watershed case, lack of trust by leadership within the farmer community initially delayed the adoption of the whole farm program. It was important for agency representatives to continue the efforts in communicating the benefits and costs, the risks and vulnerabilities, in repeated interactions to encourage the changes in attitude that led to the ultimate success of the plan.

Potentially conflicting values   The greater the variety of fundamental values or preferences, the greater the likelihood of conflict. Such conflicts can be countered by the increased capacity of the collective to generate good solutions (Page 2007). Conflicts can also be mitigated by the trust that is developed by repeated interactions over time, which is evidenced in both of the case studies. In the absence of trust, the threat of external control may still spur action toward collaboration (in the watershed case, for example, there was the threat of the potential cost of filtration requirements).

In sum, communicating vulnerability among diverse stakeholders may provide a way to enhance resilience in a variety of systems, fostering trust and practical innovation to more effectively deal with the complexity of social and environmental problems. An important role for planners in this framework is to identify the diverse vulnerabilities of those engaged in these problems, and to facilitate the dialog around these issues. The effectiveness of this framework in terms of increasing resilience remains to be tested for the cases described We will know whether this framework enhances resilience if the relationships built around the communication of vulnerability allow each community to face any future crisis and recover from the disruptions it causes, more quickly and cost-effectively. What we can say at this point, however, is that they improved social and environmental outcomes in a wider range of scales than more traditional approaches, and that institutions are set in place that are likely to repeat the successes in new situations.

Scholarly and pedagogical agendas must focus on methodological and practical issues. On the methodological side, the field would benefit from developing measures to evaluate effective communication relative to changes in belief (initial research has been conducted by Delye and Schively Slotterback 2009), and to evaluate resilience of a system in terms of the ability to transfer knowledge to new situations. Additionally, we are pursuing research into what constitutes relevant diversity, and what tools can more effectively assist in harnessing that diversity for solution building. On the practical side, planners can focus their training on facilitation skills for collective problem solving, specifically aiming at identifying individual and joint vulnerability, actively seeking diversity, and managing power imbalances.

Notes

1. Two terms to know are public goods and common goods. *Public goods* are those goods whose consumption is nonexcludable and nonrival (for example, public radio and defense). *Common goods* are those where users cannot be excluded from consumption. The consumption of common goods is rival (for example, water).

2. Note that it is understood that natural disasters may also be *encouraged* by human activity.

References

Ahnquist, J., M. Lindström, and S. P. Wamala. 2008. Institutional trust and alcohol consumption in Sweden: The Swedish National Public Health Survey, 2006. *BMC Public Health* 8:283.

Amaral, L. A. N., and J. M. Ottino. 2004. Complex networks: Augmenting the framework for the study of complex systems. *European Physical Journal B* 38:147–162.

Anderson, B. 1991. Prevalence of cryptosporidium muris-like oocysts among cattle populations of the United States: Preliminary report. *Journal of Protozoology* 38(6): 145–155.

Avery, B. K., A. Lemley, and A. G. Hornsby. 1998. Cryptosporidium: A waterborne pathogen. Gainesville, FL: Institute of Food and Agricultural Sciences, University of Florida, SL 130.

AWWA. 1998. *Cryptosporidium: Answers to questions commonly asked by drinking water professionals.* Denver, CO: American Water Works Association.

Blomqvist, K., P. Hurmelinna-Laukkanen, N. Nummela, and S. Saarenketo. 2008. The role of trust and contracts in the internationalization of technology-intensive born globals. *Journal of Engineering and Technology Management* 25:123–135.

Butzen, J. 1996. Lakefront SRO Corporation: Reviving single room occupancy housing. In *Under one roof: Issues and innovations in shared housing,* ed. G. Hemmens, C. Hoch, and J. Carp. Albany, NY: SUNY Press.

Delye, R., and C. Schively Slotterback. 2009. Group learning in participatory planning processes: An exploratory quasiexperimental analysis of local mitigation planning in Florida. *Journal of Planning Education and Research* 29:23–38.

Healey, P. 1998a. Collaborative planning in a stakeholder society. *Town Planning Review* 69(1): 1–21.

Healey, P. 1998b. Building institutional capacity through collaborative approaches to planning. *Environment and Planning. B, Planning & Design* 30:1531–1546.

Hoch, C., and R. Slayton. 1989. *New homeless and old: Community and the Skid Row Hotel.* Philadelphia: Temple University Press.

Innes, J. E., and D. E. Booher. 2003. *The impact of collaborative planning on governance capacity.* Berkeley, CA: UC Berkeley, Institute of Urban and Regional Development. Accessed 1-23-2011. Available from http://www.escholarship.org/uc/item/98k72547.

Katz, E., and P. Lazarsfeld. 1955. *Personal influence.* New York: Free Press.

Leavitt, J., and S. Saegert. 1990. *From abandonment to hope: Community households in Harlem.* New York: Columbia University Press.

Lord, C., L. Ross, and M. Lepper. 1979. Biased assimilation and attitude polarization: The effects of prior theories on subsequently considered evidence. *Journal of Personality and Social Psychology* 37(11): 2098–2109.

Miller, W. A., D. J. Lewis, M. D. G. Pereira, M. Lennox, P. A. Conrad, K. W. Tate, and E. R. Atwill. 2008. Farm factors associated with reducing cryptosporidium loading in storm runoff from dairies. *Journal of Environmental Quality* 37:1875–1882.

National Animal Health Monitoring System. 1993. *Cryptosporidium is common in dairy calves: National Dairy Heifer Evaluation Project.* Fort Collins, CO: U.S. Department of Agriculture, Animal and Plant Health Inspection Service, Veterinary Services.

Nye, J., Jr. 1997. Introduction: The decline of confidence in government. In *Why people don't trust government*, ed. J. J. Nye, P. Zelikow, and D. King. Cambridge, MA: Harvard University Press.

Page, S. E. 2007. *The difference: How the power of diversity creates better groups, firms, schools, and societies.* Princeton, NJ: Princeton University Press.

Paton, D., L. Smith, M. Daly, and D. Johnston. 2008. Risk perception and volcanic hazard mitigation: Individual and social perspectives. *Journal of Volcanology and Geothermal Research* 172:179–188.

Putnam, R. 2000. *Bowling along: The collapse and revival of American community.* New York: Simon & Schuster.

Ridgway, P., A. Simpson, F. D. Wittman, and G. Wheeler. 1994. Home making and community building: Notes on empowerment and place. *Journal of Mental Health Administration* 21(4): 407–418.

Rogers, E. M. 1982. *Diffusion of innovations.* New York: Free Press.

Shibanai, Y., S. Yasuno, and I. Ishiguro. 2001. Effects of global information feedback on diversity—Extensions to Axelrod's adaptive culture model. *Journal of Conflict Resolution* 45(1): 80–96.

United States Department of Housing and Urban Development. 1994. Priority: Home! The federal plan to break the cycle of homelessness. Washington, D.C.: U.S. Government Printing Office (HUD-1454-CPD).

Welch, E. W., and F. J. Marc-Aurele, Jr. 1999. Implementation of environmental policy in Katowice, Poland: Is there cause for concern? *International Journal of Environmental Studies* 56:259–284.

Yoder, J. S., and M. J. Beach. 2007. *Cryptosporidium surveillance 2003–2005.* Atlanta, GA: Centers for Disease Control, September 7, 2007 / 56(SS07);1–10 2007. Accessed 1-23-2011. Available from http://www.cdc.gov/mmwr/preview/mmwrhtml/ss5607a1.htm.

Zellner, M. L. 2008. Embracing complexity and uncertainty: The potential of agent-based modeling for environmental planning and policy. *Planning Theory & Practice* 9(4): 437–457.

4

Complex Systems, Anticipation, and Collaborative Planning for Resilience

Sanda Kaufman

Communities face various sudden and long-term physical and socioeconomic threats. These threats include natural catastrophes and negative consequences of human actions, such as depletion of scarce water resources, soil degradation, desertification, and climate change consequences, as well as collapse of the real estate market, sudden price surges due to shortages of key raw materials, or technology changes affecting job markets. What decision mechanisms can enhance communities' ability to sustain themselves and their physical and social environment despite such looming threats? Can collaborative forms of planning be helpful in efforts to avert irreversible damage, recover after a destabilizing shock, or adapt to new natural and social conditions? What process elements are crucial to the effectiveness of collaborative planning processes in specific situations?

Planning is essentially joint decision making. It entails responding to and shaping anticipated social and resource needs in the uncertain future (Shmueli, Kaufman, and Ozawa 2008). When collaborative, planning is inclusive of stakeholders and uses decision rules (such as consensus building) conducive to implementable solutions to jointly identified needs. Collaborative planning can contribute to wise decision making in changing contexts of increasing complexity. Whether it does so effectively hinges on our understanding of the mechanisms underlying various threats to community integrity. We also must understand how individuals and communities react to such threats at different scales. Some of these mechanisms have been identified through social-ecological systems research (for example, Abel, Cumming, and Anderies 2006; Anderies, Walker, and Kinzig 2006; Lebel et al. 2006). The mechanisms relate to three key aspects of how individuals make decisions and how they come together to make joint decisions (such as planning) within their institutional and political context. Two of these key aspects—individual/joint decision shortcomings, and difficulties in anticipating change—refer to individual and community characteristics that impact the effectiveness of their responses to serious threats and catastrophic events. The third key aspect—contextual complexity—derives from the interconnectedness of the systemic structures within which these responses have to be implemented. The three aspects will be examined in this chapter in relation to the repertory of social-ecological systems properties and reactions to drastic, rapid or slow contextual change. Resilience belongs to this repertory. It is defined by Walker et al. (2006) as the "capacity of a system to experience shocks while retaining essentially the same function, structure, feedbacks, and therefore identity, without shifting into a different regime." This chapter proposes that for planning to successfully foster resilience when necessary, it must become collaborative, and it must reckon with the obstacles presented by individual/joint decision making, failure to anticipate events effectively, and systemic complexity.

The first aspect of interest here is the nature of individual and joint decision mechanisms. Some threats to the resilience of a social system such as a community are rooted in the community members' individual actions and decisions. They are manifest, for example, in the slow-acting daily individual choices that undermine environmental sustainability, such as waste generation or driving habits. Threats to resilience are also evident in individual reactions to natural catastrophes, that appear collectively unwise in retrospect (Dörner 1989). An example is engaging individually, for extensive time periods, in agricultural or building practices causing serious soil erosion that predictably leads to severe flooding. Also at the individual decision level, several cognitive biases impede community members' ability to respond to catastrophic events in ways that sustain and restore their social system. Joint decision mechanisms can be flawed in similar ways. Certain decision processes (such as collaborative planning) have the potential to overcome some of these shortcomings.

The second aspect we need to explore is how resilience is affected by individuals' and communities' ability to anticipate at least some of the consequences of their own and others' actions or of systemic crises. Anticipation is critical to the planning and implementation of restorative responses to shocks. For example, if we did not know what happens when the price of oil escalates and its availability is curtailed, we certainly could have learned in the United States during the 1970s oil embargo. Therefore, we should have acted to prevent reoccurrence of such a predictable crisis. However, this did not happen. In the summer of 2008 oil prices skyrocketed again, dealing a shock to the global economy. The price spike caused for the first time a significant drop in the U.S. demand for oil. Nevertheless, even with a renewed interest in seeking alternative energy sources, the national resolve dissipated when, only several weeks later in the same year, oil prices dropped drastically (though only temporarily). In this case as in general, some cognitive biases impede individuals' and communities' ability to anticipate threats and act in concert to sustain their physical and social environment. Understanding these biases may enhance the effectiveness of planning tools and the ability to bring together individuals and organizations to make collaborative decisions.

The third aspect of interest in the quest to foster resilience is the complex nature of the context in which we make collective decisions. A factor playing a critical role in responses to long-brewing catastrophic events is the increasing degree of complexity in our society's organization. This increasing organizational complexity is accompanied by a growing lack of redundancy (McKenzie 2008; Bar-Yam 2006; Werfel and Bar-Yam 2004). The resulting tightly coupled economic, infrastructure, and communication systems quickly propagate shocks. Meanwhile, the lack of redundancy in these systems robs communities of their ability to cope with disasters once a vital system has been impaired. Thus a key threat to resilience is the too-efficient set of vital networks supplying communities with energy, food, water, and information. The vulnerability of these critical networks to even small disturbances has become evident in recent decades. For example, a small electrical grid disruption in the Cleveland area is credited for the 2003 blackout that extended to numerous U.S. regions and even to Canada. In a second example, hurricane events that sideline a few oil-refining installations can cause sudden shortages and sharp gasoline price surges that impede numerous activities in the United States and other countries. In both examples, some level of redundancy in the networks, while seemingly reducing their efficiency through added costs, might have averted the even-costlier disruptions following the destabilizing shocks. Besides having these direct effects, complexity also undermines individuals' and communities' ability to engage in anticipation. This is due to the fact that in complex systems relatively small shocks can cause relatively large, unpredictable changes. This consequence of complexity further reduces the effectiveness of individual and joint decisions because unintended consequences become more difficult to foresee.

This chapter examines systems' resilience and three factors affecting it: individual decisions and their dilemmas, obstacles to effective anticipation, and organizational complexity. The discussion brings together observations, concepts, and ideas from several disciplines: psychology (e.g., Dörner 1989), linguistics (e.g., Pinker 2002), social psychology (Bazerman and Watkins 2004), systems theory (e.g., Walker et al. 2002; Walker et al. 2006), complexity theories (e.g., Bar-Yam 2006), ecology (e.g., Walker and

Meyers 2004), natural resources management (e.g., Wilson et al. 1999), planning (e.g., Wallace and Wallace 2008; Shmueli et al. 2008) and public decisions (e.g., Bayley and French 2008). The need for a multidisciplinary approach has been highlighted, for instance, by Anderies et al. (2006). They note that understanding social-ecological systems—the kinds of systems within which planners work—requires accounting for relationships between actions, information processing, and the consequences of these actions (whose study spans the kinds of disciplines identified here), and more. They are also skeptical about achieving the understanding we seek; this beginning attempt is proving challenging, indeed! Nevertheless, it is worth trying because of the frequently high individual and collective stakes at play in meeting social and ecological challenges at geographic scales ranging from local to global.

This chapter proposes three arguments linking the notion of resilience in natural and social environments to collaborative planning:

1. Individual decision mechanisms, the extent of ability to foresee brewing problems, and joint decision mechanisms in (and for) a complex environment are central to whether or not collaborative planning can bolster resilience.

2. These three aspects of decision making are tightly interconnected.

3. There is encouraging multidisciplinary *consilience* regarding how these three aspects affect decision making (such as in planning) in complex contexts, and therefore how these factors impinge on resilience. According to Wilson (1998) who coined the term, *consilience* is "a jumping together of knowledge by the linking of facts and fact-based theory across disciplines to create a common groundwork for explanation."

The first section of this chapter relates the notion of resilience to how individuals, communities, and societies manage the physical and social systems in which they are embedded. The second section explores how the three aspects of decision making impinge on efforts to foster resilience. The chapter concludes by offering some insights about how collaborative planning might compensate for individual and joint decision deficiencies, to help manage resilience in the face of some current and some looming threats (as well as when change is desired).

About Resilience and Other Goals of Physical and Social Systems Management

Resilience is one among several possible system responses to change. Like *sustainability* before it, the term *resilience* has joined the ranks of meta-concepts with positive connotation: its great currency seems to obviate the need for a definition, but in fact its meaning is far from broadly shared. In the past forty years, researchers in several fields have attempted to define *resilience*, including for example Holling (1973; 1996), Adger (2000), Gunderson (2000), McCubbin (2001), and Haimes (2009), each highlighting some aspect particularly relevant to their respective fields.[1]

Holling (1973) speaks of resilience in general reference to "a system profoundly affected by change external to it." Gunderson (2000) stresses the sense of a system's transition between two states. Dealing with individuals and their capacity to recover from adversity, McCubbin (2001) highlights the numerous senses collected by the term *resilience*, calling it an "umbrella term," difficult to define and measure for either processes or outcomes. Her treatment exemplifies the implicitly positive connotation this term has acquired. Her discussion illustrates how the term is used in ways that encompass other kinds of systems' reactions to shocks (such as adaptation), which cannot but add to the definitional difficulties. Haimes (2009) examines several definitions of resilience, some of which conflate it with adaptability. The definition he favors is closest to Walker et al. (2006): "a manifestation of the states of the system. Perhaps most critically, it is a vector that is time-dependent. Resilience . . . is defined as the ability of the system to withstand a major disruption within acceptable degradation parameters and to recover within an acceptable time and composite costs and risks." Note that the acceptable time period remains undefined. This poses serious problems to planning because in some cases costs accrue first, while benefits are reaped later, sometimes by a different generation than the one that invested in recovery. Debates surrounding the formulation of health care policies or action to prevent global climate change have faced this challenge.

With perhaps most relevance to planning concerns, Adger (2000, p. 347) proposes that *resilience* is "the ability of groups or communities to cope with external stresses and disturbances as a result of social, political, and environmental change." He notes that in general resilience—a system's capacity to absorb perturbations without changing its structure and processes—has to do with the system's functioning, rather than with the stability of any of its components. He argues that the resilience of a social system and of its institutions is related to the resilience of the ecological (physical) system on which it depends.

Thus a system at any geographic scale—community, watershed, natural or political region, and so forth—can be qualified as resilient if it can weather sudden or slow change and emerge closely resembling its former state and functionality. However, the range of possible outcomes of change is broader: communities can also end, adapt, or transform. Under either sudden shock or slow change, systems such as some cities (Vale and Campanella 2005) or ecosystems (Diamond 2005) might cease to exist. Systems can adapt, as some regions of the United States have done by switching to a mix of clean industries after losing their competitiveness in heavy manufacturing. They can transform along key dimensions, as some rich ecosystems that morphed into deserts (Diamond 2005) or some Eastern European countries that, within barely twenty years of their regime changes in the 1980s, no longer resembled their former, seemingly stable economic and political orders.

Are any of the survival responses to slow or rapid change (re-emerging, adapting, or transforming) better than the others across the board? Since it is easy to see why the answer to this question is negative, we should inquire in what circumstances we should seek to foster resilience.

Useful Descriptors of Physical and Social Systems

The study (and vocabulary) of resilience is rooted in systems theory and ecology research. Its terms are useful not only for understanding the behavior of ecological systems, but also for developing managed change strategies. Such strategies are needed to respond to catastrophic events (construed as physical and social change triggers) and plan for preempting their negative effects, or to adapt to anticipated physical or social change. It is worth knowing the terms used to describe and analyze resilience in both social and ecological systems. There is, of course, a fundamental difference between systems whose main motor is purpose-driven (telic) human agency and all other systems. We should keep this difference in mind and exercise caution in directly applying results derived from ecological systems to social systems.

Based on a number of managed resource case studies, as well as others' theoretical and empirical work, Walker et al. (2006) discuss three social-ecological systems properties—resilience, adaptability, and transformability—and two types of systems dynamics—adaptive cycle and panarchy. Figure 4.1 illustrates social-ecological systems' properties and dynamics.

Together, the three properties and two dynamics form a parsimonious basis for generating and testing a surprising number of propositions about how systems change and how they react to changes inflicted on them.[2] Let us examine how these terms have been defined, beginning with the properties: resilience, adaptability, and transformability. .The first system property, *resilience*, has been defined in the last section. The second property, *adaptability*, is the capacity of actors in a system to manage resilience.

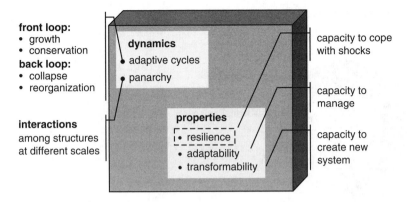

front loop:
• growth
• conservation
back loop:
• collapse
• reorganization

interactions
among structures
at different scales

dynamics
• adaptive cycles
• panarchy

properties
• resilience
• adaptability
• transformability

capacity to cope
with shocks

capacity to
manage

capacity to
create new
system

Figure 4.1
Social-ecological systems properties and dynamics. Based on Walker et al. (2006).

The third property, *transformability,* is the capacity to create a new system when the existing one has become untenable. Thus resilience and adaptability are closely related and quite different from transformability.

Let us now explore definitions of the two systems dynamics: adaptive cycle and panarchy. The first, an *adaptive cycle,* is a four-phase system dynamic characterizing any process of change (in time) of the structures and functions of ecological or social systems. It comprises a fore loop of growth (accumulation of resources and structure building, high resilience) and conservation (increasing interconnectedness at the expense of flexibility and growth, reducing resilience). It also comprises a back loop[3] of structures' collapse (release of resources) and reorganization (leading to a new cycle along the fore loop). Adaptive cycles are triggered by some event, and their reorganization component requires an infusion of resources into the system. Recent examples of such infusion as a response to crisis include the 2008 Troubled Asset Relief Program (TARP) or the 2009 American Recovery and Reinvestment Act.

The second systems dynamic is *panarchy.* It consists of (nonhierarchical) interactions among interrelated slow-changing broad structures, and smaller, faster-changing ones at different geographic/physical scales within a system (e.g., Gunderson et al. 2002). Some of the global climate change actions and proposed remedies act across scales in this way.

In various instances, resilience, adaptability, and transformability have been held as normatively desirable systemic properties (Brand and Jax 2007) in activities such as planning, design, and management of physical and social systems. However, it is possible to cast resilience (or

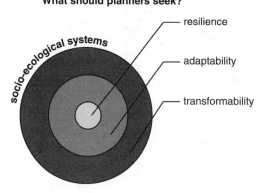

What should planners seek?

Figure 4.2
Normative dilemmas faced by planners.

transformability) as normatively either positive or negative, depending on the issue at hand. Figure 4.2 shows normative dilemmas faced by planners.

If a current social or economic state of a resilient system is undesirable, then its resilience will impede desired change. On the other hand, if the system's characteristics are valued, then resilience is necessary to its maintenance in the face of challenges. A physically decayed urban area may prompt a desire for transformation, but the U.S. urban renewal experience after World War II and some current gentrification examples suggest that transformation is at times undesirable even if the current state is unsatisfactory. Interestingly, in both urban renewal and gentrification situations, physical transformation has undercut the resilience of valued communal ties, causing unintended distress. Another example of resilience in one system undercutting transformation in another is found in Germany, after its reunification in 1990: some East German cities have undergone physical transformations that at times failed to take into account their communities' resilience.[4]

We can infer that sustainability of a (currently) valued system requires resilience, as in the case of a natural resource (the remaining wetlands or rain forests), a community, or an urban area.[5] That may not always be the case, however. When systemic sustainability requires profound change in some components, then the resilience may impede its implementation. Consider again the need for economic and transportation systems to switch toward using renewable energy sources. The well-developed, intertwined physical and management networks for delivering fossil fuel-based energy are more effective in resisting this transformation than we might wish.

Moreover, in the process of shoring up either resilience or transformability of a social or ecological system, unintended consequences (some irreversible) are apt to surface. Therefore it is imperative for planners and other interveners to develop strong anticipation capabilities.

To plan effectively for either recovery or for transformation after crises, we need to understand what factors affect a system's resilience. We might then become adept at *fostering* it when necessary, or reach consensus on the need and direction for change, and then *inhibit* resilience. Consider the previous examples: we may want to enhance the resilience of threatened ecosystems such as wetlands; on the other hand, we might seek ways to overcome the resilience of the current global systems involved in the delivery of fossil fuel energy, based on an emerging consensus around benefits of switching to alternative energy sources, whether for political, economic, or environmental reasons. From the three systems properties, two systems dynamics, several case studies, and others' current and past social-ecological systems research Walker et al. (2006) have derived a series of propositions that can be used to describe change in social-ecological systems. Several of these propositions are relevant to decision making and systems management at the community, regional, state,and national levels. Some propositions are particularly useful to the development of collective responses to catastrophic events. Figure 4.3 shows social-ecological systems characteristics that are useful to collaborative planning.

Walker et al. discuss several key resilience-related issues: cross-scale interactions, fast and slow variables, functional and response diversity, adaptability versus resilience, mental models, learning, multiple thresholds,

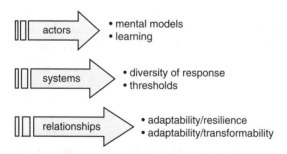

Propositions for social and ecological systems about:

actors → • mental models / • learning

systems → • diversity of response / • thresholds

relationships → • adaptability/resilience / • adaptability/transformability

Figure 4.3
Social-ecological systems characteristics useful to collaborative planning. Based on Walker et al. (2006).

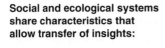

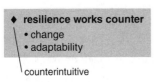

Figure 4.4
Transferability of insights. Based on Walker et al. (2006).

transformation, and (especially) the components of adaptability. Several of these issues, which will be discussed next, can be usefully linked to decision making in the public domain, such as in planning or resource management.

The proposition undergirding the arguments proposed in this chapter establishes that the ecological domain is sufficiently equivalent to the social domain. Therefore, both can be addressed in a "common conceptual, theoretical, and modeling framework," despite the unique human agency factor present in the social domain (Figure 4.4.)

Although derived independently from entirely different logics and data, the propositions of Walker et al. (2006) are consistent with (and lead to similar conclusions as) some findings at the psychological level about how people make decisions (Dörner 1989; Bazerman and Watkins 2004). The propositions are also consistent with some findings about systems' complexity (Werfel and Bar-Yam 2004), which will be discussed in the following section. This consilience of sorts is apt to increase confidence in the propositions, tentative as they may be.[6]

Exploring the Propositions of Walker et al. (2006)

According to Walker et al. (2006), systems can have functional diversity and response diversity. The type of system diversity that affects resilience is *response diversity* (also called "functional redundancy"). The response diversity proposition suggests that the availability of multiple ways of responding to crises increases the likelihood that a system will recover from a major shock. This notion is consonant with Bar-Yam's (2006) argument regarding the vulnerability of highly efficient (nonredundant) systems to even small disruptions. A notable illustration of this vulnerability is the global economy which has behaved much like a line of falling dominoes since 2008. Diversity of response is enhanced by decentralized (and therefore more locally based) decision making, as well as by increased reliance on local resources, which is akin to decentralizing the supply of certain goods. For example, one of the many perils of efficient food production is total crop loss. An untimely frost spell in Florida can destroy a year's crop of citrus (with ensuing national shortages and price rises). One remedy that is taking hold in the United States is a push toward local food production (and consumption) instead of relying on a few specialized large produce suppliers. Besides enhancing diversity of response, localized decision making also fosters direct participation and collaborative processes. These kinds of processes tend to be more difficult to sustain at larger geographic scales for lack of the direct interaction that generates the necessary trust.

Walker et al.'s discussion of the relationship between two of the systems' dynamics, adaptability and resilience, is directly relevant to decisions in the public domain. They argue that the higher the level of a system's adaptability, the less resilient it becomes! Since this may seem counterintuitive, an analogy might help. In data-based prediction, of two alternative regression models, the one with the higher R^2 is closer to the sample data and thus a "better fit." However, this model may not be the better of the two for prediction purposes (e.g., Gujarati 1995). The reason is that the closer a model is to the sample data used to estimate its parameters, the more likely it is to have been "misled" by sample quirks and therefore to fail at predicting population trends. Similarly, a system that is highly adapted to some specific conditions may be less resilient. It may be less able to swing back after experiencing conditions even slightly different from those it matches optimally. On the other hand, architects' search for functional flexibility offers an example of resilience that undermines adaptability. Users quickly find out that spaces sufficiently flexible by design to accommodate more than a single purpose are less suitable to any specific use than spaces designed for that use alone.

One reason for resilience and adaptability pulling in opposite directions is that adaptation often entails increasing the efficiency of resource use (for example, by reducing redundancies in the system), thereby reducing response diversity. The relatively slow response to the blackout of 2003 was attributed to just such a reduction (by utility companies) in alternative (redundant) electrical lines for the sake of economic efficiency.

An additional decision dilemma posed by the tug-of-war between resilience and adaptability emerges from what Walker et al. (2006) have termed (top-down and bottom-up) *cross-scale interactions among systems' components*. Suppose that at the national level, response diversity is implemented through decision decentralization and the encouragement of regional or local collaboratives. At the local scale, this strategy runs the risk of fostering too much adaptability that may come at the expense of resilience. Thus a strategy fostering resilience at one geographic scale may undermine resilience at a different scale unless decision makers are aware of this risk and try to mitigate it.

Walker et al.'s proposition regarding the role of mental models in devising successful systemic responses to change is particularly relevant to collaborative decision making. It is consistent with the roles ascribed to such models by Pinker (2002) and with some of the judgmental pitfalls to which Dörner (1989) and Bazerman and Watkins (2004) alert us. In order to trigger action, crises and threats have to affect our mental models of how systems work, and of cause and effect of behaviors and remedial actions on the systems we are trying to change. When not rooted in cause-and-effect linkages, mental models are less likely to lead to collective responses to looming threats. Such are fatidic outlooks that encourage acceptance of, and submission to, a predetermined future. Mental models rooted in a single cause-and-effect sequence may also hinder effective response to crises because they are impervious to accumulating evidence for other cause-and-effect chains. For instance, belief in creationism makes it difficult to consider evidence of evolution processes. Walker et al. (2006) acknowledge the centrality of mental models in the patterns of acquiring and using information for making decisions, including those related to the management of social-ecological systems. For example, Al Gore made global climate change a household concern at least for a while. His success may have been due in part to his effective promotion of a mental model that faults human actions for observed climate-related phenomena. Without this causal link, the worldwide mobilization around global warming in the past decade might not have occurred. Not surprisingly, debates and obstacles to concerted action to stave climate change focus on challenging this causal link and propose alternative mental models of the climate's workings. Note that the opposing sides in global warming debates are now split along political lines, suggesting that of late the respective mental models have slipped into the belief mode.

How do mental models relate to the kinds of decisions resulting from collaborative processes? Walker et al. (2006) propose that adaptability in social-ecological systems is enhanced by overlapping mental models of their structure and function. This proposition is consistent with claims that people tend to prefer evidence confirming what they already believe, and that they tend to avoid disconfirming evidence (e.g., Dörner, 1989; Bazerman and Moore, 2009). In collaborative decision processes this might result in less contentiousness among those who share mental models of the workings of the systems that they are trying to manage. Remember, however, the decision dilemma posed by adaptability countering resilience when they operate at different scales (as in national, regional, and local decisions). When mental models are shared, the increased adaptability may possibly come at the expense of a system's resilience. One reason might be that resilience entails some creative thinking ("outside the box") that is less likely to emerge from decision makers whose mental models overlap ("in the box"). Decision makers who are "on the same page" may fail to challenge each other and uncover any weaknesses in proposed solutions to problems. There is a familiar name for extensively overlapping mental models: "group think," which carries a negative connotation.

One of Walker et al.'s (2006) propositions, referring to the space of feasible alternative solutions to problems of a system in crisis, affects decision-making processes indirectly. Social-ecological systems have multiple *thresholds*[7] at different scales and for different aspects. Once thresholds for some aspects have been crossed, fewer feasible combinations of features and solutions are possible. The thresholds effect can be likened to path dependence of outcomes in negotiations (see, for example, Pierson 2000a and 2000b; Garud and Karnøe 2001; and Lamberg et al. 2008). At the outset, parties might consider that several solutions are acceptable. But as negotiators move from one proposal to the next (the path) some of the solutions initially viewed as acceptable no longer appear so to at least some of the parties. The 2009 negotiations around climate change at the Copenhagen Conference illustrate such path dependence. So do the negotiations around crafting a U.S. health care bill. In both instances, as negotiations progressed some initially broadly feasible proposals became unacceptable to some of the stakeholders. Thus the specific interim packages considered by the parties effectively reduce the field of mutually acceptable solutions. These interim packages are a good analogy to the multiple system thresholds that, once crossed, render some previously feasible fixes infeasible.

Given this threshold effect, when should we act to forestall predicted threats? Consider again the climate change example. A number of years ago it might have been possible to reverse the warming trend through concerted actions to reduce carbon emissions. But there will come a point in time when (some system thresholds having been crossed) the climate will have changed to the point that no amount of reduction in carbon emissions will avert its predicted ill-consequences. When that moment comes (if it has not already), certain solutions (such as reducing the carbon footprint of human activities) will no longer be effective. Instead, coping (adaptive) measures will become necessary. The U.S. national debt evinces a similar pattern of options narrowing in time, as certain thresholds are crossed. In terms of planning decisions, it seems that early action favors resilience, because it may reduce the severity of threats and leave open more options for tackling them. Some of these options might be preferable to the solutions left *after* thresholds have been crossed, when only adaptive or transformative actions remain possible. Therefore, climate change poses an unprecedented global conundrum. Its high level of uncertainty regarding the thresholds of no return combines with the high costs of both action and inaction and with lack of consensus around goals (whether resilience, adaptation, or transformation) to prevent global mitigation decisions. Although the U.S. national debt problem is not beset by similar levels of uncertainty, it too suffers from lack of consensus around goals and solutions.

Walker et al. view systems' adaptability and transformability both as system characteristics and as strategies for responding to crises. As a strategy, *adaptation* entails preventing a system from crossing a threshold that will force drastic change (such as would have been necessary to avert the financial markets crisis of 2008). The transformation strategy entails enacting drastic changes in response to crises (such as the government's implementation of TARP after the crisis occurred). Both are closely related to planning concerns. Walker et al.'s *adaptation* refers to all forms of capital (manufactured, financial, social, human, and natural), including the skills required of decision makers to prevent a system from reaching the brink of crisis. The factors they consider necessary relate to governance structure and to social capital: leadership, social networks, motivation for cooperation, and trust. This list may surprise by its extensive overlap with some of the conditions required for collaborative processes to emerge.

Although it too relies on governance as a crisis response strategy, *transformation* is the opposite of adaptability. In Walker et al.'s propositions *transformation* refers to a system's characteristics that enable substantial change, including incentives, cross-scale awareness, willingness to experiment, and asset reserves for resource-intensive transformations. One example is the effort begun in 2009 to remake the U.S. automotive industry. From a planning perspective, a choice between these two crisis response strategies (adaptation or transformation) requires access to a complex array of information and resources as well as process skills, and an understanding of all preceding Walker et al.'s propositions and their consequences for collective decision making.

It makes sense that Gunderson et al. (2006) consider learning to be a critical ingredient of the adaptive capacity of social-ecological systems. They define *learning* as the process of proposing conceptual models and then testing them through empirical observation. However, according to Dörner (1989) this process is predictably flawed owing to the long time periods sometimes necessary for observing any consequences of actions in social-ecological systems. Gunderson et al. discuss three types of learning that amount to how mental (cause-and-effect) models change: *incremental* (acquired through monitoring the effects of implemented policies), *lurching* (triggered by crises during which policy failures become obvious), and *transformational* (figure 4.5).

Gunderson et al. (2006) deem transformational learning to be the most profound—similar to Argyris's (1977) double-loop learning in organizations. Transformational learning spans levels of the panarchy. It includes cross-scale surprises that may challenge underlying assumptions, norms, and objectives, thus contributing to adaptability and, when necessary, system transformation. It seems then that transformational learning is both necessary and most useful to planners.

This section has explored some of the characteristics of social-ecological systems that can inform plans to avoid or respond to crises at different geographic scales. The next section reviews obstacles to making sound decisions that factor these characteristics into planning.

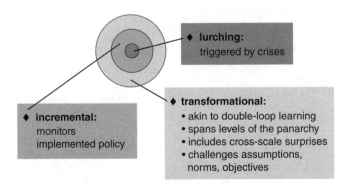

Figure 4.5
Systems learning. Based on Gunderson et al. (2006).

Decision Making (Warts and All)

Efforts to enhance the resilience of social-ecological systems can be thwarted by certain patterns of individual and collective decision making, as well as by the very nature of the systems that planning aims to impact. Any collaborative attempt to either make a system resilient, to adapt it, or to transform it has to attend to the threats discussed in this section, or risk failure.

Individual decision making is a building block of joint decision processes involved in collaborative initiatives such as might be necessary for maintaining a social-ecological system's resilience. Individuals bring to a collaborative process cognitive characteristics that have predictable effects on their joint decisions. They include judgmental biases and cognitive difficulties in handling uncertainty and the complexity of the systems whose resilience, adaptation or transformation is to be managed. In addition, individuals hold mental models of reality that affect the types of strategies and solutions they favor. The success of decisions hinges critically on these models' congruence with the reality they purport to represent. Compounding these difficulties shared by all, additional obstacles to collaboratives stem from how people's thinking relates to their context. Individuals tend to have a short attention span driven by the salience of problems (rather than, for instance, by the problems' urgency, or the magnitude of their consequences). They are susceptible to the Commons Dilemma structure of incentives present in situations involving public goods and the public interest. It should not be surprising, therefore, to find that although collaborative efforts are initiated and succeed, there are fewer such processes than there are problems waiting for solutions. Collaborative decision making requires a level of support that is often difficult to sustain in time. Such efforts tend to peter out before their usefulness is exhausted (Kaufman 2011). Time is their enemy, even in successful cases.

Cognitive Shortcomings

Cognitive biases are predictable errors of individual judgment, driven by the ways in which people handle information about complex situations. Table 4.1 summarizes some ways in which individuals' decisions may come up short. Examples (see, for instance, Kahneman, Slovic, and Tversky 1982; Bazerman and Moore 2009) include:

- Making *different* decisions about the *same* problem, depending on how the problem is presented (framed)

Table 4.1
Simple and composite individual decision shortcomings

Simple (judgmental) biases*	Composite (decision) biases**
• sensitivity to framing • mishandling probabilities • estimating through anchoring and adjustment • overconfidence in estimates • seeking/preferring confirming evidence	• favoring one-factor explanations/solutions • solving interdependent problems one by one although interrelated • tendency to simplify complex relationships • relying on trust frames • rigid understanding of technical facts • faulty mental models of reality • susceptibility to Commons Dilemma incentives

*Based on Bazerman (1994); **Based on Dörner (1989).

- Misunderstanding probabilistic concepts
- Formulating estimates by anchoring and insufficient adjustment
- Overconfidence in the estimates, even when they are based on scant knowledge
- A tendency to seek confirming evidence for one's own ideas while avoiding any disconfirming information

Dörner (1989) links some of these basic biases in very useful ways to the context characteristics that tend to trigger them. The resulting set of composite decision biases (see table 4.1) causes predictable difficulties for individual and joint decision making. He claims that these biases contribute to a "logic of failure," especially in problem solving and in planning for the uncertain future in the context of complex systems, which is what planners do.

For example, Dörner brings up our tendency to favor one-factor explanations and one-factor solutions for problems. This preference is rooted in mental strategies for coping with information overload. Various one-factor accounts of underperforming schools in urban settings and the accompanying one-factor fixes illustrate well this tendency. So does the focus on carbon as the sole culprit in global climate change, and the view that its reduction is the only (necessary and sufficient) solution. A related issue is the practice of solving problems one by one, instead of addressing the totality of issues whose interrelationships can make or break the success of solutions. The schools and climate change examples serve here as well. This observation parallels the notion advanced by negotiation theory that resolving conflict issues one by one is a worse approach than negotiating by exchanging complete (package) proposals that attend to all the issues under contention at the same time. The "package" approach in negotiations offers the possibility of identifying valuable trade-offs that make a solution attractive and eventually acceptable to more stakeholders (Shmueli et al. 2008). The analogy applies to decision making for complex systems, where working with alternatives formulated as packages of features (instead of solving problems sequentially, as people tend to do) enables similar trade-offs among the various dimensions and can yield better, implementable solutions.

Dörner also addresses a host of composite decision biases that stem from our difficulty in handling system dynamics (and their frequent intransparence or "black box" quality). We tend to add to this difficulty a tendency to simplify complex relations and reduce the number of their dimensions in order to minimize, as it were, the "cognitive energy" we must expend in problem solving. Based on Dörner's experimental results, it seems that we do manage to protect our cognitive energy, but at the expense of outcome quality. Having applied reductive hypotheses to the diagnosis of problems, we proceed to avoid or ignore any evidence that casts doubt on, or even disconfirms our conjectures. Dörner contends that we are dangerously "infatuated" with our own hypotheses because we feel they give us "power over things." This belief is a judgmental illusion confirmed experimentally by others (e.g., Bazerman and Moore 2009). Consider again the example of the 2009 Copenhagen Conference on Climate Change. Participants sought (and entertained the illusion that it was possible) to limit the global temperature rise by the end of the twenty-first century to precisely 4°C (compared to the pre-industrial era). Global warming is a complex, large-scale, and poorly understood system in which numerous actors operate at various geographical scales (within vastly diverse political regimes), with drastically different resources and stakes. The Copenhagen participants' quest and their subsequent disappointment at having to settle for a reduction of less than 4°C over the next ninety years illustrates overconfidence in estimates highly beset by uncertainty, use of reductive hypotheses about a complex system, and the illusion (bordering on hubris) of control over it.

Compounding judgmental obstacles to decision making in complex situations is our tendency to make sense of reality by using "frames." Framing is a simplifying cognitive device that brings some elements into focus while leaving out some other factors that later are difficult to reincorporate into the big picture if necessary (e.g., Elliott, Gray, and Lewicki 2003; Donohue, Rogan, and Kaufman 2011). Once established, frames filter subsequent information; they prevent us from adding new information to our understanding of complex situations and dynamics. At times our frames are quite removed from the reality they reflect, leading to errors of judgment. For example, people might cast others (frame them) in ways resistant to change during decision process interactions. Members of disadvantaged communities sometimes harbor a deep mistrust of public institutions that have failed to serve them. They may also distrust private industries that have taken advantage of them in some way in the past. These experiences lead to framing (characterizing) as untrustworthy, *anyone* working for a public agency or in industry. When they participate in a collaborative process, community members may have difficulty interacting with those they have already painted negatively with a broad brush. However, reframing, slow-paced as it may be, is one of the benefits of interaction during such processes.

A negative consequence of our reliance on frames that is relevant to decision making in complex situations is how we handle unfamiliar or complicated information, whether scientific, technical, financial, or legal. When we feel unable to evaluate certain information directly, we tend to switch to trust in the source as a measure of the information's quality, reliability, and relevance. For example, we usually accept trusted doctors' explanations of medical problems since most of us do not know enough to evaluate the merits of such information. Similarly, we may accept technical information offered by those deemed specialists and factor it into collective decisions. Our acceptance is not necessarily based on understanding the claims and their implications for our problems. Rather, it is based on trust in the producers of that information (Kaufman 2009).

Agreement among information producers often persuades us when direct evaluation of the information is too difficult. For instance, although only relatively few scientists understand climate change models, many people believe their consensus is proof of the models' veracity. Conversely, disagreement among information producers can provoke great anxiety and even conflict for those who are reduced to arguing about technical aspects of various alternative solutions in terms of trust, a weak and fickle proxy. Using such proxies also impedes people's ability to update information they do not really understand. They tend to cling to whatever they think they understood at some point, but are unable to either manipulate or update acquired wisdom. However, many argue for the centrality of transparent information in successful collaborations (e.g., Dietz, Ostrom, and Stern 2003; Turner et al. 2008). Therefore, it becomes important to develop and refine our approaches to the communication of information that is critical to the success of collaboratives, as well as the degree of uncertainty associated with it. Participants in collaborative processes might then be less disconcerted or mistrustful of information updates and more willing to welcome new data that contradict acquired wisdom.

Mental models are the cause-and-effect linkages we hold as representative of reality (Pinker 2002; 2007). According to Pinker, the tendency to search for these linkages is one of the brain's innate "gadgets." Our mental models impinge on the kinds of information we seek and the kinds of remedies we might propose for various problems. For example, those who believe poverty is the result of personal behavior are apt to propose totally different fixes than those whose mental model attributes poverty to long-term institutional and social shortcomings.

Dörner (1989) found many ways in which people's explicit and implicit mental models are prone to errors that lead to decision-making failure. He claims that our mental models of reality are very likely to be both incomplete and wrong.[8] This problem is compounded by two tendencies described by Bazerman and Moore (2009). The first is our overconfidence in our beliefs (which tends to increase the less we know). The second is our tendency to avoid seeking any-but-confirming evidence for our beliefs. Moreover, Bazerman and Watkins (2004) argue that mental models are resistant to the signs of looming crises that could trigger timely action, leading more often than necessary to "predictable surprises" and their negative consequences. Many planning and public policy failures are due, at least in part, to faulty underlying mental models of how the target systems worked, and failure to anticipate crises. Dörner has a pessimistic metaphor for decision makers in a complex situation. He likens them to two chess players who have a great surplus of game pieces, all linked to each other by rubber bands so no figure can be moved alone. Both players' pieces can move by themselves following unclear rules, about which the players may have mistaken assumptions. The pieces are surrounded by a fog that obscures their identities.

One context characteristic that this chapter has already briefly mentioned is the Commons Dilemma structure of incentives in situations involving public goods (Hardin 1968). These incentives impel individuals to act in ways that may favor them (at the expense of others) in the short term, but that in the long run end up harming them (as well as harming their community). Situations with a Commons Dilemma structure tempt us to act in ways of which we might not be proud, but that we perceive as necessary either to obtain our dues or to avoid loss because others claim theirs. Commons incentives translate in short-term goals that drive individuals to consume as much of a limited resource as they are able to secure rather than need; contribute to pollution although they would prefer to reduce it; waste resources; and fail to abide by public commitments to stop behaviors harmful to the environment.

Examples of behaviors resulting from situations with Commons incentives abound: urban residential sprawl into green areas, driving very large cars, buying products known to damage the environment, maintaining lush lawns in arid regions, and failure to curtail activities believed to contribute to climate change. When aware of the collective negative results of their dilemma-driven individual choices, we reason that others do it too; our "sacrifice" would be either "canceled out" or exploited by others who continue to abuse the limited resources or public goods; therefore, it does not make sense to behave individually in the socially responsible way unless everyone else does too—and there's the rub.

Adding insult to injury, the kinds of activities deriving from a Commons Dilemma incentive structure are difficult to monitor to ensure across-the-board compliance. So if the condition for anyone to "do the right thing" is that everyone does too, such efforts are doomed to failure as the Commons Dilemma analyses predict. The 2009 United Nations Climate Change Conference in Copenhagen illustrates this point: unable to devise trustworthy mechanisms for ensuring every country's compliance, participant nations failed to fashion (or refused to sign) a binding accord to limit emissions of greenhouse gases. This case also suggests that geographic scale might play a role in Commons-like situations. It might be easier to mitigate dilemma effects at the local rather than global levels because the local scale may be more amenable to the development of the mutual trust necessary for collective action.

As Mio, Thompson, and Givens (1993) note, simple awareness of the Commons metaphor rarely succeeds in changing behavior. It fails to alter the perception of what is in our own interest, given our prediction that others will also act selfishly. Nevertheless, at times, public debates and collaboratives help to ease the pull of the widespread and seemingly irresistible incentives of Commons-like situations (Komorita and Parks 1994). Public discussions in the framework of a collaborative process—where people know each other personally—may induce some to act against their instinct and draw satisfaction from being seen as behaving in a socially beneficial way. As well, collaboratives may be seen as tools to save resources (and contribute to social-ecological systems' resilience) by altering perceptions of incentives and of personal/collective consequences sufficiently to obtain durable behavioral changes in Commons Dilemma situations.

Trust plays a critical role in willingness to cooperate (and risk exploitation by others who fail to uphold their commitments), instead of acting unilaterally. Lack of trust undermined, in part, the 2009 Copenhagen Conference. At state, national, or global scales, where stakeholder interactions have to be mediated by representation, collaboratives may not sufficiently develop such trust, so they require more formal means of enforcing agreements. Dietz et al. (2003) are relatively optimistic about the possibility of developing governance rules and monitoring devices that can overcome the Commons incentives. Their proposed solutions also stress fit-to-scale and redundancy, which others (e.g., Mio et al. 1993) have also posited as contributors to systems' resilience.

Anticipation

Abel et al. (2006) contend that resilience of social-ecological systems is controlled mostly by slow-changing variables. The fast and slow attributes of change are roughly assessed in comparison to a human life span (one generation). Change exceeding the life span of one generation is considered slow. For example, pandemics are considered fast-changing (and occur everywhere simultaneously, as opposed to localized events such as hurricanes; Wallace and Wallace 2008). Also fast-acting are some of the causes of the destruction of cities throughout history. Vale and Campanella (2005) include examples such as Chicago's great fire of 1871, Berlin's bombing in World War II, and Mexico City's 1985 earthquake. In contrast, the causes of societal collapse in Diamond's (2005) examples (e.g., Rapa Nui or Easter Island) are considered slow-acting. Slow-changing system attributes (such as global temperature) pose a serious problem to planning, because they may go undetected or appear unthreatening until it is too late to stop or reverse their progress. Their surreptitious progress leads to "predictable" surprises (Bazerman and Watkins 2004), which we could have seen coming had we been willing to look and act.

The consequences of culturally and economically driven gender selection at or before birth, favoring boys, are examples of predictable surprises. The resulting crises emerge one or more generations after the one responsible for the choices leading to it. This slow-acting phenomenon is occurring at a staggering (continent-wide) scale and affects several large and small Asian countries. The predicted effects are twofold: one possibly desirable for global environmental sustainability and the other extremely undesirable, threatening global peace. The first effect, already noticeable, is a slow drop in previously rapid population growth rates,[9] because (all else being equal) the slow-down is directly driven by the decline, due to gender selection, in the number of available wombs. The birth rate slow-down has been sought and is welcome in China and India, though it will be predictably accompanied by the second consequence: a growing threat of unrest, social upheavals, and violence possibly leading to regional and international war. This consequence of gender selection may stem from the large numbers of frustrated young men being unable to find wives and raise families, to fulfill biologically and culturally driven reproduction goals. Those men able to find wives in these circumstances will do so by exercising either economic or physical power. Both effects—population decline and social unrest—have been recognized and predicted for a relatively long while (e.g., Sen 1990). The countries themselves, their immediate neighbors, and the global equilibrium will be affected; problems have already begun to crop up. Despite the consensus around the predicted negative consequences, there is no concerted action to mitigate effects or curb the practice of gender selection. The first war over brides is likely to surprise us all.

Another example of a looming predictable surprise is a flu pandemic. It is considered by epidemiologists not a matter of "if" but of "when," and expected much sooner than the predicted effects of global climate change. Although the flu pandemic lacks the salience and star status of global climate change, awareness of this threat is rather widespread. Therefore the general indifference to it is particularly puzzling because the pandemic will not be choosy with its numerous victims. Unlike in the climate change case, it is difficult to see oneself as likely to be spared for some reason such as geographic location. Predictions of the immediate consequences of flu pandemic paint a picture of across-the-board collapse of all vital networks. Yet there are only weak calls for preparedness.

Bazerman and Watkins (2004) have some answers to this puzzle of seeming unconcern with some threats that leads us to ignore signs of impending disasters. They contend that failure to see the coming crises is due to a combination of individual judgmental biases and institutional failures (see a summary in table 4.2). The individual judgmental biases include our positive illusion that mainly good things are in store for us in the future. Egocentrism and discounting the future make us unlikely to sacrifice now for averting a catastrophe that might happen after we are gone. The omission bias consists in preferring no action (causing damage by omission) to actions that might cause lesser damage, but by commission.[10] We may

Table 4.2
Individual and institutional obstacles to anticipatory activities*

Individual obstacles	Institutional obstacles
• positive illusions • omission bias • status quo bias • inattention to dull data	• lack of resources for data collection about emergent threats • lack of information dissemination • diffuse responsibilities • failure to learn from the past

*Based on Bazerman and Watkins (2004).

also have a preference for maintaining the status quo despite our own calls for change (Bazerman and Moore 2009). We tend to be inattentive to data that are not vivid. The last point is illustrated by Al Gore's film, *An Inconvenient Truth* (Gore 2006). The film conveyed vividly predicted consequences of global warming, generating widespread awareness, alarm, and calls for preventive action. To promote preparedness for the flu pandemic, it may be necessary to find an equally vivid channel of communication. In general, individual judgmental shortcomings are quite robust and resist change even through training (Bazerman and Watkins 2004). They play into organizational and political problems that compound our failure to detect predictable surprises.

Table 4.2 summarizes institutional blind spots that also lead to predictable surprises (Bazerman and Watkins 2004). They include: failure to devote resources to the collection of data about emerging threats, reluctance to disseminate information perceived as "too sensitive" to share, failure to integrate knowledge dispersed throughout organizations, diffuse responsibility that removes incentives to act until it is too late, erosion of institutional memory through personnel losses, and failure to capture lessons learned from the past.

An example of the latter is the one rare instance of a timely response to an impending crisis: frenetic activities and considerable resources were devoted to preventing the collapse of critical data sets as computer clocks transitioned from the twentieth to the twenty-first century (the "Y2K" crisis). The mobilization and costly preventive actions were driven by predictions of immediate and far-ranging economic and functional losses. This instance contains, embedded in its success, a germ of defeat. Instead of learning that timely and concerted collective action can avert catastrophes, many have erroneously concluded that the doom predictions did not materialize because there had been no real threat. They deemed unnecessary the preparation and resources spent avoiding the Y2K threat. Another example of this mindset relates to homeland security measures taken after 9/11. Although the absence of another attack of the same magnitude in the following decade may well have been due at least in part to those measures, it is seen by many as a sign that these measures were excessive and unnecessary.

Why are we not better able to learn from the past? In regards to institutions, Bazerman and Watkins discuss one reason: erosion of institutional memory through personnel losses. More broadly, social memory (in and among nations, for instance) is lost in much the same way, through the passing of generations. Losing those people who "knew" may account, in part, for why history repeats itself. Bazerman and Watkins contend that these institutional shortcomings are more amenable to change than judgmental ones. However, in the political arena, these shortcomings are amplified by the interplay of special interests, elected officials' short-range political goals, and their selective attention to the problems that can get them reelected (Layzer 2002).

The Y2K event illustrates pervasive obstacles to energizing people for collective preventive action. They include: difficulty in persuading people to allocate resources to solving a predicted problem, especially when it lies outside of their shared mental models, and the fact that success—which in the case of crises means they have been averted—leads people to believe that action was not really needed. Consider the global financial crisis that began in 2008. With the benefit of 20/20 hindsight (which they mistake for insight, another judgmental bias described by Bazerman and Moore 2009) many[11] now claim that they had predicted its "obvious" imminence. Many also claim the predictions should have impelled (unspecified) people to act to prevent the crisis. But had action been taken in a timely fashion, it is likely that success would have been interpreted as proof that no action had been needed, since no crisis occurred.

Adger (2000) claims surprises are inherent in ecological and social systems even when it is possible to predict changes to some extent. It would seem, then, that the systemic surprises (and the anticipation that might alert us to them in time to plan for remedies) are issues requiring attention. Anticipation is a necessary skill of planners and of those engaging in collaborative actions to build and enhance resilience in social-ecological systems. Dessai, Lu, and Risbey (2005) argue that anticipatory responses are better for resilience than reactive responses. However, according to Dörner (1989) and to Bazerman and Watkins (2004), some of our judgmental biases and some institutional biases work against early action.

Our mental models resist change in the absence of crises and even in their presence, as do our institutions.

Complexity

We examine next system complexity and its various roadblocks to resilience: scale misconceptions, scale mismatches, and unwittingly prolonging the life of maladapted systems. We discuss some tools for analyzing complexity, and a look at how redundancy makes us less vulnerable.

Unlike the decision makers' cognitive shortcomings discussed earlier, complexity is a context feature: it characterizes both ecological systems and the social systems embedded in them (within which decisions are made). It is therefore not surprising that complexity lies at the heart of resilience research. That is because the resilience of both ecological and social realms depends to a considerable extent on the ability to anticipate threats and plan responses. But in social systems, complexity not only impairs predictive and planning capacity, but it may also be a root cause of reduced resilience. Dörner's (1989) showed experimentally that when people are asked to provide solutions for problems occurring in a complex system, they tend to focus on one-factor explanations and fixes. This tendency invariably yields surprising and negative side-effects that may be even worse than the original problem.

Bar-Yam (2006) refers to the term *scale* as the level at which a specific system behavior is visible to observers. Usually scale applies to physical entities and refers to space and time. When Cumming, Cumming, and Redman (2006) speak of sociological scale, they refer to space, time, representation, and organization. Social and ecological systems are complex at all scales, whether physical or social. For instance, local planning challenges can be as intricate as regional and national ones. Wilson et al. (1999) contend that one effect of a system's complexity is that it becomes difficult to design responses to challenges. In addition, a mismatch between the scale of an ecological system and the scale at which the managing entities (institutions, collaboratives) operate can have deleterious consequences for resilience (Cumming et al. 2006). Such mismatches are also likely for social systems.

At least two aspects of scale in complex systems pose obstacles to resilience. First, Wilson et al. (1999) bring up scale misperceptions. They investigated what happens when the scale of the system dynamics that we are addressing does not match the scale of our decisions. They describe the attempt to regulate ocean fisheries. In their example, decision makers typically focus on controlling overfishing. However the fish population may be undermined by inadvertent destruction of its habitat structure at a larger scale of which decision makers remain unaware and which may doom their efforts. The 2007 financial crisis was beset by scale problems. At what level is it useful and/or appropriate to provide remedies? Would fixes at that level (e.g., country) be more effective than at another scale (e.g., international)? Other problems that pose similar conundrums include the AIDS crisis in Africa and water management in several regions of Asia. Scale misperception constitutes input to our mental models of problems and of how things work. In turn, these models affects the remedies we imagine and their chances of being effective.

The second scale aspect apt to impede resilience is scale mismatch. It may occur not necessarily due to a scale misperception of system's underlying mechanisms (i.e., in the fisheries case), but rather from the difference between the scale of a problem and that of the level at which we organize to respond (Cumming et al. 2006). The developed countries' approaches to reduce world hunger illustrate such a mismatch. Their efforts often fail or remain at band-aid level because the scale of solutions is typically smaller than the scale of the factors generating the problem. River water quality is another example. Water quality cannot be remedied in sections; it requires a watershed approach instead. Some city problems hinge on region-wide phenomena (such as unemployment) and no amount of local action will suffice to fix such troubles.

It may be difficult to distinguish whether a scale obstacle is one of misperception or mismatch because both entail solutions that fail to address the root causes of problems in complex systems. In fact, scale misperceptions constitute a subset of scale mismatches. According to Cumming et al. (2006), resolving scale mismatches is a long-term proposition involving institutional changes at several levels, and requiring social learning.

Abel et al. (2006) tackle another aspect of complexity in relation to social-ecological systems resilience: the capacity of a system to self-organize, and the sensitive balance that needs to be struck between allowing the process to occur and assisting it with external resources that may end up stifling it. Resilience means system *recovery* after a shock, rather than fundamental change. Because recovery has a positive connotation, there is the danger that an infusion of external resources—a form of "throwing good money after bad" (Gueron 2005)—prolongs the life of maladapted systems until they eventually collapse.

New Orleans in the aftermath of the hurricane Katrina (in 2005) is illustrative. The city was, arguably, maladapted to its physical context. It is below sea level, which predictably exposes it to floods; it is also located in a hurricane path. Resources might best go toward transforming New Orleans into a city that can successfully withstand effects of the severe hurricanes predicted to recur in the future. This means, for example, re-building in areas other than the low-lying ones susceptible to flooding. However, efforts, resources, and the normative discourse accompanying them were mostly directed at resilience measures aiming to restore the city to its pre-Katrina state. The U.S. automotive industry offers another example of seeking resilience instead of necessary transformation. It has been argued that by 2008 this industry, maladapted to current needs, should have been allowed to fail and possibly transform, instead of receiving an infusion of public resources to regroup. The inclination to "save" cities or large industries by helping them return to their previous state (that failed) may reflect our attachment to the status quo. It also illustrates the perils of the normatively positive connotation of resilience.

Bar-Yam (2006) proposes that the rising complexity of human societies can be modeled and analyzed with the tools used for any other complex system. This claim may seem counterintuitive given that human agency has been argued, for example by behavioral economists, to severely impede such modeling attempts. Bar-Yam sees civilization as an organism in itself, capable of more complex behaviors than its individual components. He claims this is unusual: collective behaviors are typically simpler than those of their components, especially if these components all act in the same way. This greater complexity derives from the interconnections and specializations among humans. There is also the fact that humans do not all act in the same way under the same circumstances.

Bar-Yam contends that the history of human civilization reflects an increase in complexity of large-scale behaviors. This increase derives from the coordination that accompanies increasing specialization within and across countries and regions. In time, initially hierarchical systems have given way to networked systems of societal control. A system with fixed energy and resources should compensate for increased complexity at one scale with decrease at another scale. Human society, however, has "violated" these restrictions by adding both population and energy sources, leading to increased complexity at all levels. Two consequences of the increasing complexity are directly related to resilience. First is the resulting move from hierarchical control to lateral interactions. There is a measure of turmoil during the transition (related to predictable surprises in organizations and societal systems).

A second consequence of Bar-Yam's observation is societal vulnerability. In today's world people's collective behaviors are as complex (or more) than the behaviors of individuals. As a result, societies have become vulnerable to the quick propagation of any shock throughout all scales, from local to global. Resilience is weakened by the world's high complexity and increasing efficiency (achieved by eliminating redundancies in economic, social, and supply networks). These observations have led McKenzie (2008) to the pessimistic conclusion that the demise of civilization may be inevitable because of a profound loss of resilience related to lack of redundancy in the social systems. She sees evidence of this demise in our collective environmental mismanagement. She points to our heightened vulnerability to shocks that can cascade through all societal levels, leading humanity perilously close to a tipping point, after which perhaps mostly subsistence farmers (who are the least networked) may survive.

While demise is perhaps not imminent, doing nothing about the perils of over-efficient networking is asking for a predictable surprise. It may be worthwhile to heed these warnings and act to increase redundancies even if they seem economically wasteful or unnecessary. Such redundancies might prove critical in sustaining social and ecological resilience. Collaborative processes can be helpful in making collective decisions to devote scarce resources to the preemption of predictable crises. Such decisions are rarely popular (for reasons already discussed), so they require broad consensus that political or executive decisions can rarely garner. The co-construction of the information base that is often a component of collaborative processes might help overcome the reluctance to act now to prevent future, uncertain crises.

Collaborative Processes

Let us adopt the chapter's argument that Walker et al.'s (2006) heuristics and propositions are good descriptors of how complex systems function and the ways (including resilience) in which systems respond to crises. The discussion of these propositions has surfaced some direct and indirect connections to collaborative processes, and it has described some decision-making obstacles to such processes. Let us also adopt the chapter's argument that awareness of the cognitive and institutional obstacles to decisions (presented by Dörner 1989 and. Bazerman and Watkins 2004), and understanding the perils of too-efficiently networked societies (Bar-Yam 2006) can help garner the necessary collective resolve to act.

Knowing all of this, we still have to ask: When is resilience desirable? Are collaborative processes are well suited to enhance the resilience of social and ecological systems? In what follows we will consider resilience as desirable. This is because the time span in which we operate when planning or responding to crises is usually shorter than that required to implement fundamental systemic changes (to which resilience is an impediment). However, we should not lose sight of the fact that the set of possible responses also contains adaptation and transformation, each appropriate in specific cases.

Collaborative problem-solving efforts vary from case to case and from one scale to another. These efforts have varying degrees of success in specific cases. However, they share some characteristics that are relevant to resilience. These characteristics[12] include: participation of stakeholders diverse in interests, values, skills, knowledge, societal positions, and networking; social learning; development of relationships and trust; co-construction of the information base for decisions; and inclusionary decision rules such as consensus building.

Asking whether collaboratives can enhance resilience requires exploring to what extent the characteristics of collaborative efforts are congruent with the characteristics of social and ecological systems and with our cognitive capability to understand and manage them at their various scales. Should we conclude that there is a good match between resilience needs and collaborative processes, we will be left with the tasks of making such processes happen. Figure 4.6 summarizes the congruence between resilience needs and the attributes of collaborative processes.

Based on our cognitive limitations in the face of complex information, Beratan (2007) argues that collaborative efforts are essential in dealing with social and environmental problems. She observes that there is resilience in diversity (of views, interests, preferences, values, and solutions). This parallels the systems' need for response diversity in order to be resilient. Further, given the resistance of people's mental "frames" to new information, Beratan notes that the social interaction that develops in

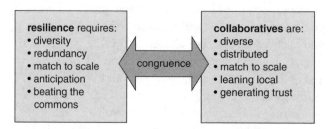

Figure 4.6
Congruence between resilience needs and attributes of collaborative processes.

collaboratives, frequently using stories, is a good vehicle for mutual frame change. This interaction can also contribute to trust building, social learning, and co-construction of a shared story. She also recognizes the usefulness of approaches developed in the context of conflict management. Her story concept, used as an effective organizer of complex information, is very similar to how others have used scenarios to capture the complex linkages and explore consequences of proposed alternative solutions to problems (e.g., Kaufman 2009).

Beratan has in mind situations at a local (place-based community) scale, where personal relationships, trust building, and co-construction of stories can readily occur. For exploring the management of global commons such as oceans or climate change, Dietz et al. (2003) stress the importance of developing the science that will enable wise decisions. They note, however, that the science has to be accompanied by wise governance that draws on social learning, trust building, and participatory mechanisms. Their conclusion is consistent with Beratan's, though it is likely that the implementation specifics will differ according to scale.

Scale matching (in all the senses described by Cumming et al. 2006) seems central to social and ecological problems and to approaches to solving them. Therefore, the scales at which we can develop successful collaboratives become a critical issue. On the one hand, it would seem that the smaller the scale of the collaborative (for example, at a neighborhood or even city or small regional level, for a limited time period), the more successful it can be. That is because the kinds of relationships necessary for success are interpersonal, direct, and immediate in nature. It may not be feasible or sustainable to develop such relationships at larger scales where representation is necessary and where Commons Dilemma effects may become more acute. Some of the successful collaborative approaches do not scale up simply. On the other hand, social and ecological problems do not happen to come at convenient scales!

Wilson et al. (1999) point out that while collaboratives are mostly local, the systems' resilience resides in higher geographic and time scales. Collaborative planning typically requires direct interpersonal interactions, building trust and relationships for the long run, balancing power differences, and finally, integrating different "knowledges," interests, and points of view. Although there have been large-scale participatory projects, the kinds of interactions on which collaborative planning is predicated are defeated if the system to be affected has a larger scale that impedes these dynamics. Wilson et al.'s proposal entails moving away from centralized management organizations and cultivating local management organizations that can deal effectively with local ecological phenomena. This is only a partial answer that does not resolve entirely the scale-mismatch problem. However it can contribute to the redundancy necessary to resilience and to better local results.

Predictable surprises pose another dilemma to collaborative action with respect to resilience. What length of time is adequate for us to see crises coming and to act to prevent them? Acting too early may fail to garner the necessary attention. In contrast, waiting for an issue to become salient enough for collective action may be too late to foster resilience. In the case of climate change, for example, early warnings came well before the term became a household notion. However, now that climate change has achieved salience, it may be too late to prevent. Therefore, instead of engaging in costly measures (possibly doomed to failure), perhaps we should plan how to adapt to the inevitable.

It seems that we require a very high level of (scientific) evidence before believing in an impending crisis enough to sacrifice today to prevent the crisis tomorrow. Therefore, we must devise ways of making the science behind predictions accessible and persuasive. Otherwise, resilience-enhancing collaboratives may be relegated to designing mostly after-the-fact responses to crises, which is suboptimal. Taking on the relationships among science, knowledge, democracy, and environmentalism, Bäckstrand (2004) has put forth the notion of civic science. This concept is very similar to Ozawa's approach to co-constructing the information base of decisions (e.g., Ozawa 1996; 2005). Bäckstrand's civic science is the reconstruction of scientific expertise in a democratic fashion. She believes this strategy is crucial for taking the kinds of collaborative actions necessary for sustainability (and therefore, for resilience).

Having concluded based on a set of case studies that collaborative efforts enhance resilience, Olsson et al. (2006) dispense a host of practical advice for how to make such efforts happen. These recommendations will sound familiar to planners but they are addressed to the generic reader, leaving unclear the issue of who should take these actions. In other words, it seems easy to agree that collaboratives are beneficial, and constitute a good approach to fostering resilience. In fact, there is a rather high level of consilience between the evidence yielded by ecosystems resilience studies (Anderies et al. 2006) and the collaborative approaches that planning and negotiation theory recommend. However, because such processes are resource- and skills-intensive and are not embedded in existing structures, making them happen remains a challenge.

Perhaps Lebel et al. (2006) have posed the most important questions we need to address in discussing how collaborative efforts can contribute to the resilience of social and ecological systems They asked: "Who decides what should be made resilient to what? For whom is resilience to be managed, and for what purpose?" The chapter has argued that collaboratives are suitable for dealing with resilience problems. But collaboratives cannot offer an answer to these questions (and neither do Lebel et al.) and thus we are left to ponder them. That is the kind of work that still lies before us.

Notes

1. Brand and Jax (2007) catalogue and classify several definitions of *resilience*, ranging from descriptive to normative, although they claim pride of coinage for the descriptive definition originating in ecological science. They warn of the meta-concept danger that has reduced the usefulness of other terms (such as *sustainability*; people agree to strive for it, while meaning different things by it).

2. According to Walker et al. (2006), this kind of work—formulating propositions that can be empirically validated and then applied—is only beginning. Their propositions are based on relatively few (15) case studies, and therefore in need of more exploration, development, and validation.

3. "Fore loop" and "back loop" refer to their respective positions in Holling's (1986) graphical representation of the adaptive cycle, which resembles a Möbius strip.

4. The examples are oversimplified here for illustrative purposes. Clearly numerous factors are at play and account for observed consequences of urban renewal, gentrification, or changes after German reunification, and they have been amply documented.

5. According to Walker et al. (2002), sustainability involves "maintaining the functionality of a system when it is perturbed, or maintaining the elements needed to renew or reorganize if a large perturbation radically alters structure and function." Resilience is thus the ability to accomplish sustainability.

6. Consilience differs from consensus in meaningful ways. *Consensus* among scientists is not necessarily a sign that a particular claim is true (Crichton 2003)—after all, there used to be consensus about the Earth being flat (and any dissenters were burned at the stake). *Consilience* characterizes streams of research in different, often unrelated fields, supporting similar or complementary findings.

7. According to Groffman et al. (2006) for example, ecological thresholds are points at which an abrupt change occurs in an ecosystem's property or quality, or where small changes in an environmental driver produce large/abrupt responses in the ecosystem. A threshold is an emergent property of complex systems. resulting from even simple interactions of the level of several driver variables, beyond which a quantitatively small change causes a qualitative change in the system, such as a shift to a different regime.

8. Pinker (2007) concurs—he contends that our metal models of the physical reality are more consistent with medieval beliefs than with contemporary scientific findings.

9. It is believed to be a chief contributor to thwarted predictions of exploding global population, whose deadline has come and gone.

10. For example, in an experiment (Ritov and Baron 1990): participants mostly prefer not to vaccinate children (letting 10 out of 10,000 die of a disease) than vaccinate (and causing 5 out of 10,000 children to die from the side-effects of the vaccine). Debates around international military intervention in countries beset by violent crises (such as Libya in 2011) reflect in part the preference for no action, to avoid loss (by commission, through potential collateral damage) of fewer civilian lives than are lost (by omission) through failure to intervene militarily to stop the continued violence.

11. According to James K. Galbraith (*New York Times Magazine,* Oct. 31, 2008), about ten to twelve of the thousands of American economists saw the mortgage crisis ahead of time.

12. In specific instances some of these characteristics are missing. Our evaluations conclude that their absence is responsible for the failure of the collaborative.

References

Abel, N. D., H. M. Cumming, and J. M. Anderies 2006. Collapse and reorganization in social-ecological systems: Questions, some ideas and policy implications. *Ecology and Society* 11(1):17. Accessed 1-31-2011. Available at http://www.ecology andsociety.org/vol11/iss1/art17/.

Adger, W. N. 2000. Social and ecological resilience: Are they related? *Progress in Human Geography* 24(3):347–364.

Anderies, J. M., B. H. Walker, and A. P. Kinzig 2006. Fifteen weddings and a funeral: Case studies and resilience-based management. *Ecology and Society* 11(1):21. Accessed 1-31-2011. Available at http://www.ecologyandsociety.org/vol11/iss1/art21/.

Argyris, C. 1977. Double-loop learning in organizations. *Harvard Business Review* 55:115–125.

Bäckstrand, K. 2004. Civic science for sustainability: Reframing the role of expert, policy makers and citizens in environmental governance. *Global Environmental Politics* 3:4.

Bar-Yam, Y. 2006. Complexity rising: From human beings to human civilization, A complexity profile. In *Encyclopedia of Life Support Systems.* Isle of Man, U.K.: UNESCO/EOLSS Publishers.

Bayley, C., and S. French 2008. Designing a participatory process for stakeholder involvement in a societal decision. *Group Decision and Negotiation* 17:195–210.

Bazerman, H. M. and D. A. Moore 2009. *Judgment in managerial decision making.* Hoboken, NJ: John Wiley.

Bazerman, M., and M. Watkins 2004. *Predictable surprises: The disasters you should have seen coming, and how to prevent them.* Cambridge, MA: Harvard Business School Press.

Beratan, K. K. 2007. A cognition-based view of decision processes in complex social–ecological systems. *Ecology and Society* 12(1):27. Accessed 1-31-2011. Available at http://www.ecologyandsociety.org/vol12/iss1/art27/.

Brand, F. S., and K. Jax 2007. Focusing the meaning(s) of resilience: Resilience as a descriptive concept and a boundary object. *Ecology and Society* 12(1):23. Accessed 1-31-2011. Available at http://www.ecologyandsociety.org/vol12/iss1/art23/.

Crichton, M. 2003. Aliens cause global warming. Lecture delivered at the California Institute of Technology, January 17.

Cumming, G. S., D. H. M. Cumming, and C. L. Redman 2006. Scale mismatches in social-ecological systems: Causes, consequences, and solutions. *Ecology and Society* 11(1):14. Accessed 1-31-2011. Available at http://www.ecologyandsociety.org/vol11/iss1/art14/.

Dessai, S., X. Lu, and J. S. Risbey 2005. On the role of climate scenarios for adaptation planning. *Global Environmental Change* 15(2):87–97.

Diamond, J. 2005. *Collapse: How societies choose to fail or succeed.* New York: Penguin Group (USA).

Dietz, T., E. Ostrom, and P. C. Stern 2003. The struggle to govern the commons. *Science* 302:1907–1912.

Donohue, W. A., R. G. Rogan, and S. Kaufman, eds. 2011. *Framing Matters: Perspecives on Negotiation Research and Practice in Communication.* New York: Peter Lang.

Dörner, D. 1989. *The logic of failure: Recognizing and avoiding error in complex situations.* New York: Metropolitan Books.

Elliott, M., B. Gray, and R. Lewicki, eds. 2003. *Making sense of environmental conflicts.* Washington, D.C.: Island Press.

Garud, R., and P. Karnøe, eds. 2001. *Path dependence and creation.* Mahwah, NJ: Lawrence Erlbaum Associates.

Gore, A. 2006. *An inconvenient truth.* [film] Beverly Hills, CA: Lawrence Bender Productions/Paramount Classics.

Groffman, P., J. Baron, T. Blett, A. Gold, I. Goodman, L. Gunderson, B. Levinson, M. Palmer, H. Paerl, G. Peterson, N. LeRoy Poff, D. Rejeski, J. Reynolds, M. Turner, K. Weathers, and J. Wiens.2006. Ecological thresholds: the key to successful environmental management or an important concept with no practical application? *Ecosystems* 9(1):1–13.

Gueron, J. M. 2005. Throwing good money after bad: A common error misleads foundations and policymakers. *Stanford Social Innovation Review* 3(3):69–71.

Gujarati, D. N. 1995. *Essentials of econometrics.* New York: McGraw-Hill.

Gunderson, L. H. 2000. Ecological resilience—In theory and application. *Annual Review of Ecology and Systematics* 31:425–439.

Gunderson, L. H., S. R. Carpenter, C. Folke, P. Olsson, and G. Peterson 2006. Water RATs (resilience, adaptability, and transformability) in lake and wetland social-ecological systems. *Ecology and Society* 11(1):17. Accessed 1-31-2011. Available at http://www.ecologyandsociety.org/vol11/iss1/art16/.

Gunderson, L. H., and C. S. Holling, eds. 2002. *Panarchy: Understanding Transformations in Human and Natural Systems.* Washington D.C.: Island Press.

Haimes, Y. Y. 2009. On the definition of resilience in systems. *Risk Analysis* 29(4): 498–501.

Hardin, G. 1968. The commons dilemma. *Science* 162 (3859): 1243–1248.

Holling, C. S. 1973. Resilience and stability of ecological systems. *Annual Review of Ecology and Systematics* 4:1–23.

Holling, C. S. 1986. Resilience of ecosystems; local surprise and global change. In *Sustainable Development of the Biosphere*, W. C. Clark and R. E. Munn, eds., 292–317, Cambridge, UK: Cambridge University Press. >

Holling, C. S. 1996. Engineering resilience versus ecological resilience. In Engineering within ecological constraints, P. C. Schulze, ed., 32–43. Washington, D.C.: National Academy of Engineering, National Academy Press.

Kahneman, D., P. Slovic, and A. Tversky, eds. 1982. *Judgment under uncertainty: Heuristics and biases.* Cambridge, U.K.: Cambridge University Press.

Kaufman, S. 2009. Risk perception and communication in public and environmental decisions. *Négociations* 11(1):159–183.

Kaufman, S. 2011. Environmental inter-organizational collaboratives and their sustainability. In *The paradox in partnerships: The role of conflict in partnership building,* H. S. Desivilya, and M. Palgi, eds. Bentham E-Book

Komorita, S. S., and C. D. Parks 1994. *Social dilemmas.* Boulder, CO: Westview Press.

Lamberg, J.-A., K. Pajunen, P. Parvinen, and G. Savage 2008. Stakeholder management and path dependence in organizational transitions. *Management Decision* 46(6):846–863.

Layzer, J. 2002. *The environmental case: Translating values into policy.* 2nd ed. Washington, D.C.: CQ Press.

Lebel, L., J. M. Anderies, B. Campbell, C. Folke, S. Hatfield-Dodds, T. P. Hughes, and J. Wilson 2006. Governance and the capacity to manage resilience. Accessed 1-31-2011. Available at http://www.ecologyandsociety.org/vol11/iss1/art19/.

McCubbin, L. 2001. On the definition of resilience in systems. Paper presented at the annual meeting of the American Psychological Association (109th, San Francisco, CA, August 24–28).

McKenzie, D. 2008. Will a pandemic bring down civilization? *New Scientist* 2650:. Accessed 1-31-2011. Available at http://www.newscientist.com/article/mg19826501.400-will-a-pandemic-bring-down-civilisation.html.

McKenzie, D. 2008. Why the demise of civilization may be inevitable. *New Scientist* 2650: Accessed 1-31-2011. Available at http://www.newscientist.com/article/mg19826501.500-why-the-demise-of-civilisation-may-be-inevitable.html.

Mio, J. S., S. C. Thompson, and G. H. Givens 1993. The Commons Dilemma as metaphor: Memory, influence, and implications for environmental conservation. *Metaphor and Symbol* 8(1):23–42. Accessed 1-31-2011. Available at http://www .informaworld.com/smpp/content~db=all~content=a785873360~frm=titlelink.

Olsson, P., L. H. Gunderson, S. R. Carpenter, P. Ryan, L. Lebel, C. Folke, and C. S. Holling 2006. Shooting the rapids: Navigating transitions to adaptive governance of social-ecological systems. *Ecology and Society* 11(1):18. Accessed 1-31-2011. Available at http://www.ecologyandsociety.org/vol11/iss1/art18/.

Ozawa. C. P. 1996. Science in environmental conflicts. *Sociological Perspectives* 39(2):219–230.

Ozawa, C. P. 2005. Putting science in its place. In *Adaptive governance and water conflict: New institutions for collaborative governance*, ed. J. T. Scholz and B. Stiftel, 185–196. Washington, D.C.: Resources for the Future Press.

Pierson, P. 2000a. Increasing returns, path dependence, and the study of politics. *American Political Science Review* 94(2):251–267.

Pierson, P. 2000b. The limits of design: Explaining institutional origins and change. *Governance: An International Journal of Policy* 13(4):475–499.

Pinker, S. 2002. *The blank slate: The modern denial of human nature.* New York: Penguin Books (USA) Inc.

Pinker, S. 2007. *The stuff of thought: Language as a window into human nature.* New York: Penguin Books (USA) Inc.

Ritov, I., and J. Baron. 1990. Reluctance to vaccinate: Omission bias and ambiguity. *Journal of Behavioral Decision Making* 3(4):263-277.

Sen, A. K. 1990. More than 100 million women are missing. *New York Review of Books* 20:61–66.

Shmueli, D., S. Kaufman, and C. Ozawa 2008. Mining negotiation theory for planning insights. *Journal of Planning Education and Research* 27(3):359–364.

Turner, N. J., R. Gregory, C. Brooks, L. Failing, and T. Satterfield 2008. From invisibility to transparency: Identifying the implications. *Ecology and Society* 13(2):7. Accessed 1-31-2011. Available at http://www.ecologyandsociety.org/ vol13/iss2/art7/.

Vale, L. J., and T. J. Campanella, eds. 2005. *The resilient city: How modern cities recover from disaster.* New York: Oxford University Press.

Walker, B., S. R. Carpenter, J. Anderies, N. Abel, G. S. Cumming, M. A. Janssen, L. Lebel, J. Norberg, G. D. Peterson, and R. Pritchard 2002. Resilience management in social-ecological systems: A working hypothesis for a participatory approach. *Conservation Ecology* 6(1):14. Accessed 1-31-2011. Available at http:// www.ecologyandsociety.org/vol6/iss1/art14/.

Walker, B. H., L. H. Gunderson, A. P. Kinzig, C. Folke, S. R. Carpenter, and L. Schultz 2006. A handful of heuristics and some propositions for understanding resilience in social-ecological systems. *Ecology and Society* 11(1):13. Accessed 1-31-2011. Available at http://www.ecologyandsociety.org/vol11/iss1/art13/.

Walker, B. H., and J. A. Meyers 2004. Thresholds in ecological and social-ecological systems: a developing database. *Ecology and Society* 9(2):3 [online] URL: http://www.ecologyandsociety.org/vol9/iss2/art3/.

Wallace, D., and R. Wallace 2008. Urban systems during disasters: Factors for resilience. *Ecology and Society* 13(1): 18. Accessed 1-31-2011. Available at http://www.ecologyandsociety.org/vol13/iss1/art18/.

Werfel, J., and Y. Bar-Yam 2004. The evolution of reproductive restraint through social communication. *Proceedings of the National Academy of Sciences of the United States of America* 101(30):11019–11024.

Wilson, E. O. 1998. *Consilience: The unity of knowledge*. New York: Knopf.

Wilson, J., B. Low, R. Costanza, and E. Ostrom. 1999. Scale misperceptions and the spatial dynamics of a social-ecological system. *Ecological Economics* 31:243–257.

5

The Study of *Slow*

Jana Carp

Like many others, I often do not have time for activities and relationships that are important and beneficial. I spend too much time doing things that, while necessary, seem trivial, bureaucratic, and unhealthful. When I have time to spare, the experience is generally pleasurable and expansive. I reconnect with my immediate surroundings and with other people in my family, reach out to friends and attend to colleagues, and feel more aware of both my human community and my ecological location. Simply put, most of my life seems compartmentalized and rushed (which can be exhilarating), while only a small part of my life feels authentic and meaningful (if sometimes tedious). Similar experiences drive the burgeoning Slow movement and its various claims that "slow life" is integral for realizing a sustainable human future.[1] This chapter sketches a foundation for seriously considering such claims, venturing into possible connections between slowing down and social-ecological resilience as a key to sustainability (Walker and Salt 2006, 9). Important perspectives on *slow* are embedded within resilience theory, within social science literature about social, economic, political, and cultural practices, and also emerge from the experience of everyday life. *Slow,* as an object of study in itself, has received comparatively little scholarly attention. However, the significance of *slow* in complex adaptive social-ecological systems may be greater than either the slow movement or resilience theory has demonstrated thus far. The chapter concludes by examining one category of professional practice for which *slow* is a central characteristic: collaborative approaches for enhancing adaptive capacity and enabling social-ecological transformation.

Resilience Theory as a Conceptual Framework for Studying *Slow*

Walker and Salt's introduction to resilience theory states the problem of unsustainability in a familiar way: "The human population is growing while its resource base declines" (2006, 4). But their diagnosis differs from the usual. While they acknowledge that compulsory overuse and willful destruction of natural resources are also to blame for our current crisis, they focus on another root cause: we do not understand how the world actually works. "It isn't just the amount of knowledge—details about species and ecosystems—it's also the kind of knowledge. It's the way we conceive of resource systems and people as part of them. The way we currently use and manage these systems ("business as usual") is no longer working and yet what we hear most of the time is that the solution lies in more of the same" (2006, 5). Walker and Salt argue that a primary misunderstanding is demonstrated in attempts to optimize a sustained effect of particular system components through controlling the system's other components. Examples are familiar: "sustainable" fish yields and timber harvest, single-species preservation, the mono-crops of industrial agriculture, conventional flood controls, highway expansion, and perhaps even biological definitions of "family" in residential zoning codes. Optimization undergirds design, policy, and management practices whose goal is to maximize efficiency of a certain output. But Walker and Salt explain that such practices overemphasize the benefits of efficiency and discount secondary impacts—in effect, inviting negative long-term effects because the world is actually "much more complex than our assumptions allow for" (Walker and Salt 2006, 7).

Unintended consequences of policy decisions in my discipline, the field of planning, occur so routinely as to be expected by practicing planners as a kind of unavoidable occupational hazard. Often in the guise of citizens' complaints, these administrative "fires" distract planners' attention from opportunities for innovative thinking and development of long-range policy. From the perspective of resilience theory, planning's unintended consequences are evidence that places, as complexly linked social-ecological systems, are constantly adapting to circumstances that are themselves constantly changing. Planning practice asserts an instrumental linkage between management (e.g., land-use regulations such as zoning) and predictable outcomes (e.g., sustainable urban development and stable property values). But in resilience theory, policies influence our social-ecological systems rather than command, control, or comprehend them. "Resilience thinking" requires more explicitly incorporating uncertainty rather than assuming that strategic control, or comprehensivity, is possible (Walker and Salt 2006). At the same time, resilience theory recognizes that it takes time for such habits of mind to change.

The interconnectedness of the social and ecological aspects of places is simultaneously tenet and growing edge for resilience science, as it is for the Slow movement. Early resilience science research concentrated on ecological systems for which social impacts were characterized abstractly as an input or a driver. Subsequently, this literature comes to include more specific attention to the social aspects of systems in terms of facilitating social and ecological change, through natural resource management practices that recognize mutual (social and ecological) benefits of resilience (e.g., Olsson and Folke 2004). Walker et al. (2006) formalize this relationship within a set of theoretical propositions, including this one: "The ecological and social domains of social-ecological systems can be addressed in a common conceptual, theoretical, and modeling framework" (p. 6). They further assert that society can and must change in order to build social-ecological health and well-being (p. 3). However, in relating particular components of system adaptability—leadership, social networks, trust, social memory—to concepts of governance and social capital, resilience scientists are limited by insufficient data on social dimensions of resilience in social-ecological systems; they encourage further research in this area (Walker et al. 2006). An example of continuing resilience science research in this direction (discussed later) involves "adaptive co-manager communities." Such communities' investment in long-term ecosystem management and the ability to deliberate about trade-offs between their short- and long-term well-being apparently improves the resilience of ecosystems (Fabricius et al. 2007; for more examples, see http://www.resalliance.org).

Attention to long-term well-being is integral to both resilience theory and the Slow movement. In resilience theory, "slow variables" are a category of analysis used in reference to both ecological and social systems. Slow variables appear to control system resilience and thus are thought to play a significant part in a system's transformability: the creation of a fundamentally new system when the existing system is untenable (e.g., Walker and Salt 2006, 59). The regime shifts that affect ecosystem resilience tend to be precipitated by such slowly changing variables as sediment concentrations or long-lived organisms (Walker et al. 2006, 5). On the social side, resilience scientists Carpenter and Gunderson (2001) identify variables that also tend to change slowly: culture, long-lived institutions, rules of law, and enduring values (p. 457).

Let us turn to the Slow movement itself. For the purposes of this chapter, it suffices to conclude that there is a fundamental social dimension to the resilience of ecological systems, and that *slow* is significant for both ecological and social aspects of social-ecological systems. The three points outlined in this section are themes of the chapter:

(1) Places are complex, adaptive, social-ecological systems.

(2) Despite uncertainty, society must change in order to build social and ecological well-being and resilience.

(3) The necessary changes to build social-ecological resilience take time.

The Slow Movement and its Diversification

Slow Food, Slow Cities, Slow Life

The worldwide Slow movement appears to be burgeoning. Slow Food is perhaps the most widely recognized and most institutionalized program of the Slow movement. Begun in Italy in 1989 by Carlo Petrini as a reaction against the industrialization of "fast food," the Slow Food movement now has well over 1,000 chapters ("convivia") in 150 countries (Slow Food International Communications 2010). Slow Food focuses on locally pro-duced, handcrafted, and traditional foods enjoyed convivially in a leisurely context. Slow Food emphasizes pleasure, particularly taste, but it also incorporates education, ecological awareness, and the politics of food pro-duction, represented by the concept of "eco-gastronomy" (Andrews 2008; Parkins and Craig 2006). Terra Madre, launched in 2004, is a recent ini-tiative of Slow Food. It is a global network of "food communities" (small producers, cooks, educators, and students) that aim to cooperatively sup-port small-scale agriculture and sustainable food production. CittàSlow ("Slow Cities") is another program closely related to Slow Food that has grown quickly since it was established in 1999. From its beginning among four Italian towns, CittàSlow has grown into a global network of 135 certified communities in twenty countries, each of which meet strict membership requirements. These include small population (under 50,000) and government policies on environmental protection, historic preservation, support for local food production, hospitality, and so forth (CittàSlow International 1999). The Italian CittàSlow website describes the overall goal in charming English:

The main goal of cittaslow [*sic*], was and still is today, to enlarge the philosophy of Slow Food to local communities and to government of towns, applying the concepts of ecogastronomy at practice of everyday life. Municipalities which join the association are motivated by curious people of a recovered time, where man is still protagonist of the slow and healthy succession of seasons, respectful of citi-zens' health, the authenticity of products and good food, rich of fascinating craft traditions of valuable works of art, squares, theaters, shops, cafés, restaurants, places of the spirit and unspoiled landscapes, characterized by spontaneity of religious rites, respect of traditions through the joy of a slow and quiet living. (*Cittaslow News* 2008)

Mayer and Knox (2006) conclude that CittàSlow represents a "sustainable" approach to urban development. Although they do not address how *slow* per se makes a difference in the towns they have studied, they observed "grassroots local implementation of the principles associated with livability and quality of life" (p. 321). These principles include community-based economic development and environmental protection of working ecosystems and associated wildlife habitat.

A different Slow initiative is emerging in Japan, a country well known for its fast pace. "Slow Life" was initiated by the Iwate Prefecture in 2001 with a "Take-It-Easy Declaration . . . to launch a movement away from the prevailing ethos of economic efficiency" (Japan for Sustainability Newsletter 2003). Soon after, Kakegawa declared itself to be a "Slow Life City," adopting a declaration with these eight themes:

SLOW PACE: We value the culture of walking, to be fit and to reduce traffic accidents.

SLOW WEAR: We respect and cherish our beautiful traditional costumes, including woven and dyed fabrics, Japanese kimonos, and Japanese night robes (yukata).

SLOW FOOD: We enjoy Japanese food culture, such as Japanese dishes and tea ceremony, and safe local ingredients.

SLOW HOUSE: We respect houses built with wood, bamboo, and paper, lasting over one hundred or two hundred years, and are careful to make things durably, and ultimately, to conserve our environment.

SLOW INDUSTRY: We take care of our forests, through our agriculture and forestry, conduct sustainable farming with human labor, and ultimately spread urban farms and green tourism.

SLOW EDUCATION: We pay less attention to academic achievement, and create a society in which people can enjoy arts, hobbies, and sports throughout our lifetimes, and where all generations can communicate well with each other.

SLOW AGING: We aim to age with grace and be self-reliant throughout our lifetimes.

SLOW LIFE: Based on the philosophy of life stated above, we live our lives with nature and the seasons, saving our resources and energy. (*Japan for Sustainability Newsletter* 2003)

Like those of Slow Food and CittàSlow, these Slow Life themes are related to sustainability principles that link social and ecological dimensions of places. Slow Life features place-based innovations that are small in scale yet achieve ambitious goals such as reducing energy consumption, facilitating collective decision-making, and supporting food self-reliance (Edahiro 2005). The Japanese movement appears to be building, if slower than the Italian-based programs; a sixth "Slow Life Summit" held in 2008 in Gifu Prefecture involved twenty-four municipalities (*Japan for Sustainability Newsletter* 2009).

The Slow movement is growing and diversifying in the United States as well. Slow Food USA has 200 chapters distributed through all fifty states, Washington D.C., and Puerto Rico (Slow Food USA 2009). After Sonoma Valley, California, became the first CittàSlow community in the country in November, 2009, it was followed in less than a year by the certification of nearby Fairfax and Sebastopol, making up a regional network that prompted the establishment of CittàSlow USA in June, 2010. In addition to these formally organized programs, other Slow initiatives seem to surface on the Internet every few months: Slow Medicine, Slow Art, Slow Poetry, Slow Sex, Voluntary Slow Reading, Slow Libraries, Slow Science, Slow Technology, Slow Exercise, Slow Housing, Slow Money, and so on. Most of these initiatives share some combination of the following: convivial events, collaborative projects, sense of place, aesthetic appreciation, regard for health and the body, improvement in the quality of lived experience, increased social justice, support for ecological integrity, and integration with local economies. Virtually all are characterized by practices designed to take time for full meaning and experience, or benefit, to emerge.

Although virtually all of the Slow programs are motivated by resistance to the speeded-up qualities of everyday life, there are some differences among them. Slow Food revolves primarily around food production and consumption and associated policy implications. Slow Cities involves Slow Food but extends its area of concern to encompass and more broadly address development systems such as infrastructure and urban form, land use, and economic development. Slow Life—while a place-based, community-oriented approach like the previous two programs—is both more comprehensive in scope and variable in scale. The myriad self-organizing Slow initiatives found on the Web are focused more narrowly and are place-neutral. Their concern is a specific activity or individual practice around which a community of interest has formed.

To some extent the Slow movement can be characterized as a "lifestyle choice": an intentionally adopted, human-scale alternative to conventional daily life for those living in a world dominated by industrial-scale technologies and economies. But the substance of this movement has deeper consequence than it may seem. The Slow movement connects people to the material conditions of existence in a way that informs and honors their relationship to their everyday surroundings. The lived experience of the senses, of personal reciprocity and exchange, of cultural diversity and history and sense of place, of health and well-being is engaged with respect to a particular social, cultural, and ecological context. The Slow movement articulates the interrelationship among natural resources, the process of making (whether it be music, sense, love, or cheese), and use. Moreover, the institutionalized programs and some of the less formal associations of the Slow movement support awareness of the natural world as interwoven into the quality and viability of everyday life. Still, the Slow movement does not fully constitute the relevance of *slow* for social-ecological resilience.

Pressing Concerns: Slow Disaster, Slow Knowledge

Attention to *slow* provides insight into differentially distributed risk, vulnerability, and recovery within a community. Patterns of environmental disparities by race, class, and other factors show that people with less wealth and people of color live with greater exposure to hazards, risks, and disasters than those who are affluent and white (Pastor et al. 2006). Pastor et al. describe how calamities such as Hurricane Katrina draw the public's morbid curiosity for a brief time. But the preexisting conditions responsible for the scale of the Katrina tragedy are themselves a "slow-motion disaster," developing over a long period of time and supported by complex factors involved in land-use planning, market dynamics, and exclusionary political decision making (Pastor et al. 2006, 9). Furthermore, these disparities persist as "a second disaster" throughout recovery and reconstruction activities. Continuation of the initial destructive event compounds the difficulties for people who are already disadvantaged due to less insurance, lower incomes, fewer savings, more unemployment, lack of affordable housing, less access to official communication and information, the intensification of their poverty, racial discrimination, and exposure to pollutants from hazardous debris disposal (Pastor et al. 2006, 24–30). Such situations demonstrate limited resilience in several aspects, both social and ecological. Unjust ecological and social conditions undermine common interests and common good regardless of geographic location or scale (Hawken 2007; Shutkin 2000). Accordingly, a social/political system that effectively addresses vulnerability requires transformation of existing power relations and even worldviews. These are expressions of "culture"—identified by resilience theorists as a slow variable for social systems (Walker et al. 2006; Turner and Berkes 2006; Berkes and Turner 2006; see also Brand 1999).

"Fast knowledge" is part of the worldview that David Orr argues is at fault in setting up the crisis situation we are trying to address now through resilience concepts. For Orr, fast knowledge is a pathology compelled by the acceleration of technological change and the global economy; the cure involves recovering "slow knowledge" as the basis for action (Orr 2002). "Shaped and calibrated to fit a particular ecological and cultural context," slow knowledge is a moral and technical practice that harmonizes human intention and ecological results (2002, 39).[2] But Orr describes formidable obstacles to adopting slow knowledge. Offering fourteen assumptions of fast knowledge, he lists established axioms such as: "Only that which can be measured is true knowledge. . . . Knowledge that lends itself to use is superior to that which is merely contemplative. . . . Whatever mistakes and blunders occur along the way can be rectified by yet more knowledge." (2002, 36–37). Orr then presents the results of our adherence to these axioms: the links among fossil fuels, acid precipitation, and climate change; between chemical manufacture, drinking water, and public health; between culverted storm water, increased flooding, and erosion; and between the "paperless office" policy, increased paper use, and more time spent managing communication. These are examples of "optimizing" intended to create gains in efficiency. Like the resilience theorists, Orr observes that this practice weakens social-ecological resilience by disregarding complex interrelationships.

The increasing velocity of knowledge is widely accepted as sure evidence of human mastery and progress. But many, if not most, of the ecological, economic, social, and psychological ailments that beset contemporary society can be attributed directly or indirectly to knowledge acquired and applied before we had time to think it through carefully. . . . We simply cannot foresee all the ways complex natural systems will react to human-initiated changes, at their present scale, scope, and velocity. (2002, 37–38)

In effect, Orr links the speed of human activities to the degradation of ecological systems, human welfare, and quality of life. Similar critiques of the speed of human activities also underlies both institutionalized and informal activities of the Slow movement (e.g., Andrews 2008).

There is a substantial interdisciplinary literature that reviews the acceleration of our technologically "driven" society and specifies the nature of its impact. Much of this literature finds that contemporary technology, the speed of technological innovation, and the exponential growth in production and dissemination of information in electronic media, have significant negative impacts on society. These affect not only our quality of life and ecological integrity, but also the quality of our decision making (e.g., Hindman 2009; Eriksen 2001; Gleick 1999; Rifkin 1987). Becoming conscious of complex interrelationships and figuring out how to respond to them take time and attention, both of which may be in short supply. However, the seemingly obvious solution—slowing down—is vexed.

Deceleration and Discontent

Interviews of emergency workers responding to Hurricane Hugo revealed that they were "unaware of the extent of the poverty in their own neighborhoods" until after the storm hit (Pastor et al. 2006, 23). It seems almost inconceivable that people—especially those attuned to helping others—could be so out of touch. An explanation may lie in the tendency to go fast at every opportunity in order to be more productive or more efficient, even elongating the workday or the workweek with the assistance of distance communication devices. A consequence, though, is to unwittingly bypass chances to connect to the places, people and things we live among. Rechtschaffen, a physician, writes, "Without taking time to really be present in our lives, to find the time to slow down, we find ourselves rushing through everything we do, riding on the surface of things. Thus we lack satisfaction in our lives, we miss a sense of connection with each other, our children, and our community" (Rechtschaffen 2002, 175–176).

High-speed travel is now customary. In the rush from one place to another, we pass quickly through other places, often without much attention. Ecologist and philosopher David Abram's story from Aboriginal Australia illustrates the intimate connection that can exist between people and their landscape, and how that relationship is affected by mode of travel. Aboriginals habitually sing while walking, using specific songs to express their bond with spiritually animate features of their landscape. Riding at speed in a motor vehicle causes their traditional chanting to occur so fast as to garble, while slowing the vehicle to walking speed allows the song to emerge comprehensibly as experience rather than merely form (Abram 1996, 173–174). We may see this practice as merely the exotic way of an indigenous people and thus irrelevant to our own lives (e.g., Anderson 2008). But awareness of interrelationship within social-ecological systems is fundamental to understanding and supporting resilience from both ecological and social standpoints. To the extent that awareness results from lived experience—being present, noticing, listening, and feeling—the time and attention afforded by slowing down becomes significant.

Anthropologist Seremetakis (1994) describes "stillness" (a version of slowing down) as a way to become conscious of other people. Her particular concern is cultural domination and postcolonial transformation: "Stillness is the moment when the buried, the discarded, and the forgotten escape to the social surface of awareness like life-supporting oxygen. It is the moment of exit from historical dust" (1994, 12). Seremetakis's contribution challenges the bulk of the literature critiquing speed. Many authors tend to generalize society in their analysis and in making recommendations for alternative practices and policies. But awareness of social differences is a prerequisite to democratic and collaborative participation. It is required not only to solve problems but also to envision a socially and ecologically resilient future. "To truly understand issues, we must hear both [sic] sides, study facts, weigh, ruminate. . . . Unless we slow down enough to realize what is truly happening in our world, we will continually repeat the mistakes of the past without taking the opportunity to learn" (Rechtschaffen 2002, 190). Democratic processes may be the most equitable and effective way to transform our contemporary situation, and it takes considerable time to think, discuss, argue, and synthesize ideas among diverse standpoints and interests.

But "fast" is compelling. It is now common sense to equate technology with speed and to believe that this combination holds significant economic advantage (Hassan and Purser 2007; Kane 2000; Gleick 1999; Rifkin 1987) and perhaps political advantage as well (Alakeson et al. 2003). Speed itself has become an experience of thrill, risk, and achievement that characterizes contemporary cultures in the developed world (Duffy 2009). The authors of *It's Not the Big that Eat the Small. It's the Fast that Eat the Slow* intend to "teach speed" as a competitive business advantage based on "secrets and tactics used by the fastest businesspeople on the planet to achieve dizzying speed and amass huge fortunes" (Jennings and Haughton 2000, 7). Speed, efficiency, and optimization exemplify the business approach appropriate for sustainable development, according to IBM's ad campaign for their "Rethinking Cities" infrastructure redevelopment initiative: "GOOD: Better. Faster. Smarter." Speed is integrated into our political economy as broadly as capitalism and as individually as the reward structure typical of business as well as higher education: the fastest and most productive workers are rewarded by both prestige and pay (Lovink 2007; Agger 2004; Kane 2000). Yet while speed is valued in our culture, it has inequitable effects that are structured into social, political, and economic systems, thus disenfranchising those who work or live slowly. The burden falls heavily on those already disadvantaged: the elderly, disabled, children, and ethnicities for whom a slower temporality is necessary to sustain culturally specific practices. Further, in a speeded-up society, endemic problems of the socially excluded tend to remain low on the agenda of those empowered by the dominant system: "In information society, the scarcest resource for people on the supply side of the economy is neither iron ore nor sacks of grain, but *the attention of others*" (Eriksen 2001, 21; italics in the original).

Discontent is not limited to the disenfranchised. Sadness, anger, frustration, grief—while inevitable responses to life for virtually everyone—prompt us to seek distractions from unpleasant emotions and dissatisfaction with the conditions in which we live, particularly when we don't see that improvement is possible (Rechtschaffen 2002). Speed itself is distracting through the focus it requires and the exhilaration that can ensue, whether it is an experience of physical movement or the exceptional productivity that can be recognized as excellence in itself. Further, distraction is made increasingly convenient by practically ubiquitous computing: elegantly portable gadgets, wireless infrastructure, and enormous server farms making information, entertainment, and social networking at hand almost anywhere, anytime. Users are occupied in a virtual space that is largely unconscious of contextual relationship in the sociality and spatialization of everyday life, whether human or ecological (Galloway 2004). Kane writes that "we are dependent on speed, and on the devices that give speed to us, even for human contact. Sometimes we use speed to fight isolation, and this is a powerful benefit that rapidity has given to us, although it may also be a technological crutch that we use to make up for a way of life that some people find does not fulfill their needs for companionship" (Kane 2000, 34). Distance communication enables instantaneous verbal contact with chosen others but disconnects us from the people and places in which we are immediately situated. It is difficult to let go of these technologies, and not just because they are so serviceable. The artifacts of speed—cars, phones, computers, and so forth—also materialize and enhance identity, prestige, and memory of individuals and, by extension, that of their organizations (Csikszentmihalyi 1993).[3]

Many aspects of speed are interrelated: its role in political economy, its place in personal identity and experience, the instantaneous delivery of information and communication through computer technology that is proliferating exponentially, and the decontextualizing effects of speed on everyday life. These aspects, combined with the link between speed and ecological degradation, form a powerful cluster of interests, habits, and secondary effects that while widespread are not entirely recognized or understood. Even those of us who are working diligently to understand and build social-ecological resilience can be unaware of the extent to which our work is influenced by and perpetuating the negative effects of speed. In his exploration of the effects of "the information revolution," anthropologist Thomas Eriksen points out that "changes which ostensibly boost efficiency and creativity may in fact do the exact opposite" (p. vii). Countering the assumption that more information will result in better decisions, he argues that the more information is available at increased speed, the more difficult it is to use cognitive skills that require narratives, orders, developmental sequences, deliberation, metaphor, and long periods of concentration (Eriksen 2001; see also Schwartz 2004). Instead of better decisions, confusion results, in part because information is decontextualized and lacks internal cohesion. Eriksen's observations are supported by studies on "information overload" that test strategies meant to optimize information processing requirements and capacities, often in relation to a time factor. While there are countermeasures that can be taken, studies have shown that people tend to simplify their responses and expend less effort when presented with more information on which to make decisions (Eppler and Mengis 2004; see also Himma 2007; Jones, Ravid, and Rafaeli 2004; and Todd and Benbasat 1992).

While we may feel that we are quickly producing information that can help solve entrenched problems and that we are working at our limit to manage and communicate this information as effectively as possible, actually "contemporary culture runs at full speed without moving an inch" (Eriksen 2001, 109). Instead of being marked by developing understanding and capacity, cultural "progress" is normally measured by the exponential growth in information and technological innovation occurring at such velocity that we are, in effect, less able to address the resilience of our social-ecological systems (Eriksen 2001, Brand 1999). For example, in reflecting on the risks of geo-engineering as a response to climate change, futurist Jamais Cascio writes: "If we start to see faster-than-expected increases in temperature, deadly heat waves and storms, crop failures and drought, the pressure to do *something* will be enormous. Desperation is a powerful driver. Desperation plus a (relatively) low-cost response, coupled with quick (if not necessarily dependable) benefits, can become an unstoppable force" (Cascio 2009). Transforming the way that we respond to these emergent conditions has a temporal dimension, but is not simply about slowing down. Change in temporality also implies, as Orr's (2002) slow knowledge suggests, engaging the human capacities fully available when working at human scale: learning, creativity, sensing, feeling, connecting, and empathizing.

Scaling Down: Connection and Transformation

The interdisciplinary literature on speed and slowness reminds us of what it means to be fully human. As well as being intelligent creatures, we are sensory, spiritual, often deeply moral, sometimes grateful for benefits of existence we have not earned or for which we did not ask or pay. We often have a sense of being part of something larger than ourselves from which emerges self-reflection, tolerance, respect, and deference. These, perhaps, are qualities of human society that have been disrupted by speed and can be uncovered by slowness. These also, perhaps, are qualities that we need to sustain in order to respond appropriately to the complexity of the questions that face us. It seems that the very technologies that mean to connect and inform us are actually, to some extent, confusing and disconnecting us. They perturb our human-scale regimes of movement and health, family and social relationships, leisure and recreation (in the literal sense of the word). They distract us from awareness of the interrelatedness of the nonhuman and the built aspects of our environments, their well-being and wholeness. Paradoxically, it may be in disconnecting from our communication technologies that we can find a connection to ourselves and others in a deeper sense, one that reclaims our capacity for resilience. As Abram (1996) writes, "it is only at the scale of our direct, sensory interactions with the land around us that we can appropriately notice and respond to the immediate needs of the living world" (p. 268). Our bodies are our most intimate experience of nature, including its durations, rhythms, and synergistic relationships.

Scaling down to direct bodily experience often results in becoming conscious of relations that were obscured by hurry and by the selective attention required of us by distance technologies, whether automobile driving, telephones, computers, or television. Recently I assigned my class of first-semester college freshmen to take forty minutes alone, in silence, without using any technology, and then to write about the experience. A handful of students (5) were unable to complete the assignment as directed. But most of them (19) reported similar responses. They first tried to wait, became bored, and then either jumped up to explore or stilled as they began to puzzle over a problem with a social relationship. Those students who explored—whether outside or indoors—were surprised to find beauty and meaning in small things they had never before noticed.

Those students who pondered relationship problems were able to come up with a response that satisfied them. The students who engaged with the assignment reported that the experience overall was surprising, difficult, but ultimately valuable and that they intended to repeat it. The students who did not enjoy the experience, however, felt that the assignment deprived them of choice, freedom, and connection to their friends and family.

People who slow down are enriched by their capacity to connect meaningfully with others and with the rhythms and cycles of nature. Yet it is also important to be quick in certain situations. Rechtschaffen (2002) advocates "timeshifting" rather than striving to function at either a fast or a slow pace. Some human capacities—such as memory, power, travel, hearing, and vision—can be technically enhanced to great individual and societal benefit. However, this enhancement is more a matter of selective augmentation than qualitative development. While having tremendous capacities, we are still limited in our ability to process information and to accurately predict the multiscalar effects of our actions. Orr (2002) describes slow knowledge as a condition of being human rather than a conscious choice (p. 42); and Eriksen (2001) advises, "One has to limit one's information out of consideration for one's knowledge" (p. 149). Similarly, resilience science includes "the rule of hand": the most important changes in a social-ecological system can be understood by analyzing between three and five key variables. "More complex models are not necessary to explain the key interesting patterns and, in fact, are likely to mask them. This is both because generally humans can only understand low-dimensional systems and because, empirically, it appears that only a few variables are ever dominant in observed system dynamics" (Walker et al. 2006, 5). The rule of hand simplifies a highly complex situation but does not obscure its fundamental qualities of change and uncertainty.

So how do we change? Our most familiar strategies and behaviors engender such serious consequences that "we are creating a world in which we do not fit" (Orr 2002, 25). If the general goal seems clear—increased social-ecological resilience—we are nonetheless uncertain about moving in that direction. Many of us would like to "create communities and places that resonate with our evolutionary past and for which we have deep affection" (Orr 2002, 26), but how? Resilience literature, as noted in the next section, abounds with management goals intent upon improving resilience. Certain cases, such as the Kristianstads Vattenrike or indigenous "management" based on traditional ecological knowledge, show that management can participate effectively in addressing problems surfaced by resilience analysis (Walker and Salt 2006; Schultz, Folke, and

Olssen 2007; Hahn et al. 2008; Turner and Berkes 2006). Yet the idea that we can strategically build social-ecological resilience is not clearly supported by research, which warns that "efforts to deliberately enhance adaptability can (unintentionally) lead to a loss of resilience" (Walker et al. 2006, 9). Insufficient evidence to guide management strategy is not just a matter of inadequate data; uncertainty about the effects of human intervention is a principle of resilience theory. As Walker et al. (2002) point out, "Not only are forecasts uncertain, the usual statistical approaches will likely underestimate the uncertainties. That is, even the uncertainties are uncertain" (p. 14). But acknowledging uncertainty does not sink the possibility of societal transformation toward increased resilience.

Paul Hawken (2007) finds reason for hope in the global proliferation of small associations working "under the radar" to achieve social justice and ecological integrity at the local scale. Calling this movement of over 110,000 organizations "Earth's immune response," he is tracking them using the WiserEarth database (Hawken 2007). When transformation such as this is a collective result rather than a top-down strategy, it occurs as self-organization, or "bugworld" rather than "cogworld" (Walker and Salt 2006). Self-organization, intentional activity occurring amid uncertainty and complexity, can result from many different motivations. To build social-ecological resilience in particular, self-organization must be directed intentionally toward community, empathy, revelation, and self-discovery. This approach involves a more variable and natural temporality than does intention to dominate (Rifkin 1987). Then, initiatives resulting from creative and synergistic opportunities must be leveraged into concerted action, which in turn requires resources and political support in order to achieve transformation (Cockerill and Carp 2009). Yet simply engaging in development work that thrives on regard for the well-being of social-ecological systems brings us in touch with what feels important, even if the way forward is unclear. A U.S. Fish and Wildlife Service official who participated in a successful collaborative effort for a fish species recovery commented, "We all trusted that we were trying to get to an end goal of harmonizing our interests. None of us knew how in the world we would get there, but we knew that if we kept at it, we'd get it figured out" (Brunner and Steelman, 2005, 299). Collaborative processes present the opportunity to use and develop those slow cognitive skills that allow us to engage complexity, become aware of the consequences of our actions, reflect, deliberate, and grow wise (Higgs 1993). Such cognitive skills may exemplify some of our most potent capabilities for intentional cultural transformation.

Slowness in Practice: Collaborative, Adaptive, and Incremental Processes of Transformation

Some practices, although they have not been identified elsewhere as part of the Slow movement, are *slow* in the sense of learning and doing in open, respectful, reciprocal relationship within a social-ecological system. Slow practices differ from those in which professionals try to optimize the output of their particular expertise, using their positional authority to make decisions that have implicit cultural, political, and ecological impacts, but without exploring, articulating, or negotiating the bases of these decisions. In contrast, decision making and policy development that takes into account human-scale knowledge and experience tends to be collaborative, take time to develop, and vary in how they are adapted to particular situations. Practices are *slow* that maintain relationship with place at the scale of direct experience while simultaneously working patiently to understand and maintain resilience that accrues through the interrelationship of the individual and other scales. Examples of other scales include: geographic location (site, watershed, bioregion), social institution (voluntary associations, professional organizations, governments), and past and future generations (native species, cultural memory, legacy). Most *slow* activities are not consistently enmeshed in collective decision making or policy development, but the demands of collaboration—thinking, discussing, arguing, and synthesizing—occur at all scales of organization. While people working on behalf of the public, such as developing the built environment, and conserving and restoring ecosystems, can seem to be ambivalent about time-intensive decision processes, they appear more and more to be necessary to ensure successful results (National Research Council 2008).

There are many activities suited to *slow* practice, such as small-scale organic agriculture, cooking, agroforestry, field science, hand-building, ecological restoration, and place-based education. Ecological design is a *slow* practice with well-articulated principles: "Any form of design that minimizes environmentally destructive impacts by integrating itself with living processes" (Van der Ryn and Cowan 1996, 18; see also Orr 2002). Another *slow* practice involves urban (re)development that combines pedestrian infrastructure, inclusive public spaces, and multiple elements of urban greening such as urban agriculture, Low Impact Development, and habitat protection. Many of these projects involve participatory design. They must be supported by urban policies, such as Smart Growth principles and green infrastructure planning, to ensure public use while protecting natural processes. These are places that encourage people to linger and enjoy their social and spatial surroundings, and thus to develop familiarity with local ecosystems, climate, and seasons. Making such places results from the combination of knowledge and experience that undergirds a sense of responsibility for, and belonging to, a social-ecological system. To the extent that these places are harmonious with natural systems, they are also places of learning by being co-present, whether passively as enjoyment and entertainment, or actively as in ecological restoration or social interaction (Hinchliffe et al. 2005; Barlett 2005). The *slow* practice in this case involves "learning to live within systems, rather than 'control' them" (Walker et al. 2002, 14).

Characteristics of *slow* practice are evident in many participatory planning and design methods, public or civic involvement processes, community development practices, and collaborative processes. Research about collaborative processes that deals specifically with social-ecological resilience has developed two conceptual frameworks: adaptive comanagement and adaptive governance. Both frameworks help guide and explain the role of local knowledge and social learning. They are helping shape the turn toward communicative, collaborative, and participatory processes in planning, management, and politics (e.g., National Research Council 2008; Brunner et al. 2005; Innes and Booher, 1999; Healey 1997). These processes take time to develop and to become effective. Though many resilience scientists (and others) would like to move faster in addressing sustainability problems, fast action does not seem to result in beneficial outcomes for ecological—and therefore human—well-being. Despite the time it takes, resilience scholars and scientists promote adaptive comanagement and adaptive governance as more realistic and practical for decision making than technical approaches focused on ecosystem management with little regard for social context.

The term *adaptive comanagement* refers to a place-based process of incremental intervention. Schultz (2009) describes it as, ideally, "performed by a diverse network of actors to enable a balance between the coordination capacity of centralized structures, and the learning capacity of decentralized structures. Core features are learning, collaboration, and multi-level governance" (p. 22).

The term *adaptive governance*, a conceptual refinement of adaptive comanagement, encompasses the concerns of ecosystem management in relation to a broader and inherently conflictual political and cultural environment. Brunner et al. (2005) offer three principles of adaptive governance: (1) the common interest is the goal of policy; (2) multiple means are necessary to advance the common interest; and (3) diffusion and adaptation of successful innovations are explicit (2005, x). As located within the conceptual framework of participatory and collaborative practices, adaptive governance is so far relatively bounded in terms of context. Cases are limited to areas with significant extent of open land and a human population economically (and culturally) dependent on the local natural resource base. However, there are aspects of the adaptive governance literature that are instructive for other *slow* practices intending to build social-ecological resilience.

Resilience researchers report that adaptive governance is slow, literally. "Natural time" is long and uncertain for both the development of human knowledge and experience in social-ecological systems and for natural ecosystems in particular (Hilderbrand et al. 2005; Brand 1999). Conservation knowledge must be learned. Berkes and Turner (2006) describe how conservation learning can occur through a depletion crisis that results from disasters or mistakes. But conservation knowledge can also be learned through increased ecological understanding, the incremental "elaboration of environmental knowledge by a group, leading to increasingly more sophisticated understanding of the ecosystem in which they dwell" (p. 482). The accumulated experience of a place-based community, their "social memory," is "the arena in which captured experience with change and successful adaptations, embedded in a deeper level of values, is actualized through community debate and decision-making processes into appropriate strategies for dealing with ongoing change" (Folke et al., 2005, 453). However, "a communal knowledge base takes a long time to develop, and practices based on such knowledge even longer" (Berkes and Turner 2006, 491). This is cultural transformation: new practices, new social norms, and new understandings of self- and of common interest must eventually become institutionalized (Goldstein 2007). While cultural transformation occurs at the slow pace of incremental learning, "our worldviews and attitudes are critical components of conservation, and may be more important than any other factor in conserving ecological integrity" (Turner and Berkes 2006, 510).

Learning processes are at the foundation for the collective action that is necessary to respond to uncertainty and social-ecological change. There are specific educational and training requirements for adaptive governance: producing and participating effectively in multistakeholder collaboration; identifying and connecting community, market, ecological, and management issues; dealing with differentially distributed capacity; evaluating local knowledge; determining how and when to scale out (or scale up) a successful project, and so forth. Even while it is the basis for adaptive governance, individual and group learning is "slow, inconsistent and/or unexpected" in these conditions (Armitage, Marschke, and Plummer 2008, 87). Adaptive governance, like other collaborative processes, requires specific capacities of participants. Participants need "broad awareness, recognition, and knowledge of sustainability and its implications, including attention to the subject of change itself" (Fazey et al. 2007, 376). But in addition, they need to learn *how to learn* in ways that enhance the community's capacity to be adaptable and flexible (Fazey et al.). Fazey et al. recommend ways of learning that are based on, for example, "elements of frequent and deliberative practice, effective reflection, and the acceptance of different perspectives [that] are themselves practiced in a variable, reflective way" (p. 378). Moreover, participants need to understand the reality of their social-ecological system more accurately. "There is a grave mismatch between the kinds of ecosystems that people want and the kinds of ecosystems that are attainable, although there may be a zone of intersection between the imagined and the possible" (Carpenter and Gunderson 2001, 456).

Learning how to collaborate on behalf of social-ecological resilience reaches beyond formal collaboratives to educational institutions, which could help prepare a citizenry for adaptive governance. Current institutional education policies based on increasing class sizes and "objective" testing methods involve pedagogical and learning strategies that depend merely on "short-term retention of information and the reproduction of the accepted products of other people's thinking" (Fazey et al. 2007, 379). In contrast, effective participation in adaptive governance and other collaborative processes requires that stakeholders recognize that their local knowledge and experience has value in the decision-making process. In addition they need to be able to share in cooperative fact-finding and sense making regarding the social-ecological system of concern. "Without their participation, achieving a collectively and socially desirable outcome is not possible, because key information resides in the knowledge and mental models of stakeholders, and because, without the inclusion that comes from participatory approaches, any proposed solution would face a legitimacy problem" (Walker et al. 2002, 14).

In addition to effective participation, leadership is an important characteristic of adaptive governance. Collaborative leadership involves shepherding a process rather than directing participants toward a predetermined outcome. This type of leadership is a new mode of professional conduct for many. It can be a creative opportunity as well as a difficult and demanding challenge. Steelman and Tucker (2005) relate a story about U.S. Forest Service (USFS) officials who decide to take the time to go door-to-door to consult with local residents, after several years of residents trying to get the attention of the USFS by using both violent and nonviolent means. The direct, personal approach—new to these officials—enabled the collaborative to finally identify a common interest for policy development. In response, the residents held a party for the USFS. An observer recalls, "Career forest people at that meeting were so choked up they could not speak because they were crying because all their careers they hoped something like this would happen and finally it did" (Steelman and Tucker 2005, 112). Leadership in adaptive governance is shared among members of a collaborative. They share creativity in implementation as well as share information in a formalized process. In a case study of a successful grass bank in the U.S. Southwest, Edwards (2005) observes that success is not measured by how quickly or broadly the innovative strategy was diffused, but by how well people "on the ground" were informed and empowered to make their own decisions. "The adapters are the experts on their own unique circumstances and more responsible decision makers as well" (p. 171). Rather than "losing control" of the project through sharing leadership, officials found that while "it takes time to coordinate people and resources within and across the various networks . . . this quasi-evolutionary process accounts for the absence of any glaring malfunctions" (p. 172). Practical support is also fundamental. Time and other resources are required to create a situation in which creative initiatives can succeed or fail on their own merits (p. 173).

Among the requirements for success in adaptive governance is assignment of resources for convening and designing the collaborative process. Some hints can be gleaned from case studies, but process design is not well covered in resilience researchers' reports. Individual skills are frequently mentioned as important characteristics of the process conveners, such as interpretive skills, listening skills, and creativity. "Essential features" of the adaptive co-management process are clearly and consistently identified: vision, leadership, trust, enabling legislation, funding, monitoring, information flow, multiple sources, sense making, and collaborative learning (e.g., Olsson and Folke 2004). However there is little mention of the groundwork, design development, group facilitation, and preparation for negotiation that are part of collaborative processes, although these aspects create the conditions conducive to success (but see Schultz et al. 2007 and Walker et al. 2002).

Designing and leading a collaborative process is a considerable under-taking. As a participant in the Natural Resources Leadership Institute, an eighteen-month training program administered by North Carolina State University, I became aware of the extent of preparation necessary for set-ting up and facilitating a collaborative process. Preparation begins well in advance of actually convening the participants. An extended situa-tion assessment is first necessary to not only gauge probable commitment to a collaborative process but also to ensure proper representation by identifying all pertinent stakeholders and issues. Then, once the formal collaboration begins, process leaders spend the time between meetings networking among participants, making detailed preparations for facili-tating the next session, and developing unique materials (such as complex scenarios) to support effective negotiation. The convener and facilitator address multiple needs throughout the process: frequent re-scheduling as well as resource requests, troubleshooting, equipment transport, and documentation of the entire effort.

Among collaboration practitioners, the insider shorthand for these de-mands is "go slow to go fast." When there is insufficient time taken to plan, prepare, include, consult, reflect, and learn before and during partici-patory decision making, the group does not arrive at the collective sense making and mutual gains that characterize collaborative achievement and it becomes unlikely that the participants will form lasting working rela-tionships. But if the preparation is adequate and sufficient time is taken for the process to be truly participatory, open, creative, and reflective, the desired results are more likely to be implemented. Since implementa-tion of collaborative agreements requires stakeholder support over time, successful implementation is largely an outcome of mutually supporting relationships that form during the collaborative process.[4]

Conclusions

We are in the midst of what appears to be a global "slow disaster" in which we are implicated but unsure how or whether to act differently. It seems clear that cultures that separate social and ecological dimensions of consciousness and responsibility need to change (the sooner, the better). Acting on our capacities at human scale—to understand, to innovate, to communicate and collaborate, to restrain and question and challenge each other, to discipline ourselves to a greater reality, to act morally and ethi-cally, to be respectful—may be where we learn how to build and sustain social-ecological resilience. It seems that to make progress in this direction as quickly as possible, we need to slow down in appropriate ways. There are many activities and practices occurring for which slowness is a central experience. These *slow* practices can enable our awareness of our social-ecological embeddedness, so that we will have more chances to consciously experience the results of our actions and to better recognize and support mutual well-being. Though slowing down is certainly difficult, it can provide benefits to society in reclaiming our connections with nature and each other. Slowing down can directly benefit ecosystems through the proliferation of small-scale actions of conservation and protection.

We need to carefully design processes that include the time for collaboration on decisions and policy development. Such processes are necessary in order to address the mutual benefit of social and ecological dimensions of places. The ensuing management strategies intervene in social and natural processes, uncertain of the long-term outcome. But this situation is exactly where restorationist Steve Packard (1993) finds hope and inspiration: "Throughout most of our species' history, we were part of nature. Our challenge now is to rediscover that role and play it well. Inherent in that opportunity are pitfalls, responsibilities, and liberations" (p. 15).

Notes

1. The word *slow* is italicized throughout the chapter when referring to "slow" as the object of this study. The term *Slow movement* refers to those formal and informal groups and initiatives that are characterized primarily by their use of "slow" as a manner of social reform.

2. Orr directly addresses the social aspects of ecological design in resilience terms: "Ecological design at the level of culture resembles the structure and behavior of resilient systems in other contexts in which feedback between action and subsequent correction is rapid, people are held accountable for their actions, functional redundancy is high, and control is decentralized" (2002, 9–10).

3. Csikszentmihalyi (1993) points out that objects associated with dominance and superiority are both dangerous and more costly in terms of resources and labor than objects associated with kinship and relatedness: "Thus the kind of selves individuals choose to build have great consequences for the material culture and for the natural environment that must be despoiled in order to create it" (p. 28).

4. However, the amount of time necessary for participatory processes can be a practical problem; both burnout and frustration at a lack of results can cripple a collaborative process (Fainstein 2000). Furthermore, participatory processes do not necessarily encompass the diversity of class, race, and ethnicity existing in many urbanized and industrialized areas where social-ecological resilience is as much an issue as it is for rural areas.

References

Abram, D. 1996. *The spell of the sensuous: Perception and language in a more-than-human world.* New York: Random House.

Agger, B. 2004. *Speeding up fast capitalism: Culture, jobs, families, schools, bodies.* Boulder, CO: Paradigm Publishers.

Alakeson, V., T. Aldrich, J. Goodman, and B. Jorgensen. 2003. *Making the Net work: Sustainable development in a digital society.* Middlesex, U.K.: Xeris Publishing Co.

Anderson, C. June 23, 2008. The end of theory: The data deluge makes the scientific method obsolete. *Wired Magazine.* Accessed 1-31-2011. Available at http://www.wired.com/science/discoveries/magazine/16-07/pb_theory.

Andrews, G. 2008. *The Slow Food story: Politics and pleasure.* Montreal, Quebec: McGill-Queen's University Press.

Armitage, D., M. Marschke, and R. Plummer. (February, 2008). Adaptive co-management and the paradox of learning. *Global Environmental Change* 18(1): 86–98.

Barlett, P. F., ed. 2005. *Urban place: Reconnecting with the natural world.* Cambridge, MA: MIT Press.

Berkes, F., and N. J. Turner. August 2006. Knowledge, learning and the evolution of conservation practice for social-ecological system resilience. *Human Ecology* 34(4): 479–494.

Brand, S. 1999. *The clock of the long now: Time and responsibility.* New York: Basic Books.

Brunner, R. D., and T. A. Steelman. 2005. Toward adaptive governance. In *Adaptive governance: Integrating science, policy, and decision-making,* eds. R. Brunner, T. A. Steelman, L. Coe-Juell, C. M. Cromley, C. A. Edwards, and D. W. Tucker, 304. New York: Columbia University Press.

Brunner, R. D., T. A. Steelman, L. Coe-Juell, C. M. Cromley, C. M. Edwards, and D. W. Tucker. 2005. *Adaptive governance: Integrating science, policy, and decision-making.* New York: Columbia University Press.

Carpenter, S. R., and L. H. Gunderson. June, 2001. Coping with collapse: Ecological and social dynamics in ecosystem management. *Bioscience* 51(6):451–457.

Cascio, J. February 9, 2009. Geo-engineering is risky but likely inevitable, so we better start thinking it through. *Grist.* Accessed 1-31-2011. Available at http://www.grist.org/article/Plan-B.

Cittaslow International. Association—Cittaslow International Charter. October 1999. Accessed 3-6-2011. Available at http://www.cittaslow.net/download/DocumentiUfficiali/2009/newcharter%5B1%5D.pdf.

Cittaslow News. Who. October 10, 2008. Accessed 3-6-2011. Available at http://cittaslow.blogspot.com/2008/10/who.html.

Cockerill, K., and J. Carp. Fall, 2009. Leveraging opportunities for campus sustainability: A case study of water resources. *Sustainability: Science, Practice, & Policy* 5(2): 28–37.

Csikszentmihalyi, M. 1993. Why we need things. In *History from things: Essays in material culture*, eds. S. Lubar and W. D. Kingery, 20–29. Washington, D.C.: Smithsonian Institution Press.

Duffy, E. 2009. *The speed handbook: Velocity, pleasure, modernism.* Durham, NC: Duke University Press.

Edahiro, J. October, 2005. The end of growth: Efforts in Japanese society and business to slow down. *Japan for Sustainability Newsletter* (038). Accessed 1-31-2011. Available at http://www.japanfs.org/en/mailmagazine/newsletter/pages/027805.html.

Edwards, C. M. 2005. Grassbanks: Diffusion and adaptation from the radical center. In *Adaptive governance: Integrating science, policy, and decision-making*, eds. R. Brunner, T. A. Steelman, L. Coe-Juell, C. M. Cromley, C. A. Edwards, and D. W. Tucker, 130–180. New York: Columbia University Press.

Eppler, M. J., and J. Mengis. November, 2004. The concept of information overload: A review of literature from organization science, accounting, marketing, MIS, and related disciplines. *Information Society* 20(5):325–344.

Eriksen, T. H. 2001. *Tyranny of the moment: Fast and slow time in the information age.* Sterling, VA: Pluto Press.

Fabricius, E., C. Folke, G. Cundill, and L. Schultz. 2007. Powerless spectators, coping actors, and adaptive co-managers: A synthesis of the role of communities in ecosystem management. *Ecology and Society* 12(1): 29. Accessed 1-31-2011. Available at http://www.ecologyandsociety.org/vol12/iss1/art29/.

Fainstein, S. A. March, 2000. New directions in planning theory. *Urban Affairs Review* 35(4):451–478.

Fazey, I., J. A. Fazey, J. Fischer, K. Sherren, J. Warren, R. F. Noss, and S. R. Dovers. September, 2007. Adaptive capacity and learning to learn as leverage for social-ecological resilience. *Frontiers in Ecology and the Environment* 5(7): 375–380.

Folke, C., T. Hahn, P. Olsson, and J. Norberg. 2005. Adaptive governance of social-ecological systems. *Annual Review of Environment and Resources* 30:441–473.

Galloway, A. March/May, 2004. Intimations of everyday life: Ubiquitous computing and the city. *Cultural Studies* 18(2/3): 384–408.

Gleick, J. 1999. *Faster: The acceleration of just about everything.* New York: Pantheon.

Goldstein, B. E. November, 2007. Skunkworks in the embers of the Cedar Fire: Enhancing resilience in the aftermath of disaster. *Human Ecology* 36(1): 15–28.

Hahn, T., L. Schultz, C. Folke, and P. Olsson. 2008. Social networks as sources of resilience in social-ecological systems. In *Complexity theory for a sustainable future*, eds. J. Norberg and G. Cumming, 119–148. New York: Columbia University Press.

Hassan, R., and R. E. Purser. 2007. *24/7: Time and temporality in the network society.* Stanford, CA: Business Books.

Hawken, P. 2007. *Blessed unrest: How the largest social movement in history is restoring grace, justice, and beauty to the world.* New York: Penguin.

Healey, P. 1997. Collaborative planning: Shaping places in fragmented societies. Vancouver, BC: University of British Columbia Press.

Higgs, E. S. 1993. The ethics of mitigation. *Restoration and management notes* 11(2): 138–143.

Hilderbrand, R. H., A. C. Watts, and A. M. Randle. 2005. The myths of restoration ecology. *Ecology and Society* 10(1): 19. Accessed 1-31-2011. Available at http://www.ecologyandsociety.org/vol10/iss1/art19/.

Himma, K. E. 2007. The concept of information overload: A preliminary step in understanding the nature of a harmful information-related condition. *Ethics and Information Technology* 9(4): 259–272.

Hinchliffe, S., M. B. Kearnes, M. Degen, and S. Whatmore. 2005. Urban wild things: A cosmopolitical experiment. *Environment and Planning D: Society & Space* 23(5): 643–658.

Hindman, M. 2009. *The myth of digital democracy.* Princeton, NJ: Princeton University Press.

Innes, J. E., and D. E. Booher. 1999. Planning institutions in the network society: Theory for collaborative planning. In *The revival of strategic spatial planning*, eds. W. Salet and A. Faludi, 175–189. Amsterdam, the Netherlands: Royal Netherlands Academy of Arts and Sciences.

Japan for Sustainability Newsletter. October, 2003. The "Slow Life" Movement: Happiness before economic efficiency. (no. 14). Accessed 1-31-2011. Available at http://www.japanfs.org/en/mailmagazine/newsletter/pages/027770.html.

Japan for Sustainability Newsletter. February 16, 2009. Slow Life Summit held in Mino, Gifu Prefecture. Accessed 1-31-2011. Available at http://www.japanfs.org/en/pages/028742.html.

Jennings, J., and L. Haughton. 2000. *It's not the big that eat the small . . . It's the fast that eat the slow: How to use speed as a competitive tool in business.* New York: HarperCollins.

Jones, Q., G. Ravid, and S. Rafaeli. June, 2004. Information overload and the message dynamics of online interaction spaces: A theoretical model and empirical exploration. *Information Systems Research* 15(2): 194–210.

Kane, H. 2000. *Triumph of the mundane: The unseen trends that shape our lives and environment.* Washington, D.C.: Island Press.

Lovink, G. 2007. Indifference of the networked presence: On time management of the self. In *24/7: Time and temporality in the network society*, eds. R. Hassan and R. E. Purser, 161–172. Stanford, CA: Stanford Business Books.

Mayer, H., and P. L. Knox. September, 2006. Slow cities: Sustainable places in a fast world. *Journal of Urban Affairs* 28(4): 321–334.

National Research Council. 2008. *Public participation in environmental assessment and decision making. Panel on public participation in environmental assessment and decision making*, eds. T. Dietz and P. C. Stern. Washington, D.C.: The National Academies Press.

Olsson, P., and C. Folke. 2004. Adaptive co-management for building resilience in social-ecological systems. *Environmental Management* 34(1):75–90.

Orr, D. 2002. *The nature of design: Ecology, culture and human intention*. New York: Oxford University Press.

Packard, S. 1993. Restoring oak ecosystems. *Restoration and Management Notes* 11(1): 5–16.

Parkins, W., and G. Craig. 2006. *Slow living*. New York: Berg.

Pastor, M., R. D. Bullard, J. K. Boyce, A. Fothergill, R. Morello-Frosch, and B. Wright. 2006. *In the wake of the storm: Environment, disaster, and race after Katrina*. New York: Russell Sage Foundation.

Rechtschaffen, S. 2002. Timeshifting. In *Sustainable planet: Solutions for the twenty-first century*, ed. J. B. Schor and B. Taylor, 175–192. Boston, MA: Beacon Press.

Rifkin, J. 1987. *Time wars: The primary conflict in human history*. New York: Henry Holt and Co.

Schultz, L., C. Folke, and P. Olssen. June, 2007. Enhancing ecosystem management through social-ecological inventories: Lessons from Kristianstads Vattenrike, Sweden. *Environmental Conservation* 34(2):142–152.

Schultz, L. 2009. Nurturing resilience in social-ecological systems: Lessons learned from bridging organizations. Thesis, Stockholms Universitet. Accessed 3-6-2011. Available at http://en.scientificcommons.org/47720432.

Schwartz, B. 2004. *The paradox of choice: Why more is less*. New York: Harper-Collins.

Seremetakis, C. N. 1994. The memory of the senses, Part I: Marks of the transitory. In *The senses still: Perception and Memory as Material Culture in Modernity*, ed. C. N. Seremetakis, 1–18. Chicago, IL: The University of Chicago Press.

Shutkin, W. 2000. *The land that could be: Environmentalism and democracy in the 21st century*. Cambridge, MA: The MIT Press.

Slow Food, USA. November 25, 2009. Local chapters: Local chapters by state. Accessed on 1-31-2011. Available at http://www.slowfoodusa.org/index.php/local_chapters.

Slow Food International Communications. June, 2010. Slow Food and Terra Madre in figures. Accessed 1-31-2011. Available in a sidebar at http://newsletter.slowfood.com/slowfood_time/2010/05/eng.html.

Steelman, T. A., and D. W. Tucker. 2005. The Camino Real: To care for the land and serve the people. In *Adaptive governance: Integrating science, policy, and decision-making*, eds. R. Brunner, et al., 91–130. New York: Columbia University Press.

Todd, P., and I. Benbasat. September, 1992. The use of information in decision-making: An experimental investigation of the impact of computer-based decision aids. *Management Information Systems Quarterly* 16(3): 373–393.

Turner, N. J., and F. Berkes. July, 2006. Coming to understanding: Developing conservation through incremental learning in the Pacific Northwest. *Human Ecology* 34:495–513.

Van der Ryn, S., and S. Cowan. 1996. *Ecological design.* Washington, D.C.: Island Press.

Walker, B., and D. Salt. 2006. *Resilience thinking: Sustaining ecosystems and people in a changing world.* Washington, D.C.: Island Press.

Walker, B., S. Carpenter, J. Aderies, N. Abel, G. Cummings, M. Janssen, L. Level, J. Norberg, G. D. Peterson, and R. Pritchard. 2002. Resilience management in social-ecological systems: A working hypothesis for a participatory approach. *Conservation Ecology* 6(1):14. Accessed 1-31-2011. Available at http://www.consecol.org/vol6/iss1/art14.

Walker, B., L. Gunderson, A. Kinzig, C. Folke, S. Carpenter, and L. Schultz. 2006. A handful of heuristics and some propositions for understanding resilience in social-ecological systems. *Ecology and Society* 11(1):13. Accessed 3-6-2011. Available at http://www.ecologyandsociety.org/vol11/iss1/art13/http://www.ecologyandsociety.org/vol11/iss/art13/.

6

Creating the Climate Change Resilient Community

John Randolph

For thousands of years, people have been learning how to manage their relationship with nature. Every generation creates a new set of circumstances: the population and economy grow, impacts on the natural environment increase, and knowledge is advanced about the consequences of our actions (and means of controlling these impacts). Every generation must adapt to those circumstances. The good news is that we continue to learn. Our evolving social and political system has enhanced our ability to make collective decisions about the use and management of the natural environment, as well as how to adapt to it.

Our latest and greatest environmental challenge is human-induced climate change. Our emission of greenhouse gases (GHG) continues. Carbon dioxide concentration in the atmosphere grows, and global temperatures increase. As a result, we are experiencing the consequences of global warming around the world, from melting glaciers, sea ice, and tundra, to extreme weather events and drought. The implications of climate change are not limited to the environmental impacts of global warming, but also include the impacts of our *response* to climate change. For example, we are saddled with higher fossil fuel and electricity prices. We also feel the disruptive effects on our economic and social systems, which now must bear the costs of conversion to a low-carbon, green economy.

Our response to climate change has thus far focused on efforts such as collaborative science to understand causes, consequences, and solutions; international consensus goal-setting; and action planning (from the national scale to the local). Action planning has emphasized climate change mitigation, or strategies to reduce GHG emissions to lessen future global warming and its consequences. People have only just begun to address climate change adaptation, or strategies to adapt to the consequences of climate change. Yet we know that these consequences will be severe, even if GHG emissions were halted *today*.

This challenge of global warming consequences is complicated by the long-term nature of climate change as well as the uncertainties about the timing, location, and extent of its impact. As such, it is an important topic for a study of resilience. This chapter uses the topic of climate change planning to explore means of building resilience to change that is long term and uncertain, and how collaborative and communicative planning approaches can enhance this effort. First, this chapter looks at the nature of adaptation and resilience in the context of climate change, and the possible ingredients of effective adaptation. The chapter reviews what climate change planning can learn from other planning arenas, those that also focus on building anticipatory capacities, including adaptive management of natural resources and natural hazard mitigation planning. Both of these disciplines are rooted in top-down, techno-economic planning. But emerging theory and practice in these fields aim to embrace social factors and build social capital through collaborative processes to enhance resilience.

The chapter includes lessons from the emerging practice of climate change planning, from international consensus building to local action plans. The experience in mitigation planning provides some lessons for collaboration. But initial experience in adaptation planning has employed more limited collaboration and capacity building. The chapter concludes by suggesting a synthesis approach drawn from these lessons for building climate change resilient communities.

The Nature of Adaptation and Resilience in the Context of Climate Change

What Is Adaptation?

Adaptation has long been studied in reference to natural hazards. More recently, adaptation has been viewed in the context of climate change. Smit and Wandel (2006) define the term *adaptation* (in the context of human dimensions of global change) as a process, action, or outcome in a system (from the scale of a household to a country) that occurs in order for the system to better cope with, manage, or adjust to some changing condition, stress, hazard, risk, or opportunity. In chapter 9 of this book, McConney and Phillips cite Armitage (2005), saying that *adaptive capacity* is about experimenting and learning to foster innovative solutions in complex social and ecological systems. Pelling and High (2005) suggest that adaptations can have different types of interventions, including infrastructural, technological, administrative, organizational, legal/legislative, regulatory, or financial. Adaptations can be reactive, concurrent, or anticipatory; spontaneous or planned; and they can be short-term tactical or long-term strategic. On this latter point, quick fixes and slow reform are not mutually exclusive; short-term reactive adjustments can be followed by longer-term strategic changes. In chapter 5 of this book, Carp discusses how slow-changing variables are an element of adaptation and social-ecological resilience. Ecological resilience is controlled by slow-changing variables, while social resilience can be affected by either fast or slow variables (Walker and Salt 2006). These facts about resilience have implications for adaptive response and resilience to climate change. We anticipate some impacts to build over several decades, such as sea level rise, while other impacts, such as extreme weather events, to manifest in short-term disasters.

Adaptation is often reactionary, coming after a dramatic change event. This reaction takes the form of recovery. Planning for disaster recovery has become a subfield of planning (Olshansky and Chang 2009). Post-disaster recovery planning is important, but such a task does not emphasize the anticipatory preparedness needed to build up the community's capacity for resilience to disaster and change. The first step in anticipatory preparedness is assessing vulnerability to hazard, disaster, or change. However, even when agencies use the concept of vulnerability to identify appropriate responses to change, they focus on physical and economic vulnerability. In contrast, to build resilience, social and political vulnerability need to be addressed as well (Heijmans 2004).

Toward More Effective Adaptation: Building Capacity for Resilience

Effective adaptation action must be anticipatory, identify vulnerabilities, stress preparedness for change, and build the capacity for resilience among those likely affected by change. Tompkins and Adger (2004) define a system's capacity for resilience as its ability to absorb perturbations without being undermined or becoming unable to adapt, self-organize, and learn. In chapter 7 of this book, Bojórquez-Tapia and Eakin point out that resilience is not only the ability of a system to "bounce back" following a crisis, but also its ability to learn and adapt so as to reduce future vulnerabilities. Other scholars define *resilience* as the capacity to experience shocks while retaining the same function, structure, and identity—without shifting into a different regime (Walker and Salt 2006).

Among scholars there is tension about whether community resilience is primarily about bouncing back to "normal" pre-existing conditions, or primarily about learning, adapting, and changing to a new regime. This controversy is important in the context of climate change. Kaufman, in chapter 4 this volume, believes that if a current social or economic system is valued and desirable, then resilience is necessary to maintain that condition. But if the current conditions are undesirable, a resilient system can impede desired and necessary change. Some impacts of climate change will be manifested in extreme weather disasters from which communities will need to bounce back; but other impacts will be exhibited in slow change with diminished capacity for water supply, coastal developments, and agricultural production. Resilience to global warming requires adaptation and transformative change not only to reduce future vulnerabilities, but also to mitigate carbon emissions (by changing the energy economy and the amount of consumption). Resilience focused on bouncing back to the status quo may actually impede necessary adaptation to climate change.

While Pelling and High's (2005) list of adaptation types (from infrastructure to financial) are primarily techno-bureaucratic, they and other scholars say that integrating the behavioral elements of adaptive action and capacity is fundamental. Social capital offers ways to understand how social attributes can contribute to building capacity for collectives and individuals to respond to change, including climate change (Pelling and High 2005; Pelling 2003; Tompkins and Adger 2003a, 2003b; Adger 2001). The characteristics of bonding, bridging, linking, and reciprocity inherent in social capital create a latent capacity that can be relied on to bind a community in times of distress, making it more resilient to change. Adger et al. (2005) believe that multi-level social networks are crucial for developing social capital and for supporting legal, political, and financial frameworks to enhance resilience.

Learning from Natural Resource Management and Natural Hazard Mitigation Planning

Although planning for adaptation to the effects of climate change is new, planning for the management of natural resources and mitigation of natural hazards is not. It is useful to review the evolution of planning in these domains to draw lessons for climate change adaptation.

Natural Resources Adaptive Management

Since the days of Gifford Pinchot (who ran the U.S. Forest Service from 1905 to 1910), natural resources planning has exemplified rational-comprehensive, top-down, technocratic planning. Cost–benefit analysis and environmental impact analysis were methods that supported this approach for public water and land resources. By the 1970s, scholars and practitioners recognized two major limitations in this approach: it did not recognize scientific and contextual uncertainty about resources and supporting ecosystems and human communities, and it did not adequately integrate public values about resource use.

Adaptive management of natural resources emerged as a planning and management approach that aimed to embrace uncertainty and to recognize the need to adapt to changing conditions and knowledge. First developed as a scientific approach (Holling 1978), adaptive management has become an integral part of ecosystem and watershed management and other environmental planning applications.

When combined with communicative and collaborative planning approaches, adaptive management expands beyond the scientific realm: it includes social dimensions in environmental problem solving, it broadens the range of potential solutions, and it builds the social capital necessary for increased resilience to change.

Critical Issues in Adaptive Natural Resources Management

Does adaptive, collaborative natural resources planning and management provide the anticipatory preparedness and social capital necessary to build capacity for resilience of natural resources and the communities they support? Two issues affect the answer to this question.

First, adaptive management has a simple premise: learn by doing. There is much uncertainty in natural and social systems. The steps of adaptive management are to implement certain actions, monitor the consequences, evaluate the effectiveness, and then modify the planned actions to respond to this new knowledge of the system. This approach has been effectively applied to complex ecosystems and has helped fine-tune management plans. However, a deficiency of the "learn by doing" approach is that it is reactive. The method requires change to occur before adapting to it. Thus, this approach is not designed to anticipate change and to build resilience to change. Adaptive management advocates have been wrestling with the challenge of reactive-versus-anticipatory adaptation for the past decade (Tschakert and Dietrich 2010; Peterson et al. 1997).

The second issue concerns effectiveness. Can stakeholder involvement and collaborative decision making be effective enough to develop the social capital sufficient to build resilience to change? Certainly stakeholder involvement is better than more limited forms of public participation, and it can lead to better decisions. But it rarely provides the level of continuing engagement required to build the bonds, bridges, and reciprocity of social capital necessary for adaptive capacity.

Emerging Practice in Adaptive Natural Resources Management

Adaptive natural resources planning and management continues to evolve. It aims to improve adaptive capacity and social capital by the enhanced collaboration and engagement of natural resources stakeholders.

A good example of enhanced collaboration is learning networks, described by Goldstein and Butler (2010) and Goldstein in this volume. Perhaps the next generation of collaborative planning, learning networks can work both horizontally and vertically at multiple spatial and jurisdictional scales. The inherent objective to learn is a fundamental means of building capacity for adaptation and resilience. Goldstein and Butler's work with fire learning networks demonstrates the benefits in applying the method to natural resources and natural hazards.

Opportunities for building social capital can be enhanced by engaging stakeholder volunteers beyond decisions in implementation of natural resources projects, such as watershed monitoring, trail maintenance, habitat enhancement, and steam bank restoration (Randolph 2004; Randolph and Bauer 2000; Margerum 1999). Resource comanagement is a similar idea, described by Tompkins and Adger (2004). In this form of collective action, resource stakeholders work together with a government agency to undertake some aspect of resource management. Tompkins and Adger offer a case study of coastal management in Trinidad and Tobago. They find that the collective action of comanagement can build both community resilience and resilient ecosystems: "By working together and consolidating spaces of dependence such as social support networks and local bonding relationships and by working with government to expand spaces of engagement or outward reaching networks," comanagement or other collective action can have "secondary benefits of building resilience to better cope with the impacts of climate change" (Tompkins and Adger 2004).

Natural Hazards Mitigation Planning

Natural hazards mitigation is relevant to climate change adaptation because many of the impacts of climate change involve natural hazards, especially those associated with extreme weather events, such as hurricanes, flooding storms, and drought. Climate change is likely to exacerbate these hazards and their secondary effects (such as forest fire hazards resulting from drought, and coastal storm surges from sea level rise). Although some see climate change impacts as gradual, adaptation to climate change risks must cope with extreme events within gradual changes in mean climate parameters (Tompkins and Adger 2004).

Like natural resources management, natural hazards mitigation has a long tradition of top-down, techno-economic planning, usually with minor public involvement. Natural hazard and disaster response focused on relief and recovery. After a hurricane, major flood, wildfire, or other disaster, government and humanitarian organizations gave relief to those impacted and gave help toward rebuilding (often rebuilding in the same place). But this rebuilding approach often put people and property back in harm's way so that when the next, often predictable disaster occurred, even greater damage would result. In the past century, this so-called disaster-relief-rebuild-disaster syndrome (D-R-R-D) was the typical pattern of response.

The Federal Emergency Management Agency (FEMA) recognized the faults of D-R-R-D. During the past two decades, FEMA has promoted these prevention policies: emergency preparedness and hazard mitigation planning that requires communities to learn from experience, better preparedness for the next disaster, damage mitigation strategies that have more stringent controls on rebuilding, and more hazard resilient communities. Figure 6.1 illustrates this prevention approach. Communities susceptible to natural hazards are required to develop a disaster mitigation plan if they are to qualify for relief. Because of uncertainty, such plans may not be sufficient to prevent impact; but each subsequent event is to provide new knowledge and trigger additional mitigation planning. That planning will reduce damage from the next event, and it will build greater

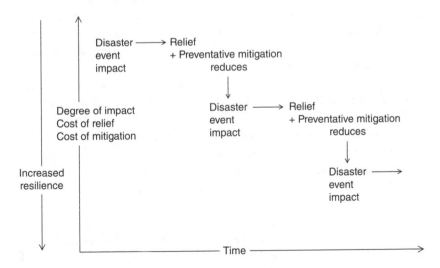

Figure 6.1
Adaptive natural hazard mitigation

resilience to the natural hazard or disaster. (You can learn more about FEMA's mitigation efforts on their Web site.)

FEMA's approach was codified in the Disaster Mitigation Act of 2000, which changed the 1988 Stafford Disaster Relief and Emergency Assistance Act's postdisaster approach to one of predisaster mitigation planning. The 2000 act requires local mitigation plans, which are to include risk assessments and mitigation strategies. The risk assessments identify structures at risk, map threatened areas by hazard type, and estimate potential disaster losses for each type of hazard. The mitigation strategies set goals and policies, prioritize mitigation projects, and identify implementation funding (Godschalk 2003; FEMA 2008).

Critical Issues in Natural Hazard Mitigation Planning

Despite FEMA's efforts, natural mitigation planning has not achieved its objective to build more hazard resilient communities because it is constrained by three critical issues.

First, there continues to be significant political pressure to try to return communities after a disaster to their former state. People err on the side of strong feelings rather than reason during recovery following an event. For example, they may rebuild where they lived previously, even though rebuilding in the same way, in the same place, may increase their future vulnerability rather than reduce it. "Experience has shown that current hazard response and mitigation practices often sustain communities as they are, and merely perpetuate the disaster-damage cycle rather than addressing the root causes of the problems . . . truly sustainable and resilient communities are not feasible in the current socio-political-economic environment" (Tobin 1999).

Adaptation is not about returning to some prior state, because natural, physical, and social systems do evolve; and in some sense, these elements co-evolve with each other over time. This evolving is especially true during a time of climate change; future events are likely not to replicate the past, increasing vulnerability and requiring recovery and reconstruction in new ways and in new locations.

The second constraint is that natural hazard mitigation continues to be a top-down intervention, centered on technology and economics (Allen 2006). Although disaster response agencies are beginning to use the concept of vulnerability to analyze processes and to identify responses, these agencies focus on physical and economic vulnerability. The social and political aspects of vulnerability are rarely addressed (Heijmans 2004). Michael Barnett was the congressional staffer instrumental in drafting a national 2003 resilience development act. He believes that the current approach to resilience is misguided; that resilience should not be conceived as a technical concept. Although the 2003 act did not get out of committee, it raised awareness of a broader concept of vulnerability and resilience among federal agencies (Mason 2006).

The third roadblock is that although the traditional emphasis of disaster planning is on technology and economics, disasters are inherently social in nature. Hurricane Katrina taught us about this factor (Kapucu 2008). Hazard mitigation and disaster planning have not engaged enough the social dimensions of preparedness, impacts, and response. Integrating social factors is needed to build social resilience. Communities are the first responders and the primary problem-solving "tools" of a nation. Social bonds and the norms of reciprocity persist during and after a disaster. These bonds prevent panic and should be incorporated in disaster preparedness, mitigation, and response planning to promote resilient communities (Mason 2006).

Emerging Practice in Natural Hazard and Disaster Mitigation Planning

There are indications from case examples and new approaches that the field of natural hazard and disaster planning is responding to the issues. The field may be evolving toward greater public engagement of social dimensions of vulnerability and disaster preparedness.

Godschalk (2003) argues for an initiative to create resilient cities, which would include expanded research, broader education and training, and increased collaboration among professional groups. His vision of collaboration would engage city planners, engineers, architects, emergency managers, and developers. While there is a need for such cooperation among professionals, this collaboration would still emphasize the technical and economic aspects of hazard and disaster planning. It does not engage a wider public dialog to integrate social and political aspects of disaster preparedness and to build the social capital necessary for resilient cities. In a more recent piece, Godschalk (2010) recognizes the social dimensions. He suggests a twofold approach for a community to become more resilient to natural disasters: (1) planning for long-term social, economic, and environmental sustainability, and (2) taking immediate action to strengthen neighborhood and organizational capacity.

The benefits of broader public involvement can be seen in case examples of disaster response in Florida and Berkeley, California. Berkeley was impacted by the 1989 Loma Pieta earthquake and the 1991 firestorm in the East Bay Hills. After these events, the city decided to engage the community in hazard mitigation. This public engagement was critical to build political support for regulatory and financial measures necessary to build resilience to future disasters. Because of this high level of public support, since 1992 the town passed six tax measures related to risk reduction and community resilience, all of which were overwhelmingly approved by citizens. Resulting tax revenues have been used to retrofit all of the city's schools, fire stations, and city buildings. Other measures provided tax credits for private building retrofits. In 2000, the city became one of the first members of FEMA's Project Impact, a community disaster resiliency program. In 2004, with the adoption of its comprehensive mitigation plan, Berkeley became the first California city to fully comply with the 2000 Disaster Mitigation Act (Mason 2006). The Berkeley case demonstrates the importance of public engagement to build political support for measures to build physical resiliency. To be sure, most of these measures still focus on the technical and economic aspects of disaster preparedness. But it is likely that the public engagement, education, and political support of this process also build social capital and social capacity for resilience.

Kapucu (2008) examined the Florida hurricanes of 2004 to assess what he calls "collaborative emergency management." He argues that better community organizing can lead to better public preparedness and response. The series in 2004 of four major hurricanes in a six-week period was unthinkable. These storms stressed communities beyond anyone's expectations. However, Florida dealt with the 2004 hurricanes with relative control and composure. Kapucu believes that the ability to respond is largely determined by what social structures and processes a community has in place when a disaster occurs.

Community coordination was a critical ingredient in Florida's even-keeled response. Successful coordination requires complex interaction among multiple agencies, nonprofits, private businesses, and citizens. Trust and relationships among these parties must be developed before a disaster hits. In Florida's case, public managers and citizens navigated the maze of response and recovery. Managers struggled to find funds to meet unexpected expenses, and residents banded together to rebuild severely damaged communities. Although these storms affected millions and killed 117, residents were able to go to multiple, coordinated sources to help rebuild their lives and the lives of their neighbors. This coordination among supporting agencies, groups, and citizens created more resilient communities (Kapucu 2008).

Allen (2006) suggests that community-based disaster preparedness (CBDP) can be an effective approach to build social capacity for resilience. (Allen's report is based on a case study in the Philippines.) A CBDP could build local coping and adaptive capacity through various means: dissemination of training and technical information; raising awareness of risk and vulnerability through mapping and participatory appraisal exercises; accessing local knowledge and resources; and mobilizing local people to implement projects such as early warning systems. Allen suggests that CBDP can be most effective when based on social capital analysis and when applied with multiple objectives for disaster prevention, sustainable development, and institution-building.

Allen argues that CBDP has a direct application to climate change adaptation. She reasons that the approach has "the potential to make a significant and long-lasting contribution to reducing local vulnerability and strengthening adaptive capacities, and by increasing emphasis on adaptation to climate change, it provides the scope for understanding and addressing a broader set of vulnerabilities than traditional disaster management." She cautions, however, that this approach may put too much responsibility on the local people, and as a result the method has the potential to unintentionally disempower as well as to empower. Allen suggests that CBDP not be operated solely as a civil society active, but rather as a civil society–government partnership.

Smit and Wandel (2006) present a similar approach: participatory vulnerability assessment (PVA). PVA is based on the participatory rural appraisal method developed in the 1970s and 1980s. It engages people in expressing and assessing realities of their own lives and conditions as a basis for plans and actions. PVA requires active involvement of community stakeholders and aims to identify adaptation strategies that are feasible and practical in communities. Like CBDP, adaptations developed in PVA are most effective when integrated or mainstreamed into other programs, such as resource management, disaster preparedness, or sustainable development.

Scenario development is a tool that can engage people to envision alternative futures. In doing so, they can anticipate change and build adaptive capacity. This tool is popularized by the Global Business Network (see, for example, GBN 2007) and presented in the context of climate change by Turnpenny, O'Riordan, and Haxeltine (2005). Scenario development embraces uncertainty and attempts to articulate alternative visions of the future based on different assumptions. The process itself is educational and the results can prompt community discussion about anticipating change and preparedness.

Tschakert and Dietrich (2010) propose that active research and learning processes (such as community-based projects, participatory appraisal, and scenario development) can foster anticipatory learning. They suggest a five-element framework to facilitate learning: (1) learn lessons from the past; (2) monitor and analyze trends to anticipate future events; (3) distinguish anticipated change from known (and potentially also cyclical) change by considering deliberate surprises, perturbations, and discontinuities; (4) measure anticipatory capacity; and (5) design decision-support tools for adaptation planning. They applied this framework to the Climate Change Collective Learning and Observatory Network Ghana (CCLONG) project. In doing so, they discovered the importance of creating "learning spaces" of iterative, experiential learning-by-doing processes of action-reflection. In such a space, alternative behaviors, visions, and scenarios about vulnerabilities can be formulated and challenged.

All of these emerging methods and approaches suggest that natural hazards and disaster planning is evolving to engage a wider range of participants to develop social capital, anticipate change, and build local capacity for adaptation and resiliency.

Learning from the Emerging Practice of Climate Change Planning

Is the current practice of planning for climate change based on traditional resources and hazards planning? Or does it reflect recent communicative planning innovations from the disciplines thus far discussed? The international framework in response to the challenge of climate change has been the most expansive and collaborative international effort ever attempted. In addition, this framework offers a unique example of a multi-scalar effort from the global, to the local, to the individual. It is useful to review components of this effort to see what lessons there are for climate change adaptation and resilience. To answer these questions we look briefly at climate change science, goal setting, and mitigation planning then address experience to date in adaptation planning.

Climate Change Science and International Goal-Setting

Consensus Science

The Intergovernmental Panel on Climate Change (IPCC) was established in 1988 and has proven to be the most comprehensive and complex collaborative scientific consensus-building exercise ever developed. In the IPCC, a huge body of scientists assess and interpret peer-reviewed research on climate change. They use a collaborative and iterative process. Over several years, four work groups each develop a major report. The reports undergo extensive review by scientists and governments; these papers serve as the basis for the IPCC assessment reports developed and approved in a plenary conference. Using this process, the IPCC has produced four assessment reports in 1990, 1996, 2001, and 2007. The six-year Fourth Assessment Report involved 450 lead authors, 800 contributing authors, and 2,500 reviewers from 130 countries (IPCC 2007).

Collaborative Agreements

The United Nations Framework Convention on Climate Change (UNFCCC) has used collaboration methods to reach major international agreements to set goals for GHG emission reduction. The IPCC's first assessment report in 1991 prompted the establishment of UNFCCC, which holds an annual Conference of Parties (COP) of participating counties. At the sixth COP in 1997 in Kyoto, the UNFCCC developed the Kyoto Protocol, the first international agreement to reduce GHG emissions. The fifteenth COP in Copenhagen in 2009 aimed to develop an agreement to supersede Kyoto. While the resulting agreement did not achieve a binding agreement for the needed GHG emission reductions, it was the first major international conference of 192 countries attended by all major chiefs of state.

Planning for Climate Change Mitigation

Climate Action Planning for Mitigation

IPCC and UNFCCC galvanized a significant international response to climate action. The European Union (EU) has become a world leader in response. On the other hand, the United States never ratified the Kyoto protocol and further has not established even its own national climate action policy. In the absence of a federal U.S. program to reduce GHG emissions, at least 32 states have responded with their own plans. These state plans have usually involved a highly public process using a specially formed commission (representing a wide range of stakeholders) and an extensive schedule of public hearings.

There has also been extensive climate action planning at the local level in the United States, usually driven by local social movements for climate action. These activities have been facilitated by two network organizations:

the 1,000 Cool Cities (including cities whose mayors have signed the Mayor's Climate Agreement), and the 450 communities that are members of ICLEI—Local Governments for Sustainability.[1] Most local climate action plans (CAP) follow ICLEI's five-step planning milestones: produce a GHG emission inventory, adopt an emissions target, develop a CAP, implement the CAP, and monitor and evaluate progress. ICLEI encourages public engagement in the plan development process, but planning can be largely top down and technocratic. However, in most localities, because the political push for a CAP often comes from the public, the planning process has been a community exercise (involving citizen groups, universities, utilities, as well as government agencies) (Wheeler et al. 2009).

Collective Action through Market Mechanisms

Carbon Cap and Trade Programs

Implementing GHG reduction on a large scale requires collective action. Several mechanisms can be employed, but an increasingly popular tool is a regulatory market network called cap and trade (C&T). Emitters are granted (or must bid for) emission allowances. They can reduce emissions to those allowances. Or, instead, they can purchase excess allowances from those emitters that have reduced their own emissions below their allowances. The system achieves the necessary reductions in a cost-effective way and establishes a market network for emission allowance trading.

The European Union established the first C&T program in 2005 among its member nations, in order to help the EU achieve their Kyoto Protocol targets. In the absence of a national system in the United States, ten northeastern states established the Regional Greenhouse Gas Initiative (RGGI) in 2006. These states are implementing a C&T program. In 2007, the Western Climate Initiative (WCI) of seven western states and four Canadian provinces began its C&T program. The U.S. House of Representatives passed a comprehensive energy and climate bill in the summer of 2009, including a C&T program. but the Senate never took a vote on the bill, and federal C&T legislation is doubtful in the near future.

Green Energy Markets

While C&T provides a regulatory market network for carbon reduction, green power provides an economic market network. Consumers can choose to purchase electricity from carbon-free renewable energy sources in lieu of their normal fossil fuel power supplier for an additional fee in three ways.

• Marketed green power from a producer (usually in a deregulated state)

• Green-priced power from their normal provider

• Certified renewable energy credits (REC) from a third-party vendor who uses the proceeds to invest in renewable power development

Planning for Climate Action Adaptation

Planning for adaptation to climate change is still in its infancy. The few adaptation plans that are being developed employ traditional rational planning models. But as you have seen in this chapter, the climate change literature is addressing the role of collaborative planning and collective action to build capacity for resilience to change. To date, adaptation to climate change has focused on two objectives:

1. Lessening the impacts using technology and planning. Examples would include seawalls to fend off sea-level rise and resulting storm surges; expanded irrigation to counter more frequent drought; and more dams and reservoirs to contain flood flows and store water supply to make up for reduced snowmelt.

2. Anticipating impacts and changing now the patterns of human settlement and agriculture so that we can live with those impacts in the future. Examples would include relocating vulnerable populations and adopting climate-adapting development designs.

The Pew Center on Global Climate Change (2009) monitors state and local climate adaptation planning activities.

State Adaptation Plans

Several countries, regions, states, and communities are beginning to develop adaptation plans. The level of activity is dependent on the state's perceived vulnerability to climate change. Florida is a case in point: a one-meter sea level rise would place a large portion of coastal Florida under water. A July, 2007 Executive Order charged the state's Action Team on Energy and Climate Change with the task of creating "adaptation strategies to combat adverse impacts to society, public health, the economy, and natural communities in Florida." The Florida planning process is traditional top-down, rational planning, stressing scientific study of possible impacts and effectiveness of different response strategies, including the following sample ideas (Bipartisan Policy Center 2007):

• *Protection*   seawalls, levees, storm surge gates

• *Retreat*   rolling easements, buyout, abandonment of facilities

• *Accommodation*   elevate, flood proof, setbacks, prohibit building in hazard zones, alternative water supplies

California released its 2009 California Climate Adaptation Strategy in response to a 2008 Governor's Executive Order (California Natural Resources Agency, 2009). A collaborative approach was used to develop the strategy, involving primarily researchers from the Energy Commission's Public Interest Energy Research group, government agencies, and local jurisdictions. (Public involvement amounted only to public comment on the draft report.) Among the guiding principles for this strategy are the following:

• Use the best available science in identifying climate change risks and adaptation strategies.

• Understand that data continue to be collected, and that knowledge about climate change is still evolving. As such, an effective adaptation strategy is "living" and will itself be adapted.

• Involve all relevant stakeholders in identifying, reviewing, and refining the state's adaptation strategy.

• Establish and retain strong partnerships with federal, state, and local governments, tribes, private business, landowners, and non-governmental organizations. Over time, develop and implement adaptation strategy recommendations.

• Give priority to adaptation strategies that initiate, foster, and enhance existing efforts that improve economic and social well-being, public safety and security, public health, environmental justice, species and habitat protection, and ecological function.

• Understand the need for adaptation policies that are effective and flexible enough for circumstances that may not yet be fully predictable.

• Ensure that climate change adaptation strategies are coordinated with other local, state, national, and international efforts to reduce GHG emissions.

Among the recommendations of the strategy are the following: establishing a Climate Adaptation Advisory panel; water conservation requirements to achieve a 20 percent reduction in per capita water use; avoidance of development in vulnerable areas; ensuring communities are healthy, to build resilience to increased spread of disease and to temperature increases; incorporating assessments of climate change impacts, vulnerability, and risk-reduction strategies in local general plans; and implementing a major public outreach effort with a new CalAdapt Web site (to synthesize climate impact research, and statewide and local climate change scenarios).

California's approach is more collaborative than Florida's, but it still is dominated by a top-down, expert-driven process. Perhaps this format is appropriate at the state level. There may be more opportunity for public engagement as localities integrate climate adaptation into their general plans.

Local Adaptation Plans

Several communities are developing adaptation plans at the local level. Two good examples are Miami-Dade County, Florida, and King County, Washington, which are both members of ICLEI—Local Governments for Sustainability's Climate Resilient Communities (CRC) program. ICLEI's CRC was launched in 2005 to assist localities to "develop their capacity to identify and reduce vulnerabilities, and thus improve resilience; to learn to use tools and develop strategies that reduce hazards and manage risk related to regulations, planning, urban design, and investments; to determine how to integrate climate preparedness strategies into existing hazard mitigation plans; to reduce costs associated with disaster relief; and to prioritize vulnerabilities" (ICLEI 2008).

Miami-Dade was one of ICLEI's pilot CRC localities, and King County, Washington, served as the basis for its Planning for Climate Change Guidebook, completed in 2007. King County formed an interdepartmental climate adaptation team in 2006 to enhance expertise in its county departments so that climate change would be considered in future planning, policy, and capital investments. With the help of the University of Washington's Climate Impact Group, the county's 2007 King County Climate Plan outlines six "Strategic Focus Areas" for future adaptation efforts, including climate science; public health; safety and emergency preparedness; surface water management, freshwater quality and water supply; land use, buildings, and transportation; financial and economic impacts (now called economic, agriculture, and forestry); and biodiversity and ecosystems.

ICLEI's guidebook (Snover et al. 2007) uses the King County experience to suggest a process and checklist for local adaptation planning:

1. Initiate your climate resiliency efforts.
   a. Scope the climate change impacts
   b. Build and maintain support to prepare for climate change
   c. Build your climate change preparedness team
   d. Identify your planning areas relevant to climate change

2. Conduct a climate resiliency study
   a. Conduct a climate change vulnerability assessment
   b. Conduct a climate change risk assessment
   c. Prioritize planning areas

3. Set preparedness goals and develop your preparedness plan
   a. Establish a vision and guiding principles
   b. Set preparedness goals
   c. Develop, select, and prioritize preparedness actions

4. Implement your preparedness plan

5. Measure your progress and update your plan
   a. Develop and track measures of resilience
   b. Update your plan

Several steps (1.b, 1.c, 2.c, 3, and 5.a) provide an opportunity for communicative planning. But the guidebook emphasizes simple outreach and public relations under step 1; it relies heavily on governmental members in the preparedness team (1.c); and it uses conventional participation throughout (e.g., external advisory committee of experts). The last step does call for developing "measures of resilience" or quantitative or qualitative "judgment" that is tracked over time to assess how a preparedness action meets the plan's goals.

There is a need for greater use of collaborative planning methods than these examples demonstrate.

Building Climate Change Resilient Communities

Climate change is perhaps the top challenge that the global community faces in this century. People must reduce GHG emissions, but even Herculean efforts will not eliminate the impacts of climate change on water supply, human health, settlement dislocation, natural hazards, agriculture, and ecosystems. We need to adapt to those environmental trends (and especially the extremes associated with them). We must also adapt to the economic and social challenges associated with converting to a low-carbon economy.

There is some evidence (from the experience in planning for climate change to-date) that collaborative processes are important (Few et al. 2006). There are attempts at collaboration and consensus building in such areas as climate change science and international agreements, in local climate change mitigation planning, in collective action through market mechanisms, and in some climate adaptation plans. But as evidenced by emerging state plans and ICLEI's Climate Resilient Communities program, most climate adaptation plans still use top-down, expert-driven, and techno-economic approaches to plan development.

Climate adaptation planners need to learn from resilience theory, as well as from emerging approaches in natural resources and natural hazards/disaster planning. Technocratic approaches may not anticipate all of the changes. As such, climate plans must become more collaborative, public engaging, proactive, and anticipatory. By engaging the public through new and established social networks, adaptation efforts can follow through on numerous tasks: to develop social capital, to expand social acceptance and political support for needed adaptive policies, and to build greater community capacity for self-organizing, learning, coping, and adapting to changes. These tasks are crucial to forming a climate resilient community.

Certainly expert judgment and scientific, engineering, and economic analysis are critical to vulnerability assessment and strategy formulation. But they should be balanced with communicative and collaborative methods to educate and engage people, in order to build social capacity to prepare for (and cope with) change. Several emerging methods that you have read about in this chapter can be used to engage people and their social networks. From adaptive management in natural resources, learning networks can provide multilevel communication and dialog to build capacity. Comanagement and other methods of stakeholder involvement in implementation also build capacity for resilience. From natural hazard and disaster planning, public engagement and civil society–government–private partnerships in the examples of Berkeley and Florida demonstrate key trends. They show that political support is needed for resilient policies and strategies, as well as an enhanced capacity to cope with major disasters. Three approaches that show promise are community-based disaster preparedness, participatory vulnerability assessment, and community scenario development. These approaches engage people in learning about (and anticipating) impacts and vulnerability. Meanwhile, the people contribute their local knowledge, develop social capital, and build resilient capacity.

If we are going to create climate resilient communities, integrating these social dimensions into climate change planning needs to be the rule rather than the exception. Social strategies for localized resilience need to become a social movement. There are some indications that it is, with blogs like "pResilience" that aim to facilitate dialog and innovation. They hope to prepare for change and build resilient capacity (see http://presilience.org/).

Good expert judgment and analysis will always be needed to anticipate and prepare for expected change, but there will also be the unthinkable and unexpected. Community resilience to change is built on social capital and capacity to learn, self-organize, and band together. In this way, we can cope with unexpected change.

Note

1. ICLEI was formerly the International Council for Local Environmental Initiatives.

References

Adger, W. N. 2001. Social capital and climate change. Working paper 8. Norwich, U.K.: Tyndall Centre for Climate Change Research.

Adger, W. N., T. Hughes, C. Folke, S. Carpenter, and J. Rockstrom. 2005. Social-ecological resilience to coastal disasters. *Science* 309:1036–1039.

Allen, K. 2006. Community-based disaster preparedness and climate adaptation: Local capacity-building in the Philippines. *Disasters* 30(1):81–101.

Armitage, D. 2005. Adaptive capacity and community-based natural resource management. *Environmental Management* 35(6):703–715.

Bipartisan Policy Center. 2007. Florida's resilient coasts: A state policy framework for adaptation to climate change. Fort Lauderdale, FL: Florida Atlantic University.

California Natural Resources Agency. 2009. 2009 California Climate Adaptation Strategy. Report to the Governor in Response to Executive Order S-13–2008. Accessed 2-2-2011. Retrieved from http://www.climatechange.ca.gov/adaptation/.

FEMA, Federal Emergency Management Agency. 2008. Local multi-hazard mitigation planning guidance. Accessed 2-2-1011. Retrieved from http://www.fema.gov/library/viewRecord.do?id=3336.

Few, R., K. Brown, and E. L. Tompkins. 2006. Public participation and climate change adaptation. Working paper 95. Norwich, U.K.:Tyndall Centre for Climate Change Research.

GBN, Global Business Network. 2007. Acting on climate change: A strategic workshop for business leaders. San Francisco, CA: Monitor Group.

Godschalk, D. 2003. Urban hazard mitigation: Creating resilient cities. *Natural Hazards Review* 4(3):136–143.

Godschalk, D. July, 2010. Viewpoint: Pick yourself up, Dust yourself off. *Planning.*

Goldstein, B., and W. Butler. 2010. Expanding the scope and impact of collaborative planning. *Journal of the American Planning Association* 76(2):238–249.

Heijmans, A. 2004. From vulnerability to empowerment. In *Mapping vulnerability: Disasters, development and people*, eds. G. Bankoff, G. Fererks, and D. Hilhorst. London: Earthscan.

Holling, C. S., ed. 1978. *Adaptive environmental assessment and management.* New York: John Wiley and Sons.

ICLELocal Governments for Sustainability. 2008. Climate Resilient Communities. Accessed 2-2-2011. Available at http://www.pewclimate.org/publications/ workingpaper/adaption-planning-whats-us-states-and-localities-are-doing.

Intergovernmental Panel on Climate Change. 2007. Fourth Assessment Report. Accessed 2-2-2011. Available at http://www.ipcc.ch/.

Kapucu, N. 2008. Collaborative emergency management: Better community organizing, better public preparedness and response. *Disasters* 32:239–262.

Margerum, R. 1999. Getting past yes: From capital creation to action. *Journal of the American Planning Association* 65(2): 181–192.

Mason, B., ed. 2006. Community disaster resilience: A summary of the March 20, 2006 workshop of the Disasters Roundtable. Washington, D.C.: National Academies Press/National Research Council. The 16th National Academies roundtable, at the Keck Center in Washington, D.C. Accessed 3-7-2011. Available at http:// www.nap.edu/openbook.php?record_id=11769

Olshansky, R., and S. Chang. 2009. Planning for disaster recovery: Emerging research needs and challenges. *Progress in Planning* 72:200–209.

Pelling, M. 2003. *The vulnerability of cities: Natural disaster and social resilience to risk.* London: Earthscan.

Pelling, M., and C. High. 2005. Understanding adaptation: What can social capital offer assessments of adaptive capacity? *Global Environmental Change* 15:308–319.

Peterson, G., G. A. De Leo, J. J. Hellmann, M. A. Janssen, A. Kinzig, J. R. Malcolm, K. L. O'Brien, et al. 1997. Uncertainty, climate change, and adaptive management. *Conservation Ecology* [online] 1(2):4.

Pew Center on Global Climate Change. 2009. Adaptation planning—What U.S. states and localities are doing. Accessed 2-2-2011. Available at http://www.icleiusa .org/programs/climate/Climate_Adaptation.

Randolph, J. 2004. *Environmental land use planning and management.* Washington, D.C.: Island Press.

Randolph, J., and M. Bauer. 2000. Improving environmental decision-making through collaborative methods. *Policy Studies Review* 16(3/4): 168–191.

Snover, A. K., L. Whitely Binder, J. Lopez, E. Willmott, J. Kay, D. Howell, and J. Simmonds. 2007. *Preparing for climate change: A guidebook for local, regional, and state governments.* Oakland, CA: ICLEI—Local Governments for Sustainability.

Smit, B., and J. Wandel. 2006. Adaptation, adaptive capacity and vulnerability. *Global Environmental Change* 16:282–292.

Tobin, G. 1999. Sustainability and community resilience: The holy grail of hazards planning? *Environmental Hazards* 1:13–25.

Tompkins, E. L., and W. N. Adger. 2003a. Defining response capacity to enhance climate change policy. Working paper 39. Norwich, U.K.: Tyndall Centre for Climate Change Research.

Tompkins, E. L., and W. N. Adger. 2003b. Building resilience to climate change through adaptive management of natural resources. Working paper 27. Norwich, U.K.: Tyndall Centre for Climate Change Research.

Tompkins, E., and W.N. Adger. 2004. Does adaptive management of natural resources enhance resilience to climate change? *Ecology and Society* 9(2): 10.

Tschakert, P., and K. A. Dietrich. 2010. Anticipatory learning for climate change adaptation and resilience. *Ecology and Society* 15(2): 11.

Turnpenny, J., T. O'Riordan, and A. Haxeltine. 2005. *Developing regional and local scenarios for climate change mitigation and adaptation. Part 2: Scenario creation*. Norwich, U.K.: Tyndall Centre for Climate Change Research.

Walker, B., and D. Salt. 2006. *Resilience thinking: Sustaining ecosystems and people in a changing world*. Washington, D.C.: Island Press.

Wheeler, S., J. London, and J. Randolph. 2009. Planning and climate change: An emerging research agenda. *Progress in Planning* 72 (1).

II
Collaborative Resilience Case Studies

A
Reaching Consensus

7

Conflict and Collaboration in Defining the "Desired State": The Case of Cozumel, Mexico

Luis A. Bojórquez-Tapia and Hallie Eakin

Introduction

Resilience is the new buzzword in disaster management and planning for natural hazards. Resilience implies the ability of a system not only to "bounce back" following a crisis, but also to learn and adapt so as to reduce future vulnerabilities. What constitutes a resilient system, and how to enhance resiliency in existing places, is still a relatively theoretical concern. Nevertheless, the rising losses associated with hazard impacts around the globe are driving a search for new approaches to hazard management that go beyond the focus on emergency prevention and preparedness. There is also an increasing interest in understanding hazards more holistically, in relation to a broad range of social-ecological interactions that occur on a daily basis (Berkes 2007). Inevitably, this means addressing hazard risk and vulnerability through the lens of social-ecological planning and ongoing resource management at various spatial scales. In practice, enhancing system resilience is challenged by conflict and disagreement among social groups over the normative dimensions of natural resource use, individual and collective economic goals, and what elements and attributes constitute an "ideal" or "desired" system.

Resilience theorists have posited that the development of a common platform for the exchange of knowledge, together with codified rules for social interaction, can help overcome the obstacles for collective action (Olsson and Folke 2003; Walker et al. 2006). If social groups share similar understandings of system functions and interactions, they may be more likely to come to agreement over approaches to resource use and management. Institutions—the rules, norms, and codes of behavior that govern social interaction—are critical in this process (Dietz et al. 2003). The existence of formal institutions for planning, for example, facilitate the formation of social networks, in which disparate social groups exchange ideas, knowledge, and viewpoints with others (Adger 2003). Evidence suggests that if such institutions are going to enhance a community's capacity to deal with stress and shocks, they should provide opportunities for diverse social groups to build relationships of trust, be inclusive, and provide access to broader decision-making processes (Adger 2003; Tompkins and Adger 2004). The absence of such inclusive and adaptive institutional frameworks makes it more likely that a disturbed system will re-organize according to engrained and persistent relationships of power, dominance, and vulnerability (Pelling 1998).

Inclusive, participatory, and iterative processes for decision making are core tenets of adaptive management. Originally conceived as an approach to improving the management of specific natural resources, adaptive management has been adopted as an approach with wider applications, including disaster preparedness, climate change adaptation, and building the overall resilience of social-ecological systems (Barnett 2001; Olsson and Folke 2003; Tompkins and Adger 2004). Adaptive management involves the integration of diverse viewpoints and values in establishing management goals (Stringer et al. 2006). In practice, adaptive management means that a society embraces the significant uncertainties and their *lack* of understanding about system interactions, while supporting flexible institutions that can adjust and respond to new knowledge and learning about the system as it occurs (Olsson and Folke 2003).

Ideally, the implementation of collaborative processes for planning not only creates such flexible institutions, but also enables participants in the planning process to form a common understanding of what is the "desired state" of a social-ecological system. When the system is disturbed, having some agreement on what is the preferred state or goal for a system can help a society avoid returning to unsustainable practices and resource use, learn from their mistakes, and improve the capacity of the system to manage future change. In practice, however, stakeholders often compete for influence over what constitutes the "desired state," and they can vehemently disagree over what represents valid knowledge or legitimate solutions for the problems they identify. While a participatory adaptive management approach aims to address such conflict, achieving agreement is not guaranteed. Participatory processes are inherently political, and in some circumstances they can have the contrary outcome of reinforcing existing inequities and vulnerabilities rather than building resilience after disturbance.

This chapter discusses the challenges faced in the implementation of a collaborative planning process in a vulnerable social-ecological system:

the island of Cozumel, Mexico. Cozumel is threatened not only by hazards such as hurricanes, but also by unrestrained tourist development, urbanization, and degradation of both terrestrial and marine ecosystems. Mexico has recently mandated that ecological ordinances (EO) be used as the primary platform for social-ecological planning at the municipal level. This new institutional framework for participatory planning aims to synthesize existing knowledge on land change dynamics, while providing avenues for continued learning and institutional adjustment as knowledge improves. EOs are designed to provide the structure for communication and decision making—in essence, a common platform for learning and planning—so that government actors and diverse elements of civil society become aware of the underlying quality and vulnerability of a region.

The EO is also, implicitly, a synthesis of what the community considers "desirable" for the social-ecological system. In a context where resource use is highly contested and political, creating a synthetic vision of the island's future is not a trivial task. We argue that instead of aiming for consensus around a pre-determined "desired state" based upon a scientific definition of risk, the EO can be conceived as an institutional framework and *process* by which a compromise vision of Cozumel's future can be negotiated, controlling as much as possible for existing disparities in economic power and resource control among participating stakeholders.

Ideals and Reality of Planning for Social-Ecological Disturbance (Hazards)

A resilient system is one that has the capacity to absorb and respond to disturbance while maintaining essential systemic functions and structure (Carpenter et al. 2001). A resilient system has the capacity to self-organize, learn, and adapt to new and potentially surprising conditions (Folke 2006). The concept of resilience thus has immediate appeal in the area of hazard management and disaster preparedness. While natural hazards are an expected threat to social and ecological system, droughts, floods, and hurricanes are often unpredictable and their impact and timing uncertain. Their impacts constitute significant shocks to ecosystems and to social and economic processes. A resilient system would be one that manages to prepare for the hazard, absorbs its impacts without social or ecological collapse, and relatively rapidly regains core functions without dependence on outside intervention (Adger et al. 2005; Berkes 2007).

How, in practice, can resilience to hazards be achieved? Much of the hazards literature focuses specifically on emergency preparedness and response, yet resilience implies more than disaster management. Making a system more resilient to shocks and crises entails an approach to natural resource management that recognizes the complex role that ecosystem processes can play in the mitigation of hazard impacts (Adger et al. 2005). Adger et al. (2005), for example, point out that the importance of mangrove forests or coral reefs in mitigating storm surge and cyclone impacts are often ignored until the crisis has occurred.

Building system resilience also means "creating the conditions for ordered rule and collective action" (Walker et al. 2006), or, in other words, the institutional structures that will facilitate exchange of knowledge, learning, and adaptation. Such institutions are not limited to addressing hazard risk, but rather can provide the space and tools for a community to share points of view, build understanding, and come to agreement on how they will approach social-ecological interactions more broadly (Cumming et al. 2005; Pahl-Wostl et al. 2007).

The existence of formal institutions coordinating collective action can mitigate vulnerability to hazards in diverse ways. First, if the institutions successfully incorporate diverse viewpoints and perspectives, and form the basis for systemic knowledge, then these institutions can be instrumental in enabling re-organization of social and economic activities following crisis. The policy challenges concerning reconstruction following Hurricane Katrina, for example, revealed the problems that emerge when there is an absence of such an institutional framework. Uncoordinated goals, conflicting administrative responsibilities, and disenfranchised segments of the public created immediate obstacles to the reconstruction effort, slowing down the process and ultimately leading to fragmented and piecemeal approaches to rebuilding (Kates et al. 2006). While New Orleans has emerged from the crisis, and lessons have been learned in emergency preparedness, it is not clear that the reconstruction effort is based on any coordinated agreement on what is desirable for the city in terms of ecological processes, social equity, and economic viability (Kates et al. 2006).

Institutions created to enhance resilience directly confront the large uncertainties and inadequacies in our understanding of social-ecological processes and interactions (Pahl-Wostl et al. 2007). Not only does science often provide an uncertain basis for making decisions, but different interests groups will often interpret the available information differently according to their distinct worldviews and political and economic objectives. These disparate frames of reference (Pahl-Wostl et al. 2007) are sources of conflict, but they also can become sources of knowledge and opportunities for learning. Fundamental differences in interpretation are often tied to group identities: self-identified "conservationists" for example, are likely to perceive and interpret available information on coral reef integrity quite differently than representatives of "the tourism industry," although ultimately the goals of these two stakeholder groups may coincide in land-use planning efforts.

Ideally, institutional arrangements facilitate an exchange of world views, knowledge, and goals, such that stakeholders come to a common understanding. This process of "social learning" provides the basis for "joint practices and collective action" (Pahl-Wostl et al. 2007). It is the availability of the common frames of knowledge and understanding that, according to Folke (2007), becomes the foundation for re-organization after crisis. Folke (2007) calls this common understanding the *institutional memory* of a social-ecological system: "that which bridges the deepest values and symbolic truths of a society and the social or ecological environment on which members of that society have to act."

Nevertheless, the creation of a collective institutional memory—and an agreement of what might be considered a common vision of what is desired from a system—is not a guaranteed outcome of a planning process, even from one that aims to be inclusive, participatory, flexible, and holistic in scope (Stringer et al. 2006). Participatory planning is inherently a complex, difficult, and political process. Stakeholders often compete for influence over what constitutes the "desired state," and they can vehemently disagree over what represents valid knowledge or legitimate solutions for the problems they identify.

In Latin America and elsewhere, the lessons from community resource management projects provide insights about the limitations of participatory and decentralized approaches to improve adaptive capacity (Eakin and Lemos 2006). Dasgupta and Beard (2007) for example, found that power relationships existing prior to a project's implementation were likely to persist, unless the institutional processes established in the management project were aimed to disperse power, provide checks and balances, and permit relatively equal participation of elites and non-elites in decision making. Nevertheless, others have found that political elite members of a community, and those with wealth, are far more likely to participate in collective planning initiatives, marginalizing those who may be the target beneficiaries (Agrawal and Gupta 2005).

Agrawal proposes that rather than mythologize "community" as a homogeneous unit with common interests and goals, it is more appropriate to focus on the institutional arrangements that can address the inevitable conflict and discord that exists within and between social groups (Agrawal and Gibson 1999). Such institutional arrangements, if designed to do so, can contain and structure social interaction to address conflict and power imbalances. Agrawal argues that institutions should be viewed as providing "provisional agreements on how to accomplish tasks" and, in the context of natural resource management, address (1) how resources will be used, managed, and conserved, (2) how rules about use and management will be implemented and enforced, and (3) how conflicts and disputes can be resolved (Agrawal and Gibson 1999). Formal government is not an adversary in this process but rather it needs to provide the legal and regulatory structure to enable broad participation in decision making, uphold the strategic goals of the policy process, and create guarantees that the outcomes of participatory planning will be inclusive of public concerns and will be defended (Assetto et al. 2003).

The tools, methods, and logistics of participatory planning may be as important as the institutional structure that circumscribes the participatory process. Techniques are required that can help make the disparate values and goals of participants explicit, and that can help participants grapple with the limitations and interpretations of the knowledge they have available. Information and communication technology can do part of the job of bridging and integrating different knowledge systems in order to help provide the material basis for building consensus (Pahl-Wostl et al. 2007).

Given the large uncertainties in the science and the likely diverse interpretations of available knowledge that emerge in a participatory process, *boundary organizations* and *boundary objects* can also be instrumental. A boundary object might be a map, a conceptual model, or some other physical object that is accepted and adopted by all participants in the process. The boundary object helps to negotiate a bridge between world views, political positions, and economic "stakes" in the problem at hand (Cash et al. 2002). Boundary institutions are the rules and procedures for interaction that enable potentially hostile actors to mediate their differences in knowledge and position, and if not come to agreement, then at least find enough common ground to engage in mutual learning (Cash et al. 2002; Stringer et al. 2006).

Case Study: Ecological Ordinance and Resilience in Cozumel, Mexico

Study Area
The island of Cozumel is located off the eastern coast of Mexico's Yucatan Peninsula. The island is administered as a *municipio* in the state of Quintana Roo, a political and administrative unit roughly the equivalent of a county in the United States. The economy of the island revolves around

beach tourism, attracting scuba divers, cruise ships, and general vacationers. The majority (81%) of the economically active population is employed in the service sector, largely serving the tourist industry. In 2004 and 2005, the island received an average of 2.6 million tourists from cruise ships. In 2003, the island had 4,010 rooms for tourist accommodation (80 percent of these in four- or five-star hotels). Nevertheless, given its contribution of approximately 80% to the municipal economy, pressure from the tourist industry to expand its spatial and economic scope has been continual. Interviews[1] in the region revealed that the general perception among tourist developers and local authorities is that Cozumel is increasingly lagging behind Cancun and Riviera Maya in the Yucatan Peninsula, as well as other tourist destinations in the Caribbean.

The island is small and flat, with a total of 48,000 hectares and a topography that does not exceed 15 meters above sea level at any point. The entire island stretches only 48 kilometers north–south and 16 kilometers east–west. Practically all tourist and urban development in the island is located on the western coast of the island. The vast majority of the population (about 80,000 inhabitants in 2005) lives in the city of San Miguel, the only urban settlement in the island. All food and manufactured supplies are shipped to the island from the Yucatan Peninsula.

Transformation of the natural cover of the island has been minimal, mainly because all development has concentrated on the western coast. The spatial pattern in development has been heavily influenced by the high exposure of the island's eastern shoreline to Atlantic hurricanes. Locals also recognize that natural vegetation provides protection from hurricanes, and that understanding has added to their reluctance to develop the eastern shoreline.

Since 1871, records show that a total of twenty-two large storms have directly affected Cozumel. The most recent large impacts were associated with hurricanes Emily and Wilma, which both hit Cozumel in 2005, on July 18 and October 21, respectively. Emily's sustained winds were 215 kilometers per hour (Category 4 on the Saffir-Simpson Hurricane Scale) when the eyewall passed directly over Cozumel. The storm surge generated waves of a height of 4 meters off Cozumel's eastern coast (CENAPRED 2006). While hurricanes are frequent off the coast of Quintana Roo, a Category 4 storm in July was unexpected. In the past, the largest storms have occurred in September or October (CENAPRED 2006).

In the state of Quintana Roo, Emily caused over US$100 million in damages largely to the tourist industry and infrastructure. The damage amounted to 1 percent of the state's gross domestic product (GDP). The damages to hotel infrastructure was estimated at US$30 million, and indirect costs to the industry were double that at US$64 million (CENAPRED 2006).

The effects of Wilma's winds that struck later in the season were even greater than those of Emily. Wilma hit Cozumel with sustained winds of 260 kilometers per hour, and the 24-hour precipitation reached 1,637 millimeters in the neighboring island of Isla Mujeres. Wilma was the second costliest hurricane in Mexican history, totaling an estimated US$1.8 billion for the state of Quintana Roo alone, 73 percent of which was in the tourism sector (CENAPRED 2006).

Despite the combined damaged caused by the two hurricanes, reconstruction after Wilma was prompt and well coordinated. Cruise ships returned within weeks and most of the tourist and urban infrastructure was restored within months. But does this return suggest that the island is *resilient*?

Ecological Ordinance

Less than a year after the hurricanes hit the island, Cozumel embarked on a formal process of land-use planning, or "Ecological Ordinance," as required of all Mexican municipios under national environmental law. Although the process was initiated independently of the experience of the municipality with the hurricanes, the process offered an opportunity to re-visit the island institutions governing land use, risk exposure, and development potential.

Ecological ordinance (EO) is defined under Mexican environmental law as a policy instrument to induce sustainable land-uses through participatory governance and multi-agency land-use management. EO is bioregional in scope and participatory in process, entailing the development of an agenda to decide what should be done, when, how, where, and by whom in a territory (DOF 2003).

Originally, EOs in Mexico were based upon what might be termed a *comprehensive/realistic planning approach* (Briassoulis 1989, 2000). Accordingly, the basic premise was that EOs should be based on apolitical (e.g., "objective") scientific information. They were designed around two basic procedural steps. First, teams of experts and scientists analyzed a defined region in terms of the relevant interconnections among the biological, physical, and socioeconomic attributes. Results were then synthesized into a zoning map consisting of a set of administrative land units, or discrete geographical entities deemed suitable for certain land-uses and unsuitable for others. Second, the zoning map was presented to authorities and stakeholders for consultation and fine-tuning. The expectation was that such a two-step process would lead to consensus-building regarding the implementation of sustainable policies and regulations.

Nevertheless, this general approach was unsuccessful. The four major shortcomings were:

- Incapacity of expert/scientific teams to unambiguously determine the suitability of the administrative land units
- Lack of articulation between the stakeholders' interests and the land attributes
- Lack of transparency in the analysis (resulting from efforts to achieve a holistic view of a region that derived in encyclopedic studies, with hidden assumptions, judgments, and values)
- Manipulation of the consultation processes through the marginalization of sectors opposing objectives of powerful economic sectors

These four drawbacks led to an implementation crisis that severely limited the role of ecological ordinances in policymaking. In essence, this approach failed to address the challenges of social learning such as those stated by Pahl-Wostl (2006) regarding the ambiguities in the problem framing, knowledge base, and the diverse ways in which the nature of the problems are perceived.

In many ways, EO was not only an unexplored area that existed between theory and practice (Gunderson 1999), but also a no man's land, in which supposedly enlightened scientists and technocrats would stake their claims, purportedly in the interest of liberating the territory from barbaric politics and vested interests. In this allegorical sense, the tacit goal of these enlightened professionals was equivalent to colonization: a science-driven territorial conquest through the imposition of environmental restrictions and guidelines so that socioeconomic progress and nature protection could be simultaneously achieved. Under this perspective, the role of experts and scientists was to determine what constitutes public interests, whereas the role of the other people was to receive information passively (Briassoulis 1989; Duncan and Lach 2006; Kelsey 2002).

This "comprehensive/realistic planning approach" was radically transformed with the decree of the federal regulations in 2003 (DOF 2003), which favored a neopragmatic perspective (Harper and Stein 1995, 2006) to EO. One crucial change was that the new regulations mandated a collaborative process to cope with the challenges of the relativistic nature of environmental policymaking (see Bojórquez-Tapia et al. 2008; Hagman et al. 2002) and the power relations inherent in the policy process (see Dietz and Stern 2008).

Theoretically, the key concern of a neopragmatic perspective, unlike the comprehensive/realistic approach, is not to determine which alternative "desired state" for a system is "the most real," but to determine which of the competing desired states are the most productive and useful for settling environmental conflicts and achieving broader sustainability. Science is thus taken as a legitimate source of authority, but not as the primary or sole authority. Moreover, the diverse perspectives, principles, values, and empirical theories are used as points of reference to broaden understanding and agreement. In other words, the neopragmatic approach focuses on achieving representations of socio-environmental systems that serve the purposes and goals of the planning process, rather than representations that correspond to an allegedly objective reality. Neopragmatism looks for the down-to-earth meaning of socio-environmental systems in relation with their purpose, so that the essential features can be used to facilitate communication among stakeholders (Harper and Stein 1995, 2006; Jamal et al. 2002). The neopragmatic approach has the potential to bridge the gap between land-use modeling and decision making, which, according to Briassoulis (2008), still afflicts planning and policymaking.

The neopragmatic perspective is of particular interest in problems concerning resilience to hazards. Within this perspective, a first step toward building resilience is to appraise the pertinence and reliability of the information that defines the stakeholders' positions. The goal is to develop a legitimate analytical framework—or boundary object—that can be used to build accurate and empirically valid geospatial representations of sectoral needs and desires. In this way, the resulting geospatial representations provide the foundation for building consensus among stakeholders who are presumed to be both rational (i.e., they look for maximizing long-run self-interest) and reasonable (i.e., they are willing to accept fair terms of cooperation and commitment).

Thus, the new regulations to EO have created an innovative legal framework for Mexico that allows the different stakeholders to bring to the table their own perspectives, information, and models to either support or oppose concrete and contentious environmental policies and land-use decisions. As such, the EO provides the necessary legal and rule-based system through which participation and collaboration can occur (i.e., as called for by Assetto et al. 2003).

In addition, the EO is designed to be conducive to social learning through these items

- The establishment of legally binding agreements between federal, state, and municipal governments, and the creation of steering committees that include nongovernmental organizations (NGO) and academia
- The introduction of a methodological framework that is transparent, systematic, and rigorous
- The creation of an environmental log or registry of the whole process

Thus not only does the EO provide a regulatory structure in which stakeholder interaction occurs, but also it provides a methodological "road map" to guide the process as suggested by Pahl-Wostl et al. (2007) and the procedural and material basis for enhancing core elements of institutional memory (Folke et al. 2007). The EO thus constitutes a boundary institution that provides a common ground for engaging stakeholders in mutual learning, mediating differences, and building consensus regarding the "desired state" to be achieved in a territory.

Achieving a Shared Vision of a "Desired State": The EO in Cozumel

The EO for Cozumel followed the new federal regulations, which mandate the implementation of collaborative framework to maximize consensus and minimize environmental conflicts among the stakeholders. Accordingly, the federal, state, and municipal governments officially installed the Ecological Ordinance Committee of Cozumel in May 8, 2006. Background studies were carried out from November, 2006 until December, 2007.

Methodologically, the EO took into consideration the issues and concerns of stakeholders through the implementation of a land suitability assessment within a participatory planning framework. Broadly defined, a *land suitability assessment* is an integrative method to determine the most appropriate spatial pattern for future land uses according to specified requirements, preferences, or predictors of human activities (see Malczewski 2004, 2006). The overall goal is to design a land-use pattern that prevents environmental conflicts through the segregation of incompatible land uses (see Bojórquez-Tapia et al. 2001; Malczewski et al. 1997).

The technical and methodological approach of the land suitability assessment for Cozumel entailed the integration of geographical information systems and multi-criteria decision analysis (GIS/MCDA) in two steps, as described in Bojórquez-Tapia et al. (2001). In the first step, a series of participatory workshops were held to develop spatially explicit models that represented the "desired state" for each stakeholder group (i.e., agriculture and cattle ranching, biodiversity conservation, fisheries, ecotourism, tourist development, and mining). The stakeholders who participated in the process responded to an open invitation posted in the local media, and thus they were, in many senses, self-selected to represent their economic sector. Through the use of GIS/MCDA, each stakeholder group identified its collective objective for land use on the island and weighted the cartographic attributes necessary for that objective. This process required that the groups substantiate their selection of attributes (e.g., the importance of a particular mangrove forest or coral reef) with the best available scientific knowledge and information. For example, the conservationist stakeholder group had as a common objective to maximize area on the island in ecological reserves, without development options. They then identified a set of criteria pertaining to geographic features such as mangrove forests, areas of significant habitat for threatened species, and so forth, drawing on the best available scientific surveys and biological inventories. Criteria that they were not able to substantiate with such information were discussed and ultimately rejected. The criteria were then associated with geographic entities in a GIS and weighted in terms of their importance for achieving the desired state of the stakeholders (e.g., maximizing area under conservation) in the GIS/MCDA process. This process resulted in a series of sector-based land suitability map layers reflecting the diverse desired states of each stakeholder group, and synthesizing the geographic attributes of the island necessary for achieving each of those states.

In a second step, the collection of map layers were synthesized through a classification procedure that aggregated land parcels into the land suitability groups shown in figure 7.1, as follows: the areas coded P1 and C2 were allocated to biodiversity protection; A1, A2 and A2a, to high-intensity tourist development; A4a-d, to moderate tourist intensity; A8 and A9, to low-intensity tourist development; A3 and A5, to agriculture and cattle ranching; and C1, to conservation, restricted development and groundwater recharge.

In mid-February, 2008, the zoning map layer was presented to the members of the EO's committee and the general public in an official meeting, in accordance with regulations that say that the committee must approve this map layer before it can be used for establishing specific policies and restrictions. The general perception of the EO committee for Cozumel was that the whole process not only had strengthened the capacity of local groups for articulating their interests, but also had improved their bargaining power vis-à-vis authorities, policy makers, and other stakeholders. For example, while in the beginning of the EO process the tourism sector and environmental conservation sector presented mutually incompatible visions for Cozumel's land use, the February meeting confirmed that the

Figure 7.1
Land suitability zoning for the island of Cozumel

final map layer delimited acceptable patterns of land uses across the island. In particular, members of the committee maintained that the results appropriately integrated the trade-offs among competing land-use objectives and enabled a sensible discussion toward solving the main environmental conflicts. The general conclusion was that the map shown in figure 7.1 represented the collective desired state of Cozumel—in essence, a "boundary object" around which integrative and adaptive planning could occur.

A series of workshops followed that official meeting and were implemented with the specific mandate of designing the specific policies and restrictions for the zoning map, to finalize at the end of March. Based upon this map, the stakeholders and the authorities openly debated the issues, proposed solutions, and devised policies in these workshops. In brief, each workshop consisted in a plenary presentation of specific technical issues concerning the rationale behind the zoning map layer, followed by breakout discussion groups to discuss the sectoral positions concerning how specific policies and restriction were needed to implement the proposed zoning scheme, and concluding with a plenary discussion about the "nuts and bolts" aspects of establishing, operating, and assessing the respective policies and restrictions. The process was recorded in formal minutes that were to be included later in the environmental registry of the EO of Cozumel.

It was at this point that the participatory process took a 180° turn. Paraphrasing Stein and Harper (1995), the EO had approximated the Habermas's ideal of a fair and legitimate process,[2] but it was immediately followed by the "Foucauldian dark side" of planning.[3] As described in the material that follows, the EO thus switched from a process in which rational argumentation predominated, to one that was distorted by coercive actions by the authorities. Because state and municipal public officials were forced to surreptitiously defend a specific project (the so-called "Trump Project"), it signified the misuse of government power disguised within the operation of the EO committee.

Following Habermas, an EO should be valid if and only if it represents genuine consensus arrived at under "ideal speech conditions." The requirements for ideal speech conditions include "openness to the public, inclusiveness, equal rights to participation, immunization against external or inherent compulsion, as well as the participants' orientation toward reaching understanding (that is, the sincere expression of utterances)" (Habermas 1996, 367). By following these conditions, the EO should in theory allow the stakeholders to express attitudes, desires, and needs among equals and in a context free of the distorting influence of power.

It was evident that until the end of March, the GIS/MCDA procedure averted some major practical impediments to ideal speech conditions. In effect, the resulting sector-based land suitability maps at this point appeared immunized against external coercion because each stakeholder group defined its sectoral "desired state" according to its own values, needs, and interests, and using the best available geospatial information. Likewise, the aggregated land suitability groups provided a basis for mutual understanding among stakeholders and enabled the definition of a collective "desired state" by consensus.

In the workshops, the different stakeholders brought to the table their own perspectives, information, and models to either support or oppose concrete and contentious zoning policies and decisions. The conclusion was that tourist development should be restricted in zone A9 to achieve the collective desired state for Cozumel. The exposure of zone A9 to hurricanes, as well as concerns about the biodiversity in the area, were sufficiently well-understood facts by all participants to achieve a consensus view that the area should be off-limits for intensive development. Even the representatives of the tourist sector concurred with the conclusion of allowing only one hotel room per hectare in this zone, implying that only small-scale developments could be authorized in zone A9.

In April, the Foucauldian "dark side" of planning emerged immediately after the final stakeholder workshop, when the process was thought to be complete. The dark side manifested itself through the conjunction of economic and political power regarding the suitability of zone A9, located at the northeastern corner of the island and thus the most exposed zone to hurricanes.

When the minutes were made available for review following the last March workshop, the members of the EO committee found that the restrictions that had been agreed on for zone A9 had been omitted or modified by state representatives without any apparent justification. By the end of March, it was evident that the state and municipal public servants responsible for the environmental registry—the basis of institutional memory of the participatory process—had modified the minutes to ensure that the zoning would be in favor of what the local media had been calling "the Trump Project," a tourist development initiative located precisely in zone A9 (figure 7.1). This project owed its name to reports that the main invited investor was Donald Trump, a well-known real estate mogul from the United States. According to the local media, the project involved the construction of 4,000 hotel rooms, condominiums with private piers that would be connected to the ocean through human-made canals, two golf courses, and a landing strip. The project had obvious economic attractions for some of the leadership in the municipal government and state government (the municipal president himself was active in the tourism development business) and for several of the island's powerful tourist developers who hoped to cash in on the project. During the EO workshops, neither the state, nor the municipal government representatives, nor the participants of the tourism sector brought up the specificities of the Trump Project in the course of the negotiation of specific land-use policies and regulations. By hiding this vision of the Cozumel's tourist future, the very elite stakeholders whose participation had enhanced the legitimacy and credibility of the EO process now risked undermining it by imposing their own version of the "desired state" in contradiction of what had been collectively decided.

By April 1, some members of the EO committee complained in writing to the municipal administration about the unauthorized changes in the minutes, and in doing so they openly opposed to the Trump Project. In contrast, the main investors of the Trump Project, who did not participate openly in the EO process (although they were aligned with some stakeholders at the EO workshops), claimed in writing that the restrictions in zone A9 were unjustified. They also alleged that scientific studies demonstrated that zone A9 was indeed suitable for the project. In an ad hoc meeting with the EO committee, a group of scientists and consultants hired by the developers tried to persuade the EO committee members that some specific restrictions to be applied in zone A9 were nonsensical from technical and scientific perspectives. Specifically, they asserted that, contrary to the common perception, the man-made canals of the Trump Project would result in improvements to mangrove ecosystems in zone A9. Despite this effort, the experts failed to convince the members of the EO committee about the alleged benefits of the Trump Project, mainly because the experts did not support the alleged benefits with empirical data and they did not address the issue of exposure to hurricanes in zone A9.

Despite pressures from the state and municipal authorities, the EO committee stood firm in its opposition to the project. The capacity of the committee to stand up to the developers was strengthened by factionalism within the tourism sector and the reality that only a subset of elite developers would be likely to benefit from the project's implementation. The EO committee was also backed in part by the federal government, which recognized that the EO process was implemented according to a legal procedure, involving substantial stakeholder participation, and a well-documented process in the committee's minutes (recorded in the environmental registry).

The clash between the two positions regarding the suitability of zone A9—one resulting from the participatory workshops and the other supported by a subset of powerful elitist interests—led to a deadlock of the EO process. The dominant perception among members of the EO committee was that the state and local governments had misused power and allegedly scientific information to support the Trump Project, justifying their unilateral intervention by arguing that there would be substantial socioeconomic benefits associated with the investment in Cozumel. In contrast, the fact that the EO followed a federally established regulatory procedure, supported by a diverse group of stakeholders and with backing by the municipal, state, and federal government, led to an impasse. Although the municipal president did an about-face to argue in support of the Trump Project, and even some of the state's environmental authorities argued for its approval, the federal government opposed the final version of the EO.

The final zoning plan, belatedly disputed by a faction of the tourism sector, was built through lengthy negotiations and transparent consideration of available data, sector goals, and environmental constraints. By constitutional law, nevertheless, an EO for a municipality such as Cozumel is formalized through a state and municipal decree. Consequently, the final responsibility for what is included in an EO lies with the local authorities. Thus, although the Trump Project advocates did not convince the EO committee that the project would be feasible according to an agreed zoning scheme, it was the local authorities who had the ultimate say. In essence, the Foucauldian "dark side" prevailed; and while the authorities did not formally approve the project, they also excluded the restrictions in the final EO that would forbid the Trump Project in zone A9.

Discussion

Under the neopragmatic umbrella, the definition of the desired state for Cozumel was built from the diverse stakeholders' environmental representations. One challenge in developing a collective desired state was that each of these representations presented distortions and different levels of precision. The articulation of the ambitions for the island reflected practical, functional, cultural, and symbolic meanings for each stakeholder group. In other words, these representations reflected the stakeholders' multiple frames of reference that are an integral part of what Duncan and Lach

(2006) call "collaborative story-making." Hence, the definition of the desired state compelled the production of a cogent synthesis of disparate goals and aspirations for land use in a highly sensitive geographic area, enabling decision makers and stakeholders become aware of the underlying quality and vulnerability of Cozumel.

Rather than attempting to achieve an allegedly "neutral" and "objective" spatial representation of the suitability of the land for the different social actors, the EO for Cozumel focused on determining the connotations of the geographical entities, which helped explain what Couclelis and Gottsengen (1997) refer as the "contested space" that arises from opposing meanings and purposes. In this way, the participatory planning process emphasized the association of meaning and purpose to biophysical entities represented in the zoning map to achieve a representation of highly polysemous geographical entities and concepts, such as "tourism of low impact" or "zone exposed to hurricanes."

Nevertheless, as the conflict over the Trump Project reveals, the process can only reflect the meanings that the stakeholders are willing to reveal at the negotiating table, and the views of those who are participating in the deliberative process. While efforts were made to ensure participation by a wide range of stakeholders, the response to the invitation was voluntary and the participants were self-selected. As a result, it is likely that some of the more politically marginal stakeholder groups failed to participate, and some very relevant and powerful players abstained from the process (only to later make their voices heard). Furthermore, the process of articulating and synthesizing "desired states" can only be achieved if stakeholders are transparent about all aspects of their aspirations, including those ambitions that are likely to be in conflict with the visions of other groups. Conflict between stakeholders over what is envisioned for a region's future will inevitably emerge at some point in the development process. Ideally, the planning process can engage directly with conflicting visions; probe for the deeper and diverse meanings associated with such visions; and use science and deliberation not to definitively resolve the conflict, but rather to agree on the criteria on which decisions should be made.

This idea points to two key challenges for defining the desired state of socio-environmental systems, similar to those factors identified by Stein and Harper (2003) in relation to environmental planning more generally. First, there is a need for a policymaking framework capable of restraining the unavoidable "undercurrents that serve certain (elite) interests other than those they purport to serve." Second, planning approaches should be capable of arriving at a collective judgment of what information is "correct" for basing land-use policies in order to achieve a collective desired state.

It should be acknowledged, however, that the process of articulating and synthesizing a desired state does not automatically indicate that the social actors are capable of reorganizing the socio-environmental system after disturbance. According to Folke et al. (2005), this capacity is contingent on the accumulation of "social memory" that captures past experiences that can be translated into "adaptive governance" or the institutional arrangements needed for sharing management power and responsibilities among stakeholders and government agencies.

While disturbance may provide an opportunity for adaptive governance to arise, Goldstein (2007) argues that social memory can, in effect, fade away once public awareness about a disturbance event recedes. This concept may explain why in Cozumel social memory regarding hurricanes Emily and Wilma in 2005 did not translated into a unanimous rejection of the Trump Project in zone A9. In effect, public awareness in Cozumel vanished once the recovery efforts by the government proved to be successful after the crisis.

Thus, the EO process plays a key role in fostering adaptive governance in Mexico where social participation in environmental policymaking is typically scant and disorganized. As the case of Cozumel shows, the EO process empowered social actors by promoting solidarity and enabling political mobilization in three ways. First, the use of a systematic and formal technique—a combination of GIS and multi-criteria decision analysis—provided structure, legitimacy and some degree of transparency in an effort to make the diverse values and goals explicit.

Second, the land suitability zoning map (figure 7.1) materialized the "common imaginary" of shared assumptions and expectations (see Goldstein and Butler 2008) regarding the desired state of the island. Formally, this imaginary took shape through the land-use guidelines and restrictions applicable to each zone.

Third, the EO process as a whole legitimized the social capital and organizational capacity needed to preserve the collective memory regarding the desired state of the island, while simultaneously fostering accountability in land-use decision making.

Although the decreed EO does not constitute a blueprint for reconstruction or postdisaster planning, the process illustrates the importance of formalizing an "institutional memory" of the deliberative process, and the collective visions of the island's future. The environmental registry—in which the minutes from the workshops and EO committee meetings are recorded—served as a break on the imposition of one unilateral vision of the island's development. The registry documented the collective concerns about the exposure of the eastern coast of the island, the specific criteria agreed upon to determine development in the area, and the scientific information on which those criteria were decided. It thus stood in opposition to the new information and criteria imposed by a subsector of the population after the process was complete. The registry thus had served as an institutionalized form of "check and balance" as argued for by Dasgupta (2007), limiting the capacity of elites to undermine and capture the participatory process.

Conclusion

Can the island of Cozumel be considered more resilient as a result of the EO process, even if that process is not complete? The case of Cozumel illustrates that achieving a collective vision of what is desired, which conceivably would facilitate reorganization and rebound following a disaster, is fraught with challenges. These challenges relate to the inherently political nature of stakeholder engagement and the participatory process advocated in adaptive management. Stakeholders are, by definition, interest groups; and even the agencies with the responsibility for overseeing and implementing the participatory process are unlikely to be neutral, and the agencies may very well have not-so-transparent agendas.

Nevertheless, the EO in Cozumel did confirm the importance of the process itself in efforts to enhance resilience around a desired state. The existence of a formal, legislated process at the federal level, and having federal, state, and local administrative involvement in the implementation of the EO, provide some degree of checks and balances, as well as legal recourse for participants dissatisfied with the process or its outcome. The process itself permitted the presentation of diverse knowledge and sources of information, and it enhanced the ability of different groups to discuss and contest the validity of each source. The environmental registry served (and is serving) as an important source of institutional memory in the current dispute over the EO outcome.

Conflict will never be eliminated, nor will the process ever be immune from the influence of significant and powerful political interests, nor should it be. The EO process does provide, however, a blueprint for how conflicts can be negotiated. In that respect, the EO process of Cozumel produced a boundary object (i.e., the land suitability map) and a boundary institution (i.e., the environmental registry) from which subsequent decisions (and conflicts) can be emerge.

But perhaps more importantly in a country like Mexico where public participation is incipient at best, the environmental registry legitimizes the institutional memory of the EO process. In the case of Cozumel, not only does the registry foster accountability in land-use decision making, but it also sets up an objective basis for determining whether or not endeavors such as the Trump Project in zone A9 are dissonant with the desired state of the island.

It is still premature to derive any conclusion regarding whether the EO process will in effect transform the spatial land-use scheme to lower the vulnerability of the island to hurricanes. Nevertheless, the EO process in effect validates the necessary framework for guiding the process of institutional learning (and potentially reconstruction and reorganization) following disaster.

Notes

1. In 2007, interviews were conducted by the lead author with stakeholders participating in the EO process

2. Jürgen Habermas (b. 1929), a German sociologist and philosopher, maintained that consensus in public matters could only be achieved under an "ideal speech situation" that requires participants to have the same capacities of discourse, social equality, and freedom from coercion.

3. Michel Foucault (1926–1984), a French philosopher, was concerned about how forms of knowledge that purport to be neutral were used in the service of power, and the misuse of government power in contemporary societies. In his work, he unmasked power within social institutions (religious, political, and economic), within organizations (factories, prisons, hospitals), and traditional conceptions (truth, rationality, morality, bureaucracy).

References

Adger, W. N. 2003. Social capital, collective action, and adaptation to climate change. *Economic Geography* 79 (4): 387–404.

Adger, W. N., T. P. Hughes, C. Folke, S. R. Carpenter, and J. Rockstrom. 2005. Social-ecological resilience to coastal disasters. *Science* 309:1036–1039.

Agrawal, A., and C. C. Gibson. 1999. Enchantment and disenchantment: The role of community in natural resource conservation. *World Development* 27 (4): 629–649.

Agrawal, A., and K. Gupta. 2005. Decentralization and participation: The governance of common pool resources in Nepal's terai. *World Development* 33 (7): 1101–1114.

Assetto, V. J., E. Hajba, and S. Mumme. 2003. Democratization, decentralization, and local environmental policy capacity: Hungary and Mexico. *Social Science Journal* 40:249–268.

Barnett, J. 2001. Adapting to climate change in Pacific island countries: The problem of uncertainty. *World Development* 29 (6): 977–993.

Berkes, F. 2007. Understanding uncertainty and reducing vulnerability: Lessons from resilience thinking. *Natural Hazards* 41:283–295.

Bojórquez-Tapia, L. A., S. Díaz-Mondragón, and E. Ezcurra. 2001. GIS-based approach for participatory decision making and land suitability analysis. *International Journal of Geographical Information Science* 15:129–151.

Briassoulis, H. 1989. Theoretical orientations in environmental planning: An inquiry into alternative approaches. *Environmental Management* 13 (4): 381–392.

Briassoulis, H. 2000. Analysis of land use change: Theoretical and modeling approaches. In *The Web book of regional science*, ed. S. Loveridge. Morgantown, WV: Regional Research Institute, West Virginia University. Accessed 2-3-2011. Available at http://www.rri.wvu.edu/regscweb.htm.

Briassoulis, H. 2008. Land-use policy and planning, theorizing, and modeling: Lost in translation, found in complexity? *Environment and Planning B: Planning & Design* 35 (1): 16–33.

Carpenter, S. R., B. H. Walker, J. M. Anderies, and N. Abel. 2001. From metaphor to measurement: Resilience of what to what? *Ecosystems* 4:765–781.

Cash, D., W. Clark, F. Alcock, N. Dickson, N. Eckley, and J. Jager. 2002. Salience, credibility, legitimacy and boundaries: Linking research, assessment, and decision-making. *Faculty Research Working Paper Series*. Cambridge, MA: John F. Kennedy School of Government.

CENAPRED. 2006. *Características e impacto socioeconómico de los principales desastres ocurridos en la república mexicana en el año 2005.* México DF. CENAPRED.

Couclelis, H., and J. Gottsegen. 1997. What maps mean to people: Denotation, connotation, and geographic visualization in land-use debates. In *Spatial information theory: A theoretical basis for GIS*, eds. S. Hirtly and A. U. Frank, 151–162. (International Conference COSIT '97, Laurel Highlands, PA.) *Lecture Notes in Computer Science* 1329. Berlin: Springer-Verlag.

Cumming, G. S., G. Barnes, S. Perz, M. Schmink, K. E. Sieving, J. Southworth, M. Binford, R. D. Holt, C. Stickler, and T. Van Holt. 2005. An exploratory framework for the empirical measurement of resilience. *Ecosystems* 8:975–987.

Dasgupta, A., and V. A. Beard. 2007. Community driven development, collective action and elite capture in Indonesia. *Development and Change* 38 (2): 229–249.

Dietz, T., E. Ostrom, and P. C. Stern. 2003. The struggle to govern the commons. *Science* 302:1907–1912.

DOF (Diario Oficial de la Federación). 2003. *Reglamento de la Ley del Equilibrio Ecológico y la Protección al Ambiente en materia de ordenamiento ecológico*, 38–54. D.F., México: Diario Oficial de la Federación.

Duncan, S. L., and D. H. Lach. 2006. Privileged knowledge and social change: Effects on different participants of using geographic information systems technology in natural resource management. *Environmental Management* 38 (2): 267–285.

Eakin, H., and M. C. Lemos. 2006. Adaptation and the state: Latin America and the challenge of capacity-building under globalization. *Global Environmental Change* 16:7–18.

Folke, C. 2006. Resilience: The emergence of a perspective for social-ecological systems analyses. *Global Environmental Change* 16:253–267.

Folke, C., T. Hahn, P. Olsson, and J. Norberg. 2005. Adaptive governance of social-ecological systems. *Annual Review of Environment and Resources* 30: 441–473.

Folke, C., J. Colding, and F. Berkes. 2007. *Building resilience and adaptive capacity in social-ecological systems*. Unpublished manuscript.

Goldstein, B. E. 2007. Skunkworks in the embers of the Cedar Fire: Enhancing resilience in the aftermath of disaster. *Human Ecology* 36 (1): 15–28.

Goldstein, B. E., and W. H. Butler. 2008. The network imaginary: Coherence and creativity within a multiscalar collaborative effort to reform US fire management. *Journal of Environmental Planning and Management* 52 (8): 1013–1033.

Gunderson, L. 1999. Resilient management: Comments on "Ecological and social dynamics in simple models of ecosystem management" by S. R. Carpenter, W. A. Brock, and P. Hanson. *Conservation Ecology* 3(2): 7. Accessed 2-3-2011. Available at http://www.consecol.org/vol3/iss2/art7.

Habermas, J. 1996. *Between facts and norms: Contributions to a discourse theory of law and democracy*, trans. W. Rehg. Cambridge, MA: MIT Press.

Harper, T. L., and S. M. Stein. 1995. Out of the postmodern abyss: Preserving the rationale for liberal planning. *Journal of Planning Education and Research* 14: 233–244.

Harper, T. L., and S. M. Stein. 2006. *Dialogical planning in a fragmented society: critically liberal, pragmatic, incremental*. New Brunswick, NJ: CUPR Press,

Jamal, T., S. M. Stein, and T. L. Harper. 2002. Beyond labels: Pragmatic planning in multi-stakeholder tourism-environmental conflicts. *Journal of Planning Education and Research* 22:164–177.

Kates, R., C. E. Colten, S. Laska, and S. P. Leatherman. 2006. Reconstruction of New Orleans after Hurricane Katrina: A research perspective. *Proceedings of the National Academy of Sciences of the United States of America* 103:14653–14660.

Kelsey, E. 2002. Implications of the nation-state system on public involvement in environmental problem-solving. In *Global environmental change and the nation state, Proceedings of the 2001 Berlin Conference on Human Dimensions of Global Environmental Change*, eds. F. Biermann, R. Brohm, and K. Dingwerth, 117–126. PIK report 80. Potsdam, Germany: Potsdam Institute for Climatic Research (PIK).

Malczewski, J. 2004. GIS-based land-use suitability analysis: A critical overview. *Progress in Planning* 62:3–65.

Malczewski, J. 2006. GIS-based multicriteria decision analysis: A survey of the literature. *International Journal of Geographical Information Science* 20:703–726.

Malczewski, J., R. Moreno-Sánchez, L. A. Bojórquez-Tapia, and E. Ongay-Delhumeau. 1997. Multicriteria group decision-making model for environmental conflict analysis in the Cape Region, Mexico. *Journal of Environmental Planning and Management* 40:349–347.

Olsson, P., and C. Folke. 2003. Adaptive comanagement for building resilience in social-ecological systems. *Environmental Management* 34(1): 75–90.

Pahl-Wostl, C. 2006. The importance of social learning in restoring the multi-functionality of rivers and floodplains. *Ecology and Society* 11, art. 10 (online).

Pahl-Wostl, C., M. Craps, A. Dewulf, E. Mostert, D. Tabara, and T. Taillieu. 2007. Social learning and water resource management. *Ecology and Society* 12(2):5.

Pelling, M. 1998. Participation, social capital and vulnerability to urban flooding in Guyana. *Journal of International Development* 10 (4): 469–486.

Stain, M. S., and T..L. Harper. 2003. Power, trust, and planning. *Journal of Planning Education and Research* 23:125–139.

Stringer, L. C., A. J. Dougill, E. Fraser, K. Hubacek, C. Prell, and M. S. Reed. 2006. Unpacking "participation" in the adaptive management of social-ecological systems: A critical review. *Ecology and Society* [online] 11(2):39.

Tompkins, E., and W. N. Adger. 2004. "Does adaptive management of natural resources enhance resilience to climate change?" *Ecology and Society* [online] 9(2):10. Accessed 2-3-2011. Available at http://www.ecologyandsociety.org/vol9/iss2/art10.

Walker, B. H., L. H. Gunderson, A. Kinzig, C. Folke, S. R. Carpenter, and L. Schultz. 2006. A handful of heuristics and some propositions for understanding resilience in social-ecological systems. *Ecology and Society* [online] 11(1):13.

8

Getting to Resilience in a Climate-Protected Community: Early Problem-Solving Choices, Ideas, and Governance Philosophy

Edward P. Weber

The potential scale, severity, and variation in the speed of the changes associated with climate change pose a series of important governance challenges to those communities seeking to become a climate-protected community (CPC). A CPC is one that is successfully connected together, such that it actively examines, understands and responds to climate change in a manner that mitigates significant climate perturbations and their damaging effects, while also sustaining local ecosystem health and the other values of importance to the community, or communities, in question. In turn, accomplishing these different goals simultaneously will be more likely to the extent a particular CPC develops the resilience—the capacity for innovation and renewal[1]—to address both long, slow significant change and rapid turbulent events (Folke et al. 2005; Hayward 2008).

How does a community develop resilience? The burgeoning literature on resilience makes it clear that getting to successful resiliency requires a high degree of flexibility and adaptability in order to foster considerable redundancies and a governance arrangement that can respond effectively to the varying speeds and types of climate change problems being encountered. This literature also accepts that flexibility and adaptability require the free flow of information, hence knowledge transfers, among and between diverse, often competing interests and experts, who necessarily must be involved given the scope and complexity of the climate change problem *if the management/mitigation effort is to be successful and sustained over time* (see also Weber 2003; Weber and Khademian 2008a). Further, facilitating such knowledge transfers requires considerable trust within the CPC, and producing *and maintaining* considerable trust requires a series of essential variables associated with institutional structure (Kickert et al. 1997; Milward and Provan 1998), entrepreneurial leadership (Danter et al. 2000; Thomas 2003), and social sources of resilience (Berkes et al. 2003; Gunderson and Holling 2002).

But what happens when decision makers are faced with a tough setting? A *tough setting* is a community lacking, or weak in the "social sources of resilience such as social capital (including trust and social networks) and social memory (including experience for dealing with change) (McIntosh 2000) [that] are essential for the capacity of social-ecological systems to adapt to and shape change" (Folke et al. 2005, 444). How does one go about developing the requisite social foundation of trust, then? Institutional structure that shapes behavior is likely to be of use (Knott and Miller 1987 Ostrom 1990), but this structure is not likely to be sufficient all by itself (Weber and Khademian 2008a, 2008b). And just as importantly, how does one transform the trust so that it is credibly and effectively focused on the public problem at issue, in this case the challenges of climate change? Stated differently, how can one integrate and shape the efforts of the diverse stakeholders such that they embrace and apply the core mission?

The short answer to rebuilding trust and focusing stakeholders in the desired policy direction in a "tough" setting involves four factors. The first one is something the public policy and administration literatures have long identified as central to ongoing policy effectiveness—an existing, credible, regulatory infrastructure that accepts and reinforces the desired policy direction. The credible regulatory infrastructure, along with deadlines for action, creates threats to the established economic and social order and imposes additional costs on regulated communities, thus creating incentives to seek less costly, more palatable, potentially more effective problem-solving alternatives such as collaboratives. Second is another basic factor long established as a "fact" for most all public problem-solving exercises and institutions: a resilient CPC must have adequate resources to design and implement public problem-solving programs.

On closer inspection, however, these two basic lessons are necessary but not sufficient conditions for moving a community from the tough original condition of low trust, weak coordination, and ineffective management to high trust, strong coordinative capacity, and effective, resilient management. Making full sense of this particular conundrum requires that we direct our attention to the concept of a robust, integrated culture capable of fomenting the kind of change in current social structures that accepts and focuses on the climate change challenge (Khademian 2002, pp. 20–21; LaPorte 1996; Selznick 1957; Wilson 1989). The right integrative culture, or social architecture, can "provide a means of managerial control, . . . [participant] loyalty, motivation, and coordination, [and overall] . . . strength and, when necessary, flexibility to organizations" and CPC governance arrangements (Khademian 2002, 18; Ouchi 1981). In turn, constructing and maintaining a robust, integrative culture, at minimum, requires three things: a common sense, strategic approach to early problem-solving choices, a set of collectively agreed ideas (North 2005; Weber 2009), and a governance philosophy that helps to facilitate the flow of communication and knowledge across interests, areas of expertise, and jurisdictions (Ludwig et al. 2001; Weber and Khademian 2008a).

Fortunately, there are existing examples of collaborative watershed communities seeking to manage complex social-ecological systems in the face of multiple challenges. These examples can be thought of as natural laboratories capable of shedding light on the CPC governance "resilience" dilemma. Drawing lessons from watershed management cases is appropriate given:

• The heavy substantive emphasis on the kinds of ecological and physical system dynamics so central to climate change debates
• The emergence of the kind of collaborative, or networked, systems of governance that are also grounded in trust and the involvement of multiple, diverse sets of interests and experts
• The shared comprehensive focus on sustaining the health of the environment, economy, and community
• The shared unstructured, cross-cutting, and relentless character of the "wicked" problem sets[2] for both watersheds and CPCs

The particular example employed here is a comprehensive collaborative watershed governance case in the Blackfoot River area of Montana. This case started in poor social soil in the early 1990s, yet ended up as an extraordinarily successful case that created a strong collaborative governance institution and enhanced collective decision capacity within the watershed for the purpose of sustaining environment, economy, and community (Ash Institute 2006). After developing details of the "tough" setting and the conclusion of collaborative governance success, the chapter moves to a detailed exploration of the variables involved in facilitating the transition.

The Blackfoot Challenge: From Tough Setting to Collaborative Success

In the summer of 1990, Greg Neudecker, a scientist and employee of the U.S. Fish and Wildlife Service (USFWS) with responsibilities for endangered species recovery programs, set foot in the Blackfoot Valley in western Montana for the first time. On his drive into the valley he drove by Jim Stone's Rolling Stone Ranch near the small town of Ovando. Stone, a third-generation Montanan and rancher seeking to maintain his livelihood and the property bequeathed to him by his father, had virtually nothing in common with Neudecker other than a mutually shared suspicion of one another and a mutual frustration at the status quo—the damage being done by the seemingly intractable series of difficult, cross-cutting, interconnected, and relentless public problems common to many rural American landscapes. At that moment in time, the federal government official and the cattleman, though unknown to each other, had come to the same conclusion—the environmental and economic sustainability of the 1.5 million acre watershed was being seriously threatened. For Stone, it was all about "his place, his home, and the home for future generations of Stones." For Neudecker in 1990, it was about finding a way to discharge his Endangered Species Act (ESA) responsibilities successfully in hopes of moving up the management ladder inside the USFWS.

By and large the problems noted by Stone and Neudecker were easy to see and easy to trace. They were a product of roughly 150 years of traditional resource use and development by private and public landowners (U.S. Forest Service; Bureau of Land Management; the State of Montana) that had, over time, significantly degraded a wide variety of natural resources and impaired the ability of the broader ecosystem to function in a healthy, much less sustainable manner. Thus, by the early 1990s, the Blackfoot watershed was home to many threatened and endangered species (i.e., bull trout, grizzly bears, wolves, Canadian lynx, westslope cutthroat trout) and was encountering severe problems with dewatered streams (insufficient and, in some cases, zero flows for at least part of the year), water quality, invasive noxious weeds, and other signs of deteriorating ecosystem health.

While traditional use decisions and methods were central to this story of decline in the Blackfoot, the large number of state and federal environmental policy initiatives passed in the 1970s and 1980s, which were typically crafted as top-down, command-and-control, single-issue (fragmented) policies, and the litigation that was a common response, failed to stop the broad-based degradation. These new laws also contributed to increasing polarization and declining trust among private landowners, government regulators, environmentalists, and other stakeholders. In addition, the scientific databases capable of understanding and monitoring the nature and extent of the relationships among the multiple resource issues in the Blackfoot fit one of four categories. They either did not exist; or, if they did exist, the databases were woefully incomplete, were fragmented and specific to the proprietary needs of the major public and private landowners in the area or were based on incompatible scientific protocols (an apples versus oranges problem). Moreover, the Blackfoot watershed, as with so many other awe-inspiring, beautiful, relatively wild locations throughout the American West, was facing growing development pressures that threatened to transform the relatively tranquil, rustic, and unspoiled area into something far different and less desirable, at least from the perspective of most Blackfoot watershed residents.

In short, in 1990, Jim Stone and Greg Neudecker faced a scenario in which the sheer complexity of trying to manage across the entire 1.5 million acre landscape was daunting, the condition of natural resource problems was extremely poor and getting worse, the scientific information needed to move forward effectively was lacking, the community fabric was in tatters, with distrust and vindictiveness replacing productive discussion and collective problem solving, and development pressures were relentless and only likely to grow (Ash Institute 2006; Weber 2009).

Working together, these two leaders were instrumental in founding the Blackfoot Challenge (BC) in 1993 as the primary vehicle for pursuing improved collective governance of, and problem resolution in, the Blackfoot watershed. The BC is a comprehensive collaborative governance arrangement that includes the USFWS along with ranchers, environmentalists, timber interests, recreation groups, state and local agency administrators, other federal agency officials, watershed landowners, and citizens. Stakeholders meet at least once monthly, with meetings open to anyone; they meet socially at their annual community barbeque in Ovando, Montana; and, in the case of massive projects, such as the Blackfoot Community Forest Project,[3] they meet weekly with the community over an extended period of time (153 weekly meetings were held on the Blackfoot Community Project alone). The BC also regularly hosts stewardship outreach (workshops), demonstration projects, and watershed/community tours (six to eight each year), while an extensive education and outreach program is used to teach citizens the value of a cooperative conservation approach. The educational outreach alone annually involves over 700 school children in a watershed with a total population of 8,000 (Ash Institute 2006).

If the clock is moved forward to July, 2006, what do we find? We find that Stone is still a Montana rancher and Neudecker still a federal regulatory official with the USFWS. However, instead of being total strangers, they are now friends and colleagues, and we find them on stage together at Harvard University's Kennedy School of Government to receive the Ash Institute's prestigious annual Innovations in American Government Award. The terrifically competitive Innovations award (with more than 1,100 applicants and only 7 winners) given to Neudecker and Stone is the result of over fifteen years of hard work as coleaders of the Blackfoot Challenge. The final site report from the Innovations competition describes the multifaceted, multistakeholder cooperative conservation endeavor as:

An exemplary collaborative effort that is engaging local communities in public problem solving and is forging strong, productive links between government agencies—both federal and state—and local expertise. . . . [It] offers an innovative and pioneering cooperative approach to the complex, and typically politically difficult, problem of restoring, managing, and sustaining the 1.5 million acre Blackfoot watershed's biologically rich natural resources, while simultaneously conserving rural lifestyles and livelihoods. If replicated across America's rural, low density watersheds, which are now recognized as being the new frontline in the battle for restoring and maintaining healthy stocks of endangered species (e.g., salmon, steelhead, bull trout, grizzlies, wolves, etc.), forest, rangeland, grassland and riparian health, and biodiversity, more generally, this significant and measurably effective cooperative program may well become a critical, and perhaps the defining, template for how successfully to marry the management of communities with the preservation and enhancement of nature. (Ash Institute 2006, 1)

How did Stone and Neudecker get to this point of high trust, strong coordination, and effective management of the watershed?

Moving Toward Resilience

The investigation of watershed governance in the Blackfoot region of Montana reveals the presence of a series of purposive steps and factors instrumental to building the foundation for resilience. Moving the watershed community from the tough original condition of low trust, poor coordination, and ineffective management to a robust, integrated culture capable of resilience required the following:

- A common sense, strategic approach to early problem-solving choices
- Collectively agreed-upon new ideas
- specific governance philosophy

Together, these three variables not only helped to solve collective problems and build trust, but also helped to foster the free flow of knowledge so central to the dynamics of flexibility, adaptability, and ultimately resilience.

A Common-Sense, Strategic Approach to Early Problem-Solving Choices

Given the diverse backgrounds, interests, and prior battles within the Blackfoot watershed community, the relationships among the stakeholders during the initial years of the Blackfoot Challenge were defined by a high degree of mistrust and a belief that they shared little in common. During this time of high risk for the nascent relationships, the leaders and stakeholders fully recognized that their first and foremost task was to rebuild the frayed relationships and establish enough trust to get people talking to each other and sharing the kinds of information necessary for managing and hopefully resolving, or minimizing, the many public problems facing the watershed community. Toward this end, the BC ended up crafting and adopting what can be labeled a *common-sense approach to early problem-solving choices* (personal interviews 2008). There are six key elements in the common-sense, early problem-solving approach.

Lead Agencies Adopt a Nonconfrontational Public Outreach Approach

Lead agencies put most of their effort into disseminating information that explains and clarifies the problem set in terms of problem severity, along with the legal parameters and obligations associated with such problems. As part of this information, agency representatives explain to stakeholders the distribution of responsibilities for resolving the problem(s), and the pros and cons to stakeholders of various alternative methods/approaches for problem resolution. Another example of this information involves the expectations for government employees assigned to work in the watershed. While this last concept developed over time out of Greg Neudecker's (USFWS) initial method for approaching the community, it is now written into job descriptions in several state and federal agencies working in the Blackfoot. The basics include the recognition that trust-based relationships are the key to long-term problem-solving success in such wicked problem settings.

The new guy in town is literally expected to get nothing or very little done programmatically for the first two years. Why? Because you have to build trust first. You cannot push things too fast and tell folks what to do in order to meet only agency-based goals. . . . And people won't listen to you, even if you are the biggest expert in the room, you have to get them to trust you by taking the proper respectful "partnership" attitude. Then they will listen and you will be amazed at how hard they will work with you to get "agency" things done. (personal interview 2008).

Adopt a Shared "Cost of Compliance" Approach and Be Persistent in the Search for Project Funding

A shared approach reinforces the "we're in this together" psychology of partnership efforts. It means that individual landowners, or those in the regulated community, do not have to shoulder the entire burden or responsibility of compliance, whether in terms of funding compliance efforts or in seeking out external funding sources.

Reduce Objective Uncertainties in the Wicked Problem Setting

The next step is collecting information, scientific and otherwise, to create a better understanding of the interdependencies and parameters of the wicked problem setting, and as "a method for minimizing, and, if we're lucky, removing politics from early decision-making by creating a common base of information" (personal interview 2006). This step is necessary for employing the discriminate decision strategy described as follows.

Exercise Pragmatism when Choosing Problems

Stated differently, pragmatism calls for attacking first those problems most likely to meet with management and implementation success. The concept, according to a Blackfoot Challenge stakeholder, is that "crawling comes before walking, and walking comes before running" (personal interview 2006). The three key parts to the pragmatic problem selection approach are the following:

1. *Think politically, tread softly.* Pursue less controversial, lower-risk problems so as not to engender political opposition from stakeholders (personal interviews 2006). This element is best captured in the Challenge's "80-20" approach to problem solving in the early years. This choice methodology focuses participant energy "on the 80 percent of problems we can all agree on, rather than the 20 percent that divide us" (personal interview 2006). As a result, the problems located in the 80 percent segment reduce uncertainty within the collective by posing limited political risks to individual participants' interests.

2. *Adopt a discriminate, or prioritized, decision strategy.* This decision strategy targets efforts and resources at areas with the highest likelihood of investment "payback." In this sense, "the new information and science [described previously] is used to help us get the biggest bang for the buck" (personal interview 2006). This decision approach explicitly acknowledges that resources, whether financial, human, or otherwise, are scarce; and the approach links ecological importance and the degradation level of the "problem" in question to the feasibility and degree of "problem" improvement likely to occur for any given amount of resources applied.

3. *Build a reputation for success.* Focus attention on more tractable, smaller problems as a way of increasing the probability of successful out-

comes, and make headway on bigger, more widespread problems through the use of "demonstration" projects. This element allows participants *and* outsiders to see tangible proof of progress, allows stakeholders and community members to benefit directly from the successful programs, and, to the extent success occurs, makes it easier to win over skeptics and build trust for future collaborative problem-solving efforts. For example, in many rural western U.S. communities, when it comes to projects designed to improve the ecology and environment, landowners are often loathe to grant physical access to their parcels of private property (Weber 2003). Yet, as was practiced in the BC case (without too much risk on the part of landowners), a small demonstration project allows landowners to see if proponents of the new collaborative approach can and will deliver on their stated promises. Will the outcomes be win-win? Will proponents really treat their property, property rights, and traditional land-uses (i.e., farming, forestry, ranching) with appropriate respect when implementing the project? Strategically, BC stakeholders viewed such demonstration projects as a critical method for convincing politically and/or ecologically important individual property owners to support and, in the best case; help build the new collaborative institution (personal interviews 2006). As part of building a reputation for success, the BC adhered to a basic concept associated with responsible fiscal stewardship—"we work hard to make sure that our resources are targeted properly and [therefore] spent effectively. This is an important reason why funders keep coming back. They like the way we manage their money" (personal interview 2008).

Forego Short-term Benefits in Isolated Cases for Potential Long-term Collective Gains

Decisions should avoid deterrence-based enforcement actions (e.g., punishment in forms of fines, bad publicity for the violator, singling out the violator as a bad apple, imprisonment) as much as possible and engage in "encouraging people to do the right thing and physical demonstrations of how such 'right things' can be done" (personal interviews 2006). The concept here is that such an approach will be more likely to elicit, or induce, the kinds of positive compliance responses required for programmatic success over the long-term. A subset of this item involves not taking advantage of voluntarily provided private information for self-interested, short-term gains, whether in terms of compliance gains or benefits particular to any one group (see also Ayres and Braithwaite 1992; Weber 1998).

Selective Partnering

The Blackfoot Challenge chooses its partners carefully. Over the years they have successfully partnered with over a hundred organizations and agencies, yet "the BC does not partner with just anyone and does not like getting involved mid-stream in other group's projects. Partners must have the watershed community's interests at heart; they must be focused on the broader public interest as defined by the BC mission" (personal interview 2008). This choice is why the BC has been "willing to refuse funding or program ideas if it means compromising our mission. We'd rather stay true to our core principles, the things that we worked out together, than risk it all for a few more dollars" (personal interviews 2006, 2008).

Collectively Agreed-Upon New Ideas

The common-sense approach to early problem solving in the Blackfoot Challenge case matters because it is directly connected to generating new-found trust among environmentalists, ranchers, recreationists (hunters, fishers, hikers, campers, rafters, off-road vehicle enthusiasts), small business owners, government officials from all three levels, timber interests, and other landowners. Many of these actors were erstwhile adversaries, while others were "cautious residents not used to working together on behalf of common causes" (personal interview 2008). By itself, however, the common-sense approach was not enough to sustain collective trust over time (personal interviews 2008). This inability was in part because rationality is not the only factor informing human choice and in part be-cause the approach does not address the full range of institutional elements affecting behavior. "A combination of formal rules, informal constraints, and their enforcement characteristics" are also critical to understanding choices and institutional change (North 1990; 2005, 5–6; Ellickson 1991; Knott and Miller 1987). North (2005), in agreement with Hayek (1952), fleshes out the concept that the informal constraint of ideas is of particular importance to understanding institutional change because they, along with formal rules, "shape our present and influence our future" (North 2005, 6).[4] In fact, a key piece of the institutional change puzzle that commands our attention in the Blackfoot watershed involves a particular set of *new ideas* around which public and private stakeholders coalesced. These new ideas, or shared norms (for understanding public problems, the commu-nity itself, and the relationships among competing ideas, interests, actors, and sectors of society) were essential to building a lasting integrative cul-ture that supports collective interests, especially those related to fostering simultaneously healthier, more sustainable natural and human systems within the watershed. Taken together they became a broad conceptual framework for guiding stakeholder interaction as participants discussed and attempted to manage and resolve the public problems facing the Blackfoot watershed. These norms were not written down; rather they served as an informal set of rules emphasizing the shared values and understandings of their "place"—the Blackfoot watershed—that then defined the parameters, hence the constraints and outer limits of the collaborative's problem-solving efforts.[5]

Importantly, the participants in the Blackfoot Challenge came together initially on the basis of very basic and general ideas—we have a series of problems, we can do better, and our "piece of Montana" is worth fighting for (personal interviews 2006). It was not until after the stakeholders—the original leaders, along with dozens of other watershed stakeholders—came together and started deliberating over a new future for the watershed, however, that the new ideas ended up being crafted, or discovered. In this way, the initial collaborative interaction of a diverse set of stakeholders that was fostered by the strategic, common-sense approach to problem solving created a constructive foundation out of which trust could emerge; and that trust set the stage for the exploration and adoption of a set of ideas that succeeded in enveloping, or cosseting, the inevitable self-interest of stakeholders by framing it as something that must *always* be balanced against others' legitimate goals (as well as against broader, collectively defined public interests). The idea-based foundation also succeeded in framing, or constraining, the behavior and messages conveyed by entrepreneurial leaders and other stakeholders by emphasizing common ground and offering a conceptual outline of what was acceptable and what was not. Moreover, each of the ideas outlined in the following material recognizes and seeks to harmonize, reconcile and better manage the inherent conflicts within the existing community. Put another way, the voluntary acceptance of new ideas for guiding the community forward emphasized shared values and a common perspective on the problems being encountered, thereby becoming a powerful, if abstract tool for facilitating mutually beneficial agreements by encouraging a community-oriented structure to frame stakeholder interaction.

In short, these new "ideas" *decreased* the risks (and hence uncertainty) associated with participant behavior within the Blackfoot Challenge collaborative, thereby fostering even more trust, the sharing of private information so critical to enduring and innovative solutions, and the willingness to sacrifice, if necessary, some personal gain for the collective good of the watershed and its inhabitants.[6] Six new ideas that help to explain the transition between poor antecedent conditions and the development of an integrative culture in the Blackfoot watershed are discussed next.

A Common, Core Vision of Place

Stakeholders in the BC "love . . . their place—the Blackfoot area. The pristine beauty, the great views, the clean air, the feeling of being connected to the natural landscape and having to depend on it for a living, [and] the solitude gave people something to fight for, to try to preserve" (personal interview 2006). Kemmis (1990) argues that a commitment to "place" can be a catalyst for self-governance. A place commitment mobilizes citizens to care enough to participate in the act of governing "their" place by reminding community members of what they share in common—reliance on the natural landscape (Kemmis 1990, 78). Sturtevant and Lange (1995, 10), for their part, find that the "strong attachment to place" drives community members to de-emphasize self-interested behavior. Members "agree to put their interests, . . . and [their] sense of duty to represent . . . [their own] particular perspective . . . aside in the interest of the collective and [the] ecosystem." Moreover, the commitment to place (especially in small-scale watershed efforts like the Blackfoot case) tends to "frame . . . watershed issues . . . as a direct relationship between watershed health and community well-being" and transforms participants' perspectives (Cheng and Daniels 2005, 30). They "beg[i]n to view themselves as members of a shared community, a new ingroup, . . . to which an individual perceives membership and attributes loyalty and a sense of belonging. Ingroup members tend to perceive one another as trustworthy and correct in their motives" (Cheng and Daniels 2005, 30).

In addition, widespread agreement on the characteristics defining the Blackfoot watershed—a common, core vision of their place—reminded BC participants that they shared more in common than they once believed possible. The shared vision centered on general characteristics capable of "attracting, and continuing to attract, people interested in a classic western landscape with rugged natural features, few people, and limited development" (personal interview, May, 2006). Key characteristics included the preservation of a rustic, rural setting, wide open spaces, a working landscape involving traditional livelihoods (e.g., ranching, farming, logging), a healthy, vibrant, visible nature (wildlife and nature-based aesthetics are part of the community experience), and limited conveniences in terms of retail shopping, restaurant diversity, and access to urban-style malls (personal interviews, May, 2006).

In short, the common, core vision of a "place" (that they were all committed to) became an idea fostering new, positive, trust-based community bonds among previously estranged Blackfoot stakeholders, thus helping to alleviate the lack of propitious socially based antecedent conditions.

The Equity-based, Holistic Mission

Blackfoot Challenge stakeholders rejected zero sum thinking in their approach to problem solving and instead embraced a new approach to problem solving grounded in equity and holism. This new way of thinking accepts that multiple policy goals each hold equal claim on the substance of decisions (see also Raymond 2003, 26–27; Weber, 2000). Specifically, stakeholders agreed that restoration and preservation of the environment, economy, and community for the long-term defined the common *policy* ground toward which each would devote his or her time, resources, and energies. The belief in positive sum (win-win) outcomes in which all stakeholders could benefit strengthened each participant's connection to each other and to the collective whole because "it promoted the idea that everyone was in it together" (personal interviews 2006). Embracing and implementing this idea did not mean that the inevitable trade-offs were ignored; rather, the BC knew that individual decisions might often favor one policy domain over another. The more important test for this idea involved the balance of outcomes over time and whether that balance adhered to the equity-based holism contained within the environment, economy, and community approach (personal interviews, May, 2006; see also Weber 2003, chapter 3). Chief among the programmatic examples of this idea in action is the Blackfoot Community Forest Project. This is a comprehensive and pioneering effort to restore the ecological and biological integrity of 88,000 acres of Blackfoot land by purchasing private land from Plum Creek Timber, deeding it over to the U.S. Forest Service (Lolo National Forest) in perpetuity, and creating a large common public, or community, area that is jointly owned and managed by community stakeholders. Another such example is the extensive application of conservation easements that allow landowners to continue working the land, while also providing environmental protection. These easements now cover 90,000 acres of the total of 300,000 privately owned acres in the watershed.[7] In addition, the easements, once signed by the landowner, are vehicles for "building trusts between the Challenge and landowners because owners see that we value them and their livelihood. This often opens the door to additional environmental restoration and water conservation projects on the property" (personal interview 2006).

Softening the Edges of the Lockean View of Property Rights

The intrinsic Lockean perspective on property rights has long been the dominant perspective in the Blackfoot watershed just as it has been throughout most of the American West.[8] Individuals stake a legal claim to a particular piece of property as owner and then can use and manage it as they see fit (subject to some basic restrictions such as nuisance, for example). With respect to water, the prior appropriations doctrine holds sway and permits those who develop and use water for certain consumptive beneficial uses (e.g., agriculture, industrial processes, domestic consumption) to have virtually complete control over the resource, with seniority of the right in question being the key to understanding the distribution of control (Raymond 2003).

The dominant Lockean perspective was challenged with a competing *instrumentalist* view on property found in many of the environmental and social policy laws crafted during the 1960s and 1970s. From this perspective, "property is simply a human institution created to further the equitable ends of society. It is therefore subject to change to meet evolving social goals. . . . Property . . . exists at the continued pleasure of the political system" (Raymond 2003, 45–46; see also Cohen 1967). As a result, the structure of property rights favored in contemporary environmental laws at both the state and federal levels tended to layer *forced* collective (social) obligations onto the intrinsic right of property ownership.

Yet, the new idea in the BC did not favor either of these fundamentally opposed property frameworks at the expense of the other. Instead, community members opted for an integrated idea that respected both as legitimate. The new balanced conception of property respects individual claims to property ownership, control, and usage to the extent they are beneficial, but voluntarily accepts the imposition of collective responsibilities on such rights per the instrumentalist framework to the extent they are not.[9] Thus explicit consideration of community needs and environmental protection is key, as illustrated by the following examples:

• Valuing endangered species as an accepted part of the larger watershed

• Allowing contractors physical access to private property for the purpose of reconstructing and restoring natural stream pathways and dynamics (in order to restore damaged riparian areas and endangered fish populations)

• Willingly sharing the sacrifices required by inadequate water resources during periods of drought

• Carving out and collectively managing a new 88,000 acre "community" forest according to collective values (privately owned but managed according to collective rules developed within the watershed) (Ash Institute 2006)

Importantly, property owners are not relaxing their intrinsic rights without conditions, or without using their property "power" to gain quid pro quo protections against the uncertainties inherent in sharing "control" over their property. In the conditions case, for example, individual ranchers and farmers with senior water rights are willing to take less than their legal share of water (property) in drought years in order to ensure that their fellow community members' livelihoods are more viable over the long-term. But they are not willing to do this scaling back if the cost of their generosity is the eventual loss of their "earned" water right (personal interviews, May, 2006). In the bargaining case, perhaps the best example in the Blackfoot involves endangered grizzly bears. Ranchers understand the aesthetic, wilderness, and ecological value grizzlies bring to this part of Montana, and they are willing to support the active encouragement of a larger population of bears—but not without specific programs taken to minimize the risks to their substantial investments in livestock (e.g., electric fences around calving yards; carcass pickups). In each case, the willingness to share control over the property right is coupled with guaranteed protections that translate the uncertainty into a manageable risk that property owners are then willing to take for the sake of the collective good.

Changes in Interpersonal Perspectives: From Adversaries to Neighbors

In the years prior to the Blackfoot Challenge, defining characteristics of interpersonal relationships within the watershed included hostile perceptions of others and "their agendas," simplistic and negative stereotypes of others with different interests and perspectives, and mutual fear (personal interviews 2006). Yet stakeholders coalesced around the idea that success in getting to the collective good required "[us] to stop thinking of everyone else as an enemy . . . [And] understand . . . that we're all in this together as neighbors" (personal interview 2006).

[B]eing neighborly focuses stakeholders on the importance of relationship-building and a desire for positive social interaction, while simultaneously reinforcing the notion that helpfulness toward others helps to facilitate collective problem solving efforts. As applied in the BC case, neighbors are those who:

- Practice reciprocity with others and willingly help others when asked,
- Recognize an obligation to some collective purpose or goal beyond the self,
- Eschew threats, intimidation, and violence, and instead embraces discussion and compromise as a primary means for achieving individual and collective goals.

• Recognize and tolerate differences with others,
• Treats others with civility, respect, honesty, and integrity (personal interviews 2006).

Redefining the Problem Set

Instead of being satisfied with public problems being defined as discrete, controllable, fixed entities, and fragmented according to their bureaucratically defined, jurisdictional "stovepipes," Blackfoot stakeholders accepted that the reality of the problem set they were dealing with had changed in fundamental ways. Problems in the watershed were "part of an integrated whole," "always connected to something else," and "loaded with uncertainty and confusion because you almost never knew when you made one part better or worse what would happen to the other parts" (personal interview 2006). Nor was it possible, according to one stakeholder, to "completely solve a problem. I mean, seriously, even if we did our best to contain the non-native noxious weed problem, or the fish population problem, does anyone think that with more and more visitors coming into the Blackfoot every year we will ever get completely on top of these and then say, OK, let's turn our attention to something else?" (personal interview 2006). Further, stakeholders (many of whom depend directly on natural systems for their livelihood's success) view nature as both a formidable ally and enemy that can never be controlled; but that nature has to be accounted for in any management plan, particularly in terms of people having enough flexibility to accommodate the "whims of mother nature" (personal interview 2006).

The idea is not new that the problems central to reversing the decline and degradation of the communities and natural resources in the watershed were overlapping and interdependent, complex, relentless, and more amenable to an experimental, integrated and adaptive approach. Nor was the concept that human systems, if they are to be effective over the long-term, need to account for and work with, rather than against, natural system processes.[10] However, consider the transition to a collaborative governance arrangement in this case. This idea *is* new and remarkable in the Blackfoot context precisely because of the arrangement's embrace across the full swath of stakeholders, whether they were environmentalists, ranchers, government officials, timber interests, or another interest group.

The Shape of Knowledge: The Kinds that Matter

Blackfoot Challenge stakeholders believe that traditional sources of knowledge such as the physical and natural sciences (e.g., silviculture, biology, ecology, chemistry) are too narrow and limited in their ability to capture the full complexity of ecological interaction. Further, that these traditional sources are incapable, by definition, of mapping or understanding the critical human dimensions—social, political, economic, and administrative—through which any scientific conclusions necessarily must be filtered. Similarly, stakeholders believed that the traditional bureaucratic and interest group repositories of information that tend to dominate formal problem-solving exercises needed leavening with the local, practical expertise of those community members most practiced, or familiar with particular problems and the capacities of the human and natural systems in question (see also Scott 1998, 309–341). The inclusion of social science and community-based "folk knowledge"[11] in problem solving processes not only brings new and valued information to the table, but also "increases the likelihood that the dynamic of human institutions . . . will be matched with that of ecological processes to the greatest extent possible, . . . [thus] produc[ing] a more robust set of alternatives for solving problems, and a more reliable and realistic estimate of the parameters affecting program success."[12]

The idea of a broad knowledge base highlights the interdependence among stakeholders by promising more effective governance outcomes *if* stakeholders will pool their knowledge assets. It also flattens power within the group by removing the knowledge monopoly enjoyed by some and elevating the value added by practice-based and human systems knowledge, thus giving a larger array of stakeholders influence within the collective decision process. Taken together, the new sense of interdependence and the acceptance of knowledge-based power sharing emanating from the broad knowledge-base idea serve as informal constraints on stakeholder behavior by favoring cooperative practices more so than other behaviors.

Governance Philosophy: The Mindset of Collaborative Capacity Builders

The knowledge sending, receiving, and integration challenges associated with wicked problems such as climate change necessarily involve multiple organizations, professions, and a wide range of participants with contrasting knowledge needs, demands, and perspectives. The key challenge is knitting together the knowledge possessed by the various actors and institutions into a coherent, usable whole (O'Toole 1997, 48). Essential lines of inquiry to address this challenge examine the dimensions, characteristics, and maturity of collaborative governance structures; whether, when, and how managers might use analytic tools; and whether, when, and how to apply particular management skills or strategies. Yet the "knowledge" challenge so central to the construction of a collaborative integrative culture that underpins resilience in Climate Protected Communities (CPC) suggests the need to push the literature to consider the "softer" aspects of collaborative management as well.

Taking from the Weber and Khademian (2008b) work on wicked problem collaboratives in urban development, environmental policy, and disaster response policy, the leaders of the Blackfoot Challenge approached the collaborative management task from the unique "mindset" of a collaborative capacity builder (CCB). A CCB is someone who either by legal authority, expertise valued within the collaborative, reputation as an honest broker, or some combination of the three, has been accorded a lead role in a collaborative's problem-solving exercises. In addition, stakeholders within the Blackfoot watershed recognize a CCB as someone having a long-term stake in and commitment to building collaborative capacity for continuously addressing wicked problems. The practical effect of the BC's perspective on CCBs means that while public managers inevitably will be involved in addressing wicked problems, CCBs do not always need to be government leaders (personal interviews 2006, 2008).

The CCB mindset helps to provide a context within which leaders consider design and function, and the application of skills, strategies, and analytics. It can be thought of as values (Selznick 1957) [a cohering logic (LaPorte 1996) or governing philosophy (Heclo 1978)] that guide the practices and behavior of organization members and that are essential to institutional success.[13] The governing philosophy focuses not only on what the organization does, but also how the organization does its work—its "distinctive competence"—and how it defines the relationship between government and society (Weber and Khademian 2008a).

The Blackfoot Challenge case provides additional confirmation of the initial CCB "mindset" framework developed by Weber and Khademian (2008a). There are five commitments that frame the task of sending, receiving, and integrating knowledge central to building resilience.[5]

A Commitment to Governance with Government

The CCB mindset suggests that in a situation where public problem interdependencies among government, private, and nonprofit sectors are inevitable, government has a responsibility to play a prominent role (Klijn and Koppenjan 2000; Weber and Khademian 2008a). The flip side of this element is the belief that government alone *cannot* "solve" wicked problems with connotations of finality.

This commitment projects a government and managerial role in collaboratives that is both less and more. The governance with government premise is less because it is *not* about government agencies bearing the entire burden of problem definition, program design, funding, and the implementation of programs designed with final solutions in mind. Indeed, this concept is fundamental to the knowledge challenge posed by wicked problems. Precisely because the definition of a problem, the design of a capacity to address it, responsibilities for funding and implementation will not be concentrated in a single government entity, the need to share, understand, and integrate diverse understandings of the wicked problem is paramount. This commitment is more, however, because it requires public managers to be accountable for the programs under their guidance, while also facilitating collaboration across organizational and government boundaries, between the public and private sectors, and among officials, professionals, and members of the public. But the authority of a government agency can also play a critical role in soliciting, sharing, and integrating knowledge among participants in a collaborative setting. From this perspective, government can be a catalyst for producing broad, enduring capacity for addressing, managing, and coping with wicked problems. It also means that managers who accept this commitment are less concerned about who, or what, agency or actor gets the credit for success but whether the problem gets addressed and, given its relentless character, continues to receive attention.

A Commitment to Govern within the Rules, Yet Think Creatively and Focus on Learning

Collaborative capacity builders accept existing rules (established by an agency, a legislative or executive mandate, or existing policy) as a necessary beginning of the process to build long-term capacities to address wicked problems, but not totally sufficient. Wicked problems, by their nature, defy categorization within a strict rules-based system that seeks to divide complex systems and problems into more manageable parts; this system assumes that the causal relationships within the wicked problem set are clear and identifiable. The complexity and uncertainty of knowledge transfer and the creation of new knowledge associated with wicked problems means that "anticipatory" rules-based actions are bound to be inadequate. This commitment reflects a balance between the public manager as "conservator" (Terry 1993) and as "entrepreneur" (Moore 1995). It is recognition of democratically defined rules that place necessary boundaries on permissible actions, combined with openness to new ideas expressed within the collaborative governance arrangement that could help to build new competencies for the long-term management of wicked problems. It is also recognition that "by the book" problem solving, or a heavy rules-oriented approach, is unlikely to create the kinds of relationships among stakeholders required for the sending, receiving, and integration of knowledge needed for long-term problem-solving capacity (Bardach and Kagan 1982).

In the collaborative Blackfoot watershed governance effort, this strategy translates into a decision culture encouraging trial and error, and the termination and/or revamping of programs midstream if they are not working well. As part of this method, mistakes are not treated as punishable offenses but rather as opportunities for learning more about the cause and effect dynamic associated with a particular set of problems. The key for programs is whether people are able to take the lessons learned and continue moving the ball forward toward agreed-upon goals. The basic decision structure of the BC supports this task. While, as one might expect, there are several standing committees, stakeholders are constantly creating new problem-specific committees for ideas that have been initially vetted and approved by the collaborative as holding high potential for successfully addressing a major collective problem(s). These committees are designed to more fully explore the costs, benefits, and potential ramifications associated with a problem(s) and then report back to the BC once feasible options have been devised (personal interviews 2008).

A Commitment to Collaboratives as Mutual-Aid Partnerships with Society
Collaborative capacity builders view citizens and other organizations, including government entities and nonprofits, as partners.[6] Potential participants in the collaborative are viewed as possible helpers who nevertheless face legitimate constraints on collective action, including narrow or limited knowledge about the scope and severity of the problem, a fear that acting alone will do little to resolve the larger problem, limited individual resources, and the fear that government authorities will not listen to, much less incorporate and allow, innovative solutions produced by those outside the agency that has formal jurisdiction over the problem. This open approach is difficult; managers under intense public scrutiny—as managers dealing with wicked problems often are—might be inclined to adopt a "fortress" mentality as a means to shut out criticism (and potentially useful problem-solving ideas) and rely on internal agency expertise and narrowly apply that expertise without public interference (Goldsmith and Eggers 2004).

In the effort to form partnerships, the CCB views authority and expertise as tools that allow managers to "serve" citizens (personal interview 2008). The flip side is that the blunt, coercive use of formal authority in collaborative scenarios is of limited value, particularly when encouraging participants to send, receive, and integrate knowledge for long-term capacity to address a wicked problem[7]—such an approach risks breeding resistance and alienating the very people necessary for successfully managing a particular wicked problem. In the Blackfoot case, stakeholders call this concept "leading from behind." "It is not about your [individual leadership] success, it's about 'we,' the group's success. The community decides how to proceed and we just facilitate that thing which is about more than yourself, it's about being part of something bigger and it is about sharing or giving credit to others" (personal interview 2008).

This commitment to servant leadership does not view experts and managers as having all the answers; expertise is one source of knowledge, and public management is just that—management of problems and decision mechanisms *within a democracy*. More specifically, the management role is understood to be facilitative (Denhardt and Denhardt 2000). A "helper," or servant manager, not only treats members of the collaborative with appropriate respect[7] and actively solicits their input, but also takes responsibility for helping build the capacities all participants need for addressing wicked problems (Reich 1990; Roberts 2002). To address the knowledge challenge, the manager as facilitator in a mutual-aid partnership is more likely to draw out different sources of knowledge to address the wicked problem, and the manager will play a role in sharing the knowledge across the collaborative governance arrangement.

The emphasis on a mutual-aid partnership has led to what one Blackfoot watershed stakeholder describes as a:

monumental change. Within a very short time after the Blackfoot Challenge started working on things, I noticed a turnaround in how the people working the land were treated by the government officials working with the Challenge. Instead of irritation and feeling like we bother them and have nothing important to add [when it comes to public problems they are responsible for], they now ask for my take on things. They ask, "How would you do this? If we were to do this, would this work on your piece of land?" Or, "How can we help you with your problems?" They always used to just present the science and tell us what we had to do to help *them* with their problems. Then they would expect us to hop to it. But now they are willing to listen to the things we know from having lived here and worked here for so long. It's really different (personal interview 2006).

The Intrinsic Inseparability of Performance, Capacity, and Accountability
Precisely because wicked problems are, by definition, hard to define and
solutions remain elusive, an important component of the CCB mindset
links performance and accountability. It does so by emphasizing the capacity of the collaborative both to produce results and demonstrate ongoing
accountability to a wide range of stakeholders whose participation in
the collaborative is essential for long-term management of the wicked
problem at issue.

The *public* in public problems requires consideration of to whom, and
to what values, a program or policy is responsive. Wicked problems typically involve large sets of stakeholders up and down the formal political
authority structure (cutting across state, local, and federal jurisdictions),
across multiple policy areas and agencies, and individual citizens within
the affected communities. The attendant complexity and interdependency
are such that coercive solutions (or solutions responsive to only a few
interests) will not provide the kind of simultaneous, broad-based accountability, or an accountability system that maintains or improves accountability to local interests, private and public, without a corresponding
diminution of accountability to broader state, regional, and national
public interests, that is necessary to keep stakeholders collaboratively and
constructively engaged over the long-term (Weber 2003, 13). And if all
stakeholders do not stay constructively engaged, it is unlikely that wicked
problem-solving capacity (i.e., producing results) can be maintained for
the long-term. From this perspective, CCB managers recognize that capacity is about finding ways to create and sustain mechanisms for participation for all stakeholders, and about finding solutions or processes that
meet the needs of stakeholders across the board, *including government
at all appropriate levels.* Such needs are likely to include, among others,
mutual gain for all within a particular decision, mutual gain stemming
from the assurance of reciprocity across decisions over time, or a reasonable, mutually agreed sharing of burdens (e.g., implementation costs,
programmatic responsibilities, time, and personnel commitments). Yet,
meeting the needs of multiple, diverse stakeholders, thus building capacity for both performance and accountability, fundamentally requires the
sending, receiving, and integration of knowledge as well as the identification of new sources of knowledge applicable to collaborative governance
problems. And this requires both trust and transparency so that all the
knowledge "cards" are shared, or on the table, and so that a shared
understanding can be created of the old, stakeholder-centric knowledge
and the new, problem-specific knowledge being discovered within the

collaborative (Feldman and Khademian 2005; Weber and Khademian 2008a).

A Passion for, and Commitment to, the Collaborative Process

As previously noted, current literature focused on management addresses the authority of managers, the skills for collaboration, and the possible resources to build and sustain collaboratives. Yet, in addition to authority, skills, and resources, CCB managers working to address wicked problems appear to benefit to the extent they have an undeniable passion and commitment to the collaborative process. In an ongoing collaborative effort, the multiple organizations, people, and groups working together are really working out a new knowledge for the purposes of the collaborative governance arrangement. There will be inevitable conflicts between the objectives and values developed within the collaborative and those of organizations and other participants. Given this reality, managers need the energy to overcome resistance within their own organizations as well as within other participating organizations, and need to get collaborative members to share the knowledge that is hard won, to receive the knowledge from others, and to create a new knowledge that will facilitate the management of wicked problems. In short, CCBs accept that they have primary responsibility for convincing the full range of affected interests to credibly commit to collaborative arrangements and the expected mutual gain results, while also demonstrating a willingness to use their authority and the resources at their disposal to promote, enforce, and protect agreements arrived at collaboratively (Miller 1992; Weber 1998).

Conclusion

Precisely because we have had limited experiences with the unfolding climate change scenario impacting human communities, along with corresponding institutional responses and consequences, it makes scientific sense to draw lessons for resilient climate-protected communities from communities wrestling with, and successfully managing, other similar public problems. This reasoning is why watershed communities that have successfully managed complex social-ecological systems in the face of multiple challenges are good candidates for shedding light on the CPC governance "resilience" dilemma. Moreover, the Blackfoot Challenge watershed effort is clearly one of the more successful community-based collaboratives to be found in the United States (Ash Institute 2006; Weber 2009). The Challenge teaches us that constructing and maintaining a robust, integrative culture, at minimum, requires three things: a common-sense, strategic approach to early problem-solving choices, a set of collectively agreed ideas, and a governance philosophy that helps to facilitate the flow of communication and knowledge across interests, areas of expertise, and jurisdictions.

Even with this advance in our understanding of making the transition from tough conditions, there is still much work that needs to be done on the specific concepts presented here, especially with respect to the ideas and governance philosophy components. For example, the new ideas found in the Blackfoot worked well. But will the ideas work equally well in other settings given the natural variation between and among communities themselves, whether it is culture, economics, politics, or other key spheres of potential difference? And what of the collaborative capacity builders central to the governance philosophy component? Are they born or made? Do they develop through trusting interaction with others in the specific setting or do they deliberately adapt the governance philosophy to the enabling conditions of the problem and community setting? Or does it have more to do with particular personality traits and/or other types of pre-existing individual qualities of the leaders themselves? Or is it some combination of factors? Currently there is not an answer to this conundrum.

As well, the analysis thus far has specifically treated the climate change "resilience" challenge in an isolated fashion that disconnects individual community resilience efforts from the larger whole. This fact is why, while it is obviously important that we need to understand the variables contributing to resiliency at the community level of analysis, we must be careful not to ignore the essential value of redundancies to long-term community and system-based resilience success (Folke et al. 2005; Ruckelshaus et al. 2008). Part of the redundancy requirement will be resolved to the extent that many communities take on the CPC challenge, and to the extent that a broader national and/or regional governance system allows for discretion and experimentation within individual CPCs. This situation is because virtually every community is grounded in a different political, economic, and ecological context, and each community will "view" climate change challenges through different prisms, thus increasing the likelihood of varied programmatic responses, even to similar climate change problems. This governance logic is not a new one; rather it has long been associated with the concept of federalism, particularly the idea that smaller units of governance (e.g., states) are valuable laboratories of democracy that can be tapped for new and innovative ideas when addressing larger, complex problems (Derthick 2001). In short, the critical role played by redundancy in the resilience equation can be fulfilled to the extent that individual CPCs are cognizant of, communicating with, and willing to consider best practices for battling climate change that have been developed elsewhere.

At the same time, not all climate change issues will fit the community scale of governance, while allowing significant community-based control also increases the likelihood that coordination will suffer and/or trans-boundary conflicts will arise between communities (as at least some will choose to resolve problems by transferring their effects to others). This situation means that fully resolving the systemic CPC conundrum requires more research into the kinds of institutional structures and variables most likely to link across scales of action and to facilitate community-to-community communication and coordinated action as needed (e.g., Gerlak and Heikkila 2011).

Recognizing these additional challenges does not obviate the lessons learned here about the factors critical to effective *individual* climate-protected communities. Long-term success at establishing and preserving such community-based resilience will require a robust, integrative culture. But just as clearly, overall success will likely require that these climate-protected communities be nested within a larger network of CPCs connected together by a federalist type of hierarchical governance structure pursuing similar goals or offering facilitation of some type (Weber 2008). In the Blackfoot watershed case, for example, Greg Neudecker's actions and central involvement in the collaborative Challenge, though nontraditional by USFWS standards, had the active support of his immediate and regional superiors inside the agency (personal interviews 2008). However, if such an overarching structure is lacking, CPC communities will, at minimum, need government entities with authority over key elements of the climate change problem to stay out of the way and allow communities to forge ahead. This last lesson is not a new one for local communities seeking to manage natural resource dilemmas successfully (e.g., Ostrom 1990), but it is a critical one that applies here.

Notes

1. Folke et al. (2005) offer a more detailed definition: "the extent to which a system can absorb recurrent natural and human perturbations and continue to regenerate without slowly degrading or even unexpectedly flipping into less desirable states" (pp. 442–443).

2. See Weber and Khademian (2008a) for an extended discussion on wicked problem characteristics and associated public management challenges.

3. This is a comprehensive and pioneering effort to restore the ecological and biological integrity of 88,000 acres of Blackfoot land by purchasing private land from Plum Creek Timber, deeding it over to the U.S. Forest Service (Lolo National Forest) in perpetuity, and creating a large common public, or community, area that is jointly owned and managed by community stakeholders according to the "community values" developed within the many weekly community-wide meetings dedicated to this topic.

4. See also Gormley (1995, 54). Raymond (2003) likewise notes that norms "are social rules that control human behavior outside the legal apparatus of government" (p. 27).

5. The shared norms discussed here are different from the participant and/or professional norms discussed in other places devoted to the study of collaborative partnerships (see, e.g., Bardach 1998; Sabatier et al. 2005). The difference is that the shared norms as ideas presented here define mutually agreeable conceptual goals enveloping the collaborative interaction among the many, diverse stakeholders, while participant norms are focused on the terms with which stakeholders deliberate and engage one another as they strive to remain true to the broader, more abstract conceptual ideas as goals.

6. See also Miller (1992) and Weber (1998) for the critical importance of reducing uncertainty with respect to the behavior of others in collective action settings.

7. The acreage total counts all private property not owned and actively managed by Plum Creek Timber.

8. British philosopher John Locke (1632–1704) wrote a treatise in 1689 about property. He said that a person can own private property from nature, as long there are enough resources left for everyone else: "Nobody could think himself injured by the drinking of another man, though he took a good draught, who had a whole river of to quench his thirst."

9. Raymond (2003, 41, 57–63).

10. See, for examples, research into adaptive management (e.g., Lee 1993)and wicked problems (Roberts 1997).

11. Examples of folk knowledge in a community-based setting include the history of watershed drainage patterns, the resilience of and changes in particular forest ecosystems over time, recollections of historical conditions promoting the health of riparian areas and fisheries, or stored memories regarding what works and what does not when it comes to managing nature.

12. Weber (2003, 247). This tenet is a key idea of the emerging field of sustainability science (see Kates, Clark et al. 2001).

13. The concept of a mindset that can influence the efforts of top managers or leaders has a basis in business literature, where the role of a mindset in the pursuit of innovation, decentralization, alternative ways of conceptualizing problems and global competitiveness, for example, is examined (e.g., McGrath and MacMillan 2000).

References

Adger, W. N., K. Brown, J. Fairbrass, A. Jordan, J. Paavola, S. Rosendo, and G. Seyfang. 2000. Governance for sustainability: Towards a "thick" analysis of environmental decision-making. *Environment and Planning A* 35(6):1095–1110.

Ash Institute. July, 2006. *Innovations in American government: Site report, Montana Partners for Fish and Wildlife*. Cambridge, MA: Harvard University.

Ayres, I., and J. Braithwaite. 1992. *Responsive regulation: Transcending the deregulation debate*. New York: Oxford University Press.

Bardach, Eugene. 1998. *Getting Agencies to Work Together: The Practice and Theory of Managerial Craftsmanship*. Washington, D.C.: Brookings Institution Press.

Bardach, E., and R. Kagan. 1982. *Going by the book: The problem of regulatory unreasonableness*. Philadelphia, PA: Temple University.

Berkes, F., J. Colding, and C. Folke, eds. 2003. *Navigating social-ecological systems: Building resilience for complexity and change*. Cambridge, U.K.: Cambridge University Press.

Berkes, F., T. P. Hughes, R. S. Steneck, J. A. Wilson, D. R. Bellwood, B. Crona, C. Folke, L. H. Gunderson, H. M. Leslie, J. Norberg, M. Nyström, P. Olsson, H. Österblom, M. Scheffer, and B. Worm. 2006. Globalization, roving bandits, and marine resources. *Science* 311:1557–1558.

Cheng, A. S., and S. E. Daniels. 2005. Getting to "we": Examining the relationship between geographic scale and ingroup emergence in collaborative watershed planning. *Research in Human Ecology* 12(1):30–43.

Cohen, M. 1967. *Law and the social order*. North Haven, CT: Archon Books.

Danter, K. J., D. L. Griest, G. W. Mullins, and E. Norland. 2000. Organizational change as a component of ecosystem management. *Society & Natural Resources* 13:537–547.

Denhardt, R., and J. V. Denhardt. 2000. The new public service: Serving rather than steering. *Public Administration Review* 60(6):549–560.

Derthick, M. 2001. *Keeping the compound republic: Essays on American Federalism*. Washington, D.C.: The Brookings Institution.

Ellickson, R. 1991. *Order without law: How neighbors settle disputes*. Cambridge, MA: Harvard University Press.

Feldman, M. S., and A. M. Khademian. 2005. The role of public managers in inclusive management. Paper presented at the Public Management Research Conference (University of Southern California, Los Angeles, CA, September 29 to October 1, 2005).

Folke, C., J. Colding, and F. Berkes. 2003. Synthesis: Building resilience and adaptive capacity in social-ecological systems. In *Navigating social-ecological systems: Building resilience for complexity and change*, eds. F. Berkes, J. Colding, and C. Folke, 352–387. Cambridge, U.K.: Cambridge University Press.

Folke, C., T. Hahn, P. Olsson, and J. Norberg. 2005. Adaptive governance of social-ecological systems. *Annual Review of Environment and Resources* (30):441–473.

Gerlak, A., and T. Heikkila. 2011. Institutional adaptation and change in collaborative watershed management: An examination of the Northwest Power and Conservation Council's Fish and Wildlife Program. In *Transboundary river governance in the face of uncertainty*, ed. B. Cosens. Corvallis, OR: Oregon State University Press.

Goldsmith, S., and W. Eggers. 2004. *Governing by network: The new shape of the public sector*. Washington, D.C.: The Brookings Institution Press.

Gormley, William T., Jr. 1995. *Everybody's Children: Child Care as a Public Problem*. Washington, D.C.: The Brookings Institution.

Gunderson, L. H., S. R. Carpenter, C. Folke, P. Olsson, and G. D. Peterson. 2006. Water RATs (resilience, adaptability, and transformability) in lake and wetland social-ecological systems. *Ecology and Society* 11(1):16. Accessed 2-11-2011. Available at http://www.ecologyandsociety.org/vol11/iss1/art16/.

Gunderson, L. H., and C. S. Holling. 2002. *Panarchy: Understanding transformations in human and natural systems*. Washington, D.C.: Island Press.

Hayek, F. A. 1952. *The sensory order: An inquiry into the foundations of theoretical psychology*. Chicago, IL: University of Chicago Press.

Hayward, B. 2008. Let's talk about the weather: Decentering democratic debate about climate change. *Hypatia* 23(3):79–98.

Heclo, H. 1978. Issue networks and the executive establishment. In *The new American political system*, ed. A. King, 88–120.Washington, D.C.: The American Enterprise Institute.

Kates, R. W., W. C. Clark, R. Corell, J. M. Hall, C. C. Jaeger, I. Lowe, J. J. McCarthy, H. J. Schnellhuber, B. Bolin, N. M. Dickson, S. Faucheux, et al. 2001. "[Policy Forum: Environment and Development] Sustainability Science." *Science* 292 (April 27): 641-642.

Kemmis, D. 1990. *Community and the politics of place*. Norman, OK: University of Oklahoma Press.

Khademian, A. M. 2002. *Working with culture: The way the job gets done in public programs*. Washington, D.C.: CQ Press.

Kickert, W. J. W., E. H. Klijn, and J. F. M. Koppenjan, eds. 1997. *Managing complex networks*. London: Sage.

Klijn, E.-H., and J. F. M. Koppenjan. 2000. Public management and policy networks: Foundations to a network approach to governance. *Public Management* 2(2):135–158.

Knott, Jack H., and Gary J. Miller. 1987. *Reforming bureaucracy: The politics of institutional choice*. Englewood Cliffs, N.J.: Prentice-Hall.

La Porte, T. R. 1996. Shifting vantage and conceptual puzzles in understanding public organization networks. *Journal of Public Administration: Research and Theory* 6(1):49–74.

Lee, K. N. 1993. *Compass and Gyroscope: Integrating Science and Politics for the Environment.* Washington, D.C.: Island Press.

Ludwig, D., M. Mangel, and B. Haddad. 2001. Ecology, conservation, and public policy. *Annual Review of Ecology and Systematics* 32:481–517.

McGrath, R.G., and I. MacMillan. 2000. *The Entrepreneurial Mindset.* Boston: Harvard Business School Press.

McIntosh, R. J. 2000. Social memory in Mande. In *The way the wind blows: Climate, history, and human action*, eds. R. J. McIntosh, J. A. Tainter, and S. K. McIntosh, 141–180. New York: Columbia University Press.

Miller, G. J. 1992. *Managerial dilemmas: The political economy of hierarchy.* Cambridge, U.K.: Cambridge University Press.

Milward, H. B., and K. Provan. 1998. Measuring network structure. *Public Administration* 76:387–407.

Moore, M. H. 1995. *Creating public value: Strategic management in government.* Cambridge, MA: Harvard University Press.

North, D. C. 1990. *Institutions, institutional change, and economic performance.* Cambridge, U.K.: Cambridge University Press.

North, D. C. 2005. *Understanding the process of economic change.* Princeton, NJ: Princeton University Press.

Ostrom, E. 1990. *Governing the commons.* New York: Cambridge University Press.

O'Toole, L. J. 1997. Treating networks seriously: Practical and research-based agendas in public administration. *Public Administration Review* 57(1):45–52.

Ouchi, W. 1981. *Theory Z: How American business can meet the Japanese challenge.* Reading, MA: Addison-Wesley.

Raymond, L. 2003. *Private rights in public resources.* Washington, D.C.: Resources for the Future Press.

Reich, R., ed. 1990. *The power of public ideas.* Cambridge, MA: Harvard University Press.

Roberts, N. C. 1997. "Public deliberation: An alternative approach to crafting policy and setting direction. *Public Administration Review* 57 (2): 124–132.

Roberts, N. C. 2002. *The transformative power of dialogue.* New York: JAI Press.

Ruckelshaus, M., T. Klinger, N. Knowlton, and D. P. DeMaster. 2008. Marine ecosystem-based management in practice: Scientific and governance challenges. *BioScience* 58:53–63.

Sabatier, P., W. Focht, M. Lubell, Z. Trachtenberg, A. Vedlitz, and M. Matlock, eds. 2005. *Swimming Upstream: Collaborative Approaches to Watershed Management.* Cambridge, MA: MIT Press.

Scott, J. C. 1998. *Seeing like a state: How certain schemes to improve the human condition have failed.* New Haven, London: Yale University Press.

Selznick, P. 1957. *Leadership in administration: A sociological interpretation.* New York: Harper and Row.

Sturtevant, V. E., and J. I. Lange. 1995. *Applegate Partnership case study: Group dynamics and community context.* Seattle, WA: U.S. Forest Service, Pacific Northwest Research Station.

Terry, L. D. 2003. *Leadership of public bureaucracies: The administrator as conservator* (2nd ed.). Armonk, NY: M. E. Sharpe.

Thomas, C. W. 2003. *Bureaucratic landscapes: Interagency cooperation and the preservation of biodiversity.* Cambridge, MA: The MIT Press.

Weber, E. P. 1998. *Pluralism by the rules: Conflict and cooperation in environmental regulation.* Washington, D. C.: Georgetown University Press.

Weber, E. P. 2000. A new vanguard for the environment: Grass-roots ecosystem management as a new environmental movement. *Society & Natural Resources* 13:237–259.

Weber, E. P. 2003. *Bringing society back in: Grassroots ecosystem management, accountability, and sustainable communities.* Cambridge, MA: The MIT Press.

Weber, E. P. 2008. Facing and managing climate change: Assumptions, science, and governance responses. *Political Science* 60(1): 133–150.

Weber, E. P. 2009. A theory of institutional change for tough cases of collaboration: "Ideas" in the Blackfoot Watershed. *Public Administration Review* 69(2): 314–327.

Weber, E. P., and A. M. Khademian. 2008a. Wicked problems, knowledge challenges, and collaborative capacity builders in network settings. *Public Administration Review* 68(2): 334–349.

Weber, E. P., and A. M. Khademian. 2008b. Managing collaborative processes: Common practices, uncommon circumstances. *Administration & Society* 40(5): 431–464.

Wilson, J. Q. 1989. *Bureaucracy.* New York: The Free Press.

9

Collaborative Planning to Create a Network of Fisherfolk Organizations in the Caribbean

Patrick McConney and Terrence Phillips

In 2004 an initiative got underway to assist local (community-based) fisher-folk organizations in about a dozen Caribbean countries to strengthen or create strong national organizations, and then network these into a regional body capable of contributing to fisheries governance, among other things, at multiple levels. This idea still seems feasible today because the initiative has made reasonable progress (McIntosh et al. 2010), but there remains a long way to go. The strengthening and networking involved participatory action research with many different kinds of actors planning together, implementing plans and learning from the processes and outcomes amid much uncertainty. It is an example of collaborative planning and applied interdisciplinary research for improving governance in a complex adaptive social-ecological system.

This chapter illustrates the resilience thinking behind the conceptual design of the fisheries networking initiative that the authors are helping to shape by combining research and development. We address the process and outputs of collaborative planning being used and adapted to accomplish the initiative, which concerns tropical marine small-scale fisheries in the English-speaking Caribbean. The lessons learned provide insight into aspects of collaborative planning and resilience thinking that should be of interest to academics and practitioners everywhere.

Collaborative Planning in a Complex Adaptive System

The global diversity of small-scale fisheries causes the emergence of a universally accepted definition of them to be elusive (Berkes et al. 2001). However, the technological, ecological, institutional, social, cultural, economic, political, and many other dimensions of this diversity (along with other characteristics) have led to the consensus that small-scale fisheries are examples of complex adaptive social-ecological systems (Mahon et al.

2008). Fisheries scientists and managers are reporting that conventional approaches to fisheries ignore this complexity and, because of this lack of attention, small-scale fisheries have not performed well (Berkes et al. 2001, Mahon et al. 2008). Conventional approaches tend to assume that fisheries (both fish and people) are much more predictable and controllable than the evidence suggests. As these approaches fail, the global fisheries crisis of catch-declines (amid increasing demand) deepens (McGoodwin 1990, Kooiman et al. 2005). In response, some scholars are examining whether complex adaptive systems concepts have the potential to reform and improve how fisheries, from small to large scale, are managed (Bavinck et al. 2005, De Young, Charles, and Hjort, 2008). Determining how these concepts (such as resilience, adaptive capacity, and networks) can be used in planning and applied in practice is the challenge we face as a work in progress.

Collaborative planning can increase the effectiveness and power of networks (Booher and Innes 2002), which can in turn serve to enhance adaptive capacity and resilience in governance (Innes and Booher 2003). In this marine resource governance initiative, collaborative planning is about fisherfolk groups and agencies involved in fisheries management and development collaborating to create, integrate, and implement plans. This task calls upon fisheries planning theory and practice, communication across knowledge bases, consensus-building, and more. Network architecture is relevant to knowing if and how actors are linked in planning and plan implementation. Collective action and learning contribute to adaptive capacity and resilience in governance systems (Innes and Booher 2003); this concept is what is being sought in the Caribbean (Chakalall et al. 2007).

Caribbean Fisheries Governance

The aim of the initiative is to create strong national organizations networked into a regional entity that can adapt, be resilient at multiple levels, and play meaningful roles in fisheries governance. Noting the deficiencies in conventional approaches to fisheries, more attention to ecosystem approaches (FAO 2003) and governance (De Young et al. 2008) is needed. Before conventional approaches firmly take root in the Caribbean, the opportunity exists to investigate, develop, test, and propose alternative approaches based on concepts and models drawn from complex adaptive system and social-ecological system perspectives. We need to determine whether new alternative directions offer greater promise of success than the conventional (CERMES 2007c). There is a growing interest in the theory and practical application of alternative perspectives, especially with regard to governance of small-scale fisheries (Bavinck et al. 2005, Kooiman et al. 2005, Mahon et al. 2008). In order to plan such innovative approaches the context and current state of fisheries governance in the Caribbean must first be understood.

The Caribbean is culturally, ecologically, geographically, institutionally, politically, socially, and otherwise diverse and complex (Chakalall et al. 2007). One of the contributors to social-ecological complexity is that most resources, exploited and nonexploited, are shared across different marine jurisdictions and resource use regimes. Although few marine boundaries have been negotiated, it is clear that there must be considerable interaction of people and issues across jurisdictions due to proximity (figure 9.1); yet the need for collaboration in fisheries governance is still often underestimated (Chakalall et al. 1998, 2007).

To address this gap in fisheries governance, the Caribbean Regional Fisheries Mechanism (CRFM) was established in 2002 by intergovernmental agreement as a body of the Caribbean Community (CARICOM). The early evolution of the mechanism is described by Haughton et al. (2004), and its mission is "to promote sustainable use of fisheries and aquaculture resources in and among member states by the development, management

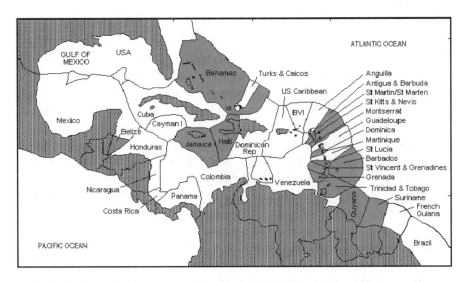

Figure 9.1
The wider Caribbean region showing hypothetical exclusive economic zones of Caribbean Community (CARICOM) countries, based on equidistance

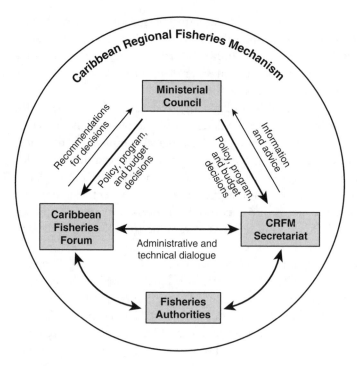

Figure 9.2
CRFM structure and relationships

and conservation of these resources *in collaboration with stakeholders* to benefit the people of the Caribbean region" (emphasis mine).

Three bodies make up the mechanism: (1) the Ministerial Council; (2) the Caribbean Fisheries Forum; and (3) the CRFM Secretariat. The first makes policy decisions and the last provides technical and administrative support. For fisheries stakeholders, most of the action takes place in the Forum, made up of full members, associate members, and observers. It is the main body to advise the Ministerial Council on fisheries policy. Observers to the Forum may include fisherfolk organizations (CRFM 2002). Figure 9.2 illustrates the mechanism's structure.

Background to Creating a Network of Fisherfolk Organizations

Despite the provision allowing observer status, up until recently fishing industry groups were unable to directly engage the mechanism's governance system. In most countries they lacked capacity at local and national levels, and collectively they had not yet formed a regional level organization. It was thought that creative networking could make a difference.

Challenges Facing Planning Participants

Fisherfolk organizations were introduced to many locations in the English-speaking Caribbean during the 1960s and 1970s. Early organizations failed in many places due to inadequate management capacity, inadequate monitoring by regulatory bodies, corruption, politics, and isolation from similar groups operating elsewhere. Fisherfolk vividly remember these failures and the reasons behind them (McConney 2007). There have been occasional revivals. Most fisherfolk organizations are small (fewer than 100 members), site-based associations or cooperatives made up mainly of small-scale boat owners and fishermen, with few or no post-harvest members. Some members may supply fishing inputs (ice, fuel, gear) and/or market the catch (finfish, lobster, conch), but few are financially comfortable. Interaction with government agencies typically concern incentives and other forms of support, funding, regulations, and market protection. Organizations leading the thrust to form a resilient regional network of national fisherfolk organizations include the Antigua and Barbuda Fisheries Alliance Inc., Barbados National Union of Fisherfolk Organizations, Belize Fishermen Co-operative Association, Jamaica Fishermen's Co-operative Union Ltd., National Association of Fisher Folk Co-Operatives of Dominica, Suriname Seafood Association, and Trinidad and Tobago Unified Fisher Folk.

These organizations face a wide range of governance challenges at several levels. One challenge common to most is the diminishing status and marginalization of fishing as an economic activity compared to tourism and other coastal uses. The contribution of fishing measured by dollar value of catch is small, but this amount does not take into account livelihoods, nutrition, and cultural values. As policy makers see better revenue-generation prospects elsewhere, it has become more difficult for small-scale fisheries to attract their attention. Consequences include low priority for technical assistance, absence of fishing agreements, inadequate physical infrastructure, limited financial services, reduced capacity development, restricted trade opportunities, and much more. Most of these issues cannot be addressed by fisherfolk as individuals or organizations. Often they require national or regional governmental action. Articulation with the state becomes a matter of necessity rather than choice for fishers who wish to sustain their livelihoods, but the strains caused by these same issues weaken the movements of collective action to resolve them.

Case studies show that past fisherfolk organization successes and failures do not accurately predict future success or failure if situations change
(Meynell 1984, 1990; Pollnac 1988). Fisheries are not easily predictable.
Some groups adapt to change and are resilient, while others become vulnerable and fail. The change that most concerns us in this chapter is the
emergence of the mechanism as a new opportunity for involving fisherfolk organizations in cross-scale governance at integrated multiple levels,
whereas previous efforts were mainly local or national (McConney et al.
1998, McConney 1999, Brown and Pomeroy 1999).

Recognizing this opportunity, the mechanism initiated a project, the
Development of a Caribbean Network of Fisher Folk Organisations, in
September 2006. The project was based on a regional needs assessment
(CRFM 2004) and subsequent regional meetings in 2004 and 2005 at
which fisherfolk organization representatives recommended forming a
regional network of national fisherfolk organizations. The aim was to
have "institutional capacities of fisher folk organizations developed at the
regional, national and community levels" (CRFM 2007b).

Researchers from the Centre for Resource Management and Environmental Studies (CERMES) at the University of the West Indies became
involved in assisting the mechanism and fisherfolk groups in collaborative
planning through a project on participatory action research to develop
capacity for marine resource governance using complex adaptive system
and social-ecological system concepts (CERMES 2007a). Following its
inception in 2006, the fisherfolk project and its partner initiatives con-
vened regional training workshops, hosted smaller meetings, benefited
from graduate student research (Tabet 2009), created a directory of fisheries stakeholders (Parsram and McConney 2008), produced newsletters
(CERMES 2007b, 2007c), spawned a fisherfolk coordinating unit (CRFM
2007b), supported fisherfolk participation in conferences (CERMES and
CRFM 2007), provided communications training (Haynes 2008), sponsored exchange visits of fisherfolk leaders and set up a networked regional
fisherfolk organization. The latter is still being worked upon. Table 9.1
provides a timeline and description of the major components. Some were
implemented by project partners and one by the fisherfolk. Although the
project was not a linear process, its three major phases were communicating concepts, collaborative planning, and network design.

Communicating Concepts
Much effort went into communicating, testing, refining, and re-interpreting
the meaning and practical significance of the concepts in collaboration

with project stakeholders. The new concepts were first introduced to stakeholders at a workshop in May, 2007, with reference mainly to the human dimensions of small-scale fisheries (CERMES 2007a). Each concept was presented and discussed in plenary; then small groups considered fisheries experiences in which the concepts could have been, or would potentially be, of practical use. These concepts were re-visited in subsequent meetings and training workshops.

Resilience was explained as the capacity of a system to receive shocks or perturbations while retaining essentially the same function, structure, feedbacks, and therefore identity, and yet not shifting into an alternate regime (Berkes and Folke 1998). Whether a particular regime is "good" or "bad" is largely a value judgment, and a substantial amount of resilience thinking is being devoted to determining how resilience benefits whom, and for what purpose (Walker and Salt 2006). For example, because resilience is not beneficial in an undesirable social and/or ecological situation, knowing what increases or reduces resilience (Walker et al. 2006), and who can engineer such system changes (Walker and Salt 2006), is important to the notion of transformation. Transformation and transformational learning (Gunderson and Holling 2002) are key aspects of resilience that incorporate human agency. However, interventions that aim to alter resilience in social-ecological systems soon confront power and governance issues (Lebel et al. 2006), as evident in the Caribbean (Pelling 1998). These issues complicate planned attempts at transformation and add to their uncertainty.

In the Caribbean much attention is paid to the ecological resilience of coral reefs to perturbations such as overfishing, hurricanes, climate change, and disease. The critical and complex roles that ecosystem components and processes play in the mitigation of anthropogenic and natural disaster impacts (Adger et al. 2005) is only now attracting attention. Yet, even less attention is being paid to the social component of the fisheries system comprising boat owners, fishers, buyers, and other stakeholders in various institutional arrangements. Institutional arrangements facilitate information and knowledge exchange, social and institutional learning, and adaptation (Walker et al. 2006). Fisheries planning authorities need to know whether stakeholder groups are, or can be, self-organized and have the adaptive capacity to sustain both fisheries resources and fisherfolk livelihoods. The latter are of particular importance to resilience in the small-scale fisheries context. A key feature of resilience is the belief that human agency can transform social and ecological conditions in order to improve the social-ecological health and well-being that are inextricably

Table 9.1
Timeline and description of the major planning components

Event/action	Link to planning process concepts
Training-of-trainers workshop for fisheries extension officers to enhance their skills (to provide better information, advisory, and training services to primary and national fisherfolk organizations). December 4–14, 2006, at St. Vincent and the Grenadines.	Shared learning and consensus-building among fisherfolk, fisheries officers, and cooperatives officers. Capacity-building. Networking across organizational and national boundaries. Learning about factors contributing to resilience of local and national fisherfolk organizations.
Marine Resource Governance (MarGov) project inception workshop. May 5–16, 2007, at Barbados.	Multistakeholder networking. Formal introduction to (and discussion of) major concepts, including practical application.
"Fisherfolk Organisations in the Caribbean: Briefing Note on Networking for Success." June, 2007.	Guidance on how to build or strengthen adaptive and resilient networks using participatory field methods.
"Fisher Folk Net" electronic newsletter started in July, 2007.	Information exchange to aid networking and collaborative decision making.
National consultations to launch national fisherfolk organizations in Dominica, Grenada, Guyana, St. Kitts, Nevis, St. Lucia, St. Vincent, and the Grenadines, in July, 2007.	Promotion of national-level networking, collaboration, and organization. Connection to policy. Promotion of institutional learning.
Regional fisheries stakeholders workshop to promote the launching of a Caribbean network of national fisherfolk organizations. Sept. 26–28, 2007, in Grenada.	Promotion of transboundary networking, collaboration, and organization. Building adaptive capacity, consensus, and group leadership. Practical use of networks.
Policy briefs: "Network Analysis in Marine Resource Governance from a Policy Perspective," April, 2007; and "Getting More Fisherfolk Into Better Fisheries Governance," September, 2007.	Information exchange that assists research to influence policy. Some capacity and consensus-building around policy aspects.
"Fisher Folk and Fisheries Scientists Linking and Learning Together" at the 60th Gulf and Caribbean Fisheries Institute (GCFI). November 5–9, 2007, at Punta Cana, Dominican Republic.	Regional networking and information exchange among fisherfolk, scientists, fisheries managers, and other actors. Build fisherfolk capacity to understand fisheries-science perspectives/methods.

Table 9.1 (continued)

Event/action	Link to planning process concepts
Small project on enhancing marine resource governance through developing capacity for communication in the Eastern Caribbean. March to June, 2008.	Build capacity for communication and fisherfolk organization advocacy. Link fisherfolk to local mass media network in several countries.
Small project on promoting the formation of national fisherfolk organizations and fishers exchange. May to June, 2008.	Fisherfolk leader-visits to strengthen links from national to regional organization levels. Learning from successful groups.
Training workshop on management, communication, and advocacy for fisherfolk organizations in CARICOM. Sept. 22 to Oct. 3, 2008, in St. Lucia.	Regional organization vision and mission statements. Capacity development in several areas. Network concepts and practical exercises. Consensus-building for regional network structure and function.
Regional symposium: "Marine Ecosystem Based Management in the Caribbean: An Essential Component of Principled Ocean Governance." Dec. 10–12, 2008, in Barbados.	Networking and knowledge acquisition by fisherfolk leaders. Capacity-building in fisheries science and management. Ecosystem-based management (EBM) "translated" into fisherfolk terms.
L. Tabet (MSc), a graduate student, presents "Fisherfolk Organisation in the Network Governance of Small-scale Fisheries in the CARICOM Region." May, 2008 to February, 2009.	Graduate research adds academic insight shared with fisherfolk in participatory action research. Builds capacity. Clarifies practical application of network concepts.
First Workshop on Regional Fisherfolk Organisations Policy Influence and Planning. January 13–15, 2009, in St. Vincent and the Grenadines.	Regional vision and mission statements refined. Policy statement for Ministerial Council. Identification of strategic objectives and priorities. Action planning. Capacity-building. Strengthening leadership, collective action, and building consensus.
Fisher exchange about Caribbean fishers collaborating on suitable gear and techniques that will contribute to sustainable fisheries. April 1–3, 2009, in Grenada.	Demonstration of fisherfolk leadership and capacity to organize. Networking among active fishers and fisher leaders. Building capacity to understand and use fisheries science/management concepts.
Second Workshop on Regional Fisherfolk Organisations Policy Influence and Planning. April 15–17, 2009, in the Commonwealth of Dominica.	Analysis of regional fisheries policy from fisherfolks' perspective, used to build capacity. Participation in fisheries policy. Medium-term strategic plan for regional fisherfolk organization, based on learning.

linked (Walker et al. 2006). Much of this evolution is accomplished through adaptation.

Adaptive capacity is about experimenting and learning in continuous cycles or loops (Gunderson and Holling 2002) to foster innovative solutions in complex social and ecological systems (Armitage 2005). In order to learn and innovate, in the process of self-organization and adaptation, systems must be open to and tolerant of failure (Anderies et al. 2006). Some experimental policy can be unattractive due to risk of failure; but adaptive capacity, good governance, and resilience are critical to sustainable development (Lebel et al. 2006). Folke et al. (2002) identify critical interacting components of adaptive capacity and resilience. These include learning to live with change and uncertainty; nurturing diversity for resilience; combining different types of knowledge for learning; and creating opportunity for self-organization toward achieving social-ecological sustainability. Social capital conceptually integrates how social assets and social networks can contribute to developing the adaptive capacity for groups and individuals to proactively or reactively respond to uncertainty and change (Pelling and High 2005). In the Caribbean, small-scale fisheries are multispecies, they use multigear, their boats are sometimes multipurpose, and the people are multioccupational. These features may suggest adaptive capacity! However, these groups are often relatively isolated locally or nationally, and they have small operational scales, limited spheres of influence (power), and fragile institutional memory. The workshop reinforced appreciation of the need for them to scale-up via networks and the use of social capital to attain and sustain adaptive capacity in order to be more effective over the entire range of fisheries resources and actors.

Networks consist of nodes (actors) and ties (relationships) in the fisheries system. Relationships may contain trust, power, information, financial aid, technical assistance, and more. Network analysis focuses on the structure of interactions between system components and the ways in which nodes and ties affect the performance and resilience of systems at multiple levels on several scales. Janssen et al. (2006) suggest that there is no "right" depiction of networks, only models and maps that are more or less useful from a particular perspective or for analyzing a specific problem. They warn that knowing network architecture is of little value unless flows through the network are also known. For example, a benevolent charity and a criminal gang may be structurally similar. In fisheries, a dense network may be good for the rapid diffusion of conservation innovations, but it may also spread unwanted practices such as irresponsible fishing. High density and strong ties may constrain learning and adaptation by individuals trapped in close-knit cliques that are resistant to adaptive change. Weak ties to distant actors can be beneficial for gaining access to power and valuable resources (Granovetter 1973). Network analysis has been applied to social systems and ecological systems, but less often to integrated social-ecological systems and governance (Bodin 2006).

Of all the concepts, the notion of networks provided deepest resonance with the various knowledge-bases of participants. The term *network* evolved from being a metaphor to attaining practical application in subsequent project components. For example, policy briefs on strategic use of networks were shared (see table 9.1) and practical networking was incorporated into several training workshops. One of the latter seemed to be a tipping point. Participants sketched a seating plan of the room and each drew lines (ties) from him or herself (the ego) to others (alters) they had come to know, being careful to the draw lines through those who had introduced them. This exercise produced sociograms in which the meeting room was a whole network from which leaders of the fisherfolk initiative emerged as hubs or bridges joining several individuals or groups (Almerigi 2008). Discussion scaled up the learning from this exercise to address organizations at various levels and transboundary links among countries. Networks became well understood. The next phase was to collaborate on determining the most desirable network characteristics.

Collaborative Planning

On geographic and jurisdictional scales, the project was expected to produce a transboundary, hierarchical regional fisherfolk organization comprising three tiers, with the lower two (national and local) being within the boundaries of member states and the highest being transboundary (figure 9.3).

In order to achieve this structure, the mechanism's strategy has been to focus upon strengthening national fisherfolk organizations that exist, while forming new ones to achieve a "critical mass" of capacity in the new networked regional fisheries organization. The approach encouraged partnerships while developing capacity through collaborative learning at various levels. For example, the project's first regional training workshop brought fisherfolk leaders, fisheries officers, and cooperatives' officers together to learn and build consensus about how to form and sustain fisherfolk organizations (CRFM 2007a). These actors do not typically meet and plan together.

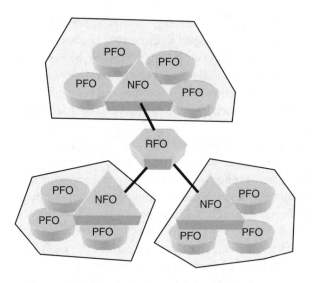

PFO = primary fisherfolk organization
NFO = national fisherfolk organization
RFO = regional fisherfolk organization

Figure 9.3
Fisherfolk organization hierarchical structure

The national consultations built upon workshop learning and linkages to promote organization formation with policy-level endorsement. Having fisheries ministers present at the consultations along with the project manager, an experienced fisheries officer as consultant, and national fisheries and cooperatives officials elevated the status of the fisherfolk organizing. Gaining policy support for national fisherfolk organizing and the regional network was important given the usually low status of small-scale fisheries. This support infused the process with policy-linked purpose, at least to start with. Sustaining momentum for the formation of the national fisherfolk organization was left largely up to the fisheries, cooperatives officers, and fisherfolk leaders as the project restrained from further intervention that could be interpreted as coercion or co-optation. However, the mechanism and regional fisherfolk leaders monitored progress and tried to promote national organization formation by way of updates in the newsletter, and by visits to countries that seemed to be faltering. The latter were critical.

Through a related project, in mid-2008 the mechanism arranged networking and promotional country visits by fisherfolk leaders from the regional coordinating unit formed at the second regional workshop (CRFM 2007b). The purpose of the visits (to Guyana, St. Kitts, Nevis, St. Vincent, and the Grenadines) was partly for the leaders to encourage national fisherfolk bodies to persevere and progress from the steering committee stage. Some (e.g., in St. Lucia and Dominica) had quickly formed secondary (umbrella) fisheries cooperatives, but others lagged. The other reason was to expose the leaders to successful fisherfolk organizations in Belize as a learning experience. These visits enhanced personal networks and created an organizational network for the coordinating unit spearheading the regional body (Tabet 2009).

As mentioned earlier, networks were mapped at the third regional training workshop (Almerigi 2008), aimed at developing leadership capacity and strengthening linkages within a pool of people from which the regional leaders would likely emerge. Options for the network design of the regional fisherfolk organization were considered at that workshop. Project staff, fisherfolk, and researchers discussed pros and cons in relation to adaptive capacity, self-organization, and resilience, among other things. The authors were participant observers in this process.

Network Design

The parties agreed that regional fisherfolk organization performance may depend upon network design. How could they develop and maintain a network over a large geographic area with transboundary social, ecological, and governance issues? Choices mainly concerned network centralization or decentralization as presented by McConney (2007) and discussed in several meetings with fisherfolk leaders during the planning process (as summarized in the following material). These hypothetical networks are not meant to suggest which specific national organizations should be in (or out) of a regional network. The ties joining the nodes contain many relations ranging from information exchange, to finance, to collaboration, and more, but the focus of this design phase was more on resilience of structure than function.

Resilience was thought of in terms of what shocks the regional fisherfolk organization could sustain (and yet remain intact) through its national organizations and the primary level members. Fisherfolk noted that the three nested tiers conferred system resilience through redundancy by allowing a strong primary organization to substitute for a national one if the latter was incapacitated. This redundancy, however, exposed the vulnerability of the national organization; it could be ignored and perhaps eliminated from the network unless it was itself resilient and quickly recovered. Hence, primary organizations contributed to adaptive capacity and resilience of national organizations as well as the reverse. Regarding the purpose of resilience, fisherfolk acknowledged governance as one dimension; but resilience for them also meant sustaining livelihoods and well-being despite social and ecological change. Fisherfolk took the concepts into consideration as they debated network design in collaboration with the other project partners. Design criteria discussed or implied included the following (put for convenience under the two other main concept headings while recognizing that most overlap):

Adaptive capacity
• Use geographic proximity as a basis for forming clusters of organizations.
• Cluster national organizations with similar resource interests to share learning.
• Invest in building hubs with sufficient capacity to function effectively.
• Rotate network leadership in order to spread capacity and promote equity.
• Focus on institutionalizing cost-effective communication at all levels.
• Facilitate face-to-face communication as a powerful learning mechanism.
• Connect organizations to national fisheries authorities and CRFM bodies.

Resilience
• Create built-in redundancy among multiple levels of organizations.
• Allow clusters to function reasonably independent of each other.
• Disperse the hubs so all is not lost through severe shocks (e.g., hurricanes).
• Experiment with cluster size in relation to vulnerability, flexibility, and so forth.
• Take into account not only governance, but also sustainability of livelihoods.
• Examine private and public sector regional agencies for working models.

Using diagrams and face-to-face discussion, the authors engaged the fisherfolk leaders at various workshops in debates on which network design was best suited. For example, the authors explained that in a centralized hub structure such as the mechanism (and in other decentralized but not devolved agencies), there is a single, easily identified node from which most relationships emanate via strong ties. Few or no places on the periphery are connected to each other by links (much like a wheel with spokes).

Fisherfolk noted that although roles and responsibilities may be rotated (so those on the periphery take turns at being the hub), this rotation is difficult because of the relatively immobile capacity (physical assets and staff) developed at the hub. Yet, having permanent "headquarters" may provide stability, aid efficiency, and encourage accountability. Fisherfolk realized that communication to and from the center must be exceptionally efficient and cost-effective for good coordination and collaboration. They were acutely aware that to develop and maintain this type of network would require very strong leadership from the center, and willingness to be lead from those at the periphery. In being led, the peripheral groups could not remain passive; rather, they would need to actively support and invest in developing adaptive capacity and resilience at the center. Many fisherfolk saw this structure as inequitable, with too much power residing in the center. It conflicted with their egalitarian preferences and was risky given the prevalence of weak leadership and distrust. At the end of one workshop, although some saw merit in investing effort into a single hub rather than spreading capacity thinly, the overriding consideration was that all would be lost if the hub should fail. Given the history of fisherfolk organization failure, this option was not seen as an encouraging path to resilience, and it was discarded.

Another structure considered briefly was that of an open or distributed network that has no center/periphery, but rather that relies upon each node or fisherfolk organization to contribute in a very egalitarian manner, with rotating or no leadership. The nodes are only loosely and perhaps temporarily connected to each other to execute specific tasks or solve problems. The structure is very much driven by self-organization. The fisherfolk discussed whether the open network would function properly in circumstances other than with strong national fisherfolk organizations that were confident about their success and that hence demanded a level of independence while agreeing to cooperate with each other. They appreciated the equity of this network along with its requirement for less sustained effort on the part of any single node to keep the structure together. They were concerned, however, that their organizations were not yet strong enough to sustain this loose structure. Fisherfolk noted that without excellent communication it would easily fall apart. If the network organizations are weak or looking externally for leadership, then the structure would be unlikely to start well or be sustainable. When the authors pointed out that resilience and adaptive capacity would need to be fairly evenly distributed throughout an open network, the fisherfolk leaders were not in favor of starting with this arrangement. It seemed more futuristic. On a more fundamental level, because it was diffuse, it was contrary to the often stated perception of fisherfolk that they need to "come together" and exercise their belief that "unity is strength" in a tangible manner. Part of creating a strong regional identity was the need to interact intensely to create a robust community of interest capable of withstanding shocks. An open network was too loose an arrangement to meet the deep need for connectedness. They also discarded this model.

The network design that came closest to meeting the structural criteria is shown in figure 9.4. It shows three geographically dispersed clusters of four national organizations each, in which the hubs are linked, and the southern hub plays the leadership role in the regional network.

Leading nodes are subregional, with cluster organizations situated geographically near to each other. Fisherfolk were told that in this arrangement resilience is increased if clusters are thought of as being small, similar, substitutable units linked to each other to form the overall regional network. Fisherfolk considered whether clusters could be developed in phases and perhaps be self-organizing, given the advantage of smaller scale and perhaps more ties (a denser network) due to similarities among neighboring countries and ecological zones. Fisherfolk were aware, however, that superficial resemblances may be misleading. It may be insufficient,

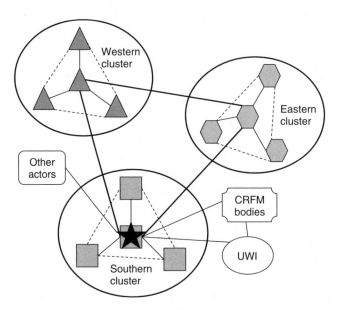

Figure 9.4
Network design option for a regional fisherfolk organization

for example, to assume affinity due to similarities in target species or fishing methods (e.g., conch in the west, reef fish in the northeast, and pelagics in the southeast islands). Even though such similarity seems reasonable, the target markets, fishing effort, and regulations may be widely different.

Fisherfolk appreciated that the multicluster model is closer to the ecosystem or eco-regional approaches recommended to ensure that political marine boundaries do not take precedence over ecological systems in designing fisheries management measures. However, to develop and maintain a multicluster network requires more overall planning and coordination than for the other two network types. Fisherfolk discussed the need to have strong, well-linked central nodes from the subregional hubs. Each cluster could be resilient once there was a constant flow of information and resources among members (perhaps facilitated by their closer geographic proximity and sharing of common goals and issues, or even conflicts). Fisherfolk also discussed how the capacity to adapt could be tailored on a smaller scale to each cluster. Leadership roles could rotate among and within clusters if needed, according to differing capacities and comparative advantages. The loss of neither an entire cluster nor a node within a cluster is likely to be fatal to the regional network. It should be able to self-organize and repair itself by taking full advantage of what the author referred to as its multi-level, polycentric structure. Fisherfolk appreciated how this semi-autonomous, almost franchise-like, model had parallels in business and could be adapted to their NGO environment. The authors pointed out that one of the major hurdles may be for them to develop a model of formal incorporation as a not-for-profit company (or similar) that is legally acceptable in one of the member states, but which allows the flexibility to function as an adaptive transboundary entity. Fisherfolk generally favored this model over the others.

The collaborative planning to implement the design choice continues while fisherfolk leaders and their organizations gain practical experience of networking within their newly formed Caribbean Network of Fisherfolk Organisations (CNFO). An example of this planning is the participation of several fisherfolk leaders in a regional symposium on marine ecosystem-based management that facilitated shared understanding of the ecosystem approach to fisheries (Fanning et al. 2009). This understanding was subsequently communicated among fisherfolk groups and incorporated into the vision of the CNFO and the fisher exchange workshop on responsible fishing gear and methods implemented by the fishers (Lay 2009). Fishers have talked about ecosystem approaches at regional scientific meetings, and this situation is significant because fisheries managers are only now tackling such concepts (CERMES and CRFM 2007).

Fisherfolk leading the CNFO have participated in meetings of the Ministerial Council (McIntosh 2009) and the Caribbean Fisheries Forum (McConney 2009). They collaborated to present statements that directly articulate the regional level interests, perspectives, and needs of fisherfolk for the first time. Other fisheries governance stakeholders have been highly supportive of their move to sit at the table with representatives of member states, international bodies, and regional organizations (McConney 2009).

Discussion

Globally, there is increasing demand for innovative resilience thinking and research that can immediately be applied by natural resource users, managers, and policymakers to real-world, complex problems (Walker and Salt 2006). In preference to following the path of conventional fisheries management that has proven to be treacherous elsewhere, Caribbean countries need to consider addressing their fisheries through new perspectives and approaches that are more people-centered and that treat fisheries as complex adaptive social-ecological systems. Many challenges facing fisherfolk organizations require active interventions from national and regional governmental authorities. Fisherfolk need to collaborate at a regional level. However, to do so is not easy.

The initiative on national fisherfolk organization strengthening and networking to improve governance contributes to the desired change in approach through bottom-up, but top-supported, participatory action research and planning. Given that resilience thinking and concepts are relatively new to fisheries (Mahon et al. 2008) there was much attention paid to communicating the concepts and relating them to actual fisheries issues and experiences. The communication was aimed mainly at fisherfolk, but also at fisheries managers, other researchers, and nongovernmental partners. We found that examples grounded in experience were useful for all target audiences. Information exchange among different stakeholders enriched the interpretation and application of the concepts. As fisherfolk grasped concepts, they sought practical use for them. The notion of network was particularly well received and subsequently incorporated into most aspects of the initiative.

Collaborative planning permitted fisherfolk, national fisheries authorities, and the inter-governmental mechanism to share information on fisheries and their organizations. This sharing enabled leaders of national fisherfolk organizations to design a networked regional fisherfolk body capable of engaging the regional fisheries governance system. In the planning process much attention was paid to building the adaptive capacity of fisherfolk leaders and groups. Mobilizing knowledge, operational planning, policy analysis, leadership training, consensus-building, and organizational management were key parts of the process. Fisherfolk pointed out that they were accustomed to dealing with ecological uncertainty in pursuit of their livelihoods (they knew how to adapt), but that the social and institutional uncertainties of governance were new to them. The project was fortunate to have working with it a fisherfolk leader (now the coordinator of the regional fisherfolk organization) who was able to apply as systematic a method of learning and testing to the entire initiative as he did to his fishing! The importance of change agents was highlighted throughout the project.

Designing the network tested understanding of the concepts. Fisherfolk had interesting insights on the trade-offs among network features within the context of their own norms and values. Because equity was important to them, very centralized networks were not acceptable, and they were keen on rotation of lead responsibility in any multicluster design of several hubs. While the researchers were primarily interested in governance, the fisherfolk emphasized the need for livelihoods to also be taken into account in the design. This emphasis linked the designs closer to resource types, uses, and management. Exposure to ecosystem-based management reinforced these linkages. When they interacted with scientists and managers, they articulated integrated approaches to both fisheries management and their involvement in all levels of governance from local to regional.

The options available for the legal-institutional structure of the preferred organization is being investigated and compared to the network design criteria. For example, a body federating the national fisheries cooperatives and associations may be viable as a network design but not feasible due to legislation on cooperatives. Conversely, a typical company structure with subsidiaries may be legally feasible, but that plan may result in a network design that is too centralized to meet adaptive capacity and resilience criteria.

The planning process illustrated that the challenges of implementing and sustaining a fisherfolk organization network from the local, through the national, to the regional level would have to be addressed by various strategies. There is need for the following tasks: to continue collaborative planning; to identify and to develop a cadre of good leaders at all levels; to ensure adequate succession planning; to strengthen organizational management; to institute regular monitoring and evaluation; to develop national interagency and inter-sectoral networks for ecosystem-based management; to support good governance throughout the network; and to identify the means to achieve sustainable financing. The fisherfolk networking initiative demonstrated the successful application of collaborative planning and resilience thinking to fisheries governance in the Caribbean.

References

Adger, W. N., T. P. Hughes, C. Folke, S. R. Carpenter, and J. Rockstrom. 2005. Social-ecological resilience to coastal disasters. *Science* 309:1036–1039.

Anderies, J. M., B. H. Walker, and A. P. Kinzig. 2006. Fifteen weddings and a funeral: Case studies and resilience-based management. *Ecology and Society* 11(1):21. Accessed 2-3-2011. Available at http://www.ecologyandsociety.org/vol11/iss1/art21/.

Almerigi, S. 2008. *Report of the training workshop on management, communication and advocacy for fisherfolk organisations in CARICOM.* Belize: Caribbean Regional Fisheries Mechanism.

Armitage, D. 2005. Adaptive capacity and community-based natural resource management. *Environmental Management* 35(6): 703–715.

Bavinck, M., R. Chuenpagdee, M. Diallo, P. van der Heijden, J. Kooiman, R. Mahon, and S. Williams. 2005. *Interactive governance for fisheries: A guide to better practice.* Delft, Amsterdam: Eburon Academic Publishers; Centre for Maritime Research (MARE).

Berkes, F., and C. Folke, eds. 1998. *Linking social and ecological systems: Management practices and social mechanisms for building resilience.* Cambridge, U.K.: Cambridge University Press.

Berkes, F., R. Mahon, P. McConney, R. Pollnac, and R. Pomeroy. 2001. *Managing small-scale fisheries: Alternative directions and methods.* Ottawa, ON: International Development Research Centre.

Bodin, Ö. 2006. A network perspective on ecosystems, societies, and natural resource management. Doctoral dissertation, Department of Systems Ecology, Stockholm University, Sweden.

Booher, D. E., and J. E. Innes. 2002. Network power in collaborative planning. *Journal of Planning Education and Research* 21:221–236.

Brown, D. N., and R. S. Pomeroy. 1999. Co-management of Caribbean Community (CARICOM) fisheries. *Marine Policy* 23:549–570.

CERMES. 2007a. Report of the MarGov Project Inception Workshop held at the UWI Cave Hill Campus, Barbados, 15–16 May 2007. MarGov Project Document 1. Barbados: Centre for Resource Management and Environmental Studies.

CERMES. April, 2007b. Network analysis in marine resource governance from a policy perspective. Barbados: CERMES Policy Perspective.

CERMES. September, 2007c. Getting more fisherfolk into better fisheries governance. Barbados: CERMES Policy Perspective.

CERMES and CRFM. 2007. Report of the Fishers Forum: "Fisher folk and fisheries scientists linking and learning together" at the 60th Gulf and Caribbean Fisheries Institute (GCFI), Punta Cana, Dominican Republic, 5–9 November 2007. MarGov Project Document 6. Barbados: Centre for Resource Management and Environmental Studies.

Chakalall, B., R. Mahon, P. McConney, L. Nurse, and D. Oderson. 2007. Governance of fisheries and other living marine resources in the wider Caribbean. *Fisheries Research* 87:92–99.

Chakalall, B., R. Mahon, and P. McConney. 1998. Current issues in fisheries governance in the Caribbean Community (CARICOM). *Marine Policy* 22:29–44.

CRFM. 2002. *Agreement establishing the Caribbean Regional Fisheries Mechanism*. Belize: Caribbean Regional Fisheries Mechanism.

CRFM. 2004. *Report of organizational needs assessment of Caribbean fisher folk organizations*. Belize: Caribbean Regional Fisheries Mechanism.

CRFM. 2007a. Report of the CTA/CRFM training of trainers workshop for fisheries extension officers to enhance their skills to provide better information, advisory and training services to primary and national fisherfolk organizations. CRFM Technical & Advisory Document No. 2007/1. Belize: Caribbean Regional Fisheries Mechanism.

CRFM. 2007b. Report of the CTA/CRFM regional fisheries stakeholders workshop to promote the launching of a Caribbean network of national fisherfolk organisations, September 26–28, 2007, St. George's, Grenada. CRFM Technical & Advisory Document No. 2007/11. Belize: Caribbean Regional Fisheries Mechanism.

De Young, C., A. Charles, and A. Hjort. 2008. Human dimensions of the ecosystem approach to fisheries: An overview of context, concepts, tools, and methods. FAO Fisheries Technical Paper No. 489. Rome: World Food and Agriculture Organization (FAO).

Fanning, L., R. Mahon, and P. McConney. 2009. Marine ecosystem-based management in the Caribbean: An essential component of principled ocean governance. Report of Caribbean Regional Symposium, University of the West Indies, Cave Hill Campus, Barbados, December 10–12, 2008. CERMES Technical Report No. 17. Barbados: Centre for Resource Management and Environmental Studies.

FAO. 2003. The ecosystem approach to fisheries. *FAO technical guidelines for responsible fisheries*, No. 4, Suppl. 2. Rome: World Food and Agriculture Organization (FAO).

Folke, C., S. Carpenter, T. Elmqvist, L. Gunderson, C. S. Holling, and B. Walker. 2002. Resilience and sustainable development: Building adaptive capacity in a world of transformations. *Ambio* 31:437–440.

Granovetter, M. 1973. The strength of weak ties. *American Journal of Sociology* 78:1360–1380.

Gunderson, L. H., and C. S. Holling. 2002. *Panarchy: Understanding transformations in human and natural systems*. Washington, D.C.: Island Press.

Haughton, M., R. Mahon, P. McConney, G. A. Kong, and A. Mills. 2004. Establishment of the Caribbean Regional Fisheries Mechanism. *Marine Policy* 28:351–359.

Haynes, C. 2008. Final summary activity report and project completion report of enhancing marine resource governance through developing capacity for communication in the Eastern Caribbean. MarGov Project Document 10. Barbados: Centre for Resource Management and Environmental Studies.

Innes, J. E., and D. E. Booher. 2003. The impact of collaborative planning on governance capacity. Berkeley, CA: UC Berkeley, Institute of Urban and Regional Development. Accessed 2-3-2011. Available at http://www.escholarship.org/uc/item/98k72547.

Janssen, M. A., Ö. Bodin, J. M. Anderies, T. Elmqvist, H. Ernstson, R. R. J. McAllister, P. Olsson, and P. Ryan. 2006. A network perspective on the resilience of social-ecological systems. *Ecology and Society* 11(1):15. Accessed 2-3-2011. Available at http://www.ecologyandsociety.org/vol11/iss1/art15/.

Kooiman, J., M. Bavinck, S. Jentoft, and R. Pullin, eds. 2005. Fish for life: Interactive governance for fisheries. MARE Publication Series No. 3. Amsterdam, the Netherlands: University of Amsterdam Press.

Lay, M. 2009. Caribbean fishers collaborating on suitable gear and techniques that will contribute to sustainable fisheries. Project summary and completion report of the Caribbean Network of Fisherfolk Organisations fishers exchange, 1–3 April 2009, Grenada. Caribbean Network of Fisherfolk Organisations.

Lebel, L., J. M. Anderies, B. Campbell, C. Folke, S. Hatfield-Dodds, T. P. Hughes, and J. Wilson. 2006. Governance and the capacity to manage resilience in regional social-ecological systems. *Ecology and Society* 11(1):19. Accessed 2-3-2011. Available at http://www.ecologyandsociety.org/vol11/iss1/art19.

Mahon, R., P. McConney, and R. Roy. 2008. Governing fisheries as complex adaptive systems. *Marine Policy* 32:104–112.

McConney, P. 2009. Report and proceedings of the CANARI/CNFO-CU/CRFM/UWI-CERMES Second Workshop on Regional Fisherfolk Organisations Policy Influence and Planning, April 15–17, 2009, Commonwealth of Dominica. CRFM Technical & Advisory Document No. 2009/3. Belize: Caribbean Regional Fisheries Mechanism.

McConney, P. 2007. Fisher folk organisations in the Caribbean: Briefing note on networking for success. Report prepared for the Caribbean Regional Fisheries Mechanism (CRFM). Belize City, Belize: Secretariat.

McConney, P. A. 1999. Organising fisherfolk in Barbados without completing a clean round. *Proceedings of the Gulf and Caribbean Fisheries Institute* 52:290–299.

McConney, P. A., A. Atapattu, and D. Leslie. 1998. Organizing fisherfolk in Barbados. *Proceedings of the Gulf and Caribbean Fisheries Institute* 51:299–308.

McGoodwin, J. R. 1990. *Crisis in the world fisheries: People, problems, and policies.* Stanford, CA: Stanford University Press.

McIntosh, S. 2009. Report and proceedings of the CANARI/CNFO-CU/CRFM/ UWI-CERMES First Workshop on Regional Fisherfolk Organisations Policy Influence and Planning, January 13–15, 2009, Saint Vincent and the Grenadines. CRFM Technical & Advisory Document—No. 2009/2. Belize: Caribbean Regional Fisheries Mechanism.

McIntosh, S., M. Lay, P. McConney, and T. Phillips. 2010. The development of a Caribbean regional network of fisherfolk organisations and its role in influencing fisheries policy. *Proceedings of the Gulf and Caribbean Fisheries Institute* 62: 298–305.

Meynell, P. J. 1984. Small-scale fisheries cooperatives—Some lessons for the future. COPAC Occasional Paper No. 2. Geneva, Switzerland: Committee for the Promotion and Advancement of Cooperatives (COPAC).

Meynell, P. J. 1990. Success and failure in fishermen's organizations. FAO Fish Circ. No. 819. Rome: World Food and Agriculture Organization (FAO).

Parsram, K., and P. McConney. 2008. Directory of fisheries stakeholders in the Caribbean. CRFM Technical & Advisory Document No. 2008/1. Prepared for the Caribbean Regional Fisheries Mechanism (CRFM). Belize City, Belize: Secretariat.

Pelling, M. 1998. Participation, social capital and vulnerability to urban flooding in Guyana. *Journal of International Development* 10(4):469–486.

Pelling, M., and C. High. 2005. Understanding adaptation: What can social capital offer assessments of adaptive capacity? *Global Environmental Change* 15:308–319.

Pollnac, R. B. 1988. *Evaluating the potential of fishermen's organizations in developing countries. International Center for Marine Resource Development.* Kingston, RI: University of Rhode Island.

Tabet, L. M. 2009. Fisherfolk organisation in the network governance of small-scale fisheries in the CARICOM region. CERMES Technical Report No. 20. Barbados: Centre for Resource Management and Environmental Studies.

Walker, B., and D. Salt. 2006. *Resilience thinking: Sustaining ecosystems and people in a changing world.* Washington, D.C., London, U.K., Covelo, CA: *Island Press.*

Walker, B. H., L. H. Gunderson, A. P. Kinzig, C. Folke, S. R. Carpenter, and L. Schultz. 2006. A handful of heuristics and some propositions for understanding resilience in social-ecological systems. *Ecology and Society* 11(1):13. Accessed 2-3-2011. Available at http://www.ecologyandsociety.org/vol11/iss1/art13/.

10

Collective Transitions and Community Resilience in the Face of Enduring Trauma

E. Franklin Dukes, Jill Williams, and Steven Kelban

Failure to remember, collectively, triumphs and accomplishments diminishes us. But failure to remember, collectively, injustice and cruelty is an ethical breach. It implies no responsibility and no commitment to prevent inhumanity in the future. Even worse, failures of collective memory stoke fires of resentment and revenge.

—Martha Minow, *Memory and Hate*

Introduction

• A student leader of African and Asian ancestry who is running for president of a major university's student council is assaulted by a white youth spewing racial epithets.

• A series of attacks on white male university students by groups of younger black males befuddles community leaders.

• An anxious, elderly African American gentleman, accompanied by his daughter and granddaughter, enters a university office to ask permission to take photographs of the building where several decades earlier he and others were assaulted and then arrested, despite their nonviolent response, as they protested the owner's defiant segregation of dining facilities.

The community of these events is Charlottesville, and the university is the University of Virginia. That building is now the office of one of the coauthors of this article. But this community could also be anywhere; the incidents, everyone's; the responses (and nonresponses) to dramatic harm, ubiquitous.

Our thesis is straightforward: First, deep trauma from substantial injustice often leaves people with losses that go unacknowledged and with impacts that can endure over years and even generations.[1] Second, historical community trauma that is not fully acknowledged and addressed leaves communities less resilient—less able to respond and adapt in the face of new stresses and harms. Third, successful transition, or the internal process of how individuals and communities respond effectively to change, can occur only when that loss is acknowledged and addressed.

In communities where such "unrightable wrongs"[2] have occurred, efforts to put the past behind that do not acknowledge and address the historical trauma or historical patterns of injustices can reinforce the original problems that led to the traumas in the first place, making the wrongs more difficult to face than they were originally. This reinforcement is so because different community members understand the historic events or patterns of injustice in different ways, if they attend to them at all; therefore, their understandings of present problems and how to deal with them are similarly divided. With a divided understanding of the nature of present problems, addressing those problems in an effective and sustainable way becomes difficult, if not impossible, for community leaders. Furthermore, as we will argue, without a collective effort to acknowledge and address the historical event or patterns, these divisions may deepen, making a community less able to respond in a unified way to new traumatic events. For a visual explanation of this cycle, see figure 10.1.

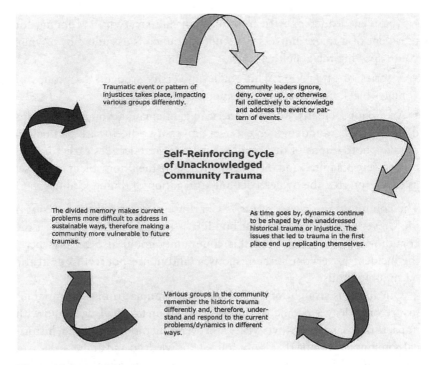

Traumatic event or pattern of injustices takes place, impacting various groups differently.

Community leaders ignore, deny, cover up, or otherwise fail collectively to acknowledge and address the event or pattern of events.

Self-Reinforcing Cycle of Unacknowledged Community Trauma

The divided memory makes current problems more difficult to address in sustainable ways, therefore making a community more vulnerable to future traumas.

As time goes by, dynamics continue to be shaped by the unaddressed historical trauma or injustice. The issues that led to trauma in the first place end up replicating themselves.

Various groups in the community remember the historic trauma differently and, therefore, understand and respond to the current problems/dynamics in different ways.

Figure 10.1
Self-reinforcing cycle of unacknowledged community trauma

How Is This Cycle Related to Resilience?

Our use of resilience follows the definition offered by Ozawa in chapter two of this volume. She notes that "a resilient community may be defined as a community that is able to respond to unexpected and unwelcomed events in ways that enable groups and individuals to work together to minimize the adverse consequences of such crises. A resilient community is adaptable, not rigid." This definition connotes self-awareness within a given community of its areas of vulnerability, along with a capacity for collaborative planning, preparation, and adaptation for crisis.

From this perspective, endurance alone is not necessarily a positive quality. As noted by Goldstein and Butler in chapter 14 and Zellner, Hoch, and Welch in chapter 3, a desired state of resilience may be blocked by problems of stability and the persistence of less-desired characteristics, and thus resistance to needed adaptive change. For instance, the economic system that enslaved black people in the United States was persistent and durable enough to survive an enormous disruption—the loss of the Civil War and Emancipation—to recover and endure for another several generations.

The communities existing within this economic system were further divided—in terms of race and class—by the endurance of the system. These entrenched divisions rendered these communities less resilient, or less able to respond, adapt, and recover in unified, sustainable ways to future traumas. So the persistence of the divisive economic system actually resulted in *less* resilient communities. Our argument is that resilience of any particular community depends upon that community's ability collectively to acknowledge, understand, and transition away from the systems that have enabled past harmful action to take place. Without that transition, the systems that led to the original and subsequent traumas will be enduring at the expense of the community's resilience.

Chaskin (2001) argues that a shared sense of community and a level of commitment among community members are basic to a community's capacity to address challenges.[3] According to Chaskin, community capacity develops as members come to see that they have a stake in the well-being of a particular community; with that stake comes a willingness to act to support that community.

Thus a community whose members have varying levels of commitment to that community is more likely to have a divided response when trauma occurs. As Putnam (2000) has documented, when community ties deteriorate, the capacity to prevent or to solve problems declines; conversely, as community bonds strengthen, so too does such capacity increase. Social capital—those connections among individuals created by shared efforts and other experiences that foster norms of reciprocity and that generate trust—must then be a key part of resilience in the face of trauma.

Thus, improving resilience requires intervening in that cycle of unacknowledged community trauma. A legitimate intervention into this cycle depends upon public knowledge, public understanding, and public acknowledgment of past events in order to avoid repeating oppression, injustice, and mistakes, and revictimizing communities and individuals still affected by the wrong.

Unfortunately, community leaders who are best positioned to facilitate such interventions may resist efforts to pay attention to these events. There can be a variety of reasons for that resistance. They may not be fully aware of that trauma or they may disagree that the trauma is linked to contemporary issues. They may see the connection but fear a loss of their own power or other interests should recognition occur. Or they may be managing many changes at once. Therefore, a significant barrier to interventions that acknowledge and address historical traumas is the challenge of developing a sense of urgency in those who resist facing the past.

Why Is It So Difficult to Face the Past?

The sense of urgency about addressing the historic event or pattern of events differs depending on, among other things, one's connection to the original injustice, pattern of injustice, or conflict. In other words, if I believe that I or my identity group continue to suffer from some legacy of the original harm, I may feel a stronger sense of urgency about addressing that original harm.[4] If, on the other hand, I either benefit from or do not feel a direct connection to the historical event (which are often one and the same), then I will feel less urgency about addressing the original harm and may even argue strongly against a process of addressing that original event or pattern of events.

In the United States, these divided understandings of history and therefore the present are never more blatant than in the face of new traumas. Consider the immediate aftermath of Hurricane Katrina; fully 90 percent of African Americans but only 38 percent of whites thought Katrina showed that racial inequities were still a problem in this country. Furthermore, 84 percent of African Americans believed that the federal government's response would have been quicker if the victims had been predominantly white, while only 20 percent of whites had that belief (Dawson 2006).

Surely it is not overly speculative to presume that most of those whites who disagreed that Katrina revealed lingering racial inequities think that the array of civil rights victories this country has seen since the mid-19th century—the Emancipation Proclamation, the desegregation of lunch counters and schools, the Voting Rights Act, or even the first black president—demonstrate that there has been sufficient progress in ending the legacies of slavery and segregation in this country. At the same time, surely most of the African Americans and whites who thought that Katrina showed that racial inequities were still a problem believe that the harmful legacy of slavery and segregation continues. The divided nature of the community's understanding of the human factors that led to the tragedy—unfair decision-making systems that disproportionately harm communities of color and poor people—simultaneously increased the resilience of these systems while decreasing the community's ability to recover from the new trauma inflicted by the storms.

A Framework for Transitions

William Bridges, a leading author and consultant in the field of organizational development, provides an explanation of resistance. Bridges (1991) draws a critical distinction between a *change* (such as the end of legal segregation) and *transition* (or the process that we go through to come to terms with that change). While the change can happen almost immediately, Bridges says, a transition can take days, weeks, years, or even decades. This distinction sheds light on the divided analyses about Hurricane Katrina mentioned previously. The whites who claim that there are no lingering racial inequities in the United States may point to the external changes of civil rights victories as markers for the end of the old way of being and the beginning of the new. But what this group fails to acknowledge or understand is the lack of a transition through which a critical mass of U.S. residents came to terms with that change. Without that transition, much of the United States remains still stuck in the old way of being; and the economic, social, and political systems that were a part of that old way of being persist in spite of other changes.

According to Bridges, the process of transition begins with an ending. People cannot begin a new project or new stage of life until they have released their hold on the way things were and have dealt with the loss of past behaviors, attitudes, beliefs, hopes, and fears. After the old ways of thinking and behaving are gone—but before the new ways have become second nature—there is an awkward in-between time called the *neutral zone*. The neutral zone is usually chaotic, and there is often a desire to return to what is old and familiar. But this zone can also be a very creative time. A new beginning takes place when people are emotionally ready to do things in a whole new way

Examples of change for individuals might be moving to a new city, losing a job, or getting married. At the organizational level, change might be new leadership, layoffs, or expansion. This change can be either positive or negative, but it is generally experienced as a particular moment in time. Bridges suggests that too often people are expected to adapt to the change without being guided through the transition processes: acknowledging what they are losing, finding their way through the chaos and creativity of the neutral zone, and finally being able to join the new beginning. At the individual level, Bridges's argument is that for a person to successfully engage that change, that individual would have to go through the endings and neutral zone in order to actually take up a new beginning.

The Andrus Family Fund (AFF) believes that the theory of transitions is as true for communities as for individuals and organizations, and that communities in conflict benefit from processes that allow them to acknowledge all the aspects of transition behind whatever change—imposed or aspirational—they are experiencing. AFF's grant-making strategy in its community-reconciliation program is to offer support to communities struggling (a) with how to come to terms with an imposed change (e.g., climate change, loss of natural resources, or budget cuts); (b) to collaboratively design changes in order to improve the community (e.g., creating systems of accountability for government institutions or creating plans to address the achievement gap in schools); or (c) most often, to do both.

The following three case studies, two of which have been funded by the Andrus Family Fund, describe three different communities where egregious harm occurred some years ago. After periods of denial or cover-up, each of those communities has made efforts to understand and address that harm. These efforts are designed to help communities come to terms with past-imposed changes while also collaboratively defining and implementing aspirational changes for the future. If our hypothesis is correct, successful efforts of this sort can lead to a transition that strengthens a community's resilience. One community, Bainbridge Island, Washington, appears to have been successful in supporting that transition. In another community,

Greensboro, North Carolina, the record is mixed. For the third community, the University of Virginia and its surroundings in Charlottesville and Albemarle County, its journey is ongoing.

Transitions and Resilience: Three Cases

Nidoto Nai Yoni: "Let It Not Happen Again"
One of the most beautiful places in the United States is also the home of one of its most shameful and painful episodes.[5]

From Bainbridge Island, home to some 23,000 people, residents possess spectacular views of Mt. Rainier, the Seattle skyline that is some twenty-five minutes away by ferry, and the Olympic and Cascade mountain ranges. On March 30, 1942, 227 Bainbridge Island men, women, and children of Japanese ancestry—more than half of whom were U.S. citizens—were not enjoying these views. Instead, they began their long trek into betrayal, as they left the island under armed guard to what was for them an unknown destination. These people were the first of more than 120,000 citizens and immigrants in the United States to be imprisoned under Presidential Executive Order 9066 and Civilian Exclusion Order No. 1. These Japanese Americans, many of them American citizens, did not know at the time that their imprisonment would last for three long years and take them from Manzanar in California's Mojave Desert to Minodoka Relocation Center in Idaho, or that only 150 of them would eventually return.

These residents had less than one week's notice to close their businesses, store their belongings, make arrangements for their homes and land, and choose which parts of their lives to fit within a single suitcase. Those who were able to return came back to find a changed landscape. A few found a welcome, and their property maintained by caring neighbors. Others found nothing remaining for them.

Fast forward some fifty years or so. Bainbridge Island is again in the news for a different type of shameful event. A creosote plant on Bainbridge Island severely contaminated the harbor with wastewater discharged directly into the water and treated timber stored in the waters, while shipyard pollution contributed dangerous chemicals and heavy metals to those same waters. The Environmental Protection Agency placed the site on the "National Priorities List," more commonly known as "Superfund," reserved for those sites most harmful to human health and the environment.

These sites typically provide significant environmental and social challenges (Dukes 2006). For many communities, discovery of the harm done to the environment and the risks to public health engender both well-founded and unfounded fears. Community members often feel betrayed by the owners of these sites as well as public officials entrusted with their safety.

This time, though, the challenge of dealing with economic loss and contamination is prompting a focus on *transition* rather than change. Besides the complex and long-term cleanup that will continue for many years, the Bainbridge Island residents are finding a way to recover both land and community. The community is taking a site that has been contaminated both physically and psychically and turning it into a place of memory and education.

The site of the memorial will be at the former Eagledale ferry landing, the very location that saw the Japanese Americans forcibly marched off of Bainbridge Island, and part of the Superfund site.[6] The words of the memorial committee demonstrate its members' recognition of the linkage between environmental and psychic contamination:

Restoration—both environmental and cultural—is the story of the Wyckoff Superfund site.

Restoring a previously contaminated environment polluted by nearly 100 years of creosote processing, and showcasing the good work of government and what technology can do to return balance and harmony with nature.

Restoring national honor by recognizing the unconstitutional treatment of American citizens in a time of war, and through reflection and interpretation, inspiring all Americans to remember, learn, and hopefully protect the constitutional rights for all. (from Wyckoff Park/Memorial Proposal, no longer accessible at original site http://www.bijac.org/)

This process of memorialization itself has fostered a transition. For Japanese Americans, it has led to a recognition and acknowledgment of their loss as they have received support from sources as diverse as the Washington State Legislature, the Suquamish Tribe, the American Legion, and Bainbridge Island City Council. For others, this process has allowed them to take pride in their community's response to the contamination and to come together over two events that could have polarized their community for many decades. We suggest that by acknowledging the history and the loss created by the removal of Japanese Americans (and the subsequent absence of widespread public recognition of that harm), the community is better able to move through the stages of the transition process and thus become more resilient.

Greensboro

Like many of its neighbors in North Carolina, the South, and the United States in general, the city of Greensboro[7] has a long history of substandard living and working conditions for people of color and poor people. This historic pattern has been regularly reinforced by laws, policies, and practices biased against these groups and by public and private institutions condoning and even provoking violence against organizers who challenge those structures. On November 3, 1979, the already divided city experienced another trauma that further divided the community.

On that day, a caravan of Klansmen and neo-Nazis confronted demonstrators planning for an anti-Klan march. The demonstrators chanted the slogan "Death to the Klan." A stickfight ensued between the demonstrators and white supremacists; then several Klansmen and neo-Nazis returned to their vehicles, retrieved their weapons, and opened fire on mostly unarmed demonstrators. While four news crews captured the unfolding events on film, the white supremacists shot and killed five demonstrators and wounded ten others. The virtual absence of the Greensboro Police Department was notable, given the parade permit the department issued to the parade organizers (a group called the Workers Viewpoint Organization that would later call itself the Communist Workers Party, or CWP). Another odd fact regarding the virtual absence of the police was that department detectives were in regular contact with their paid informant in the Klan who helped to organize the counter-demonstration.

Later, the white supremacist shooters claimed self-defense and were acquitted by all-white juries in both a state and a federal criminal trial. A third, federal civil trial jury found the shooters, as well as two Greensboro police officers and their paid Klan informant, jointly liable for the wrongful death of one of the five killed. On their behalf, the city of Greensboro paid damages of nearly $400,000 to the victim's widow and to two injured protestors.

Although decades have passed since the shootings, emotions still run high when the memory is recalled in Greensboro. Many believe that the divided memories of the events contribute to the difficulty in solving current problems. One of those community members is Carolyn Allen, Greensboro mayor from 1993 to 1999, who recalled:

In returning to the political scene here—just sort of gradually as months and years went by—I began to see that many of our racial difficulties were related to a lack of trust, and much of that all seemed to head back to the '79 events. (Allen 2005)

In 2001, community members—including Allen, surviving former CWP demonstrators, religious leaders, and others—embarked on an unprecedented grassroots effort to seek truth and work toward reconciliation around the 1979 events. With support from the Andrus Family Fund and the International Center for Transitional Justice, the group adapted the truth and reconciliation model used most famously in South Africa and Peru after oppressed groups took power.

In 2004, the Greensboro Truth and Reconciliation Commission was sworn in and began its work of seeking the truth around the context, causes, sequence, and consequence of the events of November 3, 1979. During its nearly two years of work, the Commission interviewed approximately 150 people, including former members of the Communist Workers' Party, residents of the Morningside Homes housing project, police officers, current and former Klansmen and neo-Nazis, defense attorneys, prosecutors, and even the judge in the state murder trial. The Commission hosted three two-day public hearings during which 54 speakers publicly shared their understandings of what happened, why, and what should be done to address it. The Commission also engaged the community in numerous ways—through blogs, a public access television show, a door-to-door campaign, newsletters, dialogs, and community workshops.

Divided Community Memories

Nearly everyone in Greensboro who had any memory of the 1979 event had strong feelings both about what happened and about the pending truth and reconciliation process. During a door-to-door campaign, the members and staff of the Greensboro Truth and Reconciliation Commission (GTRC) found support and opposition in both white and black communities, but the sources of that opposition and support were quite different.

Dr. Mary Johnson echoes many of her white neighbors when she says that she sees the 1979 shootings as disconnected from the city itself. As she wrote on a local blog:

As I have said before, the Greensboro I know and love and have experienced my whole life has NOTHING to do with the freakish aberration of one day in 1979. . . . Greensboro is also the home of the Woolworth's sit-ins and I daresay that is what people in San Francisco and Boston and Seattle and New York City would think of FIRST if someone would just let them. MANY RESIDENTS of Greensboro in 2006 are saying, PLEASE LET THEM.[8]

Although many white residents shared a sense that the 1979 events did not reflect a systematic problem in the local government institutions, several did support the truth and reconciliation process because of a sense that there was a need to foster better relationships between the city's white and black communities. These white residents tended to emphasize the "reconciliation" aspect of the GTRC process over the goals related to truth seeking.

For others, like Lewis A. Brandon, III, an African American civic leader who, among other things, participated in the famous sit-ins at the whites-only lunch counter at Greensboro's Woolworths in 1960, the anti-Klan march was one of many challenges to the racist and classist status quo in the city:

I don't know of any social change that occurred in this community without a struggle. . . . That's the Greensboro I know. Change doesn't come because of the goodness of people in the community. People have to struggle. People have to fight to get change in this community.[9]

Although most of Greensboro's black residents shared Brandon's sense that the 1979 events were but one example of the city's racist and classist history, many openly opposed the GTRC process. The reasons for this opposition varied widely and ranged from a lack of time to devote to the process, to a sense of hopelessness that anything would change as a result of the process, to a fear that their participation would result in retaliation from the police department, the Klan, their bosses, and landlords. Those black residents who openly supported the GTRC process, however, emphasized the importance of a collective acknowledgment of the "truth" surrounding the 1979 events.

What Does the Past Have to Do with New Traumas?

During the course of the Commission's work, more problems were brewing within the Greensboro Police Department. The department's special intelligence division was accused of targeting black officers and other black community members with a "black book" and other unethical and unfair surveillance tactics. The former mayor Carolyn Allen's observations about the lingering impacts of the divided community memories were supported as conversations about the new scandal inevitably brought up disputes about the events of November 3, 1979. (Figure 10.2 shows an illustration that one local political cartoonist drew about the events and the efforts to address the events with the community.)

What Is Reconciliation, and Has It Been Achieved in Greensboro?

Michael Ignatieff says that the best outcome a truth commission can hope for is to narrow the range of permissible lies a community tells about

Figure 10.2
Cartoon by Anthony Piraino, http://pleadthefirst.com, January 22, 2006. Reprinted with permission.

itself (Hayner 2001). If that is the ultimate goal of a TRC, then the process in Greensboro has been partially successful. Some of the inaccuracies repeated regularly in the local daily paper and anecdotally around town about the 1979 events—that the police were absent from the scene because they were confused about the starting point of the march, and because they did not realize that that white supremacists were on their way to disrupt the march—have been challenged successfully through the process, most notably with the publication and release of the GTRC's final report in May, 2006. Since that time, media accountings of the events of 1979 have included fewer inaccuracies than before the report was released.

But, so far, most would agree that the "reconciliation" aspect of the process has not been fully realized. In fact, some, mostly white, residents argue that the city is more sharply divided along race and class lines now than it was before the process was initiated. Leaders in the GTRC process believe that these people make that argument because, prior to the TRC process, most residents were unaware of the racial divides and disparities prevalent in Greensboro. The TRC process opened up the opportunity for black residents and others to talk openly about these divides; and it also thrust those issues and stories into the local media, making it impossible for many white residents to continue ignoring them.

In Bridges's terms, the process forced them into an "ending." No longer can those residents pretend that the disparities—in terms of relationships to government institutions, housing, health care, education, and so forth—do not exist. No longer can they pretend that the events of November 3, 1979, occurred in a vacuum with no connection to other parts of Greensboro's reality. Some of the discomfort being experienced by some residents now is the mourning that comes with that ending. The loss of their old way of seeing their city creates feelings of depression and anxiety. Other residents are in the neutral zone, having acknowledged and having let go of their old way of seeing the city, but not yet to a place of settling into a new way of being. It remains to be seen whether a critical mass of Greensboro's residents have sufficiently acknowledged these disparities and unjust histories and will find a new beginning sufficient to rectify the systems that have allowed these disparities and injustices to exist in the first place.

Confronting the Legacy of Slavery, Segregation, and Discrimination at the University of Virginia

One of the coauthors has been working at the university since 1990,[10] and he has been privileged in recent years to teach on the lawn of the university, in one of the pavilions originally built to house faculty and classes and still used for that same purpose.

On the first day of each class, he asks the students, "Who built this place?"

They all look uncertain; they probably think it's a trick question, because they have already been told that Thomas Jefferson built the university. So when he tells them, "This building was built with labor provided by slaves," they are taken aback.

They continue to be taken aback as they realize that not just that building, but the whole University of Virginia was built with slave labor, that the university faculty and graduates perpetuated slavery, segregation, and discrimination on many levels and for many decades, and that the legacy of that history continues today.

Many changes have been made. African Americans now hold key leadership posts at administrative and student levels. African American alumni are among the most respected and beloved names associated with the university. The graduation rate among African Americans is consistently the highest among all public universities in the entire country. The university instituted a highly regarded financial aid program to encourage greater access to all students from lower-income families.

Many in the university community take great pride in those efforts. Yet, while major change has occurred, a complete transition yet remains. The legacy of slavery and segregation has by no means been fully explored; it is not fully understood and has not been fully addressed.[11] Many African Americans and others in the community view the university not as an economic and community asset but as an uncaring and even oppressive institution. African Americans are far more likely to be found in the classrooms after hours as custodians than during class time as instructors.[12] Manifest injustices of continuing racial disparities of health, wealth and poverty, housing, and education remain highly visible in the Charlottesville community. Locally, the university continues to described as "The Plantation."

These conditions and others demonstrate a legacy that leaves the university and surrounding community less resilient. This condition is shown through incidents such as the attacks previously described and through community responses to university efforts that view such efforts through a thick lens of distrust.

Institutional Acknowledgment and the "University and Community Action for Racial Equity" Project

In spring 2007, Virginia's General Assembly concluded a bitter debate by endorsing an expression of regret—pointedly *not* an apology—that included powerful language, despite its limitations (emphasis added):

- WHEREAS, *the most abject apology for past wrongs cannot right them . . . the spirit of true repentance on behalf of a government, and, through it, a people, can . . . avert the repetition of past wrongs and the disregard of manifested injustices;*

- WHEREAS, *the story of Virginia's Native Americans and the enslavement of Africans and their descendants . . . and . . . the faith, perseverance, hope, and endless triumphs of Native Americans and African Americans . . . should be embraced, celebrated, and retold for generations to come;*

- RESOLVED . . . the General Assembly hereby *acknowledge with profound regret* the involuntary servitude of Africans and the exploitation of Native Americans . .

- RESOLVED FURTHER, . . . the General Assembly *call upon the people of the Commonwealth to express acknowledgment and thanksgiving* for the contributions of Native Americans and African Americans to the Commonwealth and this nation. . .

The Board of Visitors of the University of Virginia followed with their own endorsement of the General Assembly's action. That endorsement included this language (emphasis added):

- WHEREAS, the *Board of Visitors commends the governor and the General Assembly* for these actions and *expresses its regret* for the institution of slavery in this state; and
- WHEREAS, the *mostly anonymous laborers employed in the construction of the University were both enslaved and free,* as was the University's workforce between 1825 and 1865; and
- WHEREAS, *the board expresses its particular regret for the employment of enslaved persons* in these years;
- RESOLVED, the Board of Visitors recommits itself to the principles of equal opportunity and to the principle that *human freedom and learning are and must be inextricably linked* in this commonwealth and in this republic.

Undoubtedly, both the Virginia General Assembly and the University Board of Visitors believed that their actions provided an ending of the debate over responsibility for past actions. However, others at the University of Virginia viewed these statements not as a closed door. Rather, the statements provide an opening for a long-overdue examination of the university's history of slavery and segregation, as well as its continuing impact within and outside of the university community.

This examination is taking place as we write this chapter. A systematic, coordinated effort (involving university students, administration faculty and staff, alumni, and community members) is defining how the university community can complete the transition from its continuing legacy of slavery and segregation to a community of shared purpose. This examination, which has come to be called *University and Community Action for Racial Equity* (UCARE), is aimed at transitioning to a community in which recognition and understanding of all of the past, the bad and the good, allows the university and surrounding community to develop authentic relationships based upon integrity, trust, accomplishment, and shared purpose. The goal is to understand history but no longer to be defined by that history. As new challenges inevitably arise, the university and surrounding community will no longer be divided along racial lines in the same ways that limit its capacity. In short, they will be more resilient.

The exact nature of this work is being defined by those who become engaged in the UCARE process.[13] Many members of the University of Virginia community want to address the continuing legacy of slavery, segregation, and discrimination with honesty and courage. They want understanding and recognition of these wrongs, acknowledgment of institutional and individual roles in perpetuating these wrongs, and responsible actions that address any continuing legacy of those wrongs. They want a community in which *all* of its members, not just those of a certain race, share the same educational and economic opportunities and share the same opportunities to lead healthy, safe, and rewarding lives.

The initial convening stage for UCARE, which laid the groundwork for this effort, consisted of an entire year of quiet interviews and discussions with key university and community stakeholders. These interviews introduced parties to the project concept, helped refine the necessary scope of the project, identified a growing list of additional interested parties, generated ideas for ways of improving the process, and identified concerns and roadblocks to be addressed before moving forward.

This initial work resulted in a working vision and mission. The vision is *to move from a position of privilege and benevolence to a position of responsibility and action, in order to reconcile the past and the present.* The working mission is *for concerned University of Virginia faculty, staff, and students as well as community members to meet on a regular basis to propose actions and engage with relevant questions in order to achieve this vision.*

The rationale for that vision is to change how the university engages the community. The university already is actively engaged in the community in many ways, with activities that arguably bring many tangible benefits to that community. Yet those actions stem not from recognition that current conditions are in any way tied to the past, but instead from motivations such as a sense of active citizenship, a concern with being a good neighbor, or efforts to improve public relations. Missing from these actions is understanding and acknowledgment of the devastating and enduring impact that the university has had due to its institutional support for slavery, racial segregation, and discrimination.

That impact is real, and its legacy is seen in conditions at the university and in surrounding communities. The vision makes salient that link.

As this book goes to press, substantial work has been completed. This work includes the following activities:

• An initial series of interviews and small-group meetings, growing the project from a handful of founders to hundreds of participants

• Development of a steering committee representing community as well as university staff, faculty, and students

• A series of roundtable dialogs bringing together between twenty-five to forty-five members of the university and surrounding communities

• Several student-focused meetings with diverse student leadership

• Action Group meetings of ten to twenty people focused on three themes—truth and understanding, repair, and relationships—that developed ideas for actions that would enact the UCARE vision

• Numerous community and university administration and class presentations, discussions, and small-group meetings

This work has led to the following efforts, to date:

• *University of Virginia History: Race and Repair*   This pioneering course focused on university–community history attracted fifteen students and fifteen noncredit (no cost) community members. It was cotaught by university professors and the director of a community advocacy organization. Besides introducing students to the topic, the course conducted archival research and oral histories. It concluded with a widely attended community forum.

• *Memorializing History*   A student-led effort, endorsed by the student council, is developing a competition for a memorial for slavery and other aspects of racialized history. This memorial effort has generated considerable university and community support.

• *Orientations for Student Volunteers*   UCARE students are working with Madison House (the University clearinghouse for several thousand student volunteers each year) to improve understanding of the racial dimensions of local history, particularly concerning university–community relations, as well as cultural competency.

• *Networking Meetings*   UCARE was asked to help collect information and encourage networking of individuals and organizations who work for racial equity. Networking meetings concerning health care and housing, respectively, have been held that have allowed for people from the community and the university to meet one another, share information, and coordinate actions.

• *Charlottesville Dialogue on Race*   The Dialogue, initiated in 2009, is intended to "identify problems and propose concrete solutions and paths to action that promote racial reconciliation, economic justice and equity." UCARE had three participants on the Dialogue steering committee and provided a student intern and other assistance, and UCARE is deeply involved in follow-up actions.

• *Engaging University Administration*   UCARE participants have drafted a set of policy recommendations that recognize the influence of the university in areas such as employment and affordable housing.

The transition sought in this work is substantial. At least two major communities can be identified which have not realized an ending to date. UCARE hopes to create an ending for many white people by promoting an understanding of the consequences that racial privilege has extended, as well as an understanding that the changes UCARE seeks in fact reinforce rather than violate widespread conceptions of fairness, justice, and equity. For many members of the African American community, an ending would come from the widespread understanding and acknowledgment of the impact of slavery, segregation, and discrimination after decades of lies, obfuscation, and basic forgetting, followed by actions to address the inequities that exist today as a result of those wrongs.

Conclusions

We hypothesize that contemporary community problems may be rooted in or exacerbated by past harms. Communities that do not include some effort at collectively discerning and acknowledging what led to the original harm will not only be less resilient, but may face further entrenchment of the more resilient economic, social, and political systems that perpetuate divisions and disparities. While new challenges to communities already suffering from a legacy of unacknowledged harm can further entrench divisions, such challenges also may induce an increased willingness on the part of some formerly reluctant community members to better understand the historical antecedents of those contemporary problems. There is a saying that "reason may be clarified by disaster." For a short time at least—such as the aftermath of Hurricane Katrina, the finding of environmental contamination on Bainbridge Island, the public allegations of new scandals within the Greensboro Police Department, or a series of assaults on University of Virginia students—these new traumas can force part of the privileged group(s) to abandon their previous willingness to ignore, deny, or cover up unwelcomed aspects of their history. When community members are open to examining their myths and illusions, to acknowledging the truth of the history and its impact on the present and are open to acting to rectify the truths that were illuminated, a transition is possible that builds resilience.

But in the aftermath of trauma—particularly human-induced trauma—the tendency of leaders is usually in the opposite direction, focusing solely on immediate needs such as public safety at the expense of truth-seeking efforts. Our argument is that the oft-heard plan of "looking forward rather than backward" is a false choice. Community leaders would do well to take advantage of that increased willingness to examine the past that comes in the aftermath of trauma, if for no other reason than to be better prepared to face the future.

Notes

1. See, for example, Volkan (2004).

2. Unrightable wrongs, for purposes of this essay, refer to past injustices that (1) were systematically or intentionally inflicted upon a community or identity group, often shaped by prejudice and discrimination; (2) have historic, present, and future impacts/consequences for the parties involved and the broader community; (3) have come to involve a broad and complex set of issues and stakeholders, thus making efforts at resolution seem daunting or even impossible; (4) have spiritual, moral, emotional, social, economic, and political aspects and implications (Dukes 2009).

3. The other two elements related to capacity are, first, an ability to solve problems and to translate commitment into action, and, second, access to resources.

4. That idea may seem obvious; however, other variables may stifle or repress such interest, such as shame of victimization, fear of physical violence or re-victimization, avoidance of public conflict, and unwillingness to challenge social norms.

5. Much of this section comes from the personal experience of coauthor Frank Dukes, who worked on this project as part of the reuse planning process for the Superfund site.

6. From memorial literature (http://www.bijac.org/index.php?p=MEMORIAL OriginMessage): "the committee is guided by a vision for an evocative and contemplative memorial that will have the power to instruct future generations about the injustices of the past and to be forever vigilant about the fragility of assumed rights." Photos showing the march down the long dock to the ship that would remove them from the island portray the fear and shame of those Japanese Americans and the guards with bayoneted rifles. One particularly powerful image is that of a young boy standing stoically; that boy, now Dr. Frank Kitamoto, chaired the memorial committee. The heart of the design is a long walkway toward the water, with statuary of those families; visitors will literally stand on the same path as they did.

7. Much of the material for this section has come from the experience of one of the coauthors, Jill Williams, who served as executive director of the Commission.

8. Dr. Mary Johnson, comment to "Apology," www.edcone.com, posted 6-24-2006.

9. Lewis A. Brandon, III, Public Hearing Statement, Greensboro Truth and Reconciliation Commission, July 15, 2005.

10. Much of this section comes from the personal experience of coauthor Frank Dukes as one of the leaders of this effort.

11. As just one example, many of the university buildings and street names honor slave owners and avid segregationists and, in the case of Jordan Hall (a leader in the field of eugenics), the need for race purification. Three graduates taught by Dr. Jordan led the Public Health Service's (PHS) infamously unethical research (1932–1972) of untreated syphilis, in which African American men with syphilis in the study were left untreated and uninformed of their condition. This study, which ran from 1932 to 1972, is referred to as "The Tuskegee Study of Untreated Syphilis in the Negro Male." It ended only after national newspapers brought it to national attention. Despite a formal apology offered by President Clinton in 1997, an enduring legacy of this and other unethical medical research conducted on African Americans has been continuing distrust about health care, medical trials, and government programs in general.

12. Approximately 4 percent of the faculty is African American, in contrast to 52 percent of the service and maintenance staff.

13. Examples of participant goals include the following (UCARE Steering Committee, September 15, 2009):

Hold UVA responsible for past acts of human oppression and demand remedy proportionate to the level and degree of said oppression.

Acknowledge and address the racial disparities in our community affecting quality of life issues such as healthcare, housing, employment, and education, with primary focus on the past, present, and future impact of the University on/among the community.

Be a catalyst for actions from a broad base of participants to address the past, current and potential harms of slavery, racial injustice and inequalities that exist among UVA and the Charlottesville community.

References

Allen, C. 2005. *Statement to the Greensboro Truth and Reconciliation Commission.* Greensboro, NC: GTRC Archives at Bennett College for Women in Greensboro.

Bridges, W. 1991. *Managing transitions: Making the most of change.* New York: Addison-Wesley.

Chaskin, R. 2001. Defining community capacity: A definitional framework and case studies from a comprehensive community initiative. *Urban Affairs Review* 36(3):291–323.

Dawson, M. 2006. After the deluge: Publics and publicity in Katrina's wake. *Du Bois Review* 3(1):239–249.

Dukes, E. F. 2006. Rethinking community involvement for Superfund Site reuse: The case for consensus-building in adaptive management. In *Reclaiming the land: Rethinking Superfund institutions, methods and practices*, eds. G. Macey and J. Z. Cannon, 211–243. New York: Springer.

Dukes, E. 2009. Truth, understanding and repair. *Law and Contemporary Problems* 72(3):101–105.

Hayner, P. B. 2001. *Unspeakable truths: Facing the challenge of truth commissions.* New York: Routledge.

Minow, M. 2002. Memory and hate: Are there lessons from around the world? In *Breaking the cycle of hatred*, ed. M. Minow. Princeton, NJ: Princeton University Press.

Piraino, A. Reconciliation. (cartoon) Accessed 11-30-2009. Available at http://pleadthefirst.com/2006/01/22/cartoon-reconciliation/.

Putnam, R. 2000. *Bowling alone: The collapse and revival of American community.* New York: Simon and Schuster.

Volkan, V. 2004. Traumatized societies and psychological care: Expanding the concept of preventive medicine. In *Living with terror, working with trauma: A clinician's handbook*, ed. D. Knafo, 479–498. Oxford, U.K.: Rowman & Littlefield.

B

Advocating Change

11

Fostering Collaborative Resilience Through Adaptive Comanagement: Reconciling Theory and Practice in the Management of Fisheries in the Mekong Region

Robert Arthur, Richard Friend, and Melissa Marschke

The Mekong River runs through Vietnam, Cambodia, Thailand, Laos, Burma, and China. It originates from the Tibetan Plateau. The river is central to a region that is going through a period of rapid change. Within this context, the management of the Mekong region capture fisheries is at a critical juncture: large in scale and hugely important to local livelihoods and economies, yet also a feature of contested views of development (see, for example, Arthur and Friend 2011). These fisheries are facing a number of threats, including over-fishing (Wong et al. 2007; Allan et al. 2005), environmental degradation (Salayo et al. 2008), climate change (Ficke et al. 2007), and hydropower and other infrastructure development (Ringler and Cai 2006). Narratives of doom and an unavoidable tragedy of the commons scenario are pervasive, and fisheries scientists and managers are struggling to address these threats and (perhaps even more pressing) to demonstrate the significant developmental benefits arising from well-managed fisheries (Friend et al. 2009; Arthur and Friend 2011).

The capture fisheries of the Mekong region represent "complex systems" of dynamic, interlinked social and bio-physical elements across a range of scales, characterized by contested values and interests, in which policy decisions are made on limited information and with high stakes (see, for example Funtowicz and Ravetz 2003; van der Sluijs 2006; Verweij and Thompson 2006). Given the critical juncture of the fisheries, this chapter examines the potential for adaptive comanagement in the Mekong region.

As researchers engaged in development practice, our work has attempted to address how the Mekong capture fisheries can best be managed in order to meet the needs and aspirations of the people associated with these fisheries. We have each been involved in fisheries management and policy research in the region for some time and have seen shifts in the management approaches recommended for these fisheries. The latest focus (one that we are involved in) concerns the promise of adaptive comanagement and working toward enhanced social-ecological resilience (e.g., Garaway and Arthur 2004; Marschke and Berkes 2006; Armitage et al. 2008). Within the region, adaptive comanagement has emerged as part of a broader interest by fishers, some state officials, and nongovernmental organization (NGO) activists in exploring alternatives to state-driven approaches (e.g., Baird 1996; Garaway and Arthur 2004). In this chapter we reflect on the usefulness of this concept in the context of Mekong fisheries.

Our chapter begins with a brief overview of the Mekong capture fisheries, and then it turns to a consideration of the roots of adaptive comanagement in this region. More specifically, we present a brief overview of adaptive management and comanagement to better understand how adaptive comanagement has emerged as a potential management option for the fisheries. We pay particular attention to what adaptive comanagement is meant to do, and, in doing so, we suggest that the approach runs the risk of being too rationalist and technocratic unless particular attention is paid to issues of agency, knowledge, and power within fisheries policy and management processes. We further point out that the most important promise of adaptive comanagement lies in its potential as a process that can *create* the conditions under which management is possible. This chapter concludes with an analysis of adaptive comanagement as an approach for fisheries governance in the Mekong region and offers several recommendations for further research and deliberation.

This research stems from our work with other academics on the idea of adaptive comanagement (e.g., Garaway et al. 2006; Armitage et al. 2009) and in thinking about fisheries and fisheries management within the Mekong region (e.g., Friend et al. 2009; Arthur and Friend 2011). Our research has drawn on a combination of fieldwork in freshwater and coastal fisheries sites (in Cambodia, Lao PDR, Thailand, and Vietnam), interviews with fisheries managers, engagement in policy debates, an extensive literature review, and our collective experiences working on natural resource management issues.

The Mekong Region Fisheries

Fisheries of the Mekong region (Cambodia, Thailand, Lao PDR, and Vietnam)—inland and coastal, wild- and culture-based—are important socially and economically (Arthur and Friend 2011. For example, in 2008 the overall production of the Mekong inland capture fisheries was cited as 1.9 million tonnes with an estimated value of US$2–2.5 billion per year

(MRC 2007, 2010). In addition to the fisheries based on the main channel of the Mekong River, and the larger, more visible examples such as Tonle Sap, there is a great diversity and diffusion of small-scale fisheries in ponds, streams, and rice fields (Gregory and Guttman 1996; Garaway and Arthur 2002), as well as small-scale yet productive upland fisheries (e.g., Degen et al. 2005; Gregory et al. 2007). Aquatic resources from these fisheries systems are central to nutrition and food security, contributing between 27–78 percent of animal protein in rural diets across the Mekong basin (Meusch et al. 2003; Hortle 2007). Fisheries support many tens of thousands of small-scale entrepreneurs, ranging from shop owners and food stalls that supply fishing families to boat builders and suppliers of fishing gear (MRC 2010). Fisheries are also of particular importance to poor people partly due to the nature of fisheries as common property resources, acting as a component of diversified livelihood strategies, and as a safety-net and coping strategy (Meusch et al. 2003; Arthur and Sheriff 2008; Arthur and Friend 2011).

The fisheries systems of the Mekong region carry significant ecological importance. The inland and coastal fisheries are based on a naturally highly variable system that includes a huge number of interdependent species with different life cycles and highly seasonal abundance. Many species migrate over large distances. Added to the variability of natural systems and productivity, which are poorly understood, are the diverse and dynamic ways in which people interact with the natural system. People fish in different ways and generally not in a regular, uniform, full-time "professional" manner (Smith et al. 2005; Marschke and Berkes, 2006; Arthur and Sheriff, 2008). People also employ different gears, targeting a range of habitats, with different levels of intensity at different times of the year (e.g., Deap et al. 2003).

The complex nature of these fisheries presents a considerable management challenge. In response to this challenge, fisheries management in the region is characterized by a somewhat paradoxical combination of state absence and ineffectiveness, together with efforts at state command and control (Sneddon 2007). These efforts are hampered by notoriously weak environmental governance and hierarchical social and political structures (e.g., Ascher 2001; Blunt and Turner 2005). What is more, there is often a general incompatibility of state interests and local interests, and situations where access to and control over natural resources has been, and remains, highly contested (e.g., Sneddon 2007) with rapid encroachment and privatization of common property resources (particularly in Cambodia and Laos).

Where fisheries management does appear, across the four Mekong countries it has increasingly tended toward conservation of stocks in order to maintain production. For many, fisheries management has been based on policy and legislation that uses gear restrictions and licenses, combined with the establishment of blanket closed seasons defined for the whole country that broadly correspond with breeding and spawning seasons. However, enforcement has been highly variable, and in most cases ineffective, often causing tensions between state agents and local fishers. Within this system there appears to be significant space for political and commercial influence to determine access and control over resources (Thuon and Vannara 2005; Sneddon 2007).

Against this backdrop, there has been an increasing interest by fishers, some state officials, and NGO activists in alternatives to state-driven approaches. There have been a number of initiatives to support local involvement in resource management, sometimes with support from government actors, each with various degrees of success (e.g., Baird 2000; Garaway and Arthur, 2004), and most recently there appears to be an interest in the idea of adaptive comanagement for fisheries management (Marschke and Nong 2003; Arthur and Garaway 2005; Wilson et al. 2006).

The Emergence of Comanagement and of Adaptive Management

Adaptive comanagement has emerged from two strands of natural resource management thinking: comanagement and adaptive management (Armitage et al. 2008). *Comanagement* is concerned with issues of sharing rights and responsibilities. In contrast, *adaptive management* is an approach explicitly recognizing that natural and social-ecological systems have inherent uncertainties, and that management and policy approaches can address these uncertainties. Thus this merger—driven to a large extent by natural resource management thinking rather than development studies or public administration—is a response to the challenges of managing complex and dynamic resource systems. We will examine each concept in turn.

Comanagement emerged as a people-centered response to Hardin's (1968) "tragedy of the commons" and to the failure of centralized "command and control" approaches in resource management (Berkes 2006). Much of this thinking stems from research in the area of common pool resources (e.g., McCay and Acheson 1987; Ostrom 1990; and Oakerson 1992). Scholars of the commons have examined governance arrangements in diverse resource systems with multiple user groups often at a local scale, but also at regional and global scales (Ostrom et al. 2002; Dietz, Ostrom, and Stern 2003). The emphasis on rules of access, exclusion, and subtractability, and the identification of design principles or enabling conditions for the management of common pool resources are major contributions (Ostrom 1990; Baland and Platteau 1996; Agrawal 2002).

Theories for commons governance have continued to evolve (Armitage 2008), including the area of comanagement (e.g., Pinkerton 1989; Pomeroy et al. 2001, and Wilson et al. 2003). Comanagement is an institutional form that encourages a multilevel perspective and involves sharing the rights and responsibilities for a particular resource among several actors, usually involving some configuration of the state, resource users, and civil society (Pinkerton 1992; Armitage 2008). Common across definitions of comanagement are the notions of shared responsibility and authority for decision making in the management of natural resources (McCay and Acheson 1987; Sen and Nielsen 1996; Pinkerton 1992; Berkes et al. 2001; Borrini-Feyerabend et al. 2007). This body of thinking arose as a critique of the state's ability to understand and manage complex common pool resources on its own while recognizing the knowledge, skills, and rights of local resource users in terms of managing their own natural resources (Ostrom et al. 1999).

Comanagement arrangements vary across settings including the subject of management (which could be a single resource, such as a catfish stock, or multiple resources, such as those found within a marine protected area), the existing institutional arrangements, and the way in which comanagement is implemented or introduced, and by whom (e.g., Borrini-Feyerabend et al. 2007). For fisheries managers, comanagement offers a management approach that can potentially be viable under a variety of conditions (e.g., political, social, cultural, economic, bio-physical, and technological). Thus, comanagement could represent a less prescriptive approach for fisheries management and to resource management and institutional arrangements. By the late 1990s, the discourse of comanagement had gained in currency in the Mekong region. Comanagement was attractive to different actors for different reasons. To some, comanagement was an attractive option given that fisheries departments tended to be weak, poorly resourced, and that management institutions may exist *de facto* within "communities." While some of the motivation was to take an "asset-based" approach that builds on these local institutions and capabilities (Beck and Nesmith 2001, Garaway and Arthur 2004, Arthur and Garaway 2005), there were also undoubtedly other attractions. Poorly resourced government departments can be difficult for external agents such as researchers and NGOs to work with, while comanagement also provides opportunities to transfer the responsibility and cost of management, what Hara (2004) refers to as "instrumental comanagement."

The result of the interest and initiatives is a rhetorical policy commitment to community and comanagement of fisheries across all four Mekong countries, endorsed and promoted by the state and inter-governmental organizations. Such groups include the Food and Agriculture Organisation of the United Nations (FAO), the South East Asian Fisheries Development Center (SEAFDEC) (e.g., Brown et al. 2005); local NGOs such as the Community Based Natural Resource Management Learning Institute (CBNRM LI) in Cambodia; and academic-practitioners (e.g., Persoon et al. 2003; Pomeroy and Guieb 2005). These resulting community-state partnerships and processes for fisheries management have various names: community fisheries, community-based natural resource management, co-management, or, in a few cases, adaptive comanagement (Garaway and Arthur 2004; Marschke and Berkes 2006; Resurreccion 2006; Fennell et al. 2008). However, these names tend to be used rather loosely, with some programs emphasizing a strong governmental presence and others advocating for mostly community involvement. In practice, this looseness of terms presents some challenges when we want to talk about comanagement, because the less prescriptive nature of the approach means that the terms *comanagement* and *community-based management* can be unclear, and their application vague (see also Pinkerton 2003).

While comanagement was emerging from failures of centralized management, the literature on adaptive management was emerging in recognition of the challenges created by complex, dynamic, and uncertain natural resource systems and the rigidity of state institutions in place to manage these challenges. If not explicitly recognized and embraced, these uncertainties can lead to what Charles (2001) describes as the "illusion of certainty" and "fallacy of controllability" and unexpected, and often undesirable, outcomes (Ascher 2001; Lorenzen and Garaway 1998).

Since the 1970s, adaptive management has been advocated in situations where management of complex systems must proceed despite uncertainties and difficulties in predicting the results of management actions (e.g., Holling 1987; Walters 1986). Adaptive management can potentially address such acknowledged uncertainties and enable appropriate policies and management strategies to be identified (Gunderson et al. 1995; Lee 1993; Holling 1987; Walters 1986). In its earliest form, adaptive management was concerned more with methods for understanding the dynamics of managed fish and wildlife populations and for seeking optimum harvest policies in the face of uncertainty. Actions are developed to test alternative hypotheses aimed at reducing key uncertainties that have been identified. In this way, management can be specifically used to generate new information about the resource system dynamics *at the same time* as it is being managed, with management actions subsequently being refined based on this information.

This experimentation may be of two types, both based on contrasting variation in management actions, either temporally or spatially. These two types are passive experimentation, where the focus is on contrasting existing variation in the system such as spatial differences in management, and active experimentation, where variation is deliberately introduced into the system (Walters 1986). In both cases, experimentation is led by scientists and experts who construct the hypotheses that are tested and who present these results to decision makers. Much of the early focus was on the tools that these experts can use, for example, mathematical models and Bayesian statistics (see Walters 1986). Most examples of adaptive management stemmed from the developed world, where management agencies are relatively well resourced, where governance mechanisms are in place to allow for such dialogue among stakeholders, and where mechanisms such as independent public inquiries and expert panels are well established (e.g., Sainsbury 1988; McAllister et al. 1992). The relatively level playing fields of multistakeholder dialogue do not necessarily apply in the Mekong (Friend 2009, Arthur 2004).

The notion of what constitutes a desirable outcome of adaptive management has been influenced by thinking on systems dynamics and sustainability. Those people viewing the problem from an ecological perspective argued that the appropriate aims of management in dynamic uncertain systems should be less about stability and maximizing benefits, and more about management that maintains the structure and function of the natural system (e.g., Holling 1987; Lee 1993; Gunderson et al. 1995). This thinking has been extended to social-ecological systems and notions of managing for "resilience" (e.g., Walker and Salt 2006).

Over the past three decades the definition of *adaptive management* has shifted, becoming less explicitly focused on natural science orientated experimentation (e.g., Walters 1986; Hilborn and Walters 1992) and toward more of an iterative learning or learning-by-doing approach (e.g., Colfer 2005; Arthur 2004; Garaway and Arthur 2004; Ruitenbeek and Cartier 2001). This learning focus perhaps resulted from the difficulties and challenges experienced by people attempting to implement explicitly experimental approaches in a top-down manner (e.g., Walters 2007). The growing interest in participatory approaches (and collaborative learning in particular) is reflected in the changing emphasis in the definitions and a shift toward adaptive comanagement. Ruitenbeek and Cartier (2001, p. 8), for example, define *adaptive comanagement* as "a long-term management structure that permits stakeholders to share management responsibility within a specific system of natural resources, and to learn from their actions." Folke (2006) suggests the approach is a process by which institutional arrangements and ecological knowledge are tested and revised in a dynamic, self-organizing process of learning-by-doing.

The explicit attention given to learning in these definitions of adaptive comanagement represents an evolution that identifies the willingness of concerned stakeholders to come together in some form of dialogue, as an important aspect of management approaches and one that can be incorporated into the process of implementation.

The Promise of Adaptive Comanagement

Adaptive comanagement, a new term, emerged from academia rather than policy and practice. This term brings together strands of thinking from the comanagement and adaptive management literatures to include elements of shared management authority and iterative learning (Armitage et al. 2009). Adaptive comanagement is described as "an emergent and self-organising process facilitated by rules and incentives of higher levels, with the potential to foster more robust social-ecological systems" (Resilience Alliance 2008). Key features of adaptive comanagement include the following: (a) learning-by-doing; (b) synthesis of different knowledge systems; (c) collaboration and power sharing; (d) management flexibility. Although definitions of *adaptive comanagement* vary, embedded in this concept are ideas of collaboration and learning (Olsson et al. 2004; Arthur and Garaway 2005; Armitage et al. 2009).

In a sense, adaptive comanagement can be thought of as a resource management tool that works toward enhanced social-ecological resilience. Resilience can be defined as the capacity of a system to absorb disturbance and reorganize while undergoing change, so as to still retain essentially the same function, structure, identity, and feedbacks (Walker et al. 2004). As such, resilience is future oriented, and it is used to characterize a system's ability to deal with change (Marschke and Berkes 2006). In resilient social-ecological systems, change and renewal may nurture novelty and innovation (Folke 2006). This thinking derives from Holling's (1973) ecological research, which focused on complexity, nonlinear dynamics and dynamic interim processes. Within these complex systems, change might be slow and gradual or, at other times, large and rapid (Armitage and Johnson, 2006). Transition is a contested and dynamic process featuring inevitable uncertainty (Fischer-Kowalski and Rotmans 2009). The potential of adaptive comanagement emerges from the recognition that transition is an ongoing, responsive process based largely upon human interaction. Knowledge and communication therefore play critical roles.

In the context of the Mekong region, this approach holds an appeal within the natural resource management, scientific, and research communities (Phuong 2005; Khrutmuang et al. 2005; Armitage et al. 2009; Rojanasaeng 2008). This appeal arises as a response to the complexity and diversity of the systems, uncertainties about the effectiveness of current management arrangements, the diverse range of stakeholders, and the often unexpected outcomes from previous policies and practices (Lorenzen and Garaway 1998; Marschke and Nong 2003; Arthur and Garaway 2006; Fennell et al. 2008). Furthermore, comanagement (and now adaptive comanagement) approaches to natural resources management resonate with the regional agendas of democracy, decentralization, and devolution.

Adaptive comanagement is proposed as an evolving long-term approach, engaging actors associated with a resource in joint learning-by-doing across both scale and level (e.g., Garaway and Arthur 2004; Lebel et al. 2005; Berkes et al. 2007; Armitage et al. 2008). This approach is presented as a way of harnessing all available assets to learn and adapt and, through this process, contribute to developmental objectives. Learning (as with adaptive management) is not focused on optimization or a particular target. Rather, learning becomes a platform for developing "adaptive capacity" and "resilience," often assuming that good policy and more appropriate management outcomes will result. Both the management and learning processes can take on different forms according to the specific policy and management context (Borrini-Feyerabend et al. 2007; Armitage et al. 2009).

As with both comanagement and adaptive management, adaptive comanagement is context specific (it differs among places). While this characteristic is not necessarily problematic, there is a significant risk that it becomes difficult for us to say what adaptive comanagement is and what it is not. We are concerned that *adaptive comanagement* is in danger of becoming what Cornwall (2007) terms a "buzzword and fuzzword." Cornwall (2007, 472) aptly notes that "development's buzzwords gain their purchase and power through their vague and euphemistic qualities, their capacity to embrace the multitude of possible meanings, and their normative resonance." The core terms (*comanagement* and *adaptive*) and the focus (learning, resilience, and adaptive capacity) are intuitively appealing, and it is difficult to be against any of these things. In other words, it is difficult to place the sanctity of this goal beyond reproach (Cornwall 2007).

Perhaps it is not surprising that *adaptation* and *resilience* are currently in vogue, as these emerging buzzwords fit with concerns over the effects of humans' impacts on the natural world and the shocks and stresses these effects produce. However this appeal, together with the difficulty in being able to define any of these terms in a way that helps in practice (or how these relate to broader development goals) also means that much of what is suggested as the promise of adaptive comanagement may be left unfulfilled (see also Brand and Jax 2007).

An area that we feel is often missed in discussions (of adaptive management, comanagement, and adaptive comanagement) is the politics of resource governance. Underpinning much of the current adaptive comanagement thinking is an essentially expertized management process, which emphasizes the application of science and rational planning to management and development problems (see also Rondinelli 1993; Locke 1996). In having this emphasis, the thinking downplays the political (and historically situated) dimensions of what we see as fundamental challenges of governance and power. If adaptive comanagement is approached in this way, then it is debatable how different it really is compared with the classic "command and control" management methods. Ironically, it is perhaps by focusing on concepts of learning as a central tenant within adaptive comanagement that the political dimensions of fisheries management and the underlying conflicts have been, and can be, obscured.

There are many issues and challenges associated with learning in complex fisheries systems. Learning, as it is currently discussed in the resource management literature, however, is often a vague topic, with the literature skating over the considerable challenges of bringing together multiple stakeholders with vested, often divergent and entrenched interests in the fishery (Armitage et al. 2009). Learning is frequently presented as apolitical—a process in which different stakeholders with different interests come together to achieve consensus and some shared vision. Coming together to "learn" is assumed to occur through a sense of shared interest. Learning is less easily applied in contexts of conflict, with stakeholders of different degrees of influence and power. Furthermore, it is often assumed that this learning process will generate new knowledge that will exist independently as agreed "facts" rather than as knowledge that is ephemeral, dynamic, and embedded instead within the relationships and the actions of people (e.g., Stacey 2001). Decoupling knowledge and meaning from people and relationships acts to depoliticize and dehumanize knowledge.

Although Armitage et al. (2009) recognize power asymmetries, there remains a considerable gulf between the adaptive comanagement literature and the literature on power and knowledge in the social sciences (Nadasdy 2007; Stacey 2001). As a result, key questions that are asked in the social sciences are not being asked in the fisheries sector, namely: whose interests are being served by a certain set of arrangements, or a certain goal or goals (Wiber 2007). For example, while proponents of adaptive comanagement are critical of top-down, state-led management (see, for example Berkes 2006; Armitage et al. 2008), there appears to be little analysis of the historical context of management within this literature, or of what actually happens in adaptive comanagement arrangements in terms of distribution of power, influence, and benefits. Without explicit and careful attention to how adaptive comanagement may fit within, or alter, preexisting patterns of social, political, economic, and cultural interactions, there is a risk of inadvertently overlooking how the new "co" types of institutional arrangements being proposed may perpetuate older, socially exploitative and environmentally deleterious patterns. Moreover, there are a few research cases demonstrating that power and influence determine the outcomes of fisheries management (e.g. Vannara and Thuon 2005 to the exclusion of poorer people.

Rational Planning: A Critical Issue for Fisheries Management

There is a risk that the practice of community-based management, comanagement, adaptive management, or adaptive comanagement (these ideas blur together in practice) can become geared toward a rational-planning perspective in which context and politics are often downplayed and the emphasis is instead on finding workable solutions that can be widely implemented. An approach that calls for management actions to be used as experiments opens the door to the expertization of the process. Indeed the roles of different actors, including researchers, are rarely questioned. However, if adaptive comanagement is increasingly concerned with governance and collaborative action, then this situation and issues of how (and to what extent) the approach modifies existing power structures, need to be addressed.

Rational planning is problematic because it takes the problems of development policy as accidents or as the results of poor policy and practice, rather than considering these policy problems in their full historical and political context. Thus poverty and environmental degradation are pre-sented as technocratic challenges rather than as political challenges, and these problems are placed outside of their structural context. While complexity *is* acknowledged, in practice it is simplified to a "manageable" degree, applying a rational, problem-solving discourse to the framing of the problem and in identifying solutions (see also Rondinelli 1993). When people take this course, the approach more often than not reinforces notions of the supremacy of science and of experts, and legitimizes specific actors without adequate consideration of the contested nature of development management and policy, and the critical role of human relationships and agency.

While such approaches have their place, they make less sense in the sorts of complex, messy, and highly politicized contexts that characterize so many of the Mekong fisheries. In this situation, development challenges, contested spaces, and power struggles within and among stakeholder groups cannot be resolved simply through negotiation, facilitation, and im-proving communication to result in socially just predictable outcomes (see also Ascher 2001; Wollenberg et al. 2007). Within these contexts, these approaches lack a meaningful conceptual framework for dealing with the unpredictability of social or institutional change that shapes outcomes. However, challenging the assumptions about the approach is no trivial matter, as many of the key suppositions are contained within persuasive and persistent discourses about both the nature of research and the fishery that perpetuate these assumptions and that are rarely subject to critical review (e.g., Arthur and Friend 2011; Friend et al. 2009).

From our experience with fisheries management in the Mekong, we believe that people need to reevaluate adaptive comanagement if they are to realize its potential. From a fisheries-science perspective, there are critical assumptions being made about how management works and the linkages among policy, research, and practice (in particular about the na-ture of policy, about how decisions are made, and by whom), and about how science, research, and information influence these elements (Friend 2009). These assumptions give rise to a linear model of research and policy founded on a notion of a "plausible promise." By this notion we mean that good, often scientific, information will lead to better policy and practice outcomes. This notion manifests itself in fisheries management in some simple assumptions: that the role of research in fisheries management and policy is to diagnose, assess, and monitor, thus generating information and making policy recommendations for (often unidentified) "decision mak-ers" to implement. Even within an adaptive comanagement framework, uncertainties about policy processes are downplayed, with policy and management processes presented in an idealized way, with assumptions about the capacity and willingness to use information within these processes in the intended way (e.g., Christie et al. 2007).

For the scientific community, the problem becomes one of an information gap to be filled by scientific facts (to be generated by scientists and experts). Science and policy become biased toward "puzzle-solving," offering simple solutions and models that, it is suggested, will generate successful outcomes for what are actually complex and multidimensional issues (e.g., Ackoff 1974; Rondinelli 1993; Verweij et al. 2006; Pitcher and Lam 2010). The workings and practice of science, claims to scientific truth and neutrality, and the construction of "facts and figures" are taken at face value and the "results" are often viewed outside of the problem's own social and political context. In this construct, the role of institutions, participation, and empowerment are largely seen as instrumental and a means to an end of improved policy outcomes (e.g., Bartlett 2008).

The critical assumptions about research and policy often lead to frustration among scientists that their recommendations are not correctly taken up by the decision makers. However, much of this frustration is aimed at the perceived failings of the policy and management institutions (e.g., Christie et al. 2007; Walters 2007) and the weakness of scientists in communicating with policy makers, rather than something more fundamentally wrong with the approach itself.

Shifting the Goal Posts of Adaptive Comanagement

Fisheries face a crisis of governance, not merely a crisis of management. Addressing this crisis means moving beyond formulaic approaches couched in the politically neutral language of planning, management, and science. This linear model of information to policy change has been heavily criticized in policy-related disciplines (e.g., Court et al. 2005; van der Sluijs 2006; Shore and Wright 1997), yet there has been little introspection among the fisheries science community of the role of science and agency of scientists, with some notable exceptions (Wilson et al. 2006). While there has been considerable scientific research undertaken on fisheries (and in particular on the fish) in the Mekong, scientists have rarely braved the murky waters of policy arenas and institutional functioning (Friend 2009). This chapter, however, will do so.

Despite the acknowledgment of messiness and complexity in fisheries as social-ecological systems (Andrew et al. 2007; Armitage et al. 2008), there is little corresponding recognition of how science should respond and engage in order to have influence. People still fall back on techno-cratic rationalist approaches and their attendant tool kits, methods, and preconditions. Preconditions for success are common to adaptive coman-agement (e.g., Armitage et al. 2008), comanagement theory (e.g., Pomeroy et al. 2001), and common property theory (e.g., Ostrom 1990; Agrawal 2002). Certainly within the Mekong region there are discrete fisheries that meet the conditions of collective action and adaptive comanagement, and where it has been possible to implement forms of adaptive comanagement (Arthur 2004; Marschke and Nong 2003; Garaway and Arthur 2002). But these examples are far from representative of the majority of fisheries. Much more common are the complex fisheries described in this chapter's introduction; rather few "conditions for successful comanagement" exist at this point. For example, one condition for success is having a well-defined resource system. Achieving this condition is nearly impossible given the extent of the mobility of aquatic species. Likewise, establish-ing a context in which "participants share and draw on a plurality of knowledge" is difficult given the often hierarchical nature of relationships within the Mekong region. Creating situations where power relations are explicitly dealt with (and where local and scientific knowledge is com-bined) is a task both time-consuming and difficult (Arthur and Garaway 2006; Arthur 2004).

Does this situation mean, then, that adaptive comanagement is not appropriate to such situations? After all, Armitage et al. (2009) have rec-ognized that adaptive comanagement is not a governance panacea and will not be appropriate in all cases. Further, Borrini-Feyerabend et al. (2007) note that under some conditions, comanagement and sharing power will fail. Well, we hope not. In our context—with the importance of the fisher-ies, and with so many of the fisheries of the Mekong region not meeting these criteria—we believe that the most important promise of adaptive comanagement is actually its potential to *create* the conditions under which management is possible. For us, the major challenge for adaptive comanagement currently is to consider knowledge, power, and the role for knowledge creation through science and research in the adaptive coman-agement process. We suggest a focus on the "adaptive" and "co" elements, rather than emphasizing management aspects through meta-analyses of comanagement initiatives to find the successful models to implement. This focus requires a new research and development agenda. People must recog-nize management as a governance challenge and therefore political (about power and agency), in which contestation and struggles are recognized and seen as constructive and unavoidable parts of the process (rather than as external threats), and where linear models of research to policy may not be adequate or appropriate.

We work in a development context. We recognize that the purpose of adaptive comanagement is change through application of knowledge and in determining who does what. Yet we have found few good discussions regarding our role as researchers within the adaptive comanagement process. This lack of reflection is surprising, considering that two implications of taking on board the discourse of adaptive comanagement is that researchers are players in the process, and that researchers are also required to be adaptive. Moreover, as researchers we need to explore new roles (e.g., Arthur and Garaway 2006; Wollenberg et al. 2007).

What attracted us to notions of adaptive comanagement is that the concept is intuitively appealing. The idea implies recognition of messiness and complexity. It highlights the unpredictable outcomes of planned interventions, and it offers that people throughout the system can potentially influence change (i.e., agency). However, as a practical approach, adaptive comanagement remains fairly poorly defined. We want to revitalize this concept of adaptive comanagement by reframing what the role of science and researchers can be in generating change. In doing so we will highlight the role of people as "agents of change" (e.g., Freire 1971) or even "drivers of change," recognizing that it is not just the external environment that drives change. Change manifests itself at the local level. This level is where we see the impact of interactions with the environment, with institutions, and with the outcomes of policies. Hence we are drawn to the local level for an analysis and exploration of the crucial aspects of agency, knowledge, and power in management.

The aspect of agency is crucial. Actors are not passive recipients but are capable, even within severely restricted social spaces. They can formulate decisions, act upon them, innovate or experiment (Long and Long 1992), as well as being capable of interpreting policies and even resisting them. In addition, we have recognized our own agency. As "scientists" or "researchers," we are not neutral or without our own agendas. Even the conclusions from our work may suffer from interpretation (see, for example, Yearley 1988). Following on from this line of thought, while the importance of institutions in adaptive comanagement has been highlighted (e.g., Armitage et al. 2008), the creation and development of institutions, alliances, and networks need to be recognized themselves as dynamic political processes in which individual actors will often work to advance their own cause and in which the outcomes will reflect the political influence of those involved (e.g., Young 2002; Arce and Fisher 2007). People, as actors with agency, therefore come to be at the center of an adaptive comanagement approach (Arthur 2004).

Taking this view makes clear how limited our ability is to "fix" the system. Instead we need to accept that the world is, and will continue to be, a complex, messy, and difficult context in which our understanding and influence is limited. Within this context we believe the emphasis should be on responsive, flexible, and nonlinear research processes that are about finding "clumsy solutions," emergent innovation, and "muddling through" (e.g., Stacey 2001; McCay 2002; Verweij and Thompson 2006; Wollenberg 2007).

Working in the fisheries of the Mekong, we have found a positive role for research; that is, research as a transformative process. Research can be about the whole process of human relating and questioning. It can be about the testing of ideas and the practice, review, and analysis that is so crucial to meeting the key elements of comanagement. These elements are adaptive (reflection and change) and comanagement (roles and responsibilities, authority and power). Within this process, knowledge is not a set of "facts" that will be uncovered but rather it is the product of people's interactions, existing only in them and continuously shaped by them. People "participate" in different stages of research, but they do so actively and with agency, for different purposes, and with different outcomes—and with different insights. This process is not always a happy, straightforward method, nor is it entirely predictable. We do not see research as necessarily being a means to address conflict and to achieve a "co-evolution of stakeholder preferences," shared goals, and compromise decisions (e.g., Rammel et al. 2007). As when dealing with inequitable power relations, there will be some element of conflict.

In each of our experiences, we found that the research process became increasingly engaged with the local people. Their needs and aspirations evolved as a result, with the process itself becoming something different over time. The shifting spaces—institutional and discursive—that this engagement produces create new knowledge, interfaces, opportunities, and fault lines for change. Getting actors at these interfaces involved in doing "research" is a strategy that creates new spaces, and the task of working changes the quality of these relationships. We would argue that adaptive comanagement must create and be engaged at these interfaces, using research to create opportunities for social change. Through this method, the nature of research is changed, and so does what it means to be a "researcher."

We are therefore not saying that this approach is straightforward. In our Mekong context, this process is indeed challenging. Governance and policy processes in the region lack transparency and accountability, and scientific knowledge is intimately linked to state power in development and natural resource management. Within this region, elements of democracy appear to mix with authoritarian and traditional practices, such as a lack of rule of law and widespread patronage (Hughes 2006). The challenges these factors present should not be underestimated and are of critical importance given that we work in a context where fishers are already marginalized in policy processes, and where poor fishers are the most marginal of the marginalized (e.g., Friend et al. 2009).

We recognize the political dimension of what we are suggesting. The superior knowledge of the state is often the key to its legitimacy, particularly when dealing face-to-face with rural constituents. Some actors can be expected to actively fight against the kind of engagement we are proposing, as the method challenges their role as experts. Where rural people are often illiterate, with limited formal education, the notion of dialogue and sharing does not make sense unless people are equipped. The authority of the expert is rarely challenged, even when the expert is clearly wrong. In our experience, engaged participatory research processes can broaden the policy arena and allow for different voices to be legitimately heard. This type of approach, when facilitated correctly, can serve as a counterbalance to authority and expertise in order for management to be truly an adaptive process of comanagement.

Conclusions

Our interest in adaptive comanagement is in the specific context of developing countries going through rapid change, in which access to and control over resources are at the heart of natural resources management. We see access and control as fundamental governance and political challenges. To realize the potential of adaptive comanagement in such complex settings, it is necessary to have greater specificity and clarity concerning the meanings and outcomes ascribed to research-policy interfaces, learning, power, and agency. So what does this clarity mean for us as scientists/researchers engaged in promoting adaptive comanagement? The recent attention on adaptive comanagement as a potential model for resource governance has provided us with a useful and timely opportunity to stop and reflect on the way that fisheries management has been approached in the Mekong region. Importantly, this opportunity has enabled us to consider the implications of the development of adaptive comanagement. Thus, we offer a number of conclusions.

First, we have realized that the focus of much of the practical implementation has emphasized steps in implementation and has involved far less discussion on our role as researchers. Lessons-learned, frameworks, guidelines, and tool kits, however useful, are not enough. Despite our best intentions, this method can easily lead the nascent practitioner toward a technocratic, rationalistic approach to adaptive comanagement—the very thing we should be seeking to avoid. Knowing our role as researchers is all the more important because we do not yet really know what works, partly because there is so little written on comanagement and participatory research outside of projectized implementation.

Second, we cannot just promote adaptive comanagement as a lens through which to view and interpret our work. Rather, we must actively engage in experiments in social change, self-aware of our role and motivations—open to critical review from the "intended beneficiaries." We cannot be simply neutral experts standing outside the system and process. Our engagement should be explicitly nonlinear science and research that is recognized as constructed and value laden, and where the focus is on an inclusive transformative process to generate knowledge rather than on finding solutions or recommendations (Ramos-Martin 2003; Frame and Brown 2008). Engaging in this sort of self-aware transformative process frames the kinds of questions we should be asking, and the kinds of things we should be doing.

Third, we should be more critical of the assumptions, arguments, and discourses that shape policy approaches, building on recent work addressing policy (Roe 1991; Hajer and Versteeg 2005; Johnson 2006; Verweij et al. 2006; Shore and Wright 1997). There is a relative absence of critical reflection on the elements of adaptive comanagement's potentially progressive program. For example, are its foundational concepts such as resilience and learning sufficiently elaborated so as to really stimulate new dynamic social arrangements (Wiber 2007; Brand and Jax 2007)? The risk of not reflecting on this approach is that adaptive comanagement will merely reinforce (rather than challenge) the status quo arrangements that continue to undermine human ecology.

Fourth, we need to be careful of jumping onto a fuzzword bandwagon. Adaptive comanagement seems to provide an answer to the rigidity of management structures and limitations of systems thinking. It seems to offer a response to past failings. But the concept can also be a smokescreen for things we do when we are not sure what it is that we are doing! For both the research and development communities, the concept can become a justification for further experimentation in contexts that are poorly understood, and where outcomes of practice are uncertain, unpredictable, and provide little real insight. If our emphasis is on transformative, reflective (and by implication, transparent and accountable) social processes—against which the big obstacle is power relations—then we should be targeting these very social processes and the relationships within them. Taking on issues of power requires that we become more realistic and probably less ambitious about what can be achieved. If we do not pay careful attention to social dynamics as a critical dimension of *adaptive comanagement*, we risk having a poorly defined approach that, while intuitively appealing, is merely a set of tools and techniques, applicable in some cases, but that misses the critical dimensions of social transformation.

In reflection upon the potential of adaptive comanagement, we have found that it makes sense for us to explicitly recognize agency (including issues of knowledge and power), institutions, and discourses. We must frame adaptive comanagement as a self-aware research process that is engaged at the interface between policy and practice at the local level. Reframed in this way, we suggest that adaptive comanagement can provide a means for people to engage in dialogue over complex issues, and to develop relationships. It offers an opportunity also to explore the ways in which science and researchers can support these dialogue processes. This provides the basis for an adaptive comanagement approach that can contribute to realizing more resilient social-ecological systems.

References

Ackoff, R. 1974. *Redesigning the future: A systems approach to societal problems.* Hoboken, NJ: John Wiley.

Agrawal, A. 2002. The regulatory community: Decentralization and the environment in the Van Panchayats (Forest Councils) of Kumaon, India. *Mountain Research and Development* 21(3):208–211.

Allan, J. D., R. Abell, Z. Hogan, C. Revenga, B. W. Taylor, R. L. Welcomme, and K. Winemiller. 2005. Over-fishing of inland waters. *Bioscience* 55(12): 1041–1050.

Andrew, N. L., C. Bene, S. J. Hall, E. H. Allison, S. Heck, and B. D. Ratner. 2007. Diagnosis and management of small-scale fisheries in developing countries. *Fish and Fisheries* 8:227–240.

Arce, A., and E. Fisher. 2007. Creating natural knowledge: Agriculture, science and experiments. In *Local science vs. global science: Approaches to indigenous knowledge in international development*, ed. P. Sillitoe. New York: Berghahn Books.

Armitage, D. 2008. Governance and the commons in a multi-level world. *International Journal of the Commons* 2(1): 7–32.

Armitage, D., and D. Johnson. 2006. Can resilience be reconciled with globalization and the increasingly complex conditions of resource degradation in Asia coastal regions? *Ecology and Society* 11(1): 2.

Armitage, D., M. Marschke, and R. Plummer. 2008b. Adaptive co-management and the paradox of learning. *Global Environmental Change* 88:86–98.

Armitage, D., R. Plummer, F. Berkes, R. I. Arthur, A. Charles, I. Davidson-Hunt, A. Diduck, et al. 2008a. Adaptive comanagement for social-ecological complexity. *Frontiers in Ecology and the Environment* 7(2):95–102.

Arthur, R. I. 2004. Adaptive learning and the management of small water body fisheries: A case study in Lao PDR. PhD thesis, University of London, U.K.

Arthur, R. I., and R. M. Friend. 2011. Inland capture fisheries in the Mekong and their place and potential within food-led regional development. *Global Environmental Change* 21 (1): 219–226..

Arthur, R. I., and C. J. Garaway. 2005. Learning in action: A case from small waterbody fisheries in Lao PDR. In *Participatory research and development for sustainable agriculture and natural resource management: A sourcebook,* Vol. 3, eds. J. Gonsalves, T. Becker, A. Braun, D. Campilan, H. de Chavez, E. Fajber, M. Kapiriri, J. Rivaca-Caminade, and R. Vernooy, 191–198. CIP-UPWARD/IDRC. Los Banos, Laguna, The Philippines: International Potato Center—Users' Perspectives with Agricultural Research and Development. Ottawa, Canada: International Development Research Centre (IDRC).

Arthur, R. I., and C. J. Garaway. 2006. Role of researchers in support of fisheries comanagement. In *Rebuilding fisheries in an uncertain environment,* ed. A. L. Shriver. Proceedings of 13th Biennial International Institute of Fisheries Economics and Trade (IIFET) conference, July 11–14, 2006, in Portsmouth, U.K. Corvallis, OR: IIFET.

Arthur, R. I., and N. Sheriff. 2008. Fish and the poor. In *Poverty reduction through sustainable fisheries: Emerging policy and governance issues in Southeast Asia,* eds. R. M. Briones and A. G. Garcia. Laguna, The Philippines: Southeast Asian Regional Center for Graduate Study and Research in Agriculture (SEARCA).

Ascher, W. 2001. Coping with complexity and organizational interests in natural resource management. *Ecosystems* 4:742–757.

Baird, I. G. January, 1996. Inland community fisheries in southern Laos. *Naga, The ICLARM Quarterly* (International Center for Living Aquatic Resources Management) 1(19):13–15.

Baird, I. G. 2000. *Integrating community-based fisheries comanagement and protected areas management in Lao P.D.R.: Opportunities for advancement and obstacles to implementation.* Evaluating Eden Series. Discussion Paper No. 14. London, U.K.: International Institute for Environment and Development (IIED).

Baland, J.-M., and J.-P. Platteau. 1996. *Halting the degradation of natural resources: Is there a role for rural communities?* Oxford, U.K.: Clarendon Press.

Bartlett, A. 2008. No more adoption rates! Looking for empowerment in agricultural development programmes. *Development in Practice* 18 (4&5): 524–539.

Beck, T., and C. Nesmith. 2001. Building on poor people's capacities: The case of common property resources in India and West Africa. *World Development* 29(1): 119–133.

Berkes, F. 2006. From community-based resource management to complex systems. *Ecology and Society* 11(1):45. Accessed 2-12-2011. Available at http://www .ecologyandsociety.org/vol11/iss1/art45/.

Berkes, F., D. Armitage, and N. Doubleday. 2007. Synthesis: Adapting, innovating, evolving. In *Adaptive comanagement: Collaboration, learning and multi-level governance*, eds. D. Armitage, F. Berkes, and N. Doubleday, 308–328. Vancouver, BC: University of British Columbia Press.

Berkes, F., R. Mahon, P. McConney, R. Pollnac, and R. S. Pomeroy. 2001. *Managing small-scale fisheries: Alternative directions and methods*. Ottawa, Canada: International Development Research Center (IDRC).

Blunt, P., and M. Turner. 2005. Decentralization, democracy and development in a post-conflict society: Commune councils in Cambodia. *Public Administration and Development* 25:75–87.

Borrini-Feyerabend, G., M. Pimbert, T. Farvar, A. Kothari, and Y. Renard. 2007. *Sharing power: A global guide to collaborative management of natural resources*. London, U.K.: Earthscan.

Brand, F. S., and K. Jax. 2007. Focusing the meaning(s) of resilience: Resilience as a descriptive concept and a boundary object. *Ecology and Society* 12(1):23. Accessed 2-13-2011. Available at http://www.ecologyandsociety.org/vol12/iss1/art23/.

Brown, D., D. Staples, and S. Funge-Smith. 2005. Mainstreaming fisheries comanagement in the Asia-Pacific. Paper prepared for the AFPIC Regional Workshop on Mainstreaming Fisheries Comanagement in Asia-Pacific (Siem Reap, Cambodia, August 9 to 12, 2005). Bangkok, Thailand: Food and Agriculture Organisation of the United National Regional Office for Asia and the Pacific.

Charles, A. T. 2001. *Sustainable fishery systems*. Oxford, U.K.: Blackwell Science.

Christie, P., D. L. Fluharty, A. T. White, L. Eisma-Osorio, and W. Jantulan. 2007. Assessing the feasibility of ecosystem-based fisheries management in tropical contexts. *Marine Policy* 31(3): 239–250.

Colfer, C. J. P. 2005. *The complex forest: Communities, uncertainty and adaptive collaborative management*. Washington, D.C.: Resources for the Future Press.

Cornwall, A. 2007. Buzzwords and fuzzwords: Deconstructing development discourse. *Development in Practice* 17(4, 5): 471–484.

Court, J., I. Hovland, and J. Young, eds. 2005. *Bridging research and policy in development: Evidence and the change process*. Rugby, U.K.: ITDG Press.

Deap, L., P. Degen, and N. van Zalinge. 2003. *Fishing gears of the Cambodian Mekong: Inland Fisheries Research and Development Institute of Cambodia (IFReDI)*. Vol. IV. Phnom Penh, Cambodia: Cambodia Fisheries Technical Paper Series.

Degen, P., P. Chap, P. Swift, and M. Hang. 2005. *Upland fishing and indigenous Punong fisheries management in Mondulkiri Province.* Phnom Penh, Cambodia: Cambodia FAO/WCS.

Dietz, T., E. Ostrom, and P. C. Stern. 2003. The struggle to govern the commons. *Science* 302:1907–1912.

Fennell, D., R. Plummer, and M. Marschke. 2008. Is adaptive co-management ethical? *Journal of Environmental Management* 88:62–75.

Ficke, A. D., C. A. Myrick, and L. J. Hansen. 2007. Potential impacts of global climate change on freshwater fisheries. *Reviews in Fish Biology and Fisheries* 17:581–613.

Fischer-Kowalski, M., and J. Rotmans. 2009. Conceptualizing, observing, and influencing social-ecological transitions. *Ecology and Society* 14(2):3.

Folke, C. 2006. Resilience: The emergence of a perspective for social-ecological systems analysis. *Global Environmental Change* 16(3): 253–267.

Frame, B., and J. Brown. 2008. Developing post-normal technologies for sustainability. *Ecological Economics* 65:225–241.

Freire, P. 1971. *Pedagogy of the oppressed.* New York: Herder & Herder.

Friend, R. F., R. I. Arthur, and M. Keskinen. 2009. Songs of the doomed: The continuing neglect of capture fisheries in hydropower development in the Mekong. In *Contested waterscapes in the Mekong Region: Hydropower, livelihoods and governance*, eds. F. Molle and M. Kakönen, 23-54. London, U.K.: Earthscan.

Funtowicz, S., and J. R. Ravetz. 1993. Science for the post-normal age. *Futures* 25:739–755.

Garaway, C. J., and R. I. Arthur. 2004. *Adaptive learning: A practical framework for the implementation of adaptive comanagement. Lessons from selected experiences in South and Southeast Asia.* London, U.K.: MRAG Ltd.

Garaway, C. J., and R. I. Arthur. 2002. Community Fisheries: lessons learned from Southern Lao PDR. MRAG Ltd.

Garaway, C. J., R. I. Arthur, B. Chamsingh, P. Homekingkeo, K. Lorenzen, B. Saengvilaikham, and K. Sidavong 2006. A social science perspective on enhancement outcomes: Lessons learned from inland fisheries in southern Lao PDR. *Fisheries Research* 80(1): 37–45.

Gregory, R., and H. Guttman. 1996. Poor in all but fish: A study of the collection of ricefield foods from three villages in Svay Teap District, Svay Rieng. Working Paper 5. Bangkok, Thailand: AquaOutreach Project, Asian Institute of Technology (AIT).

Gregory, R., T. Phongphichith, and Somboun. 2007. Upland aquatic resources in Laos PDR: Their use, management and spatial dimensions in Xieng Khouang and Luang Prabang provinces. Report for the Swiss Agency for Development and Cooperation.

Gunderson, L. H., C. S. Holling, and S. S. Light, eds. 1995. *Barriers and bridges to the renewal of ecosystems and institutions.* New York: Columbia University Press.

Hajer, M., and W. Versteeg. 2005. A decade of discourse analysis of environmental politics: Achievements, challenges, perspectives. *Journal of Environmental Policy and Planning* 3(7): 175–184.

Hara, M. 2004. Beach village committees as a vehicle for community participation: Lake Malombe/Upper Shire River Participatory Programme. In *Rights, resources and rural development: Community-based natural resource management in southern Africa*, eds. C. Fabricius, E. Koch, H. Magombe, and S. Turner. London, U.K.: Earthscan.

Hardin, G. 1968. Tragedy of the commons. *Science* 162:1243–1248.

Hilborn, R., and C. J. Walters. 1992. *Quantitative fisheries stock assessment*. New York: Chapman and Hall.

Holling, C. S. 1973. Resilience and stability of ecological systems. *Annual Review of Ecology and Systematics* 4:1–23.

Holling, C. S., ed. 1987. *Adaptive environmental assessment and management*. Chichester, U.K.: John Wiley and Sons.

Hortle, K. G. 2007. *Consumption and the yield of fish and other aquatic animals from the Lower Mekong Basin*. MRC Technical Paper No. 16. Vientiane, Laos: Mekong River Commission (MRC).

Hughes, C. 2006. Cambodia. *IDS Bulletin* 37(2): 67–78.

Johnson, D. S. 2006. Category, narrative and value in the governance of small-scale fisheries. *Marine Policy* 30:747–756.

Khrutmuang, S., D. Huaisai, and L. Lebel. 2005. The emergence of an adaptive comanagement regime after a decade of conflict: A case study of water governance in the Mae Ta Chang watershed, Chiang Mai, Thailand. M-POWER Working Paper MP-2004–03. Chiang Mai, Thailand: Unit for Social and Environmental Research, Chiang Mai University.

Lebel, L., P. Garden, and M. Imamura. 2005. The politics of scale, position, and place in the governance of water resources in the Mekong region. *Ecology and Society* 10(2):18. Accessed 2-12-2011. Available at http://www.ecologyandsociety.org/vol10/iss2/art18/.

Lee, K. 1993. *Compass and gyroscope*. Washington, D.C.: Island Press.

Locke, R. R. 1996. *The collapse of the American management mystique*. New York: Oxford University Press.

Lorenzen, K., and C. J. Garaway. 1998. How predictable is the outcome of stocking? In Inland fishery enhancements, ed. T. Petr, 133–152. FAO Fisheries Technical Paper 374:133–152. Rome, Italy: Food and Agriculture Organization (FAO).

Long, N., and A. Long. 1992. *Battlefields of knowledge: The interlocking of theory and practice in social research and development*. London, U.K.: Routledge.

Marschke, M., and F. Berkes. 2006. Exploring strategies that build livelihood resilience: A case from Cambodia. *Ecology and Society* 11(1):42. Accessed 2-13-2011. Available at http://www.ecologyandsociety.org/vol11/iss1/art42/

Marschke, M., and K. Nong. 2003. Adaptive Comanagement: Lessons from coastal Cambodia. *Canadian Journal of Development Studies* 24(3): 369–383.

McAllister, M. K., R. M. Peterman, and D. M. Gillis. 1992. Statistical evaluation of a large-scale fishing experiment designed to test for a genetic effect of size-selective fishing on British Columbia pink salmon (*Oncorhynchus gorbuscha*). *Canadian Journal of Fisheries and Aquatic Sciences* 49:1294–1304.

McCay, B. 2002. Emergence of institutions for the commons: Contexts, situations, and events. In *The drama of the commons*, eds. E. Ostrom, T. Dietz, N. Dolsak, P. C. Stern, S. Stonich, and E. U. Weber, 361–402. Washington, D.C.: National Academy Press.

McCay, B., and J. M. Acheson, eds. 1987. *The question of the commons: The culture and ecology of communal resources*. Tucson, AZ: University of Arizona Press.

Meusch, E., J. Yhoung-Aree, R. M. Friend, and S. J. Funge-Smith. 2003. The role and nutritional value of aquatic resources in the livelihoods of rural people: A participatory assessment in Attapeu Province, Lao PDR. RAP Publication 2003/11. Bangkok, Thailand: Food and Agriculture Organization (FAO), Regional Office for Asia and the Pacific (RAP).

MRC (Mekong River Commission). 2007. State of the Basin Report 2007. Vientiane, Laos: Mekong River Commission.

MRC (Mekong River Commission). 2010. State of the Basin Report 2010. Vientiane, Laos: Mekong River Commission.

Nadasdy, P. 2007. Adaptive co-management and the gospel of resilience. In *Adaptive comanagement: Collaboration, learning and multi-level governance*, eds. D. Armitage, F. Berkes, and N. Doubleday, 208–227. Vancouver, BC: UBC Press.

Oakerson, R. J. 1992. Analyzing the commons: A framework. *In Making the commons work: Theory, practice and policy*, eds. D. Bromley, D. Feeny, M. McKean, P. Peters, J. Gilles, R. Oakerson, C. F. Runge, and J. Thomson, 41-59. San Francisco, CA: ICS Press.

Olsson, P., C. Folke, and F. Berkes. 2004. Adaptive comanagement for building resilience in social-ecological systems. *Environmental Management* 34(1): 75–90.

Ostrom, E. 1990. *Governing the commons: Evolution of institutions for collective action*. Cambridge, U.K.: Cambridge University Press.

Ostrom, E., J. Burger, C. B. Field, R. B. Norgaard, and D. Policansky. 1999. Revisiting the commons: Local lessons, global challenges. *Science* 284:278.

Ostrom, E., T. Dietz, N. Dolsak, P. C. Stern, S. Stonich, and E. U. Weber, eds. 2002. *The drama of the commons*. Washington, D.C.: National Academy Press.

Persoon, G., A. Diny, M. E. van Est, and P. E. Sajise, eds. 2003. *Comanagement of natural resources in Asia: A comparative perspective*. Copenhagen, Denmark: Nordic Institute of Asian Studies.

Phuong, M. V. 2005. Adaptive comanagement for social-ecological resilience: A case study in Tram Chim National Park, Vietnam. MSc thesis. Stockholm University.

Pinkerton, E., ed. 1989. *Cooperative management of local fisheries: New directions for improved management and community development*. Vancouver, BC: University of British Columbia Press.

Pinkerton, E. 1992. Translating legal rights into management practice: Overcoming barriers to the exercise of comanagement. *Human Organization* 51:330–341.

Pinkerton, E. 2003. Toward specificity in complexity: Understanding comanagement from a social science perspective. In *The fisheries comanagement experience: Accomplishments, challenges and prospects,* eds. D. C. Wilson, J. R. Nielsen, and P. Degnbol, 61–78. Dordrecht, The Netherlands: Kluwer.

Pitcher, T. J., and M. E. Lam. 2010. Fishful thinking: Rhetoric, reality, and the sea before us. *Ecology and Society* 15(2):12. Accessed 2-13-2011. Available at http://www.ecologyandsociety.org/vol15/iss2/art12/.

Pomeroy, R. S., and R. Guieb. 2005. *Fishery comanagement: A practical handbook. IDRC/CABI Publishing.* Wallingford, U.K.: Oxfordshire.

Pomeroy, R. S., B. M. Katon, and I. Harkes. 2001. Conditions affecting the success of fisheries comanagement: Lessons from Asia. *Marine Policy* 25:197–208.

Rammel, C., S. Stagl, and H. Wilfing. 2007. Managing complex adaptive systems—A co-evolutionary perspective on natural resource management. *Ecological Economics* 63:9–21.

Ramos-Martin, J. 2003. Empiricism in ecological economics: A perspective from complex systems theory. *Ecological Economics* 46:387–398.

Resilience Alliance. 2008. Factsheets. Accessed 10-2-2008. Available at http://www.resalliance.org.

Resurreccion, B. 2006. Rules, roles and rights: Gender, participation and community fisheries management in Cambodia's Tonle Sap Region. *Water Resources Development* 22(3): 433–447.

Ringler, C., and X. Cai. November/December, 2006. Valuing fisheries and wetlands using integrated economic-hydrologic modeling—Mekong River Basin. *Journal of Water Resources Planning and Management* 132(6):480–487.

Roe, E. 1991. Development narratives, or making the best of blueprint development. *World Development* 19(4): 287–300.

Rojanasaeng, N. 2008. Problems and prospects of adaptive comanagement of fishery and coastal resources in Phangnga Bay, southern Thailand. PhD. thesis, University of Wisconsin-Madison.

Rondinelli, D. A. 1993. *Development projects as policy experiments: an adaptive approach to development administration.* New York: Routledge.

Ruitenbeek, J., and C. Cartier. October, 2001. The invisible wand: Adaptive comanagement as an emergent strategy in complex bio-economic systems. CIFOR Occasional Paper No. 34. Bogor, Indonesia: Center for International Forestry Research (CIFOR).

Sainsbury, K. J. 1988. The ecological basis of multispecies fisheries, and management of a demersal fishery in tropical Australia. In *Fish population dynamics,* 2nd ed., ed. J. A. Gulland, 349–382. Hoboken, NJ: John Wiley and Sons Ltd.

Salayo, N., L. Garces, M. Pido, K. Viswanathan, R. S. Pomeroy, M. Ahmed, I. Siason, K. Seng, and A. Masae. 2008. Managing excess capacity in small-scale fisheries: Perspectives from stakeholders in three Southeast Asian countries. *Marine Policy* 32:692–700.

Sen, S., and J. Raakjaer Nielsen. 1996. Fisheries comanagement: A comparative analysis. *Marine Policy* 20(5): 405–418.

Shore, C., and S. Wright, eds. 1997. *Anthropology of policy: Critical perspectives on governance and power*. London, U.K.: Routledge.

Sneddon, C. 2007. Nature's materiality and the circuitous paths of accumulation: Dispossession of freshwater fisheries in Cambodia. *Antipode* 39(1):167–193.

Stacey, R. D. 2001. *Complex responsive processes in organizations: Learning and knowledge creation*. London, U.K.: Routledge.

Thuon, T., and T. Vannara. 2005. Making space and Access in fisheries resource management for local communities in Stung Treng Province, Cambodia. In *Commonplaces and comparisons: remaking eco-political spaces in Southeast Asia*, P. Cuasay and C. Vaddhanaphuti, eds., 219–254. Regional Center for Social Science and Sustainable Development (RCSD), Faculty of Social Sciences, Chiang Mai University

van der Sluijs, J. 2006. Uncertainty, assumptions and value commitments in the knowledge base of complex environmental problems. In *Interfaces between science and society*, ed. A. G. Pereira, S. G. Vaz, and S. Tognetti, 67–84. Sheffield, U.K.: Greenleaf Publishing.

Verweij, M., and M. Thompson, eds. 2006. *Clumsy solutions for a complex world*. Basingstoke, U.K.: Palgrave McMillan.

Verweij, M,, M. Thompson, and C. Engel. 2006. Clumsy conclusions: How to do policy and research in a complex world. In Clumsy solutions for a complex world, eds. M. Verweij and M. Thompson, 241-249. Basingstoke, U.K.: Palgrave McMillan.

Walker, B. H., and D. Salt. 2006. *Resilience Thinking: Sustaining Ecosystems and People in a Changing World*. Washington, D.C.: Island Press.

Walker, B., C. S. Holling, S. R. Carpenter, and A. Kinzig. 2004. Resilience, adaptability and transformability in social-ecological systems. *Ecology and Society* 9(2): 5.

Walters, C. J. 1986. *Adaptive management of renewable resources*. New York: Macmillan.

Walters, C. J. 2007. Is adaptive management helping to solve fisheries problems? *Ambio* 36(4): 304–307.

Wiber, M. 2007. Power, property and panarchy: Opening the black box of cultural capital. In *Cordillera in June, Essays celebrating June Prill-Brett, anthropologist*, ed. B. Tapang, 215–257. Quezon City, The Philippines: University of the Philippines Press.

Wilson, D. C., A. Ahmed, S. V. Siar, and U. Kanagaratnam. 2006. Cross-scale linkages and adaptive management: Fisheries comanagement in Asia. *Marine Policy* 30(5):523–533.

Wilson, D. C., J. R. Nielsen, and P. Degnboul, eds. 2003. *The fisheries comanagement experience: Accomplishments, challenges and prospects.* Dordrecht, The Netherlands: Kluwer Academic Publishers.

Wollenberg, E., R. Iwan, G. Limberg, M. Moelino, S. Rhee, and M. Sudana. 2007. Facilitating cooperation during times of chaos: Spontaneous orders and muddling through in Malinau District, Indonesia. *Ecology and Society* 12(1):3.

Wong, C. M., C. E. Williams, J. Pittock, U. Collier, and P. Schelle. 2007. *'World's top 10 rivers at risk.* Gland, Switzerland: World Wildlife Federation International.

Yearley, S. 1988. *Science, technology and social change.* London, U.K.: Unwin Hyman.

Young, O. 2002. Institutional interplay: The environmental consequences of cross-scale interactions. In *The drama of the commons*, eds. E. Ostrom, T. Dietz, N. Dolsak, P. C. Stern, S. Stonich, and E. U. Weber. Washington, D.C.: National Academy Press.

12

Resilient Politics and a Place-Based Ethics of Care: Rethinking the City through the District Six Museum in Cape Town, South Africa

Karen E. Till

In 2003 in Cape Town, South Africa, the skeletal remains of more than 1,400 former slaves and members of the colonial lower classes were unearthed by unsuspecting construction workers who were leveling ground to build a high-rise boutique, office, and apartment complex. The 2,800-square-meter plot, located in the chic and highly desirable inner city precinct called Green Point, was once part of a much larger set of seventeenth- and eighteenth-century informal burial grounds in what later became known as District One (Weeder 2008).

Cape Town activists claiming descendancy from those buried at Prestwich Place momentarily halted development by protesting heritage authorities' failure to provide an adequate public consultation process.[1] They appealed against the authorities' insistence that the remains be exhumed and demanded that the site be memorialized. As activist Stan Abrahams, a District Six Museum trustee, explained to me:

Stan: We kept candlelit vigils there [at Prestwich Place], letting the bones know we were there, that we were present, we were with them. As we stood, with the wind coming down from the mountain, the candles flickering, it was as though the bones were speaking to us.
Karen: And what did the bones say?
Stan: That they should not be forgotten again. They acknowledged our presence, grateful that we were with them. (Stan Abrahams, citizen activist, founding member and trustee of the District Six Museum, interview with the author, Cape Town, 2005)

The protest actions and resulting debates at Prestwich Place can be understood as engaging and creating a public sphere based upon the "right to the city."[2] By claiming these bones as the city's inheritance as well as their personal ancestors, activists charged local authorities to build material and legal environments to confront past injustices, an effort that would create social spaces for past lives and stories previously silenced. Through candlelit vigils, legal challenges, public processions, public hearings hosted by community groups, and other actions, new political organizations were formed and national heritage legislation challenged. Activists negotiated a dynamic role for community organizations to participate in future urban development and planning agendas. Ultimately, a memorial and exhibition space was established; even if this place of memory failed to realize activists' visions, their educational and public outreach work began to call attention to the significance of addressing the unresolved histories of slavery in conceptualizing and planning for the new democratic city (Jonker and Till 2009).

Planning theorists and historians have noted that the experience of the city for most residents does not match the visions, stories, or maps of planners (Hayden 1995; Sandercock 2003). The Prestwich Place case helps us understand why this incongruity occurs for at least two reasons. On the one hand, activists promoted what can be considered a resilient politics of public memory that encourages inclusive governance and planning processes. This form of politics is tied to being seen, giving voice, and making visible those particular places, people, and stories that have and continue to be physically and socially marked by histories of exclusion, displacement, and violence in the postcolonial, apartheid, and postapartheid city. As I describe in this chapter, such politics are tied to a longer-standing South African practice of citizen activism in the face of gross social injustice under both undemocratic and democratic systems. Their experiences, networking, and fundamental challenges to injustice during apartheid sustained their challenge to emerging democratic governance styles, thereby changing the planning cultures associated with interpreting and administering policy.[3]

The resilient politics of memory that animated much of the public debate about the future of Prestwich Place were tied to the significance of memory-work, a second way in which this case study can be interpreted.[4] Residents felt a moral and ethical set of obligations to this particular place. As activist Stan Abrahams mentioned previously, the ancestral spirits "acknowledged our presence, grateful that we were with them" after having been neglected and long forgotten after their entombment in the slave cemetery outside of the walls of the colonial city. Abrahams's comment draws attention to the way that debate about difficult pasts often emerges in wounded cities at zones of transition—those very places where the city becomes out of joint in Cartesian space and chronological time (Till and Jonker 2009). Capetonians demonstrated what I describe as a place-based ethics of care (Till 2010), recognizing their connections to people, lives, and landscapes through this place.[5] (Re)discovered objects, remnants from former lives, and the ruins of previous cities may speak to the living of past lives that still belong to the contemporary city, even if they are understood as occupying space-times beyond the realms of the living (Till 2005, 2011).

Thus, more was articulated by the Capetonians than current discussions of resilience (as institutional capacity-building or ensuring systems' robustness) generally allow. This chapter extends understandings of resilience by paying attention to the public politics of memory and place-based memory-work in wounded cities. The attentiveness of local residents to Prestwich Place (such as through candlelight vigils) calls for new memorial practices, and practices of caring for places and the city's inhabitants. Such practices can offer a richer and more ethical approach to understanding and planning for the postcolonial city. What these residents teach us, as planners, is to respect those who have gone before, to attend to past injustices that continue to haunt current planning and governance styles, and to treat the past as a dynamic resource in imagining different futures. These lessons in particular may help planners more successfully manage co-existence of shared spaces, create more democratic public realms, and provide more inclusive forms of communication (after Healey 1997/2006; Sandercock 2003). In other words, planners need to do more work before engaging in problem-setting or problem-solving processes, even when these processes are considered to be collaborative, adaptive, or open ended. They even need to do more than listen as Forester (1999) suggests or translate knowledge into action as Friedmann (1987) states (as cited in Healey 1997/2006, p. 219).

In Cape Town, these residents' actions and voices communicated an experience of the city—their city—as inhabited by both the dead and the living, as a reservoir of multiple histories and stories, and as offering a range of possible futures, many of which are not yet "visible" in dominant representations of the contemporary urban landscape. Inspired by their work to create a nonracial society and a more inclusive city, in this chapter I examine the resilient politics and memory work of the Hands Off District Six movement and the District Six Museum. In doing so, I wish to challenge the concept of the "resilient city," as well as the assumed positive quality of resilience according to a systems approach to urban planning and governance, by asking the following questions: What would it mean for planners to ask residents what the lived city means—before assuming that urban professionals have the ability to build more resilient cities following disastrous events, economic regional decline, or in the transition to more democratic states? What might it mean to rethink the city temporally as being wounded, as deeply marked by histories, stories, and memories rather than as a complex adaptive system moving toward robustness? Can planning practice move toward building transformative collaborations with residents such that the residents have more authority to define and decide on the spaces and times of cities in which they live? Finally, what happens when planners understand the practice of place making as always embedded in histories and geographies of power, social relations, and place-based attachments? As I suggest in this chapter, I believe that we have much to learn from the ways in which residents make and take care of particular places in their attempts to care for, remember, respect, and sometimes rebuild their cities before, during, and after traumatic change.

In the sections that follow, I use the example of the District Six in postcolonial and postapartheid Cape Town to explore temporality and place-based ethics as two new directions for current discussions about the resilient city. First, I review the ways that time is depicted in the current literature about resilient cities and resilient systems. I suggest that by paying attention to the politics of public memory, we are confronted with quite a different historical sensibility than current models of resilience allow, the latter of which impose a sort of "before and after" temporality onto planning for the future. Second, a planning practice recognizing citizen's struggles, stories, and the ways that residents care for places would entail more than a basic understanding of complex urban histories as linear processes or as "conflicts." Recognition would mean respecting all inhabitants' basic "right to the city," which includes the right to decide what the city is, how, why, and if it should be rebuilt and re-narrated (when and where), and for whom. The rest of this chapter uses the case of District Six to explore the significance and difficulties of this extended understanding of resilience according to the politics of memory and the "work" of memory, one based in caring for place and coming into contact with the range of lives attached to these places.

From the Resilient City to a Resilient Politics of Memory

According to Vale and Campanella (2005a: 5), "urban disaster, like urban resilience, takes many forms and can be categorized in many ways." Disaster can be classified according to the scale of destruction (from a single precinct to an entire city); the human toll, as measured by deaths and the disruption of lives; the presumed cause. Causes can be, for example, "uncontrollable" forces of nature (such as earthquakes); natural forces combined with human action (such as fires); deliberate human action (such as a war, a lone terrorist, regimes promoting modernization, or economic disasters). Not surprisingly, narratives of resilience vary in the face of sudden, devastating events. An episodic disruption may be depicted as both tragic and inspiring when recovery is a political goal. A faith-based element to suffering may be appended to recovery narratives; themes of forbearance and discipline in the face of adversity may be evoked. In general, however, post-disaster resilience planning narratives reframe sudden devastating events as opportunities for progress and positive change. Typically, phases of recovery (as framed by heroic narratives of resilience) end with a phase of reconstruction, which includes public forms of memorialization.

Vale and Campanella note that despite the possible range of disaster or sudden trauma they evaluated, such a framework cannot adequately deal with attenuated trauma. Moreover, as Throgmartin (this volume) describes, even particular stories of the experience of "disaster" (and I would add the spatial imaginaries of the "post-disaster" city) may vary depending upon the goals and perspectives of the teller and the historical contexts in which the story is spoken and heard. For some people, the right to represent the past is associated with a citizen's right to the city and intricately tied to the processes of democratization. Calls by the residents (of "never again," to "give voice," or to "make visible" their stories) indicate the ways that past forms of injustice constitute the present and imagined possible future. Stories about the past, moreover, are always in flux; these stories are entangled with already existing memorial topographies of a city and national histories (Boyer 1996; Nuttall and Coetzee 1998; Sturken 1997; Till 2005).

When social groups inscribe their particular perspectives and stories about the past onto and through a public space, the results are contentious. Groups and individuals often struggle with one another for authority to represent their version of the past in the built environment, the media, and in legal arenas. This "politics of memory" (Till 2003) includes the spaces and processes of negotiation about whose conception of the past should prevail in the public realm. Because the meanings of a city are not stable in time or space, the politics of memory also refers to the practices and motivations whereby groups attempt to "fix" time and identity through the material and symbolic qualities of particular places and landscapes. Indeed, some memorialization projects attempt to close off public discussion by bounding time through place, while other projects seek to keep open the process of historical reflection through dialog, changing landscape forms, and community capacity-building. Elsewhere I have described these two different approaches (in the case of Cape Town and Berlin, respectively)

(Jonker and Till 2009; Till 2005). Paying attention to the politics of memory that I have outlined here is significant for any understanding of a city, particularly in a society that has experienced difficult national histories of state-perpetrated violence and that is undergoing political and social transition. While temporal distance from past injustices may help with critical reflection, the helpfulness of distance is not always the case. Discussions about post-Katrina New Orleans well demonstrate how outside agencies and planners were not sensitive to the ongoing problems of institutional racism (and other forms of discrimination).

One might assume that current discussion of resilience as a positive quality of a complex adaptive system may be able to include the range of narratives, landscapes, social networks, and processes related to the politics of memory that I have thus far introduced. Indeed, some of the transdisciplinary dialogues in communicative planning in particular and social-ecological studies about resilience (including this book) are notable in their attempts to understand particular contexts (Goldstein 2009; Pendall, Foster, and Cowell 2010). Yet I would argue that a systems analyses, or metaphor, remains inadequate both in its assumptions about the starting point and outcomes, as well as in its understanding of diversity and interactions. Innes and Booher (2010), for example, offer an alternative to the "linear path of the rational model" of policy and planning through their "diversity, interdependence, authentic dialogue" (DIAD) model of collaborative rationality. They identify three basic conditions of the DIAD model: "full diversity of interests among participants, interdependence of the participants, who cannot get their interests met independently, and engagement of all in a face to face authentic dialogue meeting Habermas's basic speech conditions" (p. 35). Their goal is to make planning and policy processes more effective (based upon collaborative rationality) using an open systems approach that allows for adaptations in the face of complex and uncertain contexts. They highlight five features of such open systems: diverse agents connected through multiple networks; dynamic interactions resulting in a distributed system memory; nonlinear interactions with feedback loops; an open system defined by interactions, not components; and the capacity of the system to evolve, including through internal reorganization. Because collaborative rationality emphasizes "authentic dialogue," the system itself is flexible and may transform as new knowledge, policies, and practices unfold. Resilience thus is a positive quality associated with the robustness of the system (and its interconnected agents) in the face of uncertainty: "collaborative processes are resilient in the sense that they can absorb radical change in the environment and still maintain their integrity like a standing wave" (Innes and Booher 2010, 34).

The DIAD's theory and model (of collaborative rationality) privileges authentic dialogue as a way to work through conflict and uncertainty, which builds upon previous discussions about providing more inclusive planning practices. The description of particular case studies and the listing of collaborative best practices is a welcome contribution to this literature. However, because of the emphasis on authentic (Habermasian; see chapter 7) dialogue and the robustness of a system of intersecting agents, practices, and processes, the idea of resilient governance remains problematic in this work about DIAD. First, although Innes and Booher argue that the model is normative, the criteria to evaluate the system are based upon the DIAD model itself (the number of stakeholders, the diversity of interests, and the degree of authentic dialogue). In other words, if a system is open-ended and flexible, if there is authentic dialogue, if there are many agents, if interests are interrelated, it is a success (collaboratively rational). Without identifying external criteria for analyzing the system or how its agents and interactions exchange and (re)produce knowledge, this approach is teleological at best. I am thinking here of external criteria such as equality, human rights, social justice, multiculturalism, multiple forms of communication and public engagement, and so on. Second, although the label *diversity* sounds inclusive, without a basic definition of what exactly this term means to the authors, we are left to question how to evaluate a system that may have historically participated (and may still participate) in longer-standing histories of racism, oppression, exclusion, and violence. Simply by increasing the number of participants or stating that agents' interests should be diverse does not guarantee either a democratic or inclusive system. Most oppressive systems historically are indeed resilient in the sense of being robust, complex, and adaptive to changing environments. What if the system is already unjust and has done a good job of maintaining itself? What if the participants in this system do not reflect/represent subjugated and/ or minority perspectives, people, and knowledge? What if networks and intersecting interests evolve to reproduce or deepen violent forms of exclusion and oppression? Such basic questions indicate the necessity of normative evaluative criteria external to the system's ability to function in a changing environment. Third, dialogue does not always result in inclusivity. To assume so is to overlook the problems of language (literal and expert) and to undervalue nonlinguistic forms of communication. There are a range of ways humans communicate about their lives and relations with others (including with places and nonhuman lives). Fourth, because the politics of memory must include spaces, places, imaginations, narratives, behaviors, and non-narrative forms of violence and injustice, memory cannot be easily dismissed as a single "group interest," as a "political" (rather than interest-based) topic, as too emotional (not based in facts), or as rooted in the past (not focused in the present). The politics of memory are more than a "wicked problem" for deliberation and conflict resolution.

These brief overviews indicate some of the reasons why current discussions about the resilient city and resilience as a systems quality do not provide an adequate temporal or ethical framework for understanding the politics of memory in a given city. Many scholars of urban resilience largely assume that the city has either some sort of ideal (stable) equilibrium, or that the city is an adaptive complex system that moves coherently from one point in time (time = 0) to another point in time (time = 1) along a dependent temporal path. Systems interactions may be circular, such as with internal feedback loops, or linear; but the system as a whole moves from one point in time to another. Such an understanding of the temporality of the city, however, is limiting for two reasons. First, this understanding assumes an unproblematic concept of the city as somehow bound in Cartesian space. Second, this understanding assumes that one can "read" (or know) history as having a clear before and after status. The notion of nested "scales" (neighborhood, urban, regional, state, international) often stands for located space; whereas agents and networks within the open system respond to changing environments, those environments can be mapped in a Cartesian sense. This reductive approach to space does not allow for the ways in which places are part of us, functioning as a kind of exoskeleton (compare Fullilove 2005; Till 2008). Nor does this approach theorize how places are interconnected to other places across and through space. Further, such an understanding of the spatial does not come close to addressing a fundamental challenge in planning and governance that Healey (1997/2006) so clearly identifies—namely, how to manage co-existence in shared spaces in a world in which local actions matter. As Healey argues further: "As we have become aware of, and respectful of, the diversity of the ways of living, of lifestyles and cultures, so we look for ways of providing space for choice and the assertion of difference. But this brings us into conflict at the fine grain of our spatial experience as well as in our broader concern. . . . If we lose faith in governance mechanisms, these conflicts will be resolved by the power of money and landownership" (p. 201).

A focus on returning to (or creating) a new stable equilibrium, or charting the loops within a complex system from stage one to stage two, does not allow for the complex ways in which multiple pasts appear and disappear, or in which pasts continuously unfold in the present in unexpected ways. Complexity is evidenced by, for example, the legacies of slavery, colonialism, and apartheid; the living memories and inheritances of violence that are passed through generations; and the forms of institutional racism that may continue despite legal changes. The intersecting movements of temporality, including time present, time past, and time future (if they can be so easily identified as such) are fluid (compare Erasmus 2001). Crucially, understanding the temporal as path dependent, even when feedback loops are provided, means that spatial imaginaries of the future are already predictable ontologically: what is possible is defined by what is already known or expected. In other words, the present is understood to be inevitable. Such an assumption severely limits spatial-temporal imaginations of what may be possible, including more socially just cities.

I suggest a rethinking of the understanding of resilience to include a politics of memory and the work of memory. While I develop my argument from a wounded city (that is, one marked by extreme forms of state-perpetrated violence and social injustice, or what Dukes, Williams, and Kelban, in chapter 10 of this book, describe as "unrightable wrongs"), I would argue that a respect for memory and those who have gone before must be included as a basic framework for all cities.

One way that social groups have tried to make complex pasts and politically repressed stories more tangible in the built environment is through the establishment of places of memory at historic sites of cultural trauma. In this way, residents, activists, and human rights advocates reclaim national pasts and imagine more just futures in ethical ways that challenge existing understandings of how time and space work in cities. I consider these places a form of more resilient politics of memory that reflects a larger international trend. Beginning in the late 1970s, places of memory were independently established by activists and citizens in numerous countries around the world, including Bangladesh, England, Senegal, and the Czech Republic. Places such as the Topography of Terror in Berlin or Open Memory (*Memoria Abierta*) in Buenos Aires, Argentina, were envisioned to function as locales of recovery, dialogue, and storytelling for residents, citizens, and visitors. Two transnational networks were established in 2000 to call attention to this unique type of public history and memory.[6] The so-called historic sites of conscience and memorial museums in remembrance of victims of state-perpetrated crimes that have been established, as well as the networks, resources, and social capital this work has stimulated, can be seen as an important part of a resilient politics of public memory that societies and cities must face as they come to terms with difficult local and national pasts.

Historic site museums are located at sites of national trauma, yet offer more than collecting, documenting, archiving, displaying, exhibiting, and educating. I understand the sites to be "cosmopolitan places" (Entrikin 1999) that self-consciously promote progressive political agendas, including participatory democracy, social justice, and toleration. Entrikin, a geographer, defines *cosmopolitan places* as providing concrete relations that link individuals and collectives to larger social milieu on the one hand, and to a universalized "here-ness" on the other. This here-ness, explains Entrikin, centers on a "me" and "us," a potentially inclusive humanity (Entrikin 2002). His description of "overlapping, differentiated places of attachment that have relatively permeable boundaries" is echoed in the interdisciplinary literature on critical memory practices. Metaphors such as "giving voice," making visible absent presences, or uncovering forgotten pasts are used to describe these places of memory, which offer perspectives and stories distinct from those of national dominant institutions. Indeed, an important part of being a member of the International Coalition of Historic Site Museums of Conscience is the development of site- and country-specific "Dialogues for Democracy."[7]

These historic site museums of conscience are defined by an insistence on remembering difficult pasts as well as on the right to narrate those pasts. In this respect, the community capacity-building work at these places of memory can be considered a form of resilient politics that provides stability, despite the ongoing ruptures of geographies of displacement or exclusion that may occur at any particular moment in time. Particularly in cities undergoing transition, such a resilient politics signifies more than resistance to the status quo. Materially, it motivates social capital, provides a range of memorialization activities, creates new forms of public memory and is committed to intergenerational education and social outreach. It may also set into motion the possibility of creating what Healey (1997/2006) sees as a needful combination of a "hard infrastructure of a *structure of challenges*, to constrain and modify dominant centres of power, and a soft infrastructure of *relation-building* through which sufficient consensus building and mutual learning can occur to develop *social, intellectual and political capital*," which should be "locally specific and collaborative" (p. 200). In the following section I will provide a particular example of a resilient politics of public memory in District Six, Cape Town that modified hegemonic power structures. Following this discussion, I will outline the ways that place-based memory-work at the District Six Museum also includes an ethics of care and a moral obligation to others through the making and remaking of particular places.

A Resilient Politics of Memory at District Six

As I have shown thus far, in cities undergoing transition that are marked by histories of violence, public debates emerge at particular places about how, where, and in whose name to remember the past and imagine the future. District Six, on the eastern boundary of Cape Town, is such a place; it remains a symbol for many South Africans of the apartheid state's large-scale violence against domestic and communal lives.[8] More than sixteen years after the end of apartheid (in 1994), some former residents are slowly beginning to return to the area after a protracted land rights struggle. Yet District Six remains largely empty today, a physical reminder of activists' defiance in the face of injustice. (Figure 12.1 shows part of the region.)

As a place, District Six reminds us that Cape Town was the locus of the creolization and creative ferment that thrived in the least pretentious areas

Figure 12.1
District Six as "salted earth" (photograph courtesy of Andrew Tucker, 2007)

of a busy port. It emerged as a vibrant, multicultural precinct resulting from Cape Town's existence as a colonial port city. Residents included immigrants from Europe, the Caribbean, and the Americas, and slaves and freed slaves of southern African and southeast Asian origin. District Six, as it became known in the early twentieth century, inspired many of the Cape's musical, literary, and artistic legends as well its radical political discourse.

Yet apartheid laws that legislated a tripartite racial identity (of White, Colored, and Black) halted this cultural hybridity spatially by physically separating people through forced removals and areal segregation. In 1966, the apartheid Cape Town government declared that District Six was an area for whites only. By 1982, over 60,000 people had been displaced from their homes and community. Although activists were unable to stop the bulldozers that razed the neighborhood to the ground, they waged a campaign to stop redevelopment.

After the protracted forced removals had cleared the land of almost all signs of habitation, destroying families and tight community bonds, the "Hands Off District Six" activist campaign endeavored to prevent the government from rebuilding a white or even a mixed suburb on the land. For these individuals, the empty land was "salted earth," fit only for a justice to come that would bring with it the restitution of the land to those who had been removed. The organization arose from what former District Six Museum director Valmont Layne (2004) calls "a crisis of authority, of the right to speak."

During the 1980s, ex-residents of District Six began to discuss creating a museum that would both honor the people who fought against forced removals under the apartheid regime, and commemorate the history of the colorful neighborhoods that once existed in the district. During meetings of the Hands Off District Six campaign, individuals brought in photos, remnants, and other artifacts and memories about their life in the district. In 1994, the District Six Museum opened; rather than recreate the district through nostalgic narratives and exhibitions, the area instead was defined by the resilient politics of the Hands Off District Six campaign. The mission of the District Six Museum is "the documentation and imaginative reconstruction of the history, labouring life and cultural heritage of District Six. To help these residents and their children rebuild their lives, the museum offers a space to think about the community and the roles of being a citizen in a newly democratic country" (District Six Museum 2010). The goals of its exhibition are to "*re-possess the history of the area as a place* where people lived, worked, loved, and struggled" (italics added).

The museum's emphasis on ex-residents as its primary audience, and on claiming ownership of the past and of the District Six, reflects its political role as a forum for what later became a successful land restitution process.[9] The assertion of residents' right to represent the past, according to some museum staff, date back to earlier social justice movements in the district beginning roughly 125 years ago. As a non-state-funded institution, the museum still claims an alternative political space to dominant centers of power, even in postapartheid South Africa, even as planners, developers, and the state use the museum as a symbol of national heritage.[10] It continues to support a creative element in the work of public memory and history by challenging fixed and restrictive delineations of identity. In addition to documenting oral histories and engaging in local and international politics, the District Six Museum provides social outreach programs, community resources, and venues for intergenerational education (as I will describe shortly). In recent years, activists have also called for a project of "Rebuilding the City" (Figure 12.2). The museum clearly is an important social institution that provides the fabric necessary

**The District Six Museum
Celebrates its 13th Birthday**

"REBUILDING THE CITY"

Monday, 10 December 2007
The District Six Museum
25A Buitenkant Street, Cape Town

You are invited to join the staff and trustees of the Museum in celebrating 13 years of its existence in the Methodist Church building.

Please join us at 11h00 to view an exhibition of albums created by young people with their dreams and wishes for District Six.

Joe Schaffers and fellow musicians will fill the Museum with music from 09h00. They will also be joined by Tyrone Appollis and Boela Katjie.

From 15h00 young people are invited to join to Baluleka youth in the Sacks Futeran Building, 15 Buitenkant Street in celebration of their achievements in the past year. There will be poetry and performance and music.

Please call Mandy Sanger for more details 021 466 7100

Figure 12.2
A resilient politics of public memory: "Rebuilding the City" (District Six Museum public flyer, 2007)

for the growth of what urban sociologist Klinenberg (2002) describes as healthy social ecologies of place to grow.

In the next section, I discuss the memory-work at the museum as a practice of giving care to a formerly displaced community through place making. Taking care of District Six offers the possibility for communities, families, and individuals to take care of themselves and others, and to accept care. This place-based ethics of care grounded in memory-work attempts to repair the silences and pain that rip across multiple generations and through the spaces of their wounded city by offering a safe place of discovery and return.

Memory-work in Wounded Cities

The acts of citizens and activists at Prestwich Place and at District Six are grounded in a place-based ethics of care grounded in memory-work. When individuals and social groups make and remake particular places as a form of memory-work, they may also come to care for the city in ways that demand recognizing, encountering, and empathizing with others. Through making places, individuals became attached to others—the dead as well as the living, the human and the nonhuman presences that constitute their worlds and realities. Attachments to others through place making may include moral obligations, personal relations, familial ties, social networks, neighborhood and/or group identifications, and embodied co-presences.

In a context of a city wounded by longer-term histories of actual and symbolic violence, the memory-work of activists who promote a place-based ethical approach to understanding the pain of their city and that of the city's inhabitants ask residents to make difficult and self-reflexive connections to past and present inhabitants. Such an approach is qualitatively different from the narratives or educational work of public history practiced by museums, exhibitions, and archives. Moreover, it is an approach that directly challenges the place-making planning agendas typically tied to post-disaster projects, in particular urban design agendas defined by linear understandings of progress and development, and heroic narratives of recovery, reconstruction, and resilience.

Confronting transgenerational secrets that constitute the everyday fabric of our cities and nations entails creating spaces for unwanted inheritances. Giving the dead spaces to haunt the environments of the living not only gives a physical and aesthetic form to the loss of human life; it also acknowledges the spatial rights of those who have been unjustly excluded from the city to inhabit present and future urban imaginaries. For this reason, residents' demands to care for places as part of this difficult memory-work must be placed alongside of or in a higher priority to the economic demands of redevelopment. Indeed, it is work that needs to be done before development can even be considered if the city is to be socially sustainable and equitable.

Places such as the District Six Museum have the potential to be experienced as safe havens, as places to return and to feel understood, for those who have experienced what Fullilove (2005) describes as "rootshock." She defines *rootshock* as "the traumatic stress reaction to the destruction of all or part of one's emotional ecosystem" (p. 11). Citing geographers such as Doreen Massey, planners such as Jane Jacobs, and social psychologists such as Kai Erikson, Fullilove describes *place* as having a central function in one's emotional and social ecosystem.[11] Places, she argues, are a kind of exoskeleton for individuals. Through making and maintaining places, individuals maintain the external balance between themselves and the material world; they create a personal ecosystem and mazeways that are intricately linked to the larger social ecologies of a place. When this external system of protection—including everyday routines; social institutions; the fabric, taste, and scents of landscapes; symbolic systems of meaning and identity; shared memories—is damaged, individuals or groups will experience rootshock. When neighborhood structures and textures of place are demolished (such as through urban renewal or forced evictions), communities, families, and individuals will experience unhealthy living conditions. The personal damage experienced through this blow to the social ecosystem threatens the "whole body's ability to function"; in addition, the social injury from rootshock "can affect generations and generations of people" (p. 12). Fullilove reminds us that the loss of collective capacity to solve problems may become a permanently crippling one.

Fullilove's work is of critical importance to planners working in the realms of disaster management planning and in the paradigms of resilience. As planners, we need to begin theorizing about the complex spatialities involved when rootshock occurs and we must become sensitive to different forms of rootshock that result from natural-social disasters, warfare, displacements, and social violence, all the while paying attention to historical contexts of the politics of public memory. Cities become wounded in very different ways, and these differences matter, particularly in terms of intergenerational relations and silences, and the individuals' and groups' capacity for repair. Places such as the District Six Museum are important because they create social spaces for repressed memories of violence and for embodied forms of witnessing those past lives and stories. Moreover, by offering a safe place of return for those residents who have been excluded from the city, it creates the possibility for residents to imagine what it might mean to belong to and once again inhabit the city. In these ways, place making creates spaces of repair and discovery.

Places such as District Six are described by former residents as witnesses—not just in the West's legal and human rights understanding of bearing witness, of face-to-face conversation, or of opening up to public view—but also in terms of cultural temporal and spatial relations to matter, affect, social lives, personal memory, and experience. Places are described by locals as metaphysical subjects that speak to visitors and future generations as well as those touched personally by historical acts of violence. These places are distinguished from other places as being in need of care and, while being taken care of, as offering care to a larger community. Activists, museum staff, and former residents in Cape Town, for example, describe the materiality of the District Six as a silent witness of people, memories, earth, and nature, across and through distinct times and spaces. One curator-artist-activist stated that for over twenty years, the empty site and silence of the District "evoked and provoked a monumental power no physical memorial could have achieved" (Delport 2001) (recall the area's photo in figure 12.1). This emptiness and silence frames the contemporary spaces of the museum, which is housed in a Methodist church that was spared from the bulldozer. As one of the lone structures in what became a barren landscape by the 1970s, the museum functions as a physical and symbol of the District Six as place. (figure 12.3.)

The District Six Museum is understood by staff members to be a social and symbolic space, "located" somewhere between the District Six as a symbolic site and as a material landscape (Bennett and Julius 2008). An elderly ex-resident, upon visiting the museum, stated, "No matter where we are—we are here" (in Rassool and Prosalendis 2001). This resident, I believe, is responding both to the experience of entering the textured layers of the museum (which evoke the presence and landscape of the District Six), as well as to the ongoing process of making and remaking the museum—and ultimately the district—as a safe place of return. Curators describe the museum as a space of ongoing inscriptions of temporal relations; piles of earth, poetry, photos, words, artwork, sounds, and community events communicate past and present interactions with the district and the museum. The map on the floor of the museum, for example, outlines the street names and homes that existed before the Groups Areas Act. At special events, former residents are invited to identify landmarks, other residents, or simply write down memories of their

Figure 12.3
The textured space of the District Six Museum as place-making practice (photograph by
the author, 2009)

neighborhood. School tours use the map as a pedagogical tool for future generations; cultural events use the map as a stage to perform, dance, and play music. At the end of the main hall, adjacent to the map, stands a tower of actual street signs that were saved from destruction. In the museum, the historical intersects with personal memories, as does the natural landscape; the red-brown soil at the base of street signs is taken from District Six. We are reminded that this soil was also used to build up parts of the new waterfront development, which is a fairly exclusive tourism and middle class white zone today. In another room, poetry tiles grace the museum's floors. Created in a community memory workshop the poems refer to salt, sea, sand, music, and birds. Stories describe homing pigeons let loose in townships where residents were displaced that have always returned to the bare earth of the District Six. A picture of a lone palm tree standing in an empty field, A picture of a lone palm tree standing in an empty field has a special place of honor within the museum. The tree grew from the seeds Al-Noor's family took while on a pilgrimage to Mecca and planted as they were being forcibly removed from their homes; the tree stands as a reminder of the memory of displacement within the district itself.

The museum creates an aesthetic of "sounds and voices, colours and landscapes" (Layne 2008) in which past and future, memory and perception, inside and outside merge. Perhaps not surprisingly, a younger generation understands the museum as a creative process, not engaged in history in "formal ways." As one museum curator-in-training explained: "We attempt to connect history to living and personal history through sometimes ad hoc, yet artistic and concrete ways" (personal interview 2004). For her, the museum was a space of transformation.

We are dealing with injustices of the past, creating positives for the future. This is a physical and mental process. Going back to the area, coming to the District Six Museum, includes a transformation of the self through a process that includes movement [through space], but also a movement in the sense of how history is reformed, thought, and felt, and how it should be translated into a new society. We have to deal with a lot, including oppressions that still remain in one's mind, yet now we live under a new banner of freedom.

The words of this woman, who was in her twenties and pursuing a Master's in public history, beautifully demonstrate the fragile nature of places in the context of a wounded city and people. The words also describe a particular form of memory-work associated with an ethical and moral responsibility to the District Six as place.

Conclusions

Acts of witnessing and caring for place at District Six have come into conflict with land restitution, planning and development, and local and federal state institutions—in other words, more traditional public city- and state-building authorities and narratives of rebuilding. However, as one staff member explained to me, the legal fact of rebuilding the city "struggles with reality, with experience. Experience is ongoing, it is continuously interpreted. The legalistic fact can't hold the reality of the experiential fact" (personal interview 2004). The moral obligation of making and caring for places "is continuously interpreted" as the community itself grows and changes. Indeed, the District Six Museum in recent years has transitioned from caring about residents, place, and community, to giving care and receiving care, the latter of which is quite difficult. Moving from its history rooted in anti-apartheid protest and the land restitution political movement, the motto of "Hands Off District Six" changed in 2005 to indicate a new phase of making place and building community: "Hands On District Six." After hosting an international conference, "Hands On District Six: Landscapes of Postcolonial Memorialisation," the museum began conducting a series of memory methodology workshops from 2005 to 2006 with citywide and Cape Flats community leaders working on memory projects.[12] Residents shared resources and ideas, accepted ideas and possible partnerships from other neighborhood groups, and had their work acknowledged by each other, the museum, the larger community, and some international guests. People shared ideas about working in neighborhoods that remain segregated from the larger city care but that are part of the larger displaced District Six community.

In addition, the District Six Museum was active in the Prestwich Place campaign, and the museum was later identified as a community-representative in a multi-organizational city planning committee for the future of Prestwich and other projects (District Six Museum 2007). As part of this effort, they worked with other organizations to develop their concepts. They then focused on the future generation by working with local schools to develop educational outreach programs focusing on the history of slavery within the Western Cape. From 2006 to 2007, they coordinated a series of workshops with younger learners from the Cape Flats and city called "The Return: Re-imagining the City" (Sanger 2008). On December 1, 2008, they coordinated with the Institute for Justice and Reconciliation and the Prestwich Place Committee to present a 75th celebratory parade throughout the city, with poetry readings and celebrations, to commemorate Slavery Emancipation Day. As museum staff noted with respect to their work associated with the Prestwich Place Committee, their memory-work was defined by an understanding that "people return to places to which they have some sense of connection, even if the return cannot be one which is permanent and residential. This needs to be translated into an active programme through which public space can be mobilized to nurture and develop what it means *to belong*"(District Six Museum 2007, 4).

Attempting to create qualities, structures, and processes that allow for or enhance resilience is a normative goal. Yet places such as Prestwich Place and District Six in Cape Town remind us that locations, property, and urban ground are infused with unspoken (and often not publicly visible) histories, spatial hauntings, and embodied memories that put into question an understanding of rebuilding the city based upon a simplistic before/after timeframe (compare Till 2005; Jonker and Till 2009). The complex relationships between place and memory impose social and moral obligations upon planners, property owners, and future generations.

First, planners must pay attention to the political stakes of public memory, which include claims to inheritance, citizenship, and national belonging (what Lefebvre 1996 calls the right to the city). Certainly, the work of activists in creating historic site museums of conscience as a form of resilient politics grounded in public memory has already done much to create new social institutions and networks to educate about the past, as well as to provide social outreach services. In this respect, by studying and recognizing the successes and challenges of residents engaged in community capacity-building, calling for and creating more inclusive institutions, and promoting larger place-making projects tied to democratic citizenship and human rights, planners may theorize the city in more historically sophisticated ways. Doing so would provide a different approach than "rebuilding" in a "post"-event time frame: social justice, as a primary goal of defining urban social relations, would necessitate a sensitivity to competing, repressed, and difficult pasts.

Second, planners should pay more attention to the difficult work of memory that activists who promote a place-based ethics of care in wounded cities pursue. Their efforts may help frame a range of projects that may begin the work of healing and transitional justice, through transgenerational and community dialogues grounded in the making and remaking of particular places. Their emphasis upon an ethics of care, as related to how people understand "place" as a witness, may allow individuals who have experienced different forms of rootshock to have a haven for return. People need to be recognized and recognize themselves in their social environments to be able to give and accept care. When individuals visit places that have witnessed pain and violence, and yet are now cared for and may offer care to inhabitants of the city, visitors can be again surrounded by their living memories and emotional attachments. Such places may provide safe spaces for personal self-reflection, discovery, and change. On special occasions, they may even offer a supportive environment for public forms of storytelling.

As planners, we have much to learn about the resilient politics and place-making practices of residents and activists living in wounded cities, such as at the District Six Museum, whereby social spaces for repressed memories are created alongside of an ethics of care giving and receiving care. Place-making practices connect individuals to each other across time and through space. Through the creation of safe places to return, those who suffered an unjust, and even violent, displacement may communicate an emotional reality and need to others that exceed language or traditional forms of memorialization. Through the building of networks, routines, social institutions, and material textures at and through these places, the living may again begin to create healthy environments for their communities. Places such as the District Six Museum may provide the stability for individuals to begin the difficult process of repair and of again dreaming for the future.

Acknowledgments

Many thanks to Bruce Goldstein who introduced me to the conversations of communicative planning and resilient systems in planning and invited me to participate in the 2009 Virginia Tech Symposium on Resilience. Over many months, when I suggested my work did not "fit" with this volume, he patiently reassured me otherwise. I am much indebted to Gerry Kearns for pointing out the work of Joan Tronto and reminding me of the significance of temporality in my discussion of public memory.

Notes

1. My discussion of Prestwich Place is largely taken from Jonker and Till (2009). See also these sources: The District Six Museum 2007; Grunebaum 2007; Jonker 2005; Shepherd 2007; and Weeder 2008. Prestwich Place is the name given to the 2,800-square-meter plot, which is located within Green Point; Green Point is part of District One. Historically (i.e., before these names) Prestwich Place was

part of a larger seventeenth- to eighteenth-century burial ground located outside of the city's colonial walls. The name of the building for the high-rise is The Rockewell.

2. On public memory, see Sturken (1997) and Till (1999; 2005). On "right to the city," I draw upon Lefebvre's 1968 book, *Le droit à la ville*, parts of which are republished in Lefebvre (1996).

3. By noting governance styles in planning, I refer here to work by Healey (1997/2006).

4. I use the word *memory-work* in the sense of the German word *Erinnerungsarbeit* (Till 2005) and in the sense of Jelin's (2003) notion of "the labors of memory." See also Bennett, Julius, and Soudien (2008).

5. I draw upon Tronto's (1993) "ethics of care" to consider the interrelated processes of place making and memory-work.

6. See the Web sites of the International Coalition of Historic Site Museums of Conscience (hereafter ICHSMC) (http://www.sitesofconscience.org/en/) and the International Committee of Memorial Museums in Remembrance of Victims of Public Crimes http://icom.museum/who-we-are/the-committees/international -committees/international-committee/international-committee-of-memorial -museums-in-remembrance-of-the-victims-of-public-crimes.html.).

7. ICHSMC requires members to create a specific "Dialogue for Democracy Program Description." Examples and details can be obtained from the Executive Director of ICHSMC, 333 Seventh Avenue, 14th Floor, New York, NY 10001–5108.

8. Much of the description of the history of District Six Museum and Cape Town in the following paragraphs is based on the following sources: The District Six Museum (2010 Web page); Field (2003); Jeppe and Soudien (1990); Rassool and Prosalendis (2001); see also Jonker and Till (2009).

9. Although ex-residents remain the priority visitor group to the museum, it is now also a successful tourist attraction and educational site. It received major funding from the South African, Norwegian, Spanish, and Dutch governments for restoration and renovation of its building and the surrounding Buitenkant Street premises from 1999 to 2000. Working in conjunction with the two international partnerships, the International Coalition of Historic Site Museums of Conscience located in New York and the Swedish African Museum Programme, it has also hosted two conferences and attended three international conferences.

10. In June, 2004, District Six claimants were among the first granted the right to reclaim their land in the postapartheid state; Nelson Mandela symbolically gave the first returnees keys to their new homes.

11. On place, see also Yi-Fu Tuan (1977) and Till (2005, 2008).

12. With the District Six Museum staff, I received a British Academy Small Research Grant to run the workshops and learn from the museum staff about their memory pedagogy. The first workshop was with the museum staff, which was then followed by three Cape Town–wide workshops. For an overview, see Bennett et al. (2008).

References

Bennett, B., and C. Julius. 2008. Where is District Six? Between landscape, site and museum. In *City—Site—Museum*, eds. B. Bennett, C. Julius, and C. Soudien, 52–67. Cape Town, South Africa: District Six Museum.

Bennett, B., C. Julius, and C. Soudien, eds. 2008. *City—Site—Museum: Reviewing memory practices at the District Six Museum*. Cape Town, South Africa: District Six Museum.

Boyer, M. C. 1996. *The city of collective memory*. Cambridge, MA: MIT Press.

Delport, P. 2001. Signposts for retrieval: A visual framework for enabling memory of place and time. In *Recalling community in Cape Town*, eds. C. Rassool and S. Prosalendis, 31–46. Cape Town, South Africa: District Six Museum Foundation.

The District Six Museum. 2007. Prestwich research report. Paper presented to SAHRA [South African Heritage Resources Agency] in December, 2007 by the District Six Museum and the Prestwich Place Project Committee. Available at the District Six Museum research archive, Cape Town, South Africa.

The District Six Museum. 2010. Accessed 1-1-2010. Available at http://www.districtsix.co.za.

Entrikin, J. N. 1999. Political community, identity and cosmopolitan place. *International Sociology* 14:269–282.

Entrikin, J. N. 2002. Democratic place-making and multiculturalism. *Geografiska Annaler. Series B, Human Geography* 84:19–25.

Erasmus, Z., ed. 2001. *Coloured by history/shaped by place: New perspectives on coloured identities in Cape Town*. Cape Town, South Africa: Kwela.

Field, S., ed. 2003. *Lost communities, living memories: Remembering forced removals in Cape Town*. Cape Town, South Africa: David Philip.

Forester, J. 1999. *The deliberative practitioner: Encouraging participatory planning processes*. Cambridge, MA: MIT Press.

Fullilove, M. 2005. *Rootshock: How tearing up city neighborhoods hurts America, and what we can do about it*. New York: One World/Ballantine Press.

Friedmann, J. 1987. *Planning in the public domain: From knowledge to action*. Princeton, NJ: Princeton University Press.

Goldstein, B. 2009. Resilience to surprises through communicative planning. *Ecology and Society* 14(2):33. Accessed 2-12-2011. Available at http://www.ecologyandsociety.org/vol14/iss2/art33/.

Grunebaum, H. 2007. Unburying the dead in the "Mother City": Urban topographies of erasure. *Publications of the Modern Language Association (PMLA)* 122(1):210–219.

Hayden, D. 1995. *The power of place: Urban landscapes as public history*. Cambridge, MA: MIT Press.

Healey, P. 1997/2006. *Collaborative planning: Shaping places in fragmented societies*, 1st/2nd ed. Basingstoke, U.K.: Palgrave Macmillan.

Innes, J., and D. Booher. 2010. *Planning with complexity: An introduction to collaborative rationality for public policy.* London, New York: Routledge.

Jelin, E. 2003. *State repression and the labors of memory.* Minneapolis, MN: University of Minnesota Press.

Jeppe, S., and C. Soudien, eds. 1990. *The struggle for District Six, Past and present.* Cape Town, South Africa: Buchu Books.

Jonker, J. 2005. Excavating the legal subject: The unnamed dead of Prestwich Place, Cape Town. *Griffith Law Review* 14(2):187–212.

Jonker, J., and K. E. Till. 2009. Mapping and excavating spectral traces in post-apartheid Cape Town. *Memory Studies* 2(3):1–31.

Klinenberg, E. 2002. *Heat wave: A social autopsy of disaster in Chicago.* Chicago: University of Chicago Press.

Layne, V. 2004. Towards a politics of the emerging community museum sector in South Africa. Paper presented at the South African Museums Association Conference (68th, Cape Town, South Africa, June 1–3).

Layne, V. 2008. "Sounds and voices, colours and landscapes": Aesthetics for a community site museum. In *City—Site—Museum,* eds. B. Bennett, C. Julius, and C. Soudien, 76–93. Cape Town, South Africa: District Six Museum.

Lefebvre, H. 1968. *Le droit à la ville. [The right to the city.]* 2nd ed. Paris: Anthropos.

Lefebvre, H. 1996. *Writings on cities,* eds./trans. E. Kofman and E. Lebas. Oxford, U.K.: Blackwell.

Nuttall, Sarah, and Carli Coetzee, eds. 1998. *Negotiating the past: the making of memory in South Africa.* Cape Town, Oxford: Oxford University Press.

Pendall, R., K. A. Foster, and M. Cowell. 2010. Resilience and regions: Building understanding of the metaphor. *Cambridge Journal of Regions, Economy and Society* 3(1): 71–84. doi:10.1093/cjres/rsp028

Rassool, C., and S. Prosalendis, eds. 2001. *Recalling community in Cape Town: Creating community in Cape Town.* Cape Town, South Africa: District Six Museum Foundation.

Sandercock, L. 2003. *Cosmopolis II: Mongrel cities in the 21st century.* London, New York: Continuum Press.

Sanger, M. 2008. Education work in the District Six Museum: Layering in new voices and interpretations. In *City—Site—Museum,* eds. B. Bennett, C. Julius, and C. Soudien, 96–109. Cape Town, South Africa: District Six Museum.

Shepherd, N. 2007. Archaeology dreaming: Post-apartheid urban imaginaries and the bones of the Prestwich Street dead. *Journal of Social Archaeology* 7(1):3–28.

Sturken, M. 1997. *Tangled memories: The Vietnam War, the AIDs epidemic, and the politics of remembering.* Berkeley, CA: University of California Press.

Till, K. E. 1999. Staging the past: Landscape designs, cultural identity, and *erinnerungspolitik* at Berlin's Neue Wache. *Ecumene* 6(3):251–283.

Till, K. E. 2003. Places of memory. In *A companion for political geography*, eds. J. Agnew, K. Mitchell, G. O. Tuathail, 289–301. Oxford, U.K.: Blackwell.

Till, K. E. 2005. *The new* Berlin: *Memory, politics, place.* Minneapolis, MN: University of Minnesota Press.

Till, K. E. 2008. Artistic and activist memory-work: Approaching place-based practice. *Memory studies* 1(1):95–109.

Till, K. E. 2010. The limitations of resilience: The District Six Museum's place-based ethics of care. Paper presented at "Post-Apartheid Geographies of South Africa and Its Region," a session at the annual meeting of the Association of American Geographers (Washington, D.C., April, 2010).

Till, K. E., and J. Jonker. 2009. Spectral ground in new cities: Memorial cartographies in Cape Town and Berlin. In *Memory culture and the contemporary city: Building sites*, eds. U. Staiger, H. Steiner, and A. Webber, 85–105. Basingstoke, U.K.: Palgrave Macmillan.

Tronto, J. C. 1993. *Moral boundaries: A political argument for an ethic of care.* London: Routledge.

Tuan, Yi-Fu. 1977. *Space and place: The perspective of experience.* Minneapolis, MN: University of Minnesota Press.

Vale, L., and T. Campanella. 2005a. Introduction: The cities rise again. In *The resilient city: How modern cities recover from disaster*, eds. L. Vale and T. Campanella, 3–23. Oxford, U.K.: Oxford University Press.

Vale, L., and T. Campanella, eds. 2005b. *The resilient city: How modern cities recover from disaster.* Oxford, U.K.: Oxford University Press.

Weeder, M. 2008. Topographies of the forgotten: Prestwich and Cape Town's nineteenth century cemeteries. In *City—Site—Museum*, eds. B. Bennett, C. Julius, and C. Soudien, 32–49. Cape Town, South Africa: District Six Museum.

13

Shadow Networks, Social Learning, and Collaborating through Crisis: Building Resilient Forest-Based Communities in Northern Ontario, Canada

Ryan Bullock, Derek Armitage, and Bruce Mitchell

This chapter focuses on the relationship between social learning and resilience in forest-based communities in crisis in Northern Ontario, Canada. In particular, we examine how a "shadow network" (Gunderson 1999)—in this case, an informal group of town officials and their advisors—facilitated learning and mobilized resources as a critical first step in establishing a more formal collaborative forum to increase community resilience. Frame analysis is used to examine shifting perspectives of the ongoing crisis. The common framings produced to guide action reflect *social learning*, defined here as the iterative action, reflection, and deliberation of individuals and groups engaged in the sharing of experiences and ideas to collaboratively resolve complex challenges (Gray 2003; 2006; Diduck et al. 2005; Pahl-Wostl 2009). Our analysis also identifies and tracks two stages in the development of the Northeast Superior Forest Community Corporation (NSFC), from (1) an inconspicuous social network, to (2) a federally supported regional collaborative forum designed to bridge gaps in forest governance and to promote development.

The NSFC presents an ideal case to study social group frames regarding problem definitions, solutions, and forms of power in an emerging social learning setting. An emerging movement for increased local control of forest resources in Northern Ontario juxtaposes dominant and marginalized social groups with historically uneven opportunities to influence forest planning and management. The mix of experts, consultants, practitioners, and lay people provides further opportunity to assess power differentials.

A focus on shadow networks and social learning in emerging collaborations is significant because early problem and solution definitions can have a lasting effect on the resultant formal organizations. Individuals or groups with influence and/or good timing, especially during times of crisis and rapid change, can position themselves and plant or endorse preferred ideas that serve alternative interests and values. To the extent that conventionally disempowered actors can learn together in the "shadow" of a dominant, albeit failing, status quo, new opportunities can be advanced—another critical role of shadow networks. The final part of the analysis examines how actors exercise coercive and constraining power (Raik et al. 2008) to promote certain problem and solution frames, as one measure of how power relations condition learning. The outcomes of the analysis should be illuminating for other crisis situations and contexts where shadow networks may emerge or could be encouraged to perform crucial front-end work that fosters collaboration and builds community resilience.

Northern Ontario's "Forestry Crisis"

Regional Dynamics

Ontario's vast natural resources have long been a source of wealth for the province of Ontario, mainly from forestry and mining. For example, the provincial forest products sector shipped more than $18 billion in wood products in 2005 (OMNR 2008). However, a downturn in Ontario's forest economy continues to challenge communities across the province. Natural Resources Canada (NRCAN 2007) reported that Ontario has lost more forestry jobs than any other region in Canada. In Ontario between 2003 and 2007 about 8,000 direct jobs were lost through mill closures and temporary layoffs. However, the disproportionate impact of this crisis on Northern Ontario, and the resulting conflict surrounding forest policy and planning, must be considered with regard to the uneven geographical distribution of Ontario's forests and population, as well as the locus of forest governance control.

Southern Ontario is more densely populated and urbanized than the north—over 93 percent (about 11 million) of the provincial population lives in the southern area that geographically represents less than 8 percent of the province. There is also a high degree of private land ownership in southern Ontario, about 87 percent (OFA 2009), and 20 percent of the southern land base is farmland (OMAFRA 2009). Close to large U.S. markets, Southern Ontario has an economy that is heavily industrialized.

In contrast, Northern Ontario contains the overwhelming majority of Ontario's commercially productive forest lands (OMNR 2008). The provincial north is 95 percent public Crown land and 66 percent forested. Northern Ontario's boreal forest accounts for 76 percent of provincial forest land and is the backbone of the forest industry (Province of Ontario 2010). The region is home to 16 of the province's 33 pulp and paper mills.

Ontario's 25 largest sawmills produce 80 percent of the province's lumber; 22 of these mills are in Northern Ontario.

About one-third of northern communities are dependent on the forest industry (Province of Ontario 2008). Only 800,000 people live in Northern Ontario—just 7 percent of the total provincial population—yet 26,000 northerners were directly employed in Ontario's forest products industry in 2005 (Robinson 2007). This number of northerners represents 31 percent of provincial forest workers. But employment in this sector has continually dwindled due to the downturn in the forest economy. In Northern Ontario, about 2,200 direct jobs in forestry were lost between 2003 and 2005 (Minister's Council of Forest Sector Competitiveness 2005), while some people suggest that this number of lost jobs increased to 9,000 by the fall of 2007. These changes represent a loss of $869 million to the northern economy (NDP 2007). Northern forest resources and industries are important to Ontario's forest sector; however, their vital contribution to the northern economy and communities must not be overlooked.

The majority of commercially productive forests are located in Northern Ontario, and the degree of community dependence on the resource is also high. Yet forests have long been controlled by the Ontario Ministry of Natural Resources (OMNR) and the commercial forest industry through the Forest Licensing System (or "tenure system") (OMNDMF 2011). Ontario's forest policies have been developed through collaboration with large-scale pulp and forest products companies, resulting in regulatory capture and a closed policy network (Hessing et al. 2005; Robinson 2007). Historically, a provincial focus on industrial forestry and commodity exports has limited the flow of fiber to secondary manufacturing, contributing to underdevelopment in Northern Ontario.

A growing consensus among governments, communities, industry, and researchers (Haley and Nelson 2007; Robinson 2007; Rosehart 2008; Bullock 2009) is that the tenure system has constrained diversification and innovation. Access to fiber for new entrants such as local enterprise, First Nations,[1] and other communities is limited. Specifically, there are few incentives to develop nonconventional forest products and uses. Examples include food products such as berries, nuts, fiddleheads, and mushrooms; health and personal care products such as drugs, nutraceuticals, aromatherapy oils, and cosmetics; and landscape and garden products such trees, shrubs, grasses, and wildflowers (NSFC 2009). To elaborate, Ontario's current tenure policies are based on the notion of sustained yield harvesting intended to ensure steady fiber flows to designated processors

(Haley and Nelson 2007). Consequently, these policies emphasize timber harvesting rights (deemphasizing nontimber products) and long-term security for large investors through "evergreen" leases renewed every five years. Furthermore, 80 percent of annual fiber allocations are associated with large-scale processing facilities that by design require minimum fiber volumes to be economically viable, and 100 percent of the annual cut is designated to come from specific forest areas (Haley and Nelson 2007). In this rigid institutional setting, it is difficult to adjust policies, reconfigure mill operations, and redirect fiber flows without invariably impacting specific mills, towns, and forests. Current tenure policies have contributed to the decline of the forest industry in Canada as a whole, and they do not provide the flexibility needed to respond nimbly to change and shocks (Haley and Nelson 2007).

Various committees, working groups, and task forces typically agree on several key factors as contributing to the ongoing problems with the forest industry. These groups are from industry, government, labor, communities, and academe, and they include, for example, the Minister's Council on Forest Sector Competitiveness (2005), the Ontario Forestry Coalition (2006), CEP/USW Task Force on Resource Dependent Communities (Butler, Cheetham, and Power 2007), and the Northwestern Ontario Economic Facilitator (Rosehart 2008). The five key pressuring factors they identify are the following. (1) The U.S. dollar fell by 48 cents relative to the Canadian dollar between 2002 and 2007 (Bank of Canada 2009). (2) Demand for newsprint and housing materials declined (e.g., U.S. housing starts fell by more than half between 2005 and 2008, from over 2 million to 900,000) (National Association of Home Builders, 2008). (3) Increased U.S. duties on Canadian softwood lumber and increasing global competition from low-cost producers reduced demand for forest exports. (4) During the same time period, energy costs in Northern Ontario increased sharply, including a 50 percent increase in diesel costs between 2003 and 2008 (Ontario Ministry of Energy 2011) and a 30 percent increase in electricity costs between 2003 and 2006 (NRCAN 2006). (5) Finally, access to desired fiber volumes and types became problematic in Northern Ontario due to the increasing distance of supply from mills (NRCAN 2006) and a forecast 80-year supply shortage of softwood and poplar, presenting a significant future challenge (ECO 2005). Combined, these five pressures have decreased demand for provincial forest products and have increased industrial operating costs, causing the widespread layoffs and closures that have adversely affected northern communities.

Analysis of the specific impacts and social responses of residents and community leaders shows variation from place to place according to local circumstances and capacity. This chapter will highlight the local context from which an informal group emerged in response to economic and social challenges shared by a cluster of forest communities along the northeast shore of Lake Superior.

Local Impacts and Responses: The Northeast Superior Forest Community
The Northeast Superior Forest Community region includes the forest-dependent communities of Chapleau, Dubreuilville, Hornepayne, Manitouwadge, Wawa, and White River, as well as eight First Nations communities: Brunswick House, Chapleau Cree, Chapleau Ojibway, Hornepayne, Michipicoten, Missanabie Cree, Pic Mobert, and Pic River. (A map to these NSFC areas is provided in figure 13.1.) Located adjacent to the northeastern shore of Lake Superior in Northern Ontario, this

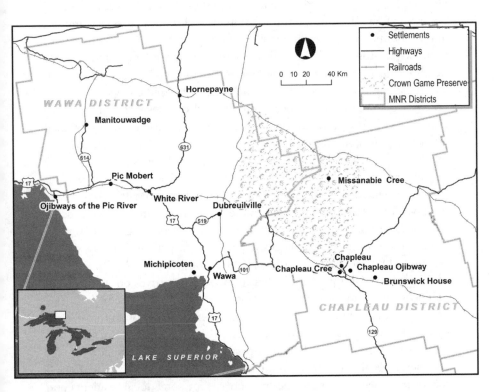

Figure 13.1
The Northeast Superior Forest Community (NSFC), Northern Ontario, Canada

roughly 60,000 km^2 region straddles the boundary between the eastern Great Lakes–St. Lawrence Forest and the northern boreal forest region (Albert et al. 2006). The region is predominantly public Crown land, and it is locally referred to as "the fiber basket," indicating a local place identity linked to forest resources and industry.

The region's communities are home to about 13,500 and 975 non-aboriginal and aboriginal people, respectively. Forest dependence is perhaps most dramatically illustrated by recent population decreases associated with several recent mill closures. Between 2001 and 2006, the region's population declined by 14.4 percent, compared to a provincial population increase of 6.6 percent (Statistics Canada 2008). More than 900 jobs were eliminated in the region with the closures of Domtar Forest Products in White River, Weyerhaeuser Oriented Strand Board in Wawa, and Dubreuil Forest Products in Dubreuilville in late 2007 and early 2008 (Economic Development Corporation of Wawa 2004). These simultaneous closures have had an added impact in that these facilities were all located approximately 100 km from one another, where local people, families, and economies are closely intertwined. The "cardhouse" structure of this regional economy and the high level of interdependence among these neighboring forest-reliant communities have become apparent as local social groups work to understand and deal with rapid change.

These communities have been grappling with widespread mill closures and job loss, population decline due to the mass outmigration of skilled labor and youth, falling real estate values and foreclosures, declining municipal tax bases, and service loss. This series of changes is typical of the downward spiral usually experienced by extractive resource-dependent towns associated with the loss of a primary industry (Beattie et al. 1981; Decter et al. 1989). However, given the number of communities affected and the extent of the decline, this combination of economic, demographic, policy, and ecological challenges is part of a larger "forestry crisis" in Northern Ontario (Stewart 2006; NOSCP 2007; Woods 2007).

As presented in the analysis that follows, perspectives on the problem and possible solutions vary, but at least two positions have emerged. The dominant and conventional view is that changing economic forces have driven the few large companies that control most of the fiber supply in Northern Ontario to scale back operations or close. "Outside" forces are therefore blamed for the industry collapse that has deeply affected forest-dependent communities. In contrast, for some local residents and forest social groups, the fundamental cause(s) of the problem is different and more pervasive. Their view is that internal resistance to change is the main problem, and that solutions will necessitate wholesale changes to the structure of regional forest economies and power relations believed to limit community resilience. Their bottom-up response to the crisis involves developing new understandings of problems and solutions through unconventional discursive forums that emerge outside of forest industry advisory committees, official plan review open houses, and government offices.

The next section highlights the conceptual links between social learning theory, particularly the idea of double-loop learning (Argyris and Schön 1978), and social framings (Gray 2003) to illustrate how problem and solution definitions are collaboratively produced amid power relations. We then turn attention to the concept of learning in shadow networks (Gunderson 1999; Olsson et al. 2006) as alternative social spaces that can provide the impetus for change and facilitate the co-production of new social framings that challenge dominant perspectives and policies during times of crisis.

Social Learning and Framings

In this section, we explain the links between social learning processes and the social framings developed to guide action and outcomes in collaborative problem domains. This discussion leads to a consideration of the implications and importance of shadow networks as alternative communicative forums and therefore as a potential source of change.

Social learning approaches (e.g., Argyris and Schön 1978; Mezirow 1994; Keen et al. 2005) to collaborative resource management and planning implicitly study the convergence of individual and organizational frames (Gray 2003, 2004; Pahl-Wostl 2009). People build shared meaning through social framings, a behavior that provides a basis for collective action (see Argyris and Schön 1978; Schusler et al. 2003; Gray 2004; Pahl-Wostl 2009).

Social learning theorists (Argyris and Schön 1978; Kim 1993) distinguish between two modes of learning. Single-loop or instrumental learning is "concerned with changing skills, practices, and actions" that affect outcomes (Keen et al. 2005, 16). This type of learning supports ongoing pursuit of current organizational policies and objectives, without changing basic values and norms (Argyris and Schön 1978; Diduck et al. 2005). Double-loop or conceptual learning results in more fundamental changes to underlying values, norms, and objectives that in turn cause change in strategies and action.

Kim (1993) highlights the difference between using "know-how" and "know-why" to influence the two aspects of "mental models" that guide action: (1) procedural routines and (2) common frameworks—the latter of which is conceptually analogous with the frame concept discussed previously. Altering frameworks through double-loop learning enables the "reframing" of problems in order to establish new routines for action. Collaboration and an inclination for conceptual learning are thought to be necessary to produce new frameworks, actions, and outcomes needed to facilitate transformation during times of turbulence and crisis (Olsson et al. 2006).

However, there is also potential for frame conflicts, as competing individuals and organizations try to assert (or do assert) their dominance. Those people with influence can affect what others (and therefore an organization or society) learn in terms of which frames are adopted to represent reality. Dominant framings of problems and solutions shape and are shaped by certain knowledge, experience and cultures, and therefore reflect the interests and values of some people or groups more than others.

Consequently, scholars (e.g., Sinclair and Diduck 2001; Keen and Mahanty 2006; Wildemeersch 2007; Armitage et al. 2008) have increasingly argued for more attention to the role of power relations (including the forms and sources of power) in social learning. Some researchers have also considered how design of process, structure, and function can contribute to collaborative forums, techniques, "new" knowledge, and decisions that can recreate hegemonic power relations (Maarleveld and Dangbegnon 1999; Schusler et al. 2003; Quaghebeur et al. 2004).

Attention must also be paid to the "embeddedness" of learning and decision-making processes within political and institutional contexts, and how political economy influences learning processes at the local scale to affect resource and environmental management outcomes (Glasbergen 1996; Diduck et al. 2005; Wildemeersch 2007). Limiting problem definitions, dissent, participation, and conflict, as well as limiting opportunities for social group discussion and reflection needed for learning, are examples of how those people with influence can intervene (Maarleveld and Dangbegnon 1999; Sinclair and Diduck 2001; Diduck and Mitchell 2003; Quaghebeur et al. 2004). Armitage et al. (2008: 11) remind us that "learning is neither value free or politically neutral."

A central theme in "critical" political ecology is the pluralism of perspectives on environmental issues. Social, cultural, political, and economic contextual influences shape perceptions, meanings, and discourses, which in turn affect practices and outcomes (Peet and Watts 1996; Escobar 1999;

Forsyth 2003). In this way, struggle is as much about whose world view will dominate as it is about institutional control and material needs (Peet and Watts 1996). Accordingly, "exploring social framings means questioning how, when, and by whom such terms were developed as a substitute for reality" (Forsyth 2003, p. 81). More recently, researchers are illustrating how civil society organizations, governments, scientists, consultants, First Nations, and other resource users are involved in local struggles for control over environmental knowledge that will be imposed through resource management institutions (e.g., Rikoon 2006; Robbins 2006; Reed and McIlveen 2006; Dengler 2007; Reed 2007).

As the processes of local organization and policy reform unfold, many social groups have a hand in shaping future outcomes. Some groups have more influence than others, due to how power is exercised and due to the stage of involvement. Experts cannot and should not be viewed as neutral consultants and objective technicians employed to advise their client social groups in situations of learning—because they bring their *own* disciplinary assumptions, tools, and reputations to the problem domain, based on certain cultures of learning. The bias and influence of scientists and professional resource managers have raised concerns about their influence on research and management agendas in, for example, wildlife management (Diduck et al. 2005), parks and protected areas (Price 1996), and forestry (Bullock 2006).

Given the immediate need for solutions and sense of dependency induced by crisis, there is high potential to adopt, unchallenged, the problem definitions and solutions of the "helpers." The point here is not to challenge the contribution of experts (policy, science, traditional knowledge, or otherwise), but to underscore their position of influence in situations of crisis and social learning. These points are discussed in the following section and are especially important to consider with regard to the timing or emergence of shadow networks during crisis and their importance during the formative stages of evolving collaborations that lead to the establishment of more visible and/or formal organizations.

The Nature of Shadow Networks
The concept of the shadow network (Gunderson 1999; Olsson et al. 2006) provides a lens to examine the emergence and potential role of the NSFC to address the conditions of crisis, facilitate social learning, and promote community resilience. Resilient communities can purposefully induce change and respond to change in order to endure disturbance without fundamental changes to their overall structure and function (Centre for

Community Enterprise 2000; Walker and Salt 2006). Resilience scholars also emphasize conditions enabling "post-event, adaptive processes that facilitate the ability of the social system to re-organize, change, and learn in response to a threat" (Cutter et al. 2008, 599). Learning is thus recognized as having a central role in enabling resilience during times of crisis and in the future recovery and adaptability of a system (Gunderson and Pritchard 2002; Cutter et al. 2008). This chapter will explore the unique characteristics of shadow networks (e.g., flexibility, propensity for innovation), which are highly amenable for collaborating and learning through crisis and for creating or reinforcing community resilience, if social equity concerns are addressed.

We share the views of Dukes, Williams, and Kelban (chapter 10 in this book) that resilient, large-scale systems that perpetuate social divisiveness, inequity, and harm are undesirable; but that the collective ability to acknowledge, understand, and embrace transition can promote positive resilience in a community context. The question(s) remains, however: transition to what, and for whom? This normative aspect of resilience requires that context and competing human interests be considered explicitly in analysis (Armitage and Johnson 2006; Walker et al. 2002). For example, in the context of corporate–community power dynamics in which hinterland community capacity is thin, industry closures are typically met with broad local support for immediate reopening, even though reopening will knowingly perpetuate the well-documented cycle of growth and decline, and heartland intervention in local politics and culture (Lucas 1971; Beattie et al. 1981; Decter et al. 1989). As Pelling (1998) points out, the engrained socio-political patterns of dominant interest and values tend to be reproduced through reorganization when adaptive and inclusive institutions do not exist. Such an outcome is not desirable.

Bojórquez-Tapia and Eakin show in chapter 7 of this book how formal and inclusive collaborative institutional frameworks that produce systemic knowledge can enable reorganization of post-event social and economic activities. We concur with their position, and we thus step back to examine the qualities of informal shadow networks as social learning forums that contribute to the later development of formal institutions supporting community resilience. Our focus is on the changing perspectives held by those within a shadow network of municipal officials, consultants, and academics who fostered the emergence of the NSFC. That is, we wanted to examine the evolving problem and solution perspectives advanced by the shadow network (and later enshrined in NSFC policy when the shadow network evolved into a formal organization).

Gunderson (1999) and later Olsson et al. (2006) discuss the importance of "shadow networks" to the emergence of adaptive governance and new organizations during periods of crisis and reorganization in social-ecological systems. But the concept has received little scrutiny in terms of its implications for practice. Below we briefly unpack what is meant by a *shadow network,* to explore what is at once a useful concept but one that warrants further definition. Gunderson (1999) first described shadow networks:

In cases of successful adaptive assessment and management, an informal network seems always to emerge. That network of participants places emphasis on political independence, out of the fray of regulation and implementation, places where formal networks and many planning processes fail. The informal, out of the fray, shadow groups seem to be where new ideas arise and flourish. It is these "skunkworks" who explore flexible opportunities for resolving resource issues, devise alternative designs and tests of policy, and create ways to foster social learning.

Shadow networks are self-organizing, informal groups of people that mobilize in response to crisis (Gunderson 1999; Olsson et al. 2006; Goldstein 2008; Sendzimir et al. 2008). They can be pre-existing or develop during a crisis, and they can form slowly or rapidly. They can also have shifting membership, consisting of different people with various training and experience at different times. Their purpose can also shift at any given time in that pre-existing networks can switch focus from problem to problem as needed. Little expectation or organizational obligations make participants free to experiment, innovate, openly discuss, create, and test policy alternatives.

Although these networks have no direct formal authority, members can hold significant or high positions within other organizations (e.g., government, universities, and nongovernment organizations) and/or belong to several networks. Individuals can also return to their formal organizational roles and apply lessons learned. Thus, shadow networks can be incubators for innovation, where new and existing ideas can be advanced by loosely coupled, and sometimes unlikely, partners advocating for change. Shadow networks that bridge multiple organizational levels (e.g., municipal to federal), geographically dispersed social groups (e.g., local to global), and resource sectors (e.g., waste management, water, forestry, and energy) are considered a source of resilience because they increase integration (Olsson et al. 2006). Table 13.1 summarizes the implications of shadow networks.

Thus, whether the shadow network evolves into a formalized, legitimate authority or inspires another organization(s) to develop further ideas originally conceived by the shadow network, the critical role of shadow

Table 13.1
Implications of shadow networks

• Shadow networks represent an alternative to the status quo, which is considered by some to be responsible for the failure(s) causing the crisis.

• Because links can exist to those who direct political agendas (depending on the extent of their influence), shadow networks can be seen also to serve "other" interests.

• The mix of individuals and organizations from different sectors and vocations implies interdisciplinarity (and the challenges associated with that approach).

• Those involved are problem solvers.

• Members presumably have a common interest in solving "the problem." But the question as to personal motivations to participate remains: how do members value and/or benefit from participation in these forums? (Possible motives include the satisfaction of doing the "right thing", the simple enjoyment of learning and interaction, a promise of prestige with group affiliation, or just for "sport.")

• The emphasis on independence, together with the absence of formal authority and obligations, provides flexibility, but also a possible lack of accountability.

• Shadow networks are considered a precursor for success with new organizations.

• As a source of expertise, ideas, memory, and communication, shadow networks are a resource.

• The timing of their emergence during crisis positions them for a pivotal role in defining problems and directions for setting alternative agendas.

---

networks is evident. As learning forums, they influence the production of social framings of regional resource problems and solutions, and they can have a lasting and significant influence on organizational mandates and practice. Given their role as a change agent, shadow networks have the potential to help communities become more resilient when hampered by failing policies and decisions. In such cases, new directions can be set for "learning the way out" of problems and solutions produced by conventional, and often dominant, thinking. As unseen learning forums with flexibility and free association (Goldstein 2008), they can challenge existing power relations, and they can present opportunities for reframing identities, problems, and solutions. They can offer alternatives to the status quo.

In the analysis, we examine the social framings collaboratively produced in a shadow network consisting of local representatives and their advisors—the Mayors' Group—that led to the development of a formal organization intended to promote community resilience in Northern Ontario. We illustrate how alternative problem and solution frames were developed and show the role of power relations in advancing certain ideas over others.

Frame Analysis

We use frame analysis to identify key frames and contrast perspectives in an evolving debate (Rein and Schön 1994; Forsyth 2003; Lewicki et al. 2003; Dewulf et al. 2005; Gray 2004) surrounding the forestry crisis in Northern Ontario. We focus on the Mayors' Group shadow network, and then on the subsequent Northeast Superior Forest Community Corporation (NSFC). Thus, we track collective frames through two stages in the development of the NSFC to see which ones emerge as alternatives within a socially constructed discourse related to the forest crisis. Collaborative decision making within the shadow network and NSFC is linked to problem and solution frames and the strategies implicitly intended to build community resilience.

The analysis and results are based on the first phase of ongoing research. A synthesis of forest social group perspectives on key forestry issues in the NSFC region is provided here. Between June and August of 2008, we conducted thirty-four semistructured interviews. These interviews were with members of the Mayors' Group and the NSFC, as well as with representatives from the forest industry; First Nations; municipal, provincial, and federal governments; forestry workers; tourism; academe; forestry consultants; and nongovernment environmental and community development organizations. Most (30 of 34) participants were long-term local residents, meaning that they lived there for more than ten years. Following the approach of Gray (2003), participants were asked open-ended questions about forestry problems in Northern Ontario and about possible solutions. Participants were also asked who they felt had the most influence over forest resources in the NSFC region and what made certain social groups powerful.

We reviewed reports, plans, and social group Web sites related to the forestry crisis, as well as over fifty newspaper and trade magazine articles covering the forestry crisis between 2001 and 2008. During the initial two-month field work season, visits were made to aboriginal and nonaboriginal communities, operating and nonoperating pulp and paper mills and sawmills, and value-added wood manufacturing facilities.

"The Mayors' Group" as a Shadow Network and the Emergence of the NSFC Corporation

The Northeastern Superior Mayors' Group emerged in February, 2000 when the mayors and other municipal representatives (from the six towns already identified) began collaborating to develop alternative solutions to common problems. This informal network had links to local government organizations and resources that could be mobilized. As well, links were developed with selected advisors and consultants (i.e., academics, media, and business people) from sectors across Northern Ontario who were engaged at various times to share different perspectives.

Known locally as "The Mayors' Group," this voluntary mayoral association began to coordinate its decision making and also developed collective strategies for dealing with government officials from provincial and federal levels. With reference to their influence, the common view among those interviewed is reflected by one member who observed: "We don't have much power; the only power [we have] is what we give ourselves" [shadow network 1][2]. However, collaboration also added to the legitimacy and capacity of their communities, which (as outlined in the NSFC Forest Communities Program proposal) "are essentially postage stamps in the middle of a vast unorganized territory" administered by the province of Ontario (Albert et al. 2006, 7). By working together with a shifting cast of advisors from within and outside its region, the group developed an understanding of common issues, of each other, and they benefited from resource sharing and a louder voice.

Recognizing common service challenges associated with rural transition, the group set out to undertake projects considered necessary to maintain and improve services and infrastructure to retain and attract residents and businesses as well as to develop the regional economy. Through links with formal governance structures both below and above them, they realized achievements to extend local cell phone service, to maintain air services and local airports, to attract health care professionals, and to establish broadband coverage throughout the region (Albert et al. 2006, 4). The initial focus was on realigning and improving services within the region to support development.

In 2005, common challenges associated with Northern Ontario's forestry crisis led the Mayors' Group to experiment with developing a shared economic strategy based on the ideas of consultants from Northern Ontario. Acknowledging the existing and future role for forests in their communities, the Mayors' Group set out to "make the forest resources of the region work for the people who live in the six communities" (Albert et al. 2006, 3)—implying the need for a greater level of local control and benefits from local forests than in the past. In developing and adopting a regional economic development strategy, coordinating decision making, and sharing project revenues, the six communities were increasing structures and functions for integrated problem solving. Through meetings and discussions, they were also developing an alternative vision of the potential relationship between forest resources and communities within their region—one that refocused on nonconventional forest products and that departed from industry control of local public forests.

Subsequently, Natural Resources Canada released a call for proposals for the Forest Communities Program during the summer of 2006. A main goal of the program was to "encourage the development of knowledge, information tools and best practices to help forest communities meet the challenges of transition in the forest sector" (NRCAN 2007). The intention was to also "foster collaborative community efforts to help communities take advantage of new economic opportunities from forest resources" (NRCAN 2007). This refocusing on forest-based communities and knowledge development sought to increase local involvement through providing funding and networking opportunities for new or existing community level organizations that integrated public/private/civic perspectives toward building resilience in forest-dependent communities.

Seeing an opportunity that matched their ongoing efforts, the Mayors' Group developed an application to the federal government based largely on consultants' work. This application resulted in successful designation and funding of $1.0 million over five years to establish research and programs aimed at generating economic opportunities, human capital, and knowledge on how to do sustainable forest management. Notably, the application accepted by the federal government stressed the perceived need for self-reliance and cultural and institutional reform, with the issues of tenure reform and the need to develop value-added processing and nontimber forest products at center stage on the first section of the proposal (Albert et al. 2006). The focus on local control of forests and on developing local talent for community economic development stood in contrast to forest industry appeals to government for increased security for industrial fiber allocations and reduced energy costs, for example, in order to create a more competitive business environment.

NRCAN representatives commented that the strengths of the application were that it represented a group of collaborating communities with a unified vision, and that the group had support from local First Nations

(NRCAN 1, 2). A major transition occurred when the Mayors' Group later became the original board of directors for the newly formed organization: the Northeast Superior Forest Community Corporation. However, interviews with First Nations representatives indicated that at the time of the NRCAN proposal, relations between the Mayors' Group and First Nations were tenuous, and that the Mayors' Group's expression of interest to collaborate with First Nations was viewed by them as "tokenism" [First Nations 1, 2, 3].

Having no previous "member" involvement in the Mayors' Group shadow network, local First Nations developed their own group as a response to the perceived failings of regional policymaking. The Northeast Superior Regional Chiefs' Forum was intended as a counterpart to critique the NSFC Strategic Plan, and the forum was initiated so that the NSFC might better reflect a legitimate collaboration with First Nations. Unsatisfied with their exclusion from the NSFC decision making, and seeing opportunity for more effective collaboration based on First Nations' traditional resource tenure and the capacity of non-aboriginal communities, First Nations indicated that they would intervene in project plans unless they were appropriately engaged. As of fall, 2009, the eight First Nations communities had selected one individual to represent them jointly as a NSFC voting board member.

Through increasing focus and formalization, the NSFC is now pursuing project work on nontimber forest products, bioenergy, and capacity-building to promote more meaningful local involvement in the management and development of public forests in Northern Ontario. The explicit goal of experimenting with new tenure regimes seems to have faded into the background, although it is still implied in the NSFC strategic plan as a prerequisite for pursuing other projects. Efforts have focused on developing the organizational capacity to manage and operate what is essentially a funding institution that supports consultant-based feasibility research. NSFC's basic approach is to develop a portfolio of feasibility studies in order to present business opportunities to would-be investors and entrepreneurs, local or otherwise. Federal money provided to foster community involvement in forestry solutions is mainly being channeled through local and nonlocal consultants who will do the preliminary work on studies intended to provide eventual returns to the communities when business opportunities are implemented.

With the need to secure a forest land base to implement their projects, NSFC staff and directors will have to develop partnerships (with industry, First Nations, and relevant provincial ministries) to arrange in-kind or lease agreements and alternative tenure policies. As of July, 2008, interviews with government representatives revealed that ongoing communication was not occurring with what they referred to as the "community forest" [province 1], indicating not only low involvement and awareness at the provincial level, but that the Ontario Ministry of Natural Resources characterizes the nascent organization as something local and isolated from the existing forestry policy arena. To explain, the community forest concept was scrapped by the province after a pilot program in Northern Ontario during the 1990s, and local control has since been vilified by opponents, as the idea of local control challenges the conventional large-scale industrial forestry model and view of communities as service centers and labor sources for extractive industries in the North.

Given NSFC's early stage of development, it is too early to tell which NSFC projects will come to fruition and what, if any, their contribution will be to sustaining the communities on the Northeast Superior region. However, the projects being initiated originate from alternative views of forestry problems and solutions—mainly the need for increased local control, value-added manufacturing, and development of nontimber forest products—rather than from mainstream concerns about conventional forest management planning. The shadow network served as a forum for the gradual development of trust, and the development of a common vision and organizational memory. The network also provided a platform for sharing ideas and resources, which metamorphosed into a formal organization to further the pursuit of problem and solution perspectives and objectives generated by the shadow network. As a successor to the Mayors' Group, the NSFC is positioned to help "learn the way out" of the crisis, if it remains open to alternative social framings and opportunities.

(Re)defining the Problem: Diagnostic Frames

Diagnostic or problem definition frames point to peoples' understanding of the problem situation as well as what has caused the problem, and the frames often target who is seen to be responsible for the problem (Gray 2003). As illustrated in the prior discussion, a drive for self-reliance and to "do things differently" led to the formation of the shadow network that subsequently evolved into the NSFC. The emergence of the Mayors' Group and NSFC is linked to the efforts of collaborating individuals who, questioning the apparent failures of policy and management, engaged in conceptual learning to reframe the problem and identify promising new paths.

All participants explained the current forestry crisis in terms of the many economic factors (outlined previously) affecting the existing industry, thereby acknowledging substantive facts emanating from the dominant social framings of the problem provided by industry/government reports and the media. However, rather than passively accepting this diagnosis and the prescribed actions to fix the existing industry, shadow network members pressed to identify more fundamental causes of the overall problem and, through double-loop learning, developed their own nuanced understanding. A change in the vision and policies surrounding forest tenure were judged to be at the heart of the matter. At least three participants referred to tenure as a taboo issue: "that nasty word called *tenure*" [shadow network 2].

Citing the failure of provincial forest policy and the Crown tenure system, participants underscored what they saw as the more fundamental aspects of the "real" problem (that is, a lack of local control). This framing of the problem explains the focus of the NSFC strategic plan on projects for nontimber forest products, bioenergy, and tenure innovation. The ideas were conceived through "straight dialogue" [shadow network 2] in an alternative forum and through double-loop learning modes intended to "do the right thing" for communities. For example, the focus shifted from solving the problems of the current forest industry to redefining community relationships with forest ecosystems, and to how they ought to be managed and used in order to benefit northern populations.

Now that the NSFC is fully operational, the routine is to award funding to consultants who can use their "know how" for instrumental or single-loop learning on how to "do the things right." In other words, they hire consultants to develop the technical aspects of project development to support alternatives proposed and fostered by the NSFC board and advisors. Notable examples to date include developing business plans for commercial blueberry production and feasibility assessments for sustainably harvesting and processing nontimber forest products such as ground hemlock (*Taxus canadensis*) and fireweed (*Epilobium angustifolium*) for their medicinal qualities (NSFC 2009). However, this pattern reflects a practical challenge faced by the NSFC directors and its consultants—to get out of and avoid a "lock-in trap" (Allison and Hobbs 2004) created when significant investments of time and money preclude ongoing reflection and conceptual learning. To avoid this trap, the fine-tuning and application of "new" ideas and solutions cannot be treated as end points, but rather as entry points to pursue additional opportunities.

Accordingly, while each side accepts some responsibility for its own shortcomings in terms of capacity to deal with the problem, both shadow network members and those in industry often externalize the main causes of the problem. Shadow network members blame industry and senior government for being inflexible and unaccountable to communities. The forest industry and labor groups [e.g., the Ontario Forestry Coalition; the Communications, Energy, and Paperworkers Union of Canada (CEP), and the United Steelworkers (USW)] blame global forces as well as federal and provincial governments for being unresponsive or not doing enough, bad policymaking, and red tape. For their part, government representatives point to the constraints of existing policy with respect to what can be done, as well as the possible range of responses.

The Solutions: Prognostic Frames

Peoples' prognostic or solution frames identify preferred strategies and tactics for solving the problem, including who should be responsible to act (Gray 2003). The possible solutions depend on how the problem is framed. Given that lack of local control was considered by the shadow network members to be the root of the problem, it is not surprising that all of those interviewed from the shadow network believed that increased local control was part of the solution. More specifically, participants suggested that increased local control could take on a variety of tenure forms; but such control was mainly envisioned as being through municipal involvement or as creating more opportunities for local business and other social groups by securing timber allocations for specialized value-added manufacturing, rather than for conventional, large-scale commodity-based operations such as sawmills.

Some participants were unsure about the benefits of total local control or forest ownership [shadow network 2], emphasizing instead the need for more meaningful collaboration between industry and municipalities, and specifically, municipal involvement in Crown timber allocation processes. Others were more absolute about the need to "wrestle control away from industry" [shadow network 8]. Another member stated "if it were me, and I were a Mayor, I'd say 'you're God damn right I want [forest tenure]'. Absolutely . . . but I'm not" [shadow network 1]. Other members were more open to any combination that would create conditions to have a viable forest economy [shadow network 3, 6]. Whatever the solution was, they believed that the onus was on the local people to make it happen because industry and government were not seen to be motivated to support change [shadow network 1, 3, 4, 8, 9]. A shift away from the conventional thinking about and acceptance of industry-dominated forests and communities is indicative of double-loop learning processes among network participants.

Network members said they had gained an appreciation for the complexity of forestry in Northern Ontario and specifically in their region. Both aboriginal and nonaboriginal members said they had learned that they had to work together with the other communities, instead of competing with one another [shadow network 1, 2, 8, 9]. They expressed a preference and need for regional social groups to collaborate in order to overcome what were seen as "northern problems" [shadow network 2, 4, 5, 9]. This call to "get everyone together" [shadow network 5] was certainly not restricted to elites from industry and government, but rather the call was intended to move the discussion into an accessible public forum where diverse perspectives and ideas could be integrated into public policy.

In part, the emergence of the Mayors' Group and the later formation of the NSFC represent such a forum. While mainstream debates among industry, labor, and government entertained instrumental learning solutions (such as how to lower energy prices and delivered wood costs, and how to tweak fiber flows to improve the competitiveness of existing industry), the shadow network set out to develop solutions to diversify the forest economy. These solutions to diversify later took the form of NSFC projects for identifying new products (e.g., nontimber forest products) and changing the culture of forest communities. Emerging from a bottom-up collaborative, the problem was framed as a challenge caused by limited local access to fiber, a limitation that in turn stifled innovation and northern talent. Following that framing, the network placed additional value on the need to develop local solutions rather than only focusing on attracting the next industry investor to the region.

Power Frames

Raik et al. (2008, 730) consider the concept of power in natural resource management research. They examine it as a nuanced concept with latent implications for practice, rather than as an idea that is obvious and "inherently understandable." Two main views of power are portrayed. First, the agent-centered view explains power on the basis of coercion and constraint, or the ability of one actor to either cause or limit certain behaviors in another. Coercive power can be exercised to force actors to do things they do not want to do. Constraining power works to limit action through, for example, limiting discourse or dialogue to prevent what *could* happen and "ensure inaction on issues" (Raik et al. 2008, 733). Second, the structural view considers power as separate from individuals, to instead emanate from social structures that embody certain interests and, therefore, to reproduce social structures that do not represent the interests of the other. According to Raik et al. (2008, 734), "The structural view understands power as forces above and external to the individual (e.g., race, gender, class) that operate unacknowledged to influence people and their behavior." Both views of power are relevant to how social learning and framing occurred in the evolution of the NSFC, from shadow network to formal organization.

Participants were asked who they thought had the most power over Crown forests in the Northeast Superior region, and how that power was gained. Most participants, whether part of the shadow network or part of wider private/public/civic groups, considered either the provincial government or forest industry to have the most power, followed by First Nations. The sources of power most often identified were the legal authority of the provincial government and of First Nations, with the latter's rights being recognized by the Supreme Court decisions: "Aboriginal people have pre-existing inherent rights to the land that they grant to the Crown, not the other way around" [NSFC 8]. However, the view that industry had the capacity to unduly influence due to its political affiliation and capital/resources always seemed to arise:

In terms of forestry I think that companies still have way too much influence. They hold the [Sustainable Forest Licences]. They're the ones who hold the factories and the assets. They're the ones who employ the people. [Ministry of Natural Resources] has influence of course, but then again it's the forestry companies who are contributing to the campaigns. [Shadow network 1]

Nearly all shadow network participants believed that industry had too much power and that communities were excluded from decision making. This frame was linked closely with problem and solution frames for tenure reform and support for alternative wood uses, both thought to be constrained by current institutional arrangements. Indeed, legal authority and sheer resources (e.g., capital, financial, human) suggest a capacity to influence through coercion or forced action, but the ability to constrain potential actions was more important. Specifically, the ability of industry to control government forest policy agendas and ensure inaction was a central observation among those who perceived the need for tenure reform.

Legal authority and resources were identified as the dominant sources of power at work in forest management and policy in the NSFC region. The municipalities and federal government were not seen as powerful social groups relative to the Ontario Ministry of Natural Resources and the forest industry. The view was that municipalities were powerless because industry and government did not consult them or ignored them altogether [shadow network 1, 2] (again an example of power as constraint). Shadow network participants did not consider themselves to have much influence on the only agenda that really mattered (i.e., forestry).

Ironically, they overlooked that the federal government had endorsed their unconventional project plans—a vision developed by the early discursive work of the shadow network—by providing considerable funding and links to an international research network. This project later helped create a formal collaborative forum (the NSFC) right in the shadow of the region's traditionally dominant social groups (i.e., the forest industry and Ontario Ministry of Natural Resources). As the network and its thinking evolved, it gained power and legitimacy through its individual municipal affiliations as well as its association with one another, the aboriginal communities, and the federal government, which supported their vision for local control. The formation of these relationships between traditionally marginalized social groups served to subvert the power of conventional forest management structures by creating new structures and learning agendas. As a result, even though the shadow network, and subsequently the newly formed NSFC, had no formal authority over forest resource management decision making, they were not powerless and indeed were a source of community resilience.

Changing power dynamics within the shadow network also led to the eventual downgrading of relationships with consultant members. Once a formal organization was established and was backed with federal funding, municipal representatives took on more of a leadership role. Consultants and other advisors were disengaged due to potential conflicts of interest and the perceived need to maintain complete local control over the organization. Certain pet project ideas were left to "die off"—intentionally dropped to remove any vestige of former consultant control, and to distance rejected ideas from the "new" organizational identity (NSFC 1). The Mayors' Group continues to meet in its original form, with the NSFC as a stand-alone corporation with hired management and staff.

Conclusions

We have provided an examination of the shadow network that contributed to the successful establishment of the NSFC. A frame analysis was used to analyze the shadow network as a formative source of learning and community resilience in a setting of crisis and conflict. In particular, the analysis illustrated a two-part dynamic in the evolution of alternative ideas associated with an increasingly structured social organization. Shadow network participants went beyond instrumental learning to collectively reframe the forestry problem and to promote related solutions as a counterpoint to conventional views of the crisis. This reframing inspired the formation of a regional collaborative organization focused on innovative solutions to forest-related regional development. Our analysis has also presented evidence related to how power relations influenced social learning and the alternative framing of problems and solutions in forest-based communities in Northern Ontario, Canada. There are some implications and lessons for enhancing social learning and building resilience in forest-based communities, which this chapter will now present.

The initial emergence of the shadow network created a space for discussion among individuals from different backgrounds. Together, they identified and constructed a more complete view of their shared problems. This insight and understanding took forestry debates away from the usual topics (e.g., energy and transportation costs, licensing and permits, fiber flows) associated with conventional power brokers, such as the provincial government, forest companies and labor groups. Initially under the radar, the shadow network was able to advocate contentious ideas about tenure reform and about directing control away from major forest companies. The network was able to encourage these ideas to take hold as a way to promote regional development. This outcome is consistent with the role of shadow networks as incubators for alternative ideas and learning in response to the failings of existing policies (Gunderson 1999; Olsson et al. 2006; Goldstein 2008).

The shadow network performed critical front-end work for the development of what emerged as a form of regional governance. Beginning as an informal association, members were able to act on a shared vision and pool physical and human resources to capitalize on an opportunity; this work later enshrined their agenda in the NSFC's formal organizational policies. The early discursive work of the shadow network was pivotal to the success of this collaboration, which now stands as one alternative to standard forestry problem responses.

Collaboration was one local response to significant economic and social change experienced at the local level. However, the shadow network and later the NSFC deliberately remained separate from industry and the province to ensure the level of autonomy needed to pursue their own agenda. Developing regional partnerships, attracting new funding opportunities, and creating new governance institutions was facilitated by coordinating existing capacity and pooling existing resources and ideas. They meant to induce change as directed by priorities established within the Mayors' Group. The ability to respond to change, to reframe problems and solutions, and in turn to build additional capacity based on newly adopted views suggests that community resilience was enhanced by double-loop learning processes facilitated by the shadow network. Serving the local towns rather than the dominant industry, this forum provided opportunities to reflect on doing what was perceived as right for communities in the Northeast Superior region; and in doing so, the forum developed solutions that diverged significantly from those proposed by the forest industry and the province of Ontario.

However, NSFC (and similar organizations) must continue to think about what is the right thing to do and move toward other types of economic activities (whether in bioenergy or NTFPs), rather than exclusively trying to improve how to do better what has already been done. Indeed, one challenge with maintaining double-loop learning processes in organizations is that people tend to put more emphasis and value on doing rather than thinking, especially when awaiting returns on past investment. It is also relatively easy to continue doing what is familiar with respect to daily organizational routines (Levitt and March 1988). Such "lock-in" (Allison and Hobbs 2004) and "competency" traps (Levitt and March 1988) present challenges for newly forming organizations, in that it can be difficult to balance the temptation to "concentrate" on developing continuity and "doing things right," with the need for ongoing reflection. A caution is that community resilience depends on a continuous rethinking of problems and solutions for the ability to respond to rapid change and therefore eventually to be undermined by entrenched actions.

In addition, without meaningful ties to industry and forest management decision-making authority, local representatives engaged (via alternative structures and processes) to pursue their common interest when pressed for solutions. The leadership of local elected officials who were committed to living and working in the region supported a truly bottom-up approach to governance innovation within the conventional political economy of this resource hinterland. But this forum was still not without power dynamics. The early influence of consultants was central to encouraging the Mayors' Group to further pursue the notion that local control could address many of their existing concerns related to regional development. The idea to employ consultants also enabled some consultants to embed their own pet projects on the agenda as part of the later NSFC proposal to NRCAN.

Acknowledging that "learning is neither value free nor politically neutral" (Armitage et al. 2008), this chapter further clarifies that shadow networks are not necessarily neutral discursive forums, nor are double-loop learning processes inherently "good." These spaces and processes do indeed serve particular interests. In this sense, both shadow networks and learning must be observed with regard to the extent that they work to overcome dominant and/or negative power relations involving conventionally disempowered social groups.

Note

1. In Canada the term *First Nation*(s) is increasingly used in place of both Indian(s) and band and to distinguish aboriginal individuals and groups from other aboriginal peoples in Canada, namely the Inuit and Métis.

2. To maintain confidentiality where interviewees' ideas and direct statements are included, interviewees are identified by their group association and a randomly assigned number, which appears in brackets [ ] following the material that has been directly quoted or summarized.

References

Albert, S., D. Robinson.. L. Duchesne, and D. DeYoe. 2006 Chapleau, Ontario: Transition Strategy for the Northeast Superior Forest Community.

Allison, H. E., and R. J. Hobbs. 2004. Resilience, adaptive capacity, and the "Lock-in Trap" of the western Australian agricultural region. *Ecology and Society* 9(1):3.

Argyris, C., and D. A. Schön. 1978. *Organizational learning: A theory of action perspective*. Reading, MA: Addison-Wesley.

Armitage, D., and D. Johnson. 2006. Can resilience be reconciled with globalization and the increasingly complex conditions of resource degradation in Asian coastal regions? *Ecology and Society* 11(1). Accessed 3-2-2011. Available at http:// www.ecologyandsociety.org/vol11/iss1/art2/.

Armitage, D., M. Marschke, and R. Plummer. 2008. Adaptive co-management and the paradox of learning. *Global Environmental Change* 18(1):86–98.

Bank of Canada. 2009. Rates and statistics: Exchange rates. Accessed 3-1-2011. Available at http://www.bank-banque-canada.ca/en/rates/exchange_avg_pdf.html.

Beattie, K., W. Bond, and E. Manning. 1981. *The agricultural use of marginal lands: A review and bibliography*. Ottawa, ON: Lands Directorate, Environment Canada.

Bullock, R. 2006. An analysis of community forest implementation in British Columbia, Canada. Unpublished MES thesis. Waterloo, ON: Wilfrid Laurier University, Department of Geography and Environmental Studies.

Bullock, R. 2009. *Stakeholder perceptions of Ontario's Crown Forest Tenure System, Northeast Superior Forest Community*. Chapleau, ON: Prepared for the Northeast Superior Forest Community Corporation.

Butler, J., B. Cheetham, and M. Power. 2007. *A solutions agenda for Northern Ontario's forest sector*. Communications, Energy, and Paperworkers Union of Canada (CEP), and the United Steelworkers (USW) Taskforce on Resource Dependent Communities.

Centre for Community Enterprise (CCE). 2000. *Community resilience: A resource for rural renewal and recovery*. Port Alberni, BC: CCE Publications.

Cutter, S., L. Barnes, M. Berry, C. Burton, E. Evans, E. Tate, and J. Webb. 2008. A place-based model for understanding community resilience to natural disasters. *Global Environmental Change* 18:598–606.

Decter, M. B., D. R. Miller, F. Lamontagne, and the Canadian Association of Single-Industry Towns. 1989. *What we can do for ourselves. Diversification and single industry communities: The implications of a community economic development approach*. Ottawa, ON: Economic Council of Canada.

Dengler, M. 2007. Spaces of power for action: Governance of the Everglades Restudy process (1992–2000). *Political Geography* 26:423–454.

Dewulf, A., M. Craps, R. Bouwen, T. Taillieu, and C. Pahl-Wostl. 2005. Integrated management of natural resources: Dealing with ambiguous issues, multiple actors and diverging frames. *Water Science and Technology* 52(6):115–124.

Diduck, A., N. Bankes, D. Armitage, and D. Clark. 2005. Unpacking social learning in social-ecological systems: Case studies of polar bear and narwhal management in northern Canada. In *Breaking ice: Renewable resource and ocean management in the Canadian north*, ed. F. Berkes, 269–290. Calgary, AB: University of Calgary Press.

Diduck, A. P., and B. Mitchell. 2003. Learning, public involvement and environmental assessment: A Canadian case study. *Journal of Environmental Assessment Policy and Management* 5(3):339–364.

Economic Development Corporation of Wawa. 2004. *Wawa economic development profile 2004*. Wawa, ON: Economic Development Corporation of Wawa.

Environmental Commissioner of Ontario. 2005. *2004–2005 Annual report: Planning our landscape*. Toronto, ON: Environmental Commissioner of Ontario.

Escobar, A. 1999. After nature: Steps to an antiessentialist political ecology. *Current Anthropology* 40(1):1–30.

Forsyth, T. 2003. *Critical political ecology: The politics of environmental science*. London, U.K. / New York: Routledge.

Glasbergen, P. 1996. Learning to manage the environment. In *Democracy and the environment: Problems and prospects*, eds. W. M. Lafferty and J. Meadowcroft, 175–193. Cheltenham, U.K. / Brookfield, VT: Edward Elgar.

Goldstein, B. 2008. Skunkworks in the embers of the Cedar Fire: Enhancing societal resilience in the aftermath of disaster. *Human Ecology* 36(1):15–28.

Gray, B. 2003. Framing of environmental disputes. In *Making sense of environmental conflicts: Concepts and cases*, eds. R. Lewicki, B. Gray, and M. Elliot, 11–34. Washington, D.C.: Island Press.

Gray, B. 2004. Strong opposition: Frame-based resistance to collaboration. *Journal of Community & Applied Social Psychology* 14:166–176.

Gray, B. 2006. Frame-based interventions for promoting understanding in multiparty conflicts. In *Inside networks*, eds. T. Gössling, L. Oerlemans, and R. Jansen, 223–250. Cheltenham, U.K.: Edward Elgar.

Gunderson, L. 1999. Resilience, flexibility, and adaptive management—Antidotes for spurious certitude? *Conservation Ecology* 3(1): 7.

Gunderson, L., and L. Pritchard. 2002. *Resilience and the behavior of large scale ecosystems. SCOPE volume.* Washington, D.C.: Island Press.

Haley, D., and H. Nelson 2007. Has the time come to rethink Canada's Crown forest tenure systems? *Forestry Chronicle* 83(5): 630–641.

Hessing, M., M. Howlett, and T. Summerville. 2005. *Canadian natural resource and environmental policy: Political economy and public policy*, 2nd ed. Vancouver, BC: University of British Columbia Press.

Keen, M., V. A. Brown, and R. Dyball. 2005. *Social learning in environmental management: Towards a sustainable future*. London, U.K. / Sterling, VA: Earthscan.

Keen, M., and S. Mahanty. 2006. Learning in sustainable natural resource management: Challenges and opportunities in the Pacific. *Society & Natural Resources* 19:497–513.

Kim, D. 1993. The link between individual and organizational learning. *Sloan Management Review* 35(1): 37–50.

Levitt, B., and J. G. March. 1988. Organizational learning. *Annual Review of Sociology* 14:319–340.

Lewicki, R., B. Gray, and M. Elliot. 2003. *Making sense of environmental conflicts: Concepts and cases*. Washington, D.C.: Island Press.

Lucas, R. 1971. *Minetown, milltown, railtown: Life in Canadian communities of single industry*. Toronto, ON: University of Toronto Press.

Maarleveld, M., and C. Dangbegnon. 1999. Managing natural resources: A social learning perspective. *Agriculture and Human Affairs* 16:267–280.

Mezirow, J. 1994. Understanding transformation theory. *Adult Education Quarterly* 44(4):222–232.

Minister's Council on Forest Sector Competitiveness. 2005. *Final report—May, 2005*. Report to the Minister of Natural Resources. Accessed 2-13-2011. Available at http://www.mnr.gov.on.ca/stdprodconsume/groups/lr/@mnr/@forests/documents/document/mnr_e000248.pdf.

National Association of Home Builders. 2008. *Housing Starts 1978–2007*. Accessed 9-8-2008. Available at http://www.nahb.org/generic.aspx?sectionid=819&genericcontentid=554& channelID=311.

Natural Resources Canada (NRCAN). 2006. *Canada's forests*. Accessed 3-2-2011. Available at http://canadaforests.nrcan.gc.ca/?lang=en.

Natural Resources Canada (NRCAN). 2007. *Forest communities program announcement.* Accessed 3-2-2011. Available at http://www.nrcan-rncan.gc.ca/media/newcom/2007/200761-eng.php.

New Democratic Party. 2007.*Forestry announcement just a re-annoucement: Bisson accuses Liberals of pre-election desperation.*. Accessed 3-2-2011 Available at http://gillesbisson.com/newsitem.php?id=434 .

Northeast Superior Forest Community. 2009. *Opportunities in the non-timber forest products industry.* Sault Ste Marie, ON: Forest BioProducts. Accessed 12-1-2009. Available at http://www.nsfc.ca/uploaded/Opportunities%20in%20NTFP%20Industry%20v3.pdf.

Northern Ontario Sustainable Communities Partnership. 2007. Accessed 8-20-2008. Available at http://noscp.greenstone.ca/.

Olsson, P., L. Gunderson, S. Carpenter, P. Ryan, L. Lebel, C. Folke, and C. S. Holling. 2006. Shooting the rapids: Navigating transitions to adaptive governance of social-ecological systems. *Ecology and Society* 11(1):18.

Ontario Forestry Association (OFA). 2009. Accessed 3-1-2011. Available at http://www.oforest.ca/index.php/awareness.Ontario Forestry Coalition. 2006. *Enhancing the economy of northwestern Ontario.* Thunder Bay, ON: Northwestern Ontario Municipal Association.

Ontario Ministry of Agriculture, Food and Rural Affairs (OMAFRA). 2009. *Southern Ontario region at a glance.* Accessed 11-12-2009. Available at http://www.omafra.gov.on.ca/english/stats/county/southern_ontario.htm.

Ontario Ministry of Energy. 2011. *Fuelling Ontario: Oil and gas, Fuel prices.* Accessed 3-1-2011. Available at http://www.mei.gov.on.ca/en/energy/oilandgas/..

Ontario Ministry of Northern Development, Mines and Forestry (OMNDMF). 2011. *Ontario's tenure and licensing system.* Accessed 3-2-2011. Available at: http://www.mndmf.gov.on.ca/forestry/tenure_licensing_e.asp.

Pahl-Wostl, C. 2009. A conceptual framework for analysing adaptive capacity and multi-level learning processes in resource governance regimes. *Global Environmental Change* 19: 354–365.

Peet, R., and M. Watts. 1996. *Liberation ecologies: Environment, development, social movements.* London: Routledge.

Pelling, M. 1998. Participation, social capital and vulnerability to urban flooding in Guyana. *Journal of International Development* 10(4):469–486.

Price, M. F. 1996. People in biosphere reserves: An evolving concept. *Society & Natural Resources* 9:645–654.

Province of Ontario. 2010. *Ontario's north, Industry sectors: Forest Sector and value-added products.* Accessed 3-2-2011. Available at http://www.sse.gov.on.ca/medt/investinontario/en/Pages/industry_forest.aspx. .

Quaghebeur, K., J. Masschelein, and H. H. Nguyen. 2004. Paradox of participation: Giving or taking part? *Journal of Community & Applied Social Psychology* 14(3):154–165.

Raik, D., A. Wilson, and D. Decker. 2008. Power in natural resources management: An application of theory. *Society & Natural Resources* 21(8):729–739.

Reed, M. G. 2007. Uneven environmental management: A Canadian comparative political ecology. *Environment and Planning* 39(2):320–338.

Reed, M., and K. McIlveen. 2006. Toward a pluralistic civic science? Assessing community forestry. *Society & Natural Resources* 19:591–607.

Rein, M., and D. Schön. 1994. *Frame reflection: Toward the resolution of intractable policy controversies.* New York: Basic Books.

Rikoon, J. S. 2006. Wild horses and the political ecology of nature restoration in the Missouri Ozarks. *Geoforum* 37:200–211.

Robbins, P. 2006. The politics of barstool biology: Environmental knowledge and power in greater Northern Yellowstone. *Geoforum* 37:185–199.

Robinson, D. 2007. *The social foundations for sustainability: Carbon, creativity and the failure of Canadian forestry strategy.* Unpublished manuscript.

Rosehart, R. 2008. *Northwestern Ontario: Preparing for change.* Northwestern Ontario Economic Facilitator Report. Accessed 2-13-2011. Available at http://www.scribd.com/doc/2324266/The-Rosehart-Report .

Schusler, T. M., D. J. Decker, and M. J. Pfeffer. 2003. Social learning for collaborative natural resource management. *Society & Natural Resources* 16(4):309–326.

Sendzimir, J., P. Magnuszewski, Z. Flachner, P. Balogh, G. Molnar, A. Sarvari, and Z. Nagy. 2008. Assessing the resilience of a river management regime: Informal learning in a shadow network in the Tisza River Basin. *Ecology and Society* 13(1):11.

Sinclair, A. J., and A. P. Diduck. 2001. Public involvement in EA in Canada: A transformative learning perspective. *Environmental Impact Assessment Review* 21(2):113–136.

Statistics Canada. 2008. *2006 Community Profiles.* Accessed 9-1-2008. Available at http://www12.statcan.ca/english/census06/data/profiles/community/Index.cfm?Lang=E.

Stewart, N. December 1, 2006. *Forest industry spiralling crisis.* Northern Ontario Business. Accessed 2-13-2011. Available at http://www.highbeam.com/doc/1G1-156555660.html.

Walker, B., S. Carpenter, J. Anderies, N. Abel, G. S. Cumming, M. Janssen, L. Lebel, J. Norberg, G. Peterson, and R. Pritchard. 2002. Resilience management in socioecological systems: A working hypothesis for a participatory approach. *Conservation Ecology* 6(1):14. Accessed 3-2-2011. Available at http://www.ecologyandsociety.org/vol6/iss1/art14/.

Walker, B., and D. Salt. 2006. *Resilience thinking: Sustaining ecosystems and people in a changing world.* Washington, D.C.: Island Press.

Wildemeersch, D. 2007. Social learning revisited: Lessons learned from North and South. In *Social learning: Towards a sustainable world*, ed. A. E. J. Wals, 99–116. Wageningen, The Netherlands: Wageningen Academic Publishers.

Woods, J. 2007. Harper views Ontario forest industry crisis. *The Canadian Press.* Accessed 2-13-2011. Available at http://www.ctv.ca/CTVNews/Canada/20071027/harper_forestry_071027/.

14

Collaborating for Transformative Resilience: Shared Identity in the U.S. Fire Learning Network

Bruce Evan Goldstein and William Hale Butler

Wildland fire management in the United States has been in a frustrated transition for nearly forty years. In the 1970s, fire managers agreed to end the war against fire on the wildlands that had dominated U.S. fire management policy and practice for nearly a century (Pyne 2004). However, despite changes in agency rhetoric and fire management policy, fire suppression continues to be reinforced through incentive structures, agency budgets, and professional practice (Arno and Allison-Bunnell 2002). Land management agencies devote increasing resources to suppressing fires that continue to grow in extent and intensity. The system remains self-reinforcing and unable to innovate and adapt, a condition that Gunderson and Holling (2002) call a "rigidity trap."

Record-setting wildland fire seasons around the turn of the twentieth century created a new opportunity for policy change. Once-insular fire management agencies became subject to greater public scrutiny and congressional oversight, and the agencies unveiled the National Fire Plan in 2001. In addition to these top-down responses, The Nature Conservancy (TNC), USDA Forest Service (USFS), and the land management agencies of the U.S. Department of Interior (DOI) created the U.S. Fire Learning Network (FLN) to build fire managers' capacities to engage in ecological fire restoration. The FLN enlists participants to develop landscape-scale ecological restoration plans for fire-adapted ecosystems, necessitating collaboration across organizational and administrative boundaries. The network facilitates this collaborative approach and enables learning across scales by operating at landscape, regional, and national levels. Since its inception, the FLN has included some 750 partner organizations distributed across over 130 landscape collaboratives connected to 15 regional networks.

Within this multiscalar structure, the FLN uses technologies, planning guidelines, and various forms of media that shape, transmit, and reinforce assumptions and expectations for engaging in collaborative ecological fire restoration planning and management. We contend that these assumptions and expectations articulate a network-wide social imaginary (Taylor 2004) that coordinates site-based collaboratives without hierarchal authority or mutually supporting social relationships. As professionals enact practices associated with this imaginary, they directly address some of the core challenges that perpetuate the rigidity trap in fire management and influence the conditions that prevent restoration of fire-adapted ecosystems. This chapter focuses on how the FLN has fostered a collective identity among fire professionals, allowing them to speak and act autonomously but with a coherent purpose and set of practices. By engendering the adoption of ecological fire restoration principles and practices among fire professionals, the FLN has the potential to catalyze a "social cascade" (Baumgartner 2006) from within the land management agencies, the primary purveyors of wildland fire management across the nation. In so doing, it may offer a way to spring fire management's rigidity trap.

The chapter offers an overview of our case study methodology and a brief review of social-ecological resilience and rigidity traps. Then the chapter outlines the potential of multiscalar collaborative networks to spring the trap. We suggest that a "social imaginary" may facilitate the coordination of multiple collaboratives and shape common identities across a distributed network. Next, we specify characteristics of the rigidity trap within fire management. The chapter describes how the FLN was created in response to the fire management crisis and outline how the circulation of people and planning products within and across organizational scales fosters the emergence of a network imaginary that binds participants to assumptions and expectations of landscape-scale ecological fire restoration. Finally, we describe how the FLN serves as an incubator of change, creating the potential for fire management professionals to initiate social change from within fire management agencies. The chapter concludes with broader implications of pursuing multiscalar collaboration to promote social-ecological resilience.

Methods

We have been engaged in the study of the FLN since 2005, focusing on network design, function, and accomplishments. Our research to-date has included more than 140 interviews with network leaders, participants, and high-level staff in participating organizations involved in the formation and continuation of the network. We have attended and recorded audio at sixteen regional and national level workshops and leadership meetings. Along with our analysis of interview and workshop transcripts, we have reviewed hundreds of documents including fire restoration plans, geographic information systems (GIS) maps and models, interorganizational agreements, meeting agendas and summaries, network newsletters, listserv communications, and media reports.

We have drawn our analytical insights about how the FLN operates as a multiscalar collaborative network from this case study approach, using qualitative methods, aided by NVIVO analysis software, to develop codes and categories to define common interpretations of network action at all levels of the network (Charmaz 2006; Yin 2003). This chapter represents a synthesis of much of our other work, as we have developed new interpretations from the data and analysis. For descriptions of methods we have used to analyze specific aspects of network action, we refer you to our previous publications on the FLN (Goldstein and Butler 2009, 2010a, 2010b; Goldstein, Butler, and Hull 2010).

Resilience and the Social Imaginary

Social-Ecological Resilience and Rigidity Traps

Proponents of social-ecological resilience use a systems vocabulary to define *resilience* as an outcome of interaction between unsettling events and a bioculture that could assume multiple stable states. Resilient social-ecological systems respond to disturbances by maintaining structural and functional complexity within a variety of potential system configurations (Folke et al. 2002; Walker, Holling, Carpenter, and Kinzig 2004). Thus, resilience is not just stability, but it also is the ability to withstand loss and recover identity and structural and functional complexity. Greater resilience is associated with self-organization and capacity to integrate learning and adaptation to restore system functions in the face of perturbation or change (Berkes, Colding, and Folke 2002). These qualities are independent of the temporal, spatial, and organizational scale of analysis, and they can encompass firms, communities, states, and societies.

Gunderson and Holling (2002) developed the concept of "panarchy" to describe how social-ecological systems can change, either gradually or suddenly, across multiple scales through the emergence of adaptation within the system. Panarchy links multiple scales in a system in an interconnected adaptive cycle of crisis (Ω), reorganization/renewal (α), growth (r), and conservation (K) (see figure 14.1 to see an illustration of three-scale panarchy). The adaptive cycle of a panarchy relies on the circulation of

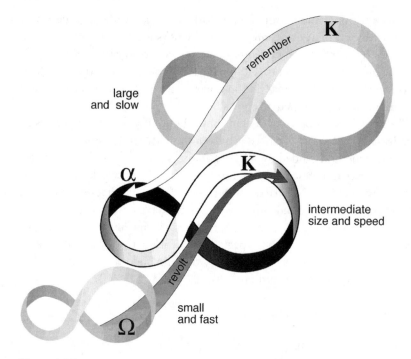

Figure 14.1
Three-scale panarchy, reprinted with permission from Resilience Alliance, http://www.res alliance.org/593.php

innovation across nested scales to engender transformative change. Smaller scales are more nimble and generate innovation through experimentation, while larger and slower-moving scales stabilize the system. Smaller scales can initiate "revolts" that can lead to the destabilization of the larger system. New perspectives and practices get folded into the larger scales. At these scales, continuity and conservation stabilize the system, applying characteristics of the "revolt" to broader system dynamics molded by the process of "remember." As smaller systems initiate revolts, the potential for the larger system to undergo transformative change increases as new practices are codified and institutionalized, and the larger system applies the wisdom of accumulated memory (Berkes et al. 2002; Gunderson and Holling 2002).

Stable and durable institutions can be an obstacle to broader social-ecological resilience, because they maintain themselves through shocks or perturbations that might otherwise catalyze adaptive change (Allison and Hobbs 2004; Carpenter and Brock 2008). Without innovation and adaptation, a system can get caught in a "rigidity trap" (Gunderson and Holling 2002), unable to break free from the stage of conservation that maintains the status quo. These systems are characterized as self-reinforcing and tightly connected, unable to adapt even in the face of crisis (Carpenter and Brock 2008, p. 41). Rigidity traps were first described in natural resource management bureaucracies that perpetuate themselves at the expense of the productivity and vitality of the ecosystems that they manage (Gunderson and Holling 2002). Resource managers reduce natural variation because dependent industries require predictability and productivity maximization of certain resources. This reduced variation enables the bureaucracy to persist, but negative ecological feedbacks increase the likelihood of catastrophic events and dramatic, unanticipated change (Holling, Gunderson, and Ludwig 2002).

This process can be self-correcting when extreme events such as wildfire or hurricanes foster change in long-established rules and practices (Schusler, Decker, and Pfeffer 2003). However, extreme events may also be accompanied by feedbacks that maintain the status quo, such as financial and/or political support that accompanies continued crisis management. Even when resource managers recognize that things would improve if they approached their work differently, change can be undermined by persistent institutional processes (Repetto and Allen 2006). Change can be threatening as it can disrupt familiar procedures and ways of knowing, require new training, and increase uncertainties associated with reorganization (Goldstein 2007).

Social Cascades

People's willingness to change the status quo is conditioned by the willingness of others to do so, a phenomena that Baumgartner (2006, 43) calls a "social cascade." People tend to coalesce around certain ideas or frames based on the beliefs of those people they respect, the information they obtain to legitimize a point of view, and the relative number of people who hold that point of view (Bikhchandani, Hirshleifer, and Welch 1998; Sunstein 1999). A cascade occurs when a critical mass begins to form around a common set of beliefs, perspectives, or interpretations and "a rivulet ends up as a flood" (Sunstein 1999, p. 8). Social cascades can lead to broader social change and have been cited in cases such as the anti-slavery and environmental movements in the United States, the rise of Nazism in Germany, and the fall of communism in Eastern Europe (Sunstein 2000).

Collaboration to Initiate a Cascade and Spring the Trap

Some resilience researchers have suggested that multistakeholder collaboration can spring rigidity traps because these processes are inclusive, well-suited to building trust and social capital, and they can enhance innovation by providing a multitude of testing grounds for establishing new relationships and exploring alternative work practices (Cash et al. 2006; Pahl-Wostl et al. 2007; Walker et al. 2002). Multistakeholder collaboration developed as a way to solve disputes that stymied regulatory agencies, representative assemblies, and the courts (Gray 1989; Weber 1998). Collaborative relationships not only enhance problem solving, but they also enable agreements to be implemented, as stakeholders remain engaged with one another and implement the solutions they had devised (Booher and Innes 2002; Healey 1997).

In addition, collaboration can provide an opportunity for individuals to align themselves around new and potentially common notions of how they view themselves and the social worlds around them (Booher and Innes 2002; Hardy, Lawrence, and Grant 2005; Inkpen and Tsang 2005). Participants may come to see themselves as interconnected in new ways and may change how they view their relationships to each other and to the biosphere (Bryan 2004; Poncelet 2004; Roling and Maarleveld 1999). Booher and Innes (2002, 231) suggest that "a central outcome [of collaboration] is that participants in dialogue build a sense of shared identity as part of a system or community." As collaborators try out new roles and consider new ways of making sense of their experiences, they can build a new individual and shared identity within a place and community (Booher and Innes 2002; Hardy et al. 2005; Healey 1999).

Our work explores how shared identity can be cultivated within a multiscalar collaborative network in order to address challenges that are beyond single-sited place-based stakeholder collaboration. Our prior analysis of the FLN traced how participants in a collaborative network develop common assumptions and expectations that enable them to act autonomously in the service of a common purpose (Goldstein and Butler 2009, revised and resubmitted 2010a). The idea of a "social imaginary" provides a framework to understand how a network of disparate participants might build solidarity and foster a common identity, and in so doing, initiate a social cascade to engender more fundamental change in fire management practice.

Common Identity through Imaginary

Anderson (1983, p. xxxi) proposes that the ties of nationality constitute an imagined community, stating that "members of even the smallest nation will never know most of their fellow-members, meet them, or even hear of them, yet in the minds of each lives the image of their communion." Taylor (2002, 2004), expanded the concept describing a "social imaginary" as a dispersed collective expectation of how things work now, how they are supposed to work, and how to engage with others to make them work that way. Individuals who adhere to a common imaginary can reinforce solidarity within a group with common struggles and pleasures, despite the absence of personal relationships among all members of the group.

Taylor (2001a) emphasizes that the imaginary is not analogous to institutional rules and norms. An imaginary is an implicit and pre-conscious background, a common sense that ties a community together and legitimates certain communal practices. Rather than constraining individuals, an imaginary provides a framework for their routines, enabling them to exercise judgment and select alternatives within a particular field of action. It subtly articulates the assumptions and expectations of people operating in certain social spheres, shaping who they are, what practices they engage in, and how they judge the actions of others.

Our analysis focuses on how an imaginary can enhance agency by shaping the conditions of possibility for collective action, generating the potential for a social cascade to initiate a "revolt" in the fire management panarchy. We suggest that an imaginary can unify and motivate a distributed network of collaboratives by drawing together dispersed participants around a shared identity. To make this link, we examine how a network imaginary formed within the FLN and describe the practices through which the imaginary is expressed and reproduced among network participants. Then, we suggest how this shared identity can enable a social cascade to initiate a "revolt" throughout the larger system of fire management.

Fire Management's Rigidity Trap

Wildland fire management in the United States emerged with the establishment of public land management agencies around the turn of the twentieth century. The fledgling agencies were invested in a utilitarian conservationist ethic that focused on maintaining resource production (Hays 1999). In this context, fire was considered an enemy to be eliminated from the landscape (Langston 1995; Pyne 2004). The USFS took the lead and created a national system of fire prevention and suppression (Pyne, Andrews, and Laven 1996).

Since the 1970s, a social-ecological crisis has been growing in the nation's forests. Fire suppression led to accumulation of woody biomass that stoked large conflagrations, promoted disease and pest outbreaks, and reduced species diversity. Land management agencies were overstretched and unable to respond to an ever-worsening crisis caused by their overzealous efforts to eliminate fire (Pyne 2004).

In the late 1990s and early 2000s, conflagrations of record frequency and intensity led Congress and the public to scrutinize the previously insular world of fire management (Davis 2006; National Interagency Fire Center 2009). New wildland fire policies emphasized ecosystem restoration, fuels reduction, and community protection (Steelman and Burke 2007). Both the National Fire Plan (USDA Forest Service & U.S. Department of Interior 2001) and the Healthy Forests Restoration Act (U.S. House of Representatives 2003) aimed to curb the cycle of declining ecological health and ballooning fire control budgets by calling for ecologically informed management approaches.

While these new policies highlighted the importance of ecologically informed fire management, they left unchanged the organizational incentives, budget priorities, and professional practices of agency land managers (Arno and Allison-Bunnell 2002; Kennedy and Quigley 1998; USDA Office of the Inspector General 2006). Fire suppression continued to be the agency priority, with 98 percent of all forest fires suppressed, regardless of ignition source (USDA Office of the Inspector General 2006). Despite near-universal recognition of the need for change and a continued crisis in fire management, the system resists reorganization. As Pyne (2004, 52) concludes, "the issue is not that we have failed to cross the divide, but that we have so little to show for having breached it decades ago."

While various institutional factors play a role in maintaining this rigidity trap, the persistent identity among wildland fire managers as firefighters hinders change on the ground. For more than a century, fire professionals examined the means, not the ends, of fire management. They worked on "imagining new concepts to guide fire protection planning, inventing better tools for firefighting, devising better techniques to detect and hit fires quickly" (Pyne 2004, 93). Despite rhetorical and policy-level support for ecological fire restoration, change was slow to come as ecological restoration required a different set of capacities and range of practices than fire fighting. Jim Hubbard (personal communication, April 27, 2007), the director of State and Private Forestry for the USFS, asserts that although the agencies understood eco-regions and landscape-scale restoration prior to the FLN, "that did not translate through to the land managers making priority decisions . . . where the landscape context was being considered as it should be."

Officials in the Forest Service have highlighted this difficulty of reorienting fire management professionals acculturated to the assumptions, expectations, and practices of fire suppression as a core challenge in engaging in more ecologically informed fire management practice. As the Education Committee of the Association for Fire Ecology asserts, the "changing scope of fire management" requires a corresponding shift in training, education, and experience to "incorporate new knowledge of fire ecology, fire behavior, and social sciences to tackle the multifaceted issues [fire professionals] will face" (Kobziar et al. 2009, 340). Jim Hubbard identifies the need to "change behavior, change thinking, and change approaches over time," particularly among fire professionals, in order to build the capacities and practices necessary to achieve landscape restoration goals on the ground (personal communication April 27, 2007). It is this shift in thinking and behavior—an identity shift—that these officials identify as a necessary step to bring about more fundamental change in fire management practice.

U.S. Fire Learning Network

Responding to this lack of capacity among fire professionals to address the fire crisis, TNC, USFS, and the DOI signed a cooperative agreement in 2001 creating the FLN. Federal agencies allotted nearly $1 million a year to the agreement and TNC hired network coordinators and support staff. Initially, twenty-five landscape collaboratives across the United States took part in a two-year planning process to generate ecological restoration plans on landscapes ranging from 100,000 to 11 million acres. FLN staff grouped landscapes into regional networks in 2003 (Fire Learning Network, March, 2003). As of late 2010, more than sixty landscapes linked through eight regional networks worked to develop collaborative landscape-scale ecological restoration plans for fire-adapted ecosystems. (A map of the active landscapes is shown in figure 14.2.)

Cross-scale Circulation
FLN organizers sought to "foster innovation and transfer lessons learned to other landscape projects . . . to accelerate the implementation of ecologically based and culturally acceptable fuels reduction and fire regime restoration" (TNC U.S. Fire Learning Network 2009). Linking collaborative planning processes across the nation, the network enhances fire managers' capacities to develop ecological fire restoration plans, facilitates innovation, and increases the application of ecological fire restoration on the ground (Goldstein et al. 2010).

348   *Bruce Evan Goldstein and William Hale Butler*

Figure 14.2
Map of the active U.S. FLN landscapes and regions, courtesy of the FLN's director, 2010

The FLN links multiple place-based collaboratives together into a larger network at regional and national scales (see figure 14.3). At the landscape level, diverse stakeholders collaboratively develop ecological fire restoration plans and modeling or mapping tools for those plans. They generate new ideas, field test new practices and share resources to enable landscape-scale management. Regional networks bring together leading landscape participants to compare plans, discuss how they produced these plans, and exchange ideas about overcoming barriers to plan implementation. Through these exchanges, regional participants enhance their capacities in collaboration and in ecological restoration planning and management (Goldstein and Butler 2010a). The national network staff provides funding and support to enable landscape- and regional-level meetings, guide planning processes, and ensure cross-scalar communication and learning.

These activities do not occur in isolation at each level, as both participants and material objects circulate throughout the network. Landscape representatives attend regional workshops to present landscape-level work and obtain feedback as they collectively analyze their respective planning products and generate new ideas. Regional leaders attend landscape-level gatherings to facilitate collaborative planning processes or to disseminate innovative practices emerging from other landscapes and regional forums.

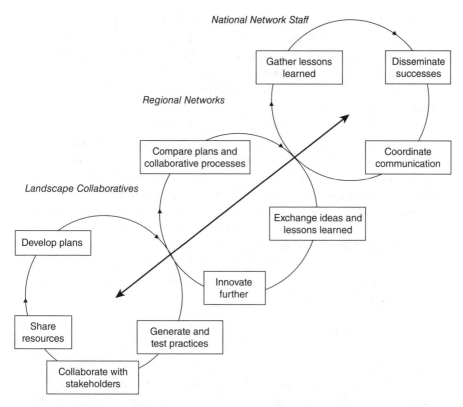

Figure 14.3
Multi-scalar network action in the FLN; cross-scalar circulation of FLN participants, planning products, and media throughout the network

Regional and landscape leaders gather in national meetings to provide input into the design and activities of the overall network, to highlight and share practices with each other, and to seek to develop creative responses to common challenges across the nation. National leaders present at regional meetings and counsel regional leaders as they shape agendas and guide planning processes.

This circulation of people is accompanied by a circulation of planning products, modeling tools, and representations that focus network action and serve as translating devices across network levels. In particular, the FLN relies on a four-step series of planning guidelines and modeling systems based on Fire Regime Condition Class (FRCC) to facilitate decision making in the planning process. The planning guidelines help participants develop a narrative that describes idyllic historic conditions,

sources of present-day decline, and the potential to chart a future of renewal (Goldstein and Butler 2010b). FRCC, a three-part scale that denotes
departure from a reference or historic ecological conditions, reinforces
the narrative as desired future conditions are often tied to how closely
existing conditions can approximate the historic condition (Goldstein and
Butler 2009).

FLN leaders maintain network communications through newsletters,
field guides, and briefing documents, and by conducting presentations and
interactive landscape tours at national and regional meetings. Regional
leaders also conduct presentations, host field excursions, publish workshop summaries and tout success stories among their members. Web sites,
databases, video conferences and other remote means of communication
serve as repositories of network products and communication forums to
highlight specific innovations. In this way, both print and performative
media serve the function of what Anderson (1983) calls "representations,"
conveying and reinforcing a common understanding of appropriate action
(Goldstein and Butler 2009).

The FLN Imaginary

In previous work, we describe how the use of certain technologies, in
particular planning guidelines and modeling protocols, reinforced shared
assumptions and expectations among network participants (Goldstein and
Butler 2009). The assumptions and expectations constitute more than
a common story about landscape-scale fire restoration, or a set of ecological goals shared by the FLN founders and sponsors. They include an
understanding of the historical basis of the problem (largely linked to
past fire suppression) and the appropriate strategic and tactical response
highlighting ecological restoration planning and management. In addition,
they are collectively oriented toward overcoming organizational barriers
to restoration action, and they share tacit agreement that fire managers
possess the credibility and legitimacy to participate in FLN collaborative
efforts. Taken as a whole, these assumptions and expectations support
an imaginary among network participants that defines how to engage in
landscape-scale ecological restoration of fire-adapted ecosystems. It provides an implicit common understanding that enables partners to carry
out the collective practices of the FLN, to identify exemplary planning
and management activities among network members, and to discern legitimate practices associated with landscape-scale ecological restoration
of fire-adapted ecosystems (Goldstein and Butler 2009).

Shaping Identity

The FLN imaginary helped to define a new professional identity among fire managers. Wildland fire managers share in firefighters' reputation as heroic defenders against an elemental danger. The FLN offered fire managers the chance to be heroes again, although heroes of a different sort, adapting to dynamic landscape conditions to restore ecological health and to protect human communities. As fire managers participated in the FLN, they developed planning products and sought to redeem fire management by undoing a century of fire suppression, removing barriers to restoration, and applying fire to protect communities and to heal landscapes. In the process, FLN participants expressed their desire for ecological and institutional transformation and their belief that they had the capacity to affect change. Identification with the roles, values, and knowledge of ecological restoration allowed fire managers to redefine the meaning of their professional practice and to gain a renewed sense of purpose and orientation for action. As one fire manager put it, "If you are a status quo person, you are going to be very uncomfortable in the Fire Learning Network" (John Andre, USFS, personal communication, March 12, 2009).

FLN assumptions and expectations that sustain the network imaginary do guide individual action, but not in the same way an individualistic ethic does. The FLN imaginary provides a bridge between the fire manager and the emergent collective. A shared goal and purpose provides FLN participants with an understanding of what it means to be a member of the group and with a sense of their role in shared community life, a horizon and context for action that delimits appropriate behavior for self and others in the pursuit of ecological fire restoration. This understanding reinforces their solidarity within a group with common struggles and pleasures, despite limited personal ties or mutual accountability among FLN partners. As one participant points out, the FLN provided a framework for addressing "All the things that I had been wondering about for years that hadn't added up" and helped him to make "a shift in focus from issue-based land management . . . to ecosystem management" (Jim McCoy, personal communication, March 14, 2007).

Rather than provide a set of explicit rules, the FLN imaginary indicates what the rules should be (and the relationship between these rules) by informing partner's self-understandings, practices, and common expectations. While the FLN was founded on the premise that there is a nationwide problem with the degradation of ecological health in fire-adapted ecosystems (The Nature Conservancy 2001), the planning guidelines and technologies enabled each landscape collaborative to situate the FLN imaginary in participants' own experience and context, through their own actions, collective reasoning, and choices. Rather than being an outgrowth of theory, the imaginary was "nourished in embodied habitus" through practices that were engendered by FLN guidelines and technologies (Taylor 2001b, 189). Practices are possible and make sense within the imaginary's assumptions and expectations of one another, while carrying and legitimating the imaginary. This dialectic supports a "repertory" of collective actions. As Taylor (2002, 106–107) notes, "These understandings are both factual and normative; that is, we have a sense of how things usually go, but this is interwoven with an idea of how they ought to go, of what missteps would invalidate the practice." What the FLN offered to land management professionals and organizations was the opportunity to work through a planning process that would "make them stop and sit down and think through this . . . and apply it to the processes that they work with" in their own organizational and ecological contexts (Jim Hubbard, personal communication, April 27, 2007). This process allowed managers to collaboratively develop plans that were locally applicable and to coalesce around a common framework for validating ecological fire restoration practice.

Initiating a Revolt through Environmental Subjects

As the FLN imaginary facilitated the emergence of new ecological restoration subjectivities among fire managers, it laid the foundation for more fundamental change. Agrawal (2005) describes a similar identity formation process in the forests of the Kuamon state in India. Agrawal proposes that the making of environmental subjects can occur through the dispersal of power, knowledge, and regulation to allow people to reconstruct their identities and to associate themselves with the surrounding natural environment. His concept, which he labels "environmentality," derives from the decentralization of control from government to local populations, allowing the latter to become accomplices in governance by enabling the co-management of ecological landscapes. As Agrawal (2005, 100) contends, "The manufacture of interest and the redefinition of subjectivities play a key role in the construction of fresh beliefs about what kinds of practices are most attractive." Thus, unlike traditional understandings of power as a controlling influence, Agrawal suggests that the "individuality that is supposed to be constrained by the exercise of power may actually be its effect" (Agrawal 2005, 217). He suggests that environmentality can be exercised through more decentralized approaches to governance that encourage co-management and self-regulation to reshape and solidify human subjects as protectors of environmental quality of natural land-scapes (Agrawal 2005).

Extending beyond this reading of localized governance of environmental systems, the FLN shapes subjectivities that introduce new perspectives and practices into the larger governance system. In some cases, FLN participants inform policy-level changes to incorporate more opportunities for ecological fire restoration at the federal or state level (Butler and Goldstein 2010). In other cases, participants introduce ecological restoration perspectives and practices into land management planning efforts in their respective organizational units. For example, Jim McCoy (personal communication, March 14, 2007) joined the Land Between the Lakes National Recreation Area staff, having participated in the network, and thus he "was able to bring FLN information and technology into the process [of land management plan revisions]. I was able to infuse that document with the tenets of landscape-scale prescribed fire ecosystem-based management." His supervisor, Bill Lisowsky, recalls that McCoy played a fundamentally important role in the plan revisions, bringing "a new source of energy" and a level of fire expertise to the process, infusing the plan with "ecological restoration and fire restoration principles" (Bill Lisowsky, personal communication, November 28, 2007).

Not only did FLN participants spread ecological restoration practices into their respective workplaces, but also the FLN shaped new professional capacities and spread to new locations. The FLN imaginary helped create and maintain the collaborative network, entraining individuals as they circulated through the network in association with planning guidelines, technologies, and media. Fire restoration ideas and practices circulated between landscapes and regions, enabling participants to become experts in landscape-scale ecological fire restoration. As these professionals built capacity in collaborative and technical expertise, acolytes became leaders and mentors in their own right, fostering a growing cadre of fire management professionals dedicated to and capable of engaging in collaborative landscape-scale ecological fire restoration. As they circulated through landscape and regional networks, they expanded the scope of the FLN, establishing and supporting new sites and bringing new members into the network over time (Goldstein and Butler 2010a). The network expanded from twenty-five landscape collaboratives to having included more than 130 landscapes and 750 partner groups over its first eight years.

In the panarchy associated with fire management, the FLN facilitates cross-scalar circulation of ecological fire restoration perspectives and practices. Through the multiscalar structure of the network, innovation and experimentation becomes introduced into the larger system at multiple levels. FLN participants catalyze the potential transformation at larger scales. Many FLN participants work within the federal agencies involved in fire management (in particular, the USDA Forest Service). As they refine their perspectives and practices in landscape-scale ecological fire restoration within the network, they are able to return to their roles in fire management agencies as ecological restorationists, promoting new ideas and possibilities within their work units. Moreover, as the network itself expands to new locations and new participants are introduced to the network imaginary and its associated practices, the potential for transformation of the system increases.

Conclusion

Place-based multistakeholder collaboration is particularly effective at resolving disputes, generating consensus-based agreements, and fostering learning, change, and identity formation (Gray 1989; Healey 1997; Innes and Booher 1999). However, a bounded and place-based multistakeholder process may not provide resilience to catastrophic events because it cannot bring about structural change across spatial, temporal, and organizational scales. Fainstein (2000) suggests that collaborative planning facilitates changing speech and rhetoric but cautions that more fundamental or structural change requires social mobilization to overcome power imbalances that cannot be effectively erased through "talk" alone.

We contend that the FLN offers a model for how a network of collaboratives might foster the potential for structural change. Like a multistakeholder collaborative, a network of collaboratives relies on communication and deliberation to foster learning and cultivate new identities among participants. What distinguishes a multiscalar network is that it connects multiple sites, fostering the potential to diffuse innovation and to respond to common challenges across geographic space and organizational scales. Such a network can catalyze a social cascade from within rather than through protest and oppositional tactics that frequently characterize social movements.

This process of social change is not sudden. As Jim Hubbard (personal communication, April 27, 2007) suggests, "This is not going to be revolutionary. It will evolve over time. And we will have to have the patience and the determination and persistence to stay with it." While adaptations within the larger system have been initiated by FLN participants in specific locations, the metaphorical rivulet has yet to build into a flood. None-theless, the movement is growing, both within the network and beyond. Transformation of fire management from its focus on suppression to more ecologically informed alternatives is underway. While the FLN has not reached the tipping point, it has catalyzed changes in policies, plans, and practices at multiple scales in fire management agencies and organizations (Butler and Goldstein 2010), pushing the system closer and closer to more fundamental change.

References

Agrawal, A. 2005. *Environmentality: Technologies of government and the making of subjects*. Durham, NC: Duke University Press.

Allison, H. E., and Hobbs, R. J. 2004. Resilience, adaptive capacity, and the "lock-in trap" of the Western Australian Agricultural Region. *Ecology and Society* 9(1):3.

Anderson, B. 1983. *Imagined communities: Reflections on the origin and spread of nationalism*. New York: Verso.

Arno, S. F., and S. Allison-Bunnell. 2002. *Flames in our forest: Disaster or renewal?* Washington, D.C.: Island Press.

Baumgartner, F. R. 2006. Punctuated equilibrium theory and environmental policy. In *Punctuated equilibrium and the dynamics of US environmental policy*, ed. R. Repetto, 24–46. New Haven, CT: Yale University Press.

Berkes, F., J. Colding, and C. Folke, eds. 2002. *Navigating social-ecological systems: Building resilience for complexity and change*. Cambridge, U.K.: Cambridge University Press.

Bikhchandani, S., D. Hirshleifer, and I. Welch. 1998. Learning from the behavior of others: Conformity, fads, and informational cascades. *Journal of Economic Perspectives* 12 (3): 151–170.

Booher, D. E., and J. E. Innes. 2002. Network power in collaborative planning. *Journal of Planning Education and Research* 21 (3): 221–236.

Bryan, T. 2004. Tragedy averted: The promise of collaboration. *Society & Natural Resources* 17:881–897.

Butler, W. H., and B. E. Goldstein. 2010. The US fire learning network: Springing a rigidity trap through multi-scalar collaborative networks. *Ecology and Society* 15 (3): 21.

Carpenter, S. R., and W. A. Brock. 2008. Adaptive capacity and traps. *Ecology and Society* 13(2):40. Accessed 2-14-2011. Available at http://www.ecologyandsociety.org/vol13/iss2/art40/.

Cash, D. W., W. N. Adger, F. Berkes, P. Garden, L. Lebel, P. Olsson, et al. 2006. Scale and cross-scale dynamics: Governance and information in a multilevel world. *Ecology and Society* 11(2):8. Accessed 2-14-2011. Available at http://www.ecologyandsociety.org/vol11/iss2/art8/.

Charmaz, K. 2006. *Constructing grounded theory: A practical guide through qualitative analysis.* Thousand Oaks, CA: Sage Publications.

Davis, C. 2006. Western wildfires: A policy change perspective. *Review of Policy Research* 23:115–127.

Fainstein, S. S. 2000. New directions in planning theory. *Urban Affairs Review* 35(4):451–478.

Fire Learning Network. March, 2003. *Improved collaboration advances implementation of fire restoration strategies.* Boulder, CO: The Nature Conservancy.

Folke, C., S. Carpenter, T. Elmqvist, L. Gunderson, C. S. Holling, and B. Walker. 2002. Resilience and sustainable development: Building adaptive capacity in a world of transformations. *Ambio* 31 (5): 437–440.

Goldstein, B. E. 2007. The futility of reason: Incommensurable differences between sustainability narratives in the aftermath of the 2003 San Diego Cedar Fire. *Journal of Environmental Policy and Planning* 9(4):227–244.

Goldstein, B. E., and W. H. Butler. 2009a. The network imaginary: Coherence and creativity within a multiscalar collaborative effort to reform U.S. fire management. *Journal of Environmental Planning and Management* 52 (8): 1013–1033.

Goldstein, B. E., and W. H. Butler. 2010a. Expanding the scope and impact of collaborative planning: Combining multi-stakeholder collaboration and communities of practice in a learning network. *Journal of the American Planning Association* 76(2): 238–240.

Goldstein, B. E., and W. H. Butler. 2010b. The U.S. Fire Learning Network: Providing a narrative framework for restoring ecosystems, professions, and institutions. *Society and Natural Resources* 23 (10): 1–17.

Goldstein, B. E., W. H. Butler, and R. B. Hull. 2010. The Fire Learning Network: A promising conservation strategy for forestry. *Journal of Forestry* 108 (3): 120–125.

Gray, B. 1989. *Collaborating: Finding common ground for multiparty problems.* San Francisco, CA: Jossey-Bass Publishers.

Gunderson, L., and C. S. Holling. 2002. *Panarchy: Understanding Transformations in human and natural systems.* Washington, D.C.: Island Press.

Hardy, C., T. B. Lawrence, and D. Grant. 2005. Discourse and collaboration: The role of conversations and collective identity. *Academy of Management Review* 30 (1): 58–77.

Hays, S. P. 1999. *Conservation and the gospel of efficiency.* Pittsburgh, PA: University of Pittsburgh Press.

Healey, P. 1997. *Collaborative planning: Shaping places in fragmented societies.* London, U.K.: MacMillan Press.

Healey, P. 1999. Institutionalist analysis, communicative planning and shaping places. *Journal of Planning Education and Research* 19:111–121.

Holling, C. S., L. H. Gunderson, and D. Ludwig. 2002. In quest of a theory of adaptive change. In *Panarchy: Understanding transformations in systems of humans and nature,* eds. L. H. Gunderson and C. S. Holling, 25–62. Washington, D.C.: Island Press.

Inkpen, A. C., and E. W. K. Tsang. 2005. Social capital, networks, and knowledge transfer. *Academy of Management Review* 30 (1): 146–165.

Innes, J. E., and D. E. Booher. 1999. Consensus building and complex adaptive systems: A framework for evaluating collaborative planning. *Journal of the American Planning Association* 65 (4): 412–423.

Kennedy, J. J., and T. M. Quigley. 1998. Evolution of USDA Forest Service organizational culture and adaptation issues in embracing an ecosystem management paradigm. *Landscape and Urban Planning* 40:113–122.

Kobziar, L. N., M. E. Rocca, C. A. Dicus, C. H. Sugihara, A. E. Thode, J. M. Varner, et al. 2009. Challenges to educating the next generation of wildland fire professionals in the United States. *Journal of Forestry* 107 (7): 339–345.

Langston, N. 1995. *Forest dreams, forest nightmares: The paradox of old growth in the inland west*. Seattle, WA: University of Washington Press.

National Interagency Fire Center. (2009). Wildland fire statistics. Accessed 7-1-2009. Available at http://www.nifc.gov/fire_info/fires_acres.htm.

Pahl-Wostl, C., J. Sendzimir, P. Jeffrey, J. Aerts, G. Berkamp, and K. Cross. 2007. Managing change toward adaptive water management through social learning. *Ecology and Society* 12(2):30. Accessed 2-14-2011. Available at http://www.ecologyandsociety.org/vol12/iss2/art30/.

Poncelet, E. C. 2004. *Partnering for the environment: Multistakeholder collaboration in a changing world*. Lanham, MD: Rowman and Littlefield Publishers, Inc.

Pyne, S. J. 2004. *Tending fire: Coping with America's wildland fires*. Washington, D.C.: Island Press.

Pyne, S. J., P. L. Andrews, and R. D. Laven. 1996. *Introduction to wildland fire*. New York: John Wiley & Sons, Inc.

Repetto, R., and R. B. Allen. 2006. On social traps and lobster traps: Choppy waters on the voyage toward fisheries' harvesting rights. In *Punctuated equilibrium and the dynamics of US environmental policy*, ed. R. Repetto, 110–136. New Haven, CT: Yale University Press.

Roling, N., and M. Maarleveld. 1999. Facing strategic narratives: An argument for interactive effectiveness. *Agriculture and Human Values* 16:295–308.

Schusler, T. M., D. J. Decker, and M. J. Pfeffer. 2003. Social learning for collaborative natural resource management. *Society & Natural Resources* 15:309–326.

Steelman, T. A., and C. A. Burke. 2007. Is wildfire policy sustainable? *Journal of Forestry* 105 (2): 67–72.

Sunstein, C. R. 1999. The law of group polarization. John M. Olin Law and Economics Working Paper, No. 91, 30. Accessed 2-14-2011. Available at http://www.law.uchicago.edu/Publications/Working/index.html.

Sunstein, C. R. 2000. Deliberative trouble? Why groups go to extremes. *Yale Law Journal* 110 (1): 71–119.

Taylor, C. 2001a. On social imaginary. Accessed 11-20-2008. Available at http://blog.lib.umn.edu/swiss/archive/Taylor.pdf.

Taylor, C. 2001b. Two theories of modernity. In *Alternative modernities*, ed. D. P. Gaonkar, 172–196. Durham, NC: Duke University Press.

Taylor, C. 2002. Modern social imaginaries. *Public Culture* 14 (1): 91–124.

Taylor, C. 2004. *Modern social imaginaries.* Durham, NC: Duke University Press.

The Nature Conservancy. 2001. *Proposal to promote restoration of fire-adapted ecosystems through education and community-based partnerships.* Arlington, VA: The Nature Conservancy, Conservation Science Division.

TNC U.S. Fire Learning Network. 2009. Global fire initiative: Training and networks: U.S. Fire Learning Network. Accessed 9-22-2009. Retrieved from http://www.tncfire.org/training_usfln.htm.

USDA Forest Service, & U.S. Department of Interior. 2001. *A collaborative approach for reducing wildland fire risks to communities and the environment: 10-Year comprehensive strategy.* Washington, D.C.: USDA Forest Service and U.S. Department of Interior.

USDA Office of the Inspector General. 2006. *Forest Service large fire suppression costs.* Accessed 2-14-2011. Available at http://www.usda.gov/oig/webdocs/08601-44-SF.pdf.

U.S. House of Representatives. 2003. Healthy Forest Restoration Act of 2003, (P.L. 108-148). Accessed 2-14-2011. Available at http://www.fs.fed.us/wild ecology/HFRA.pdf.

Walker, B., S. Carpenter, J. Anderies, N. Abel, G. Cumming, M. Janssen, et al. (2002). Resilience management in socialecological systems: A working hypothesis for a participatory approach. *Conservation Ecology* 6(1), 14. Accessed 2-14-2011. Available at http://www.consecol.org/vol6/iss1/art14.

Walker, B., C. S. Holling, S. R. Carpenter, and A. Kinzig. 2004. Resilience, adaptability and transformability in socialecological systems. *Ecology and Society* 9(2).

Weber, E. P. 1998. *Pluralism by the rules: Conflict and cooperation in environmental regulation.* Washington, D.C.: Georgetown University Press.

Yin, R. 2003. *Case study research: Design and methods,* 3rd ed., vol. 5. Thousand Oaks, CA: Sage Publications.

15

Conclusion: Communicative Resilience

Bruce Evan Goldstein

This book has explored how collaboration can promote adaptive and transformative resilience. Crises can be catalytic, providing opportunities to work around existing institutions and experiment with alternatives that, in ordinary times, would not even be considered or, if they were, would meet powerful opposition. These approaches have great potential during times of rapid transformation, when existing governance and planning models often fail. However, realizing this potential is not inevitable, because crises also produce pressure to restore prior conditions, even if they were unjust and unsustainable. It takes hard work in social mobilization and collective engagement to reflect on the causes of vulnerability and to organize in order to pursue opportunities a crisis may offer.

At the 2008 symposium at Virginia Tech, "Resilience to Catastrophic Events through Communicative Planning" (an event organized in response to the campus shootings), natural resource management and planning scholars considered how collaborative processes could promote resilience by fostering trust and cognitive capacity to understand and cope with complexity. Drawing on breakout discussions from that symposium, the preceding chapters of *Collaborative Resilience*, and the broader literature, I'd like to suggest that while planning and natural resource management are converging in response to their crises of over-confident managerialism (described in the introductory chapter), their complementarity must address the two fields' different assumptions about practice, theory, and methodology. Planners tend to focus on place-based multistakeholder collaboration as a means to "bounce back" from immediate crisis. Planners have much to learn from efforts by natural resource managers to enhance social-ecological resilience through capacity-building and institutional change across multiple sites and scales. In turn, collaborative planners challenge natural resource managers to move beyond rational actor theory in order to understand how collaboration can reshape collective knowledge, identity, and governance possibilities. I suggest that this productive tension informs "communicative resilience," which is not the intersection between these two fields but rather a product of their differences. Communicative resilience is an empowerment discourse that often functions outside state control and challenges state legitimacy; as such, it challenges the persistent managerialism of both planning and natural resource management.

New Possibilities in Collaborative Process and Design

The idea of resilience has been around for a long time—the term has Latin roots meaning "to jump, leap, or bounce back"—although until recently its definition was limited to the idea of rebounding from an external force. For example, engineers describe material resilience as the capacity to absorb energy during deformation and bounce back by releasing this energy elastically (Hollnagel, Woods, and Leveson 2006). As a metaphor for social action, resilience focuses attention on an immediate crisis that threatens the integrity of a bounded community, challenging its capacity for decision making and coordinated action. Resilience is a community's ability to regain equilibrium and return to normal, for instance when cities recover after destructive shocks such as hurricanes or coordinated attacks (Vale and Campanella 2005).

But the metaphor is too simplistic, because the dynamics of a bouncing ball and a society in crisis are not the same. The concept of social-ecological resilience developed in *Collaborative Resilience* addresses these differences by providing a less deterministic and more creative definition of a system's capacity to absorb disturbance and reorganize while undergoing change. This definition is intentionally not a conservative one of "bouncing back"; it emphasizes that resilient systems can adapt or transform. It draws on advances in systems theory that acknowledge that, rather than seeking the highest degree of system efficiency at a single equilibrium point, systems respond to disturbance by maintaining structural and functional complexity within a variety of potential configurations. Social-ecological resilience implies an adaptive system and the term is associated with self-organization, the capacity to integrate learning and adaptation, and an ability to restore system function and structure in the face of perturbation or change (Berkes and Folke 1998).

This redefinition of resilience to encompass transformative learning parallels changes in thinking about what collaboration can achieve. Initially, collaborative techniques were developed to address intractable conflicts that could not be solved by agencies, legislatures, or the courts. These crises were resolved through consensus, allowing a return to normal modes of decision making. However, collaborative agreements were often impossible to implement within institutions where the conflicts had originated (Amy 1987; Flyvbjerg 1998). Scholars began to consider whether collaboration could catalyze new institutional relationships that addressed root causes of conflict (Booher and Innes 2002; Healey 1997).

Many of the contributors to this volume share an interest in collaborative governance, and in *Collaborative Resilience* they have engaged with resilience to address a wide variety of collaborative possibilities beyond dispute resolution and crisis recovery. These possibilities include learning networks (chapter 14), shadow networks (chapter 13), community reconciliation processes (chapter 10), social movements (chapter 5), comanagement (chapter 11), and site-based interaction occurring in museums (chapter 12) and cooperative housing (chapter 3). These collaborative approaches differ in four ways from the stakeholder-based consensus processes that are a mainstay of collaborative conflict resolution:

- From right now to temporal bridging
- From places to cross-scale
- From problem solving to capacity-building
- From stability to change

From Right Now to Temporal Bridging
The chapters consider a wide range of temporalities for collaboration beyond response to an immediate crisis or threat. While some authors address urgent crises, such as that confronting the watershed collaborative in upstate New York (chapter 3), others address situations that are slower to build, such as the decline of Ontario Canada's timber-based economy (chapter 13), or are future-oriented, such as climate change (chapter 6) and coastal protection from hurricanes (chapter 7). Some even focus on crises that occurred long ago and are remembered in different ways (when they are remembered at all), such as the legacy of segregation in Bainbridge Island, Washington, and in southern cities (chapter 10), or the destruction of a community during South Africa's apartheid era (chapter 12). In these cases, the point of collaboration is not to resolve an immediate crisis so much as to provide therapeutic awareness of past injustice in order to increase community capacity and solidarity. Other chapters also deliberately frame problems over long time periods. Carp (chapter 5) ties together past and future in her exploration of the recovery of such age-old cultural patterns as "slow" regionally obtained food. These revivals

cultivate a collective feeling of presence and capacity for appreciating local context, as well as a means to respond to such looming challenges as peak oil. In the case study I cowrote with Butler (chapter 14), collaborators were encouraged to create a fire narrative spanning from the pre-Columbian past to the distant future, to imagine how their profession could help solve a continuing fire management crisis.

This range of temporal concerns often is associated with longer periods of collaborative interaction. Some collaboratives continue on for years or even decades, providing governance capacity (chapter 8), sustaining a community of practice (chapter 14), providing the basis for community mutual aid and economic self-sufficiency (chapter 3), and promoting fundamental social change (chapter 5). Others that are short-lived feed into other governance processes, such as Bojórquez-Tapia and Eakin's (chapter 7) environmental assessment in Cozumel Mexico, and Bullock, Armitage, and Mitchell's (chapter 13) shadow networks.

From Places to Cross-scale

While place-based multistakeholder collaborative processes have been used to good effect in bounded communities with distinct cultures, ecologies, and economies, these approaches cannot address the cross-scale dynamics of social-ecological resilience. Responding to these limits, several chapters address issues that concern spatially delimited communities, while also engaging with processes that operate at different spatial, temporal, and organizational scales. For example, Weber (chapter 8) considers how a network of watershed-based collaboratives could foster climate adaptation, and Arthur and colleagues (chapter 11) address how governmental policy and global trade relations affect fishing villages within the Mekong River delta. Others consider collaborative relations that operate at multiple scales, such as McConney and Phillip's (chapter 9) effort to organize a participatory design process for a cross-scale fisherfolk network, Randolph's (chapter 6) discussion of integrating local with global climate adaptation, and my and Butler's (chapter 14) examination of how a collaborative network can influence resilience dynamics across scales. We suggest that cross-scale networks can promote overall coherence while providing individual collaboratives with the independence required to innovate.

From Problem Solving to Capacity Building

Rather than focus on immediate problem solving, many of the chapters emphasize that efforts to solve a crisis speedily can, ironically, impede resilience. For example, Ozawa (chapter 2) suggests that the city officials' decision to cover Portland Oregon's reservoirs to reduce the risk of poisoning by terrorists after the 9/11 attacks threatened the deliberative civic culture that nourished the city's resilience. Other chapters look beyond specific crises to identify the systemic conditions that nurtured vulnerability. For example, Zellner, Hoch, and Welch (chapter 3) examine chronic homelessness and watershed degradation as the end result of relationship failures that arise from complexity and uncertainty so overwhelming as to disable effective coordination. Bojórquez-Tapia and Eakin (chapter 7) describe how a land suitability map can be created even in the absence of agreement among stakeholders, and how it can provide a means of preserving institutional memory after the collaborative process ends. Weber (chapter 8) even suggests that organizers of collaboratives be called "collaborative capacity builders" rather than facilitators, because their success depends on their ability to nurture institutional capacity, rather than mediate specific disputes.

From Stability to Change

Some chapters go beyond institutional capacity-building and consider how collaboration fosters institutional change that addresses the root cause of episodic crises. For example, Bullock, Armitage, and Mitchell (chapter 13) describe the way local "shadow networks" in forest-dependent communities develop ideas for land tenure reform that challenge how provincial government, labor groups, and forest companies organize the region's political economy and ecology. Contrary to the assumption that resilience means regaining stability, these authors suggest that destabilizing an inequitable and harmful system may increase resilience, even if this transition requires partial loss of system function. Conversely, Butler and I (chapter 14) describe how resilience is lost through stabilization of an untenable condition, as when fire managers during the past century suppressed forest wildfires that renewed ecological health.

Both of these chapters describe collaboratives that deliberately do not include all potential stakeholders. The purpose of the fire learning network remains to enhance social learning among fire managers, who comprise nearly all of the active participants, just as participation in the "slow food" movement (chapter 5) only includes those who are motivated to take part in a community of shared interest. Bullock and colleagues' shadow networks (chapter 13) are by definition not inclusive of representatives of provincial and corporate authorities whose dominance they seek to challenge, just as Arthur, Friend, and Marschke (chapter 11) advocate organizing comanagement arrangements that can resist powerful national elites. These exclusive and sometimes secretive collaborative processes intentionally violate the common dictum in the collaborative planning literature that communicative processes be maximally inclusive and transparent (Innes and Booher 2010).

Contribution to Resilience Thinking

In addition to exploring new possibilities for collaborative process and design, this book offers ideas about the impact of communicative action on human agency, knowledge, and institutions. The findings are potentially useful to resilience scholars, who have noted (Walker 2006) that they lack understanding about how resilience is enhanced by dialogue, trust, and social memory. However, the interpretive methods in many of these chapters are grounded in a different perspective on subjectivity and agency than in most resilience scholarship. Let us reflect on these differences, before considering the broader conceptual and practical implications of the encounter between collaborative planning and resilience studies.

Resilience scholars have focused on the usefulness of collaborative processes in mobilizing collective action and compressing the time required to develop new institutional rules and behavioral routines (Gunderson and Holling 2002; Berkes and Turner 2006). Following Ostrom's classic analysis of common property resource regimes (1990), scholars have tended to emphasize identifying generalizable rules or design principles for structuring interaction so that individuals make rational choices in favor of a social-ecological common good. This methodological positivism is consistent with the natural sciences, particularly ecosystem analysis (Holling 1978). Sharing this approach, resilience scholars can claim that "ecological and social domains of social-ecological systems can be addressed in a common conceptual, theoretical, and modeling framework" (Walker et al. 2006).

Collectively, the preceding chapters suggest that a rational choice perspective is an inadequate foundation for understanding how collaboration can enhance resilience. The authors of this book apply a wide variety of theoretical and methodological lenses to collaborative interaction to consider such questions as how empathetic storytelling facilitates group learning about history and place (Carp, chapter 5), how diverse perspectives facilitate trust-building (Kaufman, chapter 4), and how social worlds mark limits to intersubjective understanding (Bojórquez-Tapia and Eakin, chapter 7). The authors of *Collaborative Resilience* are able to consider a broader range of communicative possibilities because they do not test falsifiable hypotheses in the way that resilience scholars do. Their research is, as Geertz (1973) puts it, "not an experimental science in search of law, but an interpretive one in search of meaning." What Berger and Luckman (1967) call a social constructivist epistemology is particularly well suited to studying how identity, knowledge, and the social order emerge from within collaborative processes. This approach is attentive to what Kaufman (chapter 4) refers to as the role of human agency or "telos" in creating a combined social-ecological perspective. It follows a pragmatic middle way between a positivistic commitment to science as holding a mirror to nature and a social relativism that says that all knowledge is a product of social interests. Knowledge is a partial perspective on the external world, reliable when grounded in subjects who conduct the work that sustains meaningful truths (Haraway 1990).

These chapters offer social-ecological resilience scholarship the possibility of understanding social interaction as more than a system component that modelers treats as a "black box" in which something good but mysterious takes place. What is required is a pragmatic acceptance of epistemic diversity, an ability simultaneously to accept that resilience is good, reliable science and that resilience thinking is a perspective on the external world, reliable when grounded in knowing subjects who conduct the work that sustains meaningful truths. However, this understanding has a price that most resilience scholars are probably unwilling to pay—abandoning positivism, which has functioned to unify disparate disciplines and fields but is not well-suited to examining the dialectical relationships among identity, knowledge, and the social order.

Communicative Resilience

In these chapters, planning and social-ecological resilience researchers show how they are learning from each other's fields and expanding their domains of interest and practice. However, the paradigm differences noted previously present limits to interdisciplinarity, and these limits are associated with the difference between the fields' core interests. Communicative planning, with its post-positivist interpretive methods, focuses on the construction of meaning and identity, while resilience research seeks to understand system dynamics to enhance prediction and control, within the limits of complexity thinking. Rather than suggesting that we elide these differences to develop a unified research framework, *Collaborative Resilience* underscores the potential to take advantage of them to engage in "communicative resilience." This idea both draws upon and challenges the fields of collaborative planning and social-ecological resilience studies.

Just as *social-ecological resilience* was deliberately not termed *socio-ecological resilience* so as not to imply that the social was a subordinate modifier of the ecological (McDonald 2007), communicative resilience is not just a method for achieving resilience through collaboration. Instead, it is a framework for communities to both define and pursue resilience through collaborative dialog, rather than solely through expert analysis. A resilient system emerges as participants debate and define ecological and social features of the system and appropriate scales of activity. Poised between collaborative practice and resilience analysis, communicative resilience is both a process and an outcome of collective engagement with social-ecological complexity.

Communicative Resilience as Process

Resilience can mean various things beyond merely survival, because there are many ethical, political, cultural, and ecological possibilities for life. Communicative resilience is a process that enables a corresponding interpretative flexibility as participants consider questions such as "Why do we want to be resilient?" and "What will we make resilient?" These questions involve trade-offs, because one person's resilience may be another's vulnerability, and resilience at one scale may compromise it at another. These queries enable participants to distinguish whether different resilient outcomes are desirable or undesirable. They also open up transformative possibilities beyond the customary domain of collaborative conflict resolution.

As a number of chapters emphasize, these alternative framings can take the form of narratives or storylines, through which actors spell out the origins of the problem, how it might be addressed, and by whom. Stories about the past, present, and future have various contexts, positioned assumptions, and interpretations, dividing a community in ways that cannot be understood within a single temporal or spatial framework. As Dukes, Williams, and Kelban (chapter 10), Till (chapter 12), Arthur, Friend, and Marschke (chapter 11), and others suggest, collaborative interaction can provide potent spaces for reshaping multiple frames and truths, enabling participants to re-examine their ways of thinking and revise assumptions that inform institutional norms, rules, and practices.

This reframing is more than a challenge to their creativity, because the distribution of power influences how certain narratives dominate others, rooting threats to resilience in an officially forgotten past. The authors of *Collaborative Resilience* describe how collaboration can alter these power dynamics by enhancing participants' ability to uncover alternative, suppressed, or hidden framings. Collaboration can help them to understand how responsibility and accountability are assigned and why some pathways to resilience are pursued while others are avoided. Some of the collaborative approaches in *Collaborative Resilience* resemble social movements in which conflict is accepted as constructive and unavoidable (chapters 11 through 13), rather than as obstacles to mutual understanding to be redressed through inclusive dialogue overseen by a neutral facilitator. Even highly inclusive and state-sponsored consensus-building activities, such as Bojórquez-Tapia and Eakin (chapter 7) and Weber (chapter 8) describe, can become part of larger transformative political projects of struggle and resistance—the kind of projects that create and sustain resilience by challenging powerful actors and institutions and by holding them accountable.

While scientific advice—including from resilience scientists themselves—is a critical part of communicative resilience, it requires careful integration in a collaborative. As Arthur, Friend, and Marschke (chapter 11) note, experts who engage in a collaborative process as apolitical puzzle-solvers may reinforce an unfair and unresilient status quo by displacing the focus from political "what to do" questions to technical "how to" questions, obscuring underlying conflict over what are fundamentally challenges of governance and power sharing. Resilience thinking, like any other kind of expertise, is situated and invested in a specific culture and politics, and such thinking may reinforce the power of those who sponsor its production and distribution. While none of the chapters address this directly, a close analogy is provided in Hajer's (2003) account of how government agencies and environmental NGOs used an ecological vocabulary and storyline about "ecological corridors" and "target types" to justify expansion of central authority in rural Holland. This account underscores the need for resilience scholars to make a distinction between pursuit of what is scientifically rigorous within their research community and engaging community members in ways that foster autonomy and creativity, as well as broader coherence and cross-site and cross-scale integration.

As Arthur, Friend, and Marschke suggest, experts can cultivate a reflexive awareness of their own influence and remain open to critical review from their intended beneficiaries. In addition, there are joint fact-finding techniques (Karl and Susskind 2007) that enable experts to engage directly with stakeholders while facilitating inclusion of multiple forms of expertise, including local knowledge. Zellner, Hoch, and Welch (chapter

3) describe one effort to do this technique through a series of workshops organized by the Skaneateles Lake Watershed Agricultural Program. As Weber (chapter 8) notes when describing the inclusion of different sorts of knowledge in the Blackfoot Challenge, joint fact-finding "flattens power within the group by removing the knowledge monopoly enjoyed by some and elevating the value added by practice-based and human systems knowledge, thus giving a larger array of stakeholders influence within the collective decision process."

Linking scientific expertise with other ways of knowing can help collaborators conceive of diverse social and ecological components and connections that might prove resilient, from resource dependencies and cultural traditions to market interactions, reciprocal obligations, and emotional ties. This creative process can be seen in the slow food movement (chapter 5), which focuses on local food production and consumption as a means to foster understanding of local dependencies and promote community solidarity and wisdom. Participants in such processes do not establish the meaning and identity of system definitions and relationships before collaborative interaction takes place, in part because of the unique admixture of different kinds of knowledge, in part because system conditions are defined and reshaped by collaborative interaction. McConney and Phillips (chapter 9) provide an example in which fisherfolk decided that independence and equity were core characteristics for a cooperative network that would identify and defend their interests at a regional scale.

Communicative Resilience as Outcome

Communicative resilience is not just about collaborative inquiry into resilience processes. Communicative resilience also involves defining system attributes and properties and developing our capacity to identify appropriate goals and the obstacles to achieving them. As participants engage with one another, they develop common language and practices that enable them to assist one another in pursuing shared objectives. Collaboratives are potent spaces for reshaping both knowledge and the knowers, as participants re-examine their ways of thinking and revise assumptions from which institutional norms, rules, and practices are derived. As Ozawa (chapter 2) writes, collaboration "is not only about gathering data, conducting analyses, generating alternatives and recommending an optimum course, the objects of planning. It is also about the subjects of planning—the decision makers, the implementers, the people affected by the decision or plan, and the planners and public managers—and their relationships. Substance, process and relationships are intertwined." Communicative resilience is similar in certain respects to what Pahl-Wostl (2009) and others have described as triple-loop learning, a process that questions and transforms values, norms, and world views underlying a regime. However, communicative resilience places stronger emphasis on collective transformation, the process of discovery that not only reshapes the regime but also reshapes those who participate in the collaborative. The purpose is not just to engage in critical learning but rather to co-produce more resilient associations between individuals and their social identity, knowledge practices, and institutions.

My chapter and related work (Goldstein and Butler 2009; Butler and Goldstein 2010; Goldstein and Butler 2010a, 2010b) focus specifically on the potential for greater resilience through collaborative co-production. Butler and I describe how the Fire Learning Network (FLN) fosters resilience by building solidarity around an ecologically grounded professional identity, by developing skills and knowledge to support that identity, and by creating institutional relationships that increase collective capacity to embark on new, potentially risky management approaches to restoring fire-adapted ecosystems. Taking advantage of the availability of federal funding and a willingness to try new approaches after a series of destructive wildfires in the early 2000s, the FLN organized hundreds of fire managers around the nation into multijurisdictional, landscape-scale learning cooperatives. The FLN's coordinators publicized exemplary practices and provided common analytical tools to landscapes, to link these independent collaboratives at a national scale. This strategy gave participants a sense that they shared in the life of a community, despite not knowing all the members of the far-flung network. Within each collaborative, participants described their landscape's healthy distant past, degraded present, and a future of either continued decline or ecological recovery. This storytelling helped forge a common purpose, developed a shared repertoire of knowledge and skills, and laid the groundwork for cross-jurisdictional collaboration. The FLN's capacity to promote change lay not only in the plans it produced but also in its ability to disrupt old assumptions and habits and engender routines that formed the groundwork for new institutional relationships, while enabling the entire network to speak autonomously with a unified voice.

Conclusion

The convergence of the fields of planning and natural resource management on collaboration for social-ecological resilience is an opportunity for mutual learning. *Collaborative Resilience* examines a variety of ways to build resilience to violence, hazards, and resource decline. These collaborative methods range from consensus-based stakeholder agreements to collective mobilization for change in durable institutions that are dysfunctional and inequitable. This book illustrates how planning research is grappling with the implications of resilience for a broader domain of collaborative practice and striving to integrate ecological and social concerns. Across this range of practice, the authors consider how collaboratives foster trust and cognitive capacity to understand complex interactions and foster mutual reinvention; and how, in so doing, they create new kinds of knowledge, identity, relationships, communities, and institutions. Such research can enable scholars of social-ecological resilience to confront the limits of considering collaboration in terms of institutional conditions, rules, and practices.

Beyond mutual learning, this engagement suggests the possibility of communicative resilience, which is not an interdisciplinary synthesis but rather something new that emerges through productive tension between the two fields. Communicative resilience goes beyond suggesting that joint fact-finding and collective sensemaking can help a community better understand social-ecological relationships. It suggests that the system does not preexist the collaborative, which draws on diverse knowledge practices and storytelling to define it, their place in it, and its preferred condition. It is a coproductive dynamic, as system conditions are determined and reshaped through collaborative interaction.

Providing content and process expertise to support communicative resilience challenges the conventional practical engagements of both collaborative planning and resilience thinking. Resilience scientists need to engage in dialogic processes to define resilience as opposed to providing a definition themselves. This engagement requires deference to other forms of knowledge. For collaborative planners, communicative resilience invokes a spectrum of activities, from stakeholder-based collaboration to a more antagonistic politics of collective resistance and struggle against powerful actors and networks. This range of collaborative possibilities transcends widely accepted conditions and principles for good collaborative design, such as facilitator neutrality (e.g., chapters 11 and 13) and maximum inclusivity (e.g., chapters 13 and 14). In exchange for sacrificing comfortable assumptions about their managerial authority and prerogatives, practitioners can occupy new roles and contribute not only to a more resilient future but also to one that is more in tune with collective preferences arrived at through deliberation. They can contribute to a just social-ecological resilience.

References

Amy, D. J. 1987. *The politics of environmental mediation.* New York: Columbia University Press.

Berger, P. L., and T. Luckman. 1967. *The social construction of reality.* Garden City, NJ: Anchor Books, Doubleday.

Berkes, F., and C. Folke. 1998. *Linking social and ecological systems.* Cambridge, U.K.: Cambridge University Press.

Berkes, F., and N. J. Turner. 2006. Knowledge, learning and the evolution of conservation practice for social-ecological system resilience. *Human Ecology* 34 (4): 479–494.

Booher, D. E., and J. E. Innes. 2002. Network power in collaborative planning. *Journal of Planning Education and Research* 21:221–236.

Butler, W. H., and B. E. Goldstein. 2010. The US Fire Learning Network: Springing a rigidity trap through multi-scalar collaborative networks. *Ecology and Society* 15(3):21. Available at http://www.ecologyandsociety.org/vol15/iss3/art21/.

Flyvbjerg, B. 1998. *Rationality and power: Democracy in practice*, trans. S. Sampson. Chicago, IL: University of Chicago Press.

Geertz, C. 1973. *The interpretation of cultures.* New York: Basic Books.

Goldstein, B. E., and W. H. Butler. 2009. The network imaginary: Coherence and creativity within a multiscalar collaborative effort to reform U.S. fire management. *Journal of Environmental Planning and Management* 52(8):1013–1033.

Goldstein, B. E., and W. H. Butler. 2010a. Expanding the scope and impact of collaborative planning: Combining multi-stakeholder collaboration and communities of practice in a learning network. *Journal of the American Planning Association* 76(2): 239–249.

Goldstein, B. E., and W. H. Butler. 2010b. The U.S. Fire Learning Network: Providing a narrative framework for restoring ecosystems, professions, and institutions. *Society & Natural Resources* 23(10): 935–951.

Gunderson, L., and C. S. Holling. 2002. *Panarchy: Understanding transformations in human and natural systems.* Washington, D.C.: Island Press.

Hajer, M. 2003. A frame in the fields: Policymaking and the reinvention of politics. In *Deliberative policy analysis: Understanding governance in the network society*, eds. M. Hajer and H. Wagenaar, 88–112. Cambridge, U.K.: Cambridge University Press.

Haraway, D. J. 1990. Situated knowledges: The science question in feminism and the privilege of a partial perspective. In *Simians, cyborgs, and women: The reinvention of nature*, D. J. Haraway, 183–202. New York: Routledge.

Healey, P. 1997. *Collaborative planning: Shaping places in fragmented societies.* London: MacMillan Press.

Holling, C. S. 1978. *Adaptive environmental assessment and management.* New York: John Wiley and Sons.

Hollnagel, E., D. D. Woods, and N. G. Leveson. 2006. *Resilience engineering: Concepts and precepts.* Aldershot, U.K.: Ashgate.

Innes, J. E., and D. E. Booher. 2010. *Planning with complexity: An introduction to collaborative rationality for public policy.* New York: Routledge.

Karl, H. A., and L. E. Susskind. 2007. A dialogue, not a diatribe: Effective integration of science and policy through joint fact finding. *Environment: Science and Policy for Sustainable Development* 49(1): 20–34.

McDonald, T. 2007. Resilience thinking: Interview with Brian Walker. *Ecological Management & Restoration* 8(2):85–91.

Ostrom, E. 1990. *Governing the commons: The evolution of institutions for collective action.* Cambridge, U.K.: Cambridge University Press.

Pahl-Wostl, C. 2009. A conceptual framework for analysing adaptive capacity and multi-level learning processes in resource governance regimes. *Global Environmental Change* 19 (3): 354–365.

Vale, L. J., and T. J. Campanella. 2005. *The resilient city: How modern cities recover from disaster.* New York: Oxford University Press.

Walker, B., L. Gunderson, A. Kinzig, C. Folke, S. Carpenter, and L. Schultz. 2006. A handful of heuristics and some propositions for understanding resilience in social-ecological systems. *Ecology and Society* 11(1), 13. Available at http://www.ecologyandsociety.org/vol11/iss1/art13.

Walker, B. S. D. 2006. *Resilience thinking: Sustaining ecosystems and people in a changing world.* Washington, D.C.: Island Press.

Index

Caribbean Regional Fisheries Mechanism (CRFM), 209–212, 217–220, 224
Carlson, C., 21
Carp, Jana, 9, 99–125, 129, 361–362, 364
Carpenter, S., 21, 117, 155, 341–343
Carroll, M. S. H., 3
Carter, Jimmy, 25
Cartier, C., 261–262
Cascio, Jamais, 110
Case, C., 29
Cash, D., 158, 344
Cassell Coliseum, 2, 12
Centre for Resource Management and Environmental Studies (CERMES), 208, 212–213, 224
CEP-USW Task Force on Resource Dependent Communities, 312
Chakalall, B., 208–209
Chang, S., 129
Charles, A., 208, 227, 260
Charmaz, K., 341
Chaskin, R., 233
Cheating, 41
Cheetham, B., 312
Cheng, A. S., 188
Chernobyl, 24
Cho, Seung-Hui, 2, 4
Christie, P., 267
CH2MHill, 28
CittàSlow, 102–104
Civic science, 92
Civilian Exclusion Order No. 1, 237
Civil War, 233
Clamshell Alliance, 24
Climate action plans (CAPs), 139–140
Climate Adaptation Advisory panel, 142–143
Climate change, 362
  adaptation and, 127–132, 137–138, 141–145
  anticipatory learning and, 138
  carbon cap and trade programs and, 140
  climate action planning and, 139–140

complex systems and, 61, 65, 67, 72–74, 77–83, 91–92
consensus and, 127–128, 138–139, 144
consequences of, 127–128
Cool Cities and, 140
Copenhagen Conference and, 73, 78, 81, 139
disaster-relief-rebuild-disaster (D-R-R-D) syndrome and, 133
ecological issues and, 128–129, 142
electricity prices and, 127
emerging practice and, 138
Federal Emergency Management Agency (FEMA) and, 133–134, 136
fossil fuels and, 127, 140
global warming and, 72, 78, 84, 127–130
Gore and, 72, 84
green energy markets and, 140–141
greenhouse gases (GHG) and, 127, 139–144
human-induced, 127
ICLEI–Local Governments for Sustainability and, 140, 143–145
Intergovernmental Panel on Climate Change (IPCC) and, 138–139
international goal-setting and, 138–139
Kyoto Protocol and, 139–140
local adaptation plans and, 143–144
mitigation of, 139–140
natural hazard mitigation planning and, 132–138
natural resources management and, 130–132
networks and, 130, 132, 137–140, 145
Regional Greenhouse Gas Initiative (RGGI) and, 140
resilience and, 128–130
safety and, 142–143
scenario development and, 137–138
social capital and, 128–132, 135–138, 145–146
state adaptation plans and, 141–143
trust and, 136

Olsson, P. L. (*continued*)
  Mekong region and, 262
  Slow movement and, 101, 113, 118
Ontario, 11
  consensus and, 311
  First Nations and, 311, 313, 317,
    321–324, 329, 333n1
  forest-based communities and,
    309–333
  forestry crisis of, 310–315
  The Mayor's Group and, 320–330
  Minister's Council on Forest Sector
    Competitiveness and, 312
  Natural Resources Canada
    (NRCAN) and, 310, 312, 323–324,
    332
  pulp/paper mills and, 310–311, 321
  regional dynamics of, 310–313
  shadow networks and, 12, 309–310,
    315–333, 361–363
  tenure system and, 311–312,
    323–331
  U.S. dollar and, 312
Ontario Forestry Coalition, 312, 327
Ontario Ministry of Natural Re-
  sources (OMNR), 310–311, 325,
  329–330
O'Riordan, T., 137
Orr, David, 106, 110–112, 114,
  120n2
Ostrom, E., 7, 79–80, 258–259, 268,
  364
O'Toole, L. J., 193
Ottino, J. M., 40
Ouchi, W., 178
Oyster Shell Alliance, 24
Ozawa, Connie P., 8, 19–38, 61, 92,
  363, 368

Packard, Steve, 120
Paddison, R., 21–22
Page, S. E., 44, 55–56
Pahl-Wostl, C., 156–158, 161, 163,
  309, 315, 344, 369
Panarchy, 66–67, 75, 341–342, 345,
  353
Parkins, W., 102

Parks, C. D., 81
Parsram, K., 212
Participatory appraisal, 137–138
Participatory vulnerability assessment
  (PVA), 137
Pastor, M., 105, 107
Paternalism, 22
Paton, D., 43
Patton, B., 22, 32
Peace Corps, 3
Pear District Neighborhood Associa-
  tion, 29
Peet, R., 316–317
Pelling, M., 128, 130, 154, 213, 216,
  318
Pendall, R., 288
Persoon, G., 260
Perspectives, 44
Peterson, G., 131
Petrini, Carlo, 102
Pew Center on Global Climate
  Change, 141
Pfeffer, M. J., 343
Philadelphia Inquirer, 26
Philippines, 137
Phillips, Terrence, 10, 128, 207–229,
  362, 368
Phuong, M. V., 263
Physical resilience, 45
Pierson, P., 73
Pinchot, Gifford, 130
Pinker, S., 63, 72, 80, 94n8
Pinkerton, E., 259–260
Pitcher, T. J., 267
Planning
  anticipating change and, 61–81,
    84–87, 90–92, 93n7
  anticipatory learning and, 138
  carbon cap and trade programs and,
    140
  Caribbean fisherfolk and, 207–226
  cheating and, 41
  climate change and, 61, 65, 67,
    72–74, 77–83, 91–92, 139–140
  collaboration and, 44–45, 49–50,
    54–55
  comanagement and, 255–273

risky technologies and, 8, 19–27,
31–33, 36
Slow movement and, 9, 101, 113,
118
Three Mile Island and, 8, 24–27,
31–33
transparency and, 35–36, 364 (*see
also* Transparency)
trauma and, 234, 238–239, 244–
245, 250n11
violation of, 2–4
vulnerability and, 8, 39–46, 49–57
Tschakert, P., 131, 138
Tucker, D. W., 118
Tuler, S., 23, 31
Turner, M., 257
Turner, N. J., 80, 106, 113, 116, 364
Turnpenny, J., 137
Tversky, A., 76

Union Carbide, 24
United Nations Framework Conven-
tion on Climate Change (UN-
FCCC), 139
United States
carbon cap and trade programs and,
140
climate action planning and,
139–140
Cool Cities and, 140
dollar depreciation and, 312
Fire Learning Network (FLN) and,
339–355
National Fire Plan and, 339, 346
United Steelworkers (USW), 327
University and Community Action for
Racial Equity (UCARE), 244–248
University of Virginia, 11, 231, 237,
243–248, 250n11
Unrightable wrongs, 11, 232, 249n2,
291
Urban planning, 285
Ury, W., 22, 32
U.S. Department of the Interior
(DOI), 339, 346–347
U.S. Fish and Wildlife Service (US-
FWS), 113, 179–183, 201

U.S. Forest Service (USFS), 118, 130,
180, 339, 345–347, 351

Vale, L. J., 66, 82, 286–287, 360
Van der Ryn, S., 114
Van der Sluijs, J., 255, 267
Vannara, T., 258
Veilleux, R. E., 4
Versteeg, W., 272
Verweij, M., 255, 267, 270, 272
Victims
Cape Town and, 291–292, 304n6
complex systems and, 83
higher purpose and, 4–5
trauma and, 234–235, 239, 249n4
Virginia Tech murders and, 1–5,
12–13
vulnerability and, 55
Virginia Tech Center for Peace Studies
and Violence Prevention, 4
Virginia Tech murders, 1–5, 12–13,
303, 359
Voting Rights Act, 235
Vulnerability
adaptability and, 39–41
community commitment and, 52
community-individual perspectives
and, 52–53
complex systems and, 39–45, 48–49,
53, 55, 57, 63, 70, 86–89
conflict and, 41–44, 56–57
consensus and, 52, 55
ecological ordinances (EOs) and,
155, 158–173
flexible authority and, 52
heuristics and, 44
homeless people and, 7–8, 39,
46–50, 55–56, 363
interpretations and, 44
networks and, 43, 48
participatory vulnerability assessment (PVA) and, 137
perspective and, 44
physical resilience and, 45
planning and, 40–57
power imbalances and, 56
predictive models and, 44